Let's Dance a Waltz

1

Natsumi Ando

Contents

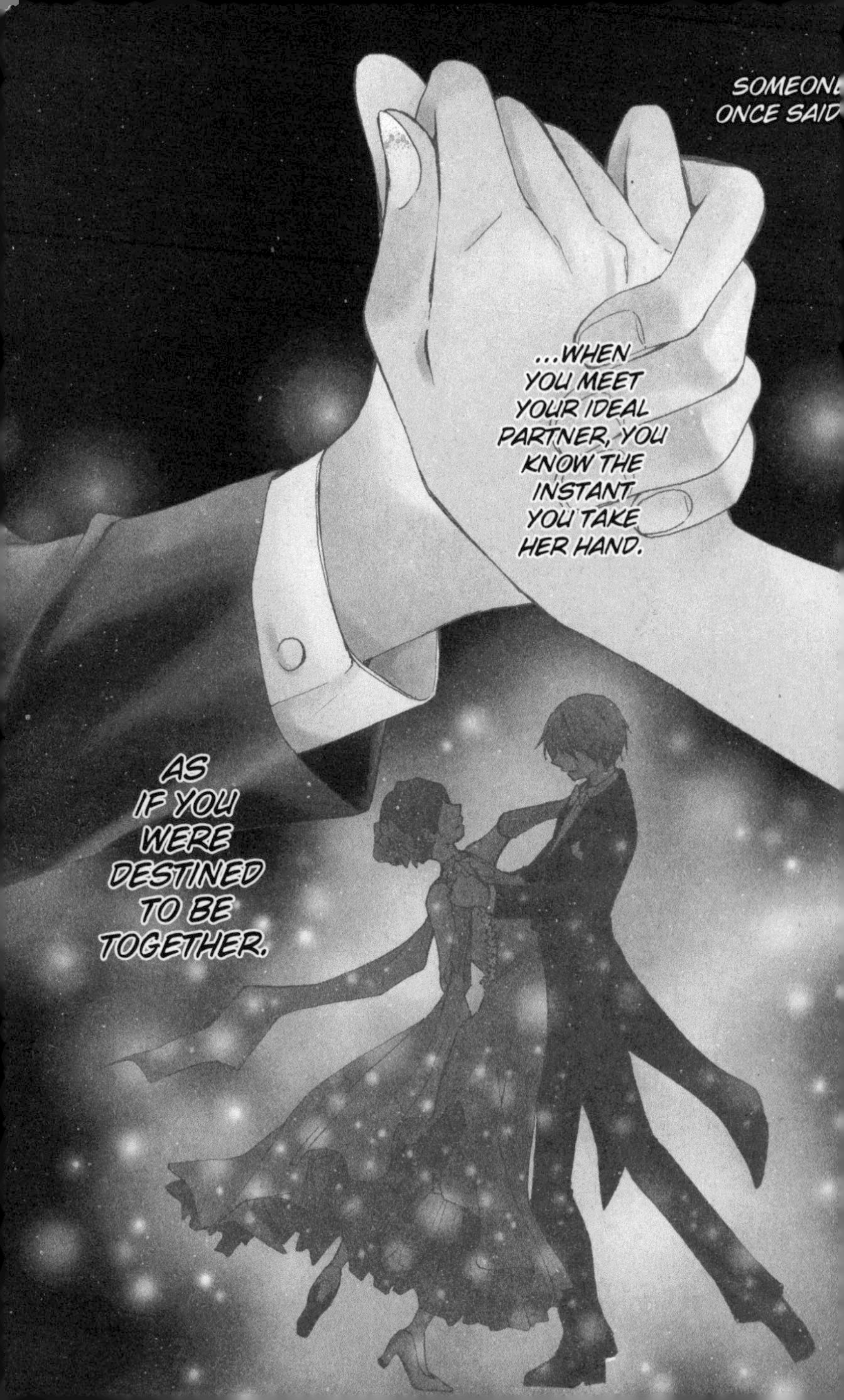
SOMEONE ONCE SAID
...WHEN YOU MEET YOUR IDEAL PARTNER, YOU KNOW THE INSTANT YOU TAKE HER HAND.
AS IF YOU WERE DESTINED TO BE TOGETHER.

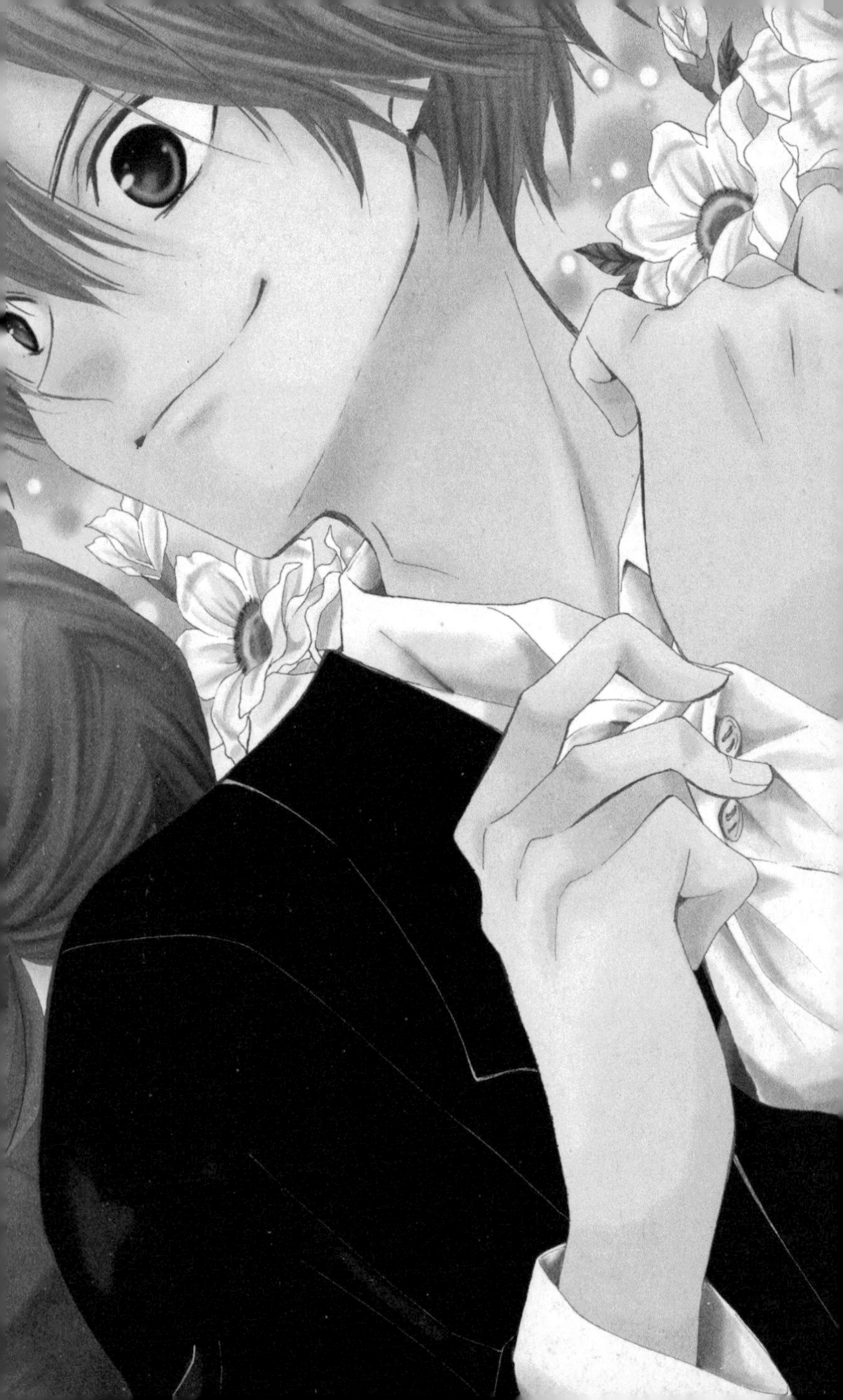

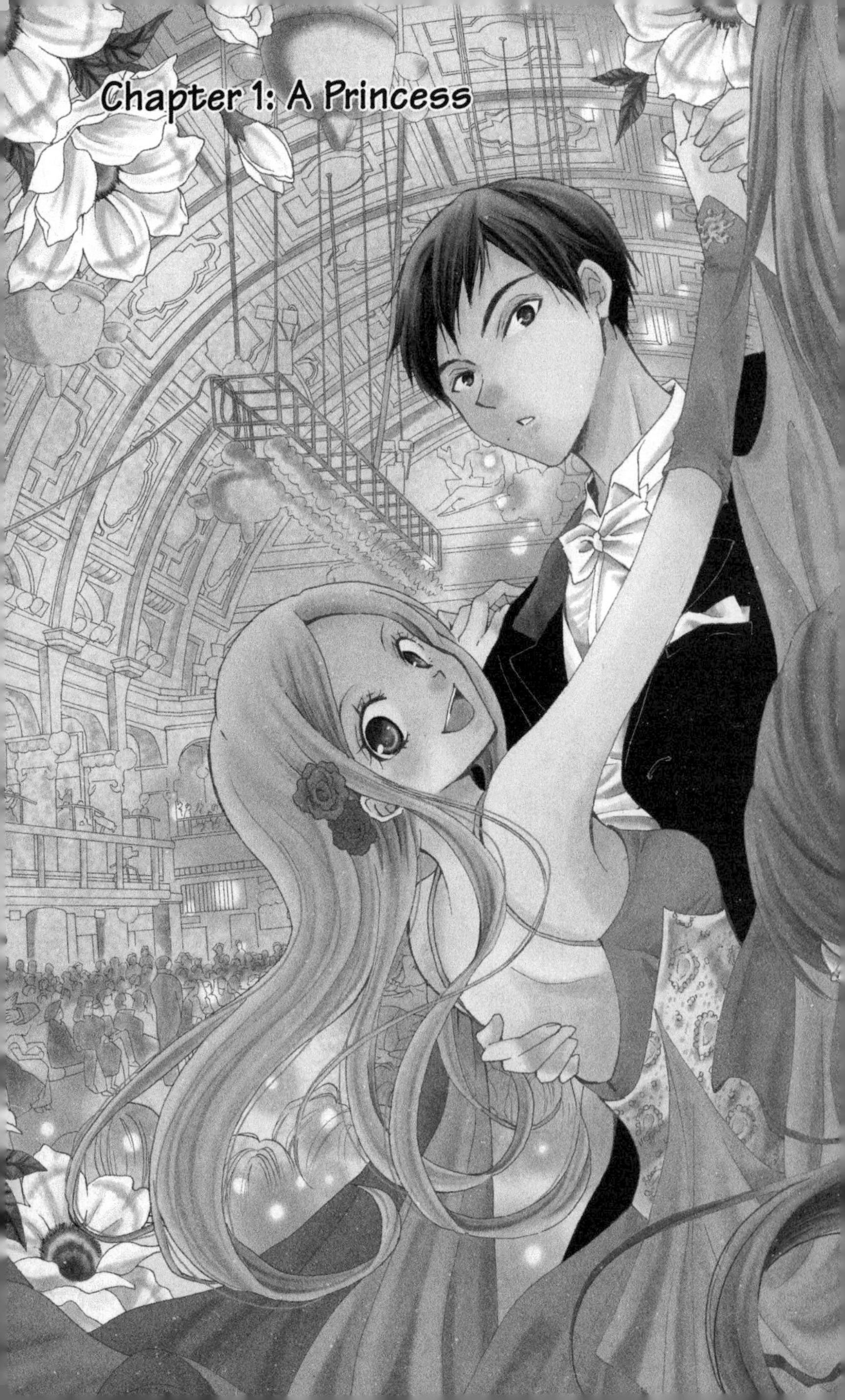
Chapter 1: A Princess

Let's Dance a Waltz.

Volume one, yo! ♪

Thank you very much for picking up volume one of
Let's Dance a Waltz!! This is my first graphic novel
in a long time, so I'm a little extra excited. \\^o^/

I had a nice long break after my last series ended, so
I had all kinds of fantasies about, "I'm gonna do **this!**"
"I'm gonna go **there!**" "I'm gonna eat **that!**" But in the end,
I feel like I spent almost my whole vacation staring into space...

Oh! But I have one experience to add to the things that
I'll probably remember for the rest of my life. **I climbed Mt. Fuji!!**
I went to the highest point in all Japan. Oh, man, but it was tough....
If I were to count the events that exhausted me the most in my life,
climbing Mt. Fuji would probably be in the first three fingers. When
I finally made it back down the mountain, I almost got down on my
knees and apologized to the mountain for underestimating it.

I also went to the Izumo-Taisha shrine, and got as close to the
gods as I could. And went on the bakery tour of my dreams.
...I guess I did a lot after all.

Anyway, I got a full recharge, and now my head is filled with
Let's Dance a Waltz. (And about 10% full of bread... with some
space left over for desserts and buffets... *mumble mumble*...)

I'll work hard so that lots of people can enjoy this new world!!

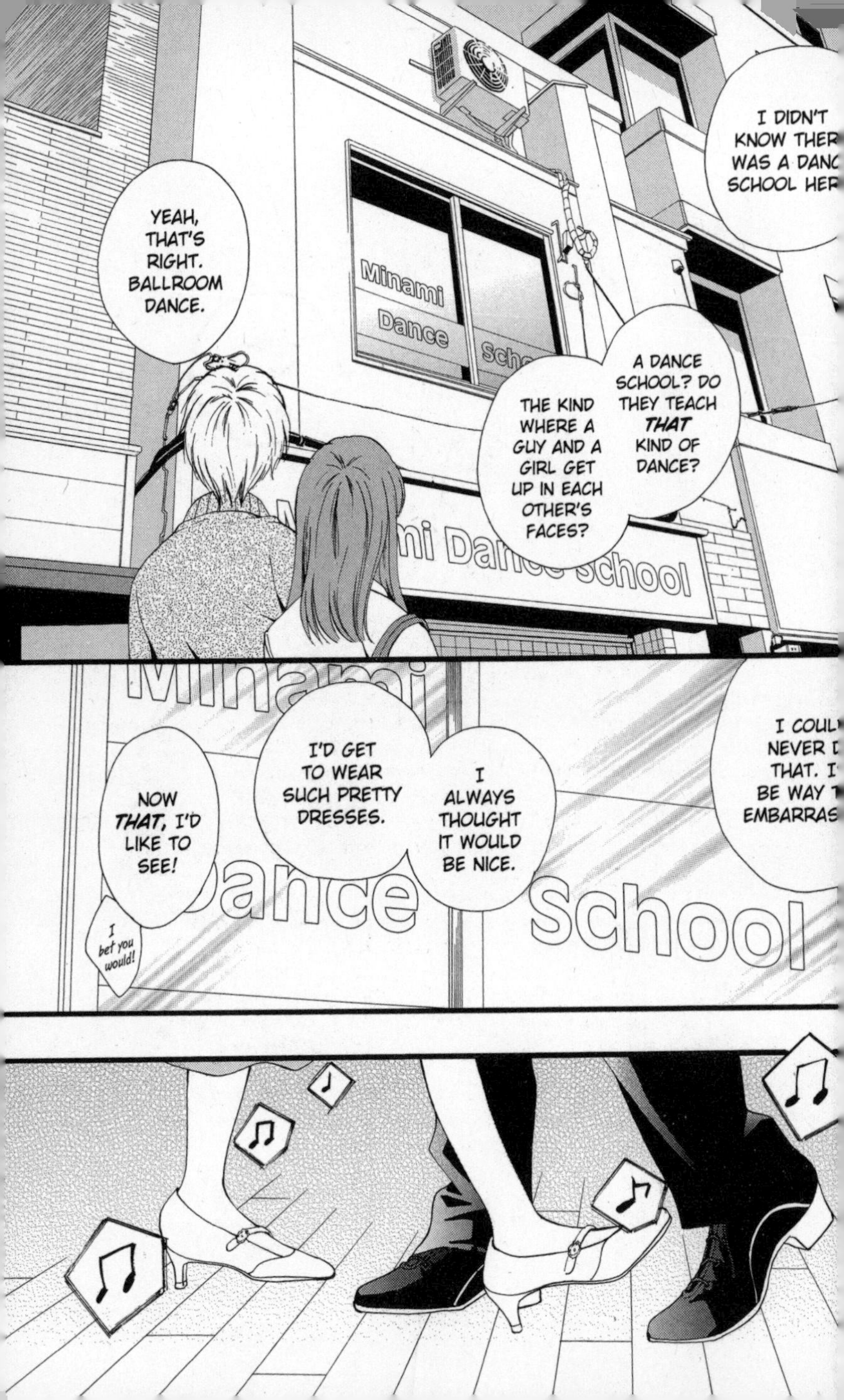
I DIDN'T KNOW THER WAS A DANC SCHOOL HER
A DANCE SCHOOL? DO THEY TEACH *THAT* KIND OF DANCE?
THE KIND WHERE A GUY AND A GIRL GET UP IN EACH OTHER'S FACES?
YEAH, THAT'S RIGHT. BALLROOM DANCE.
I COUL NEVER D THAT. I' BE WAY T EMBARRAS
I ALWAYS THOUGHT IT WOULD BE NICE.
I'D GET TO WEAR SUCH PRETTY DRESSES.
NOW *THAT*, I'D LIKE TO SEE!
I bet you would!

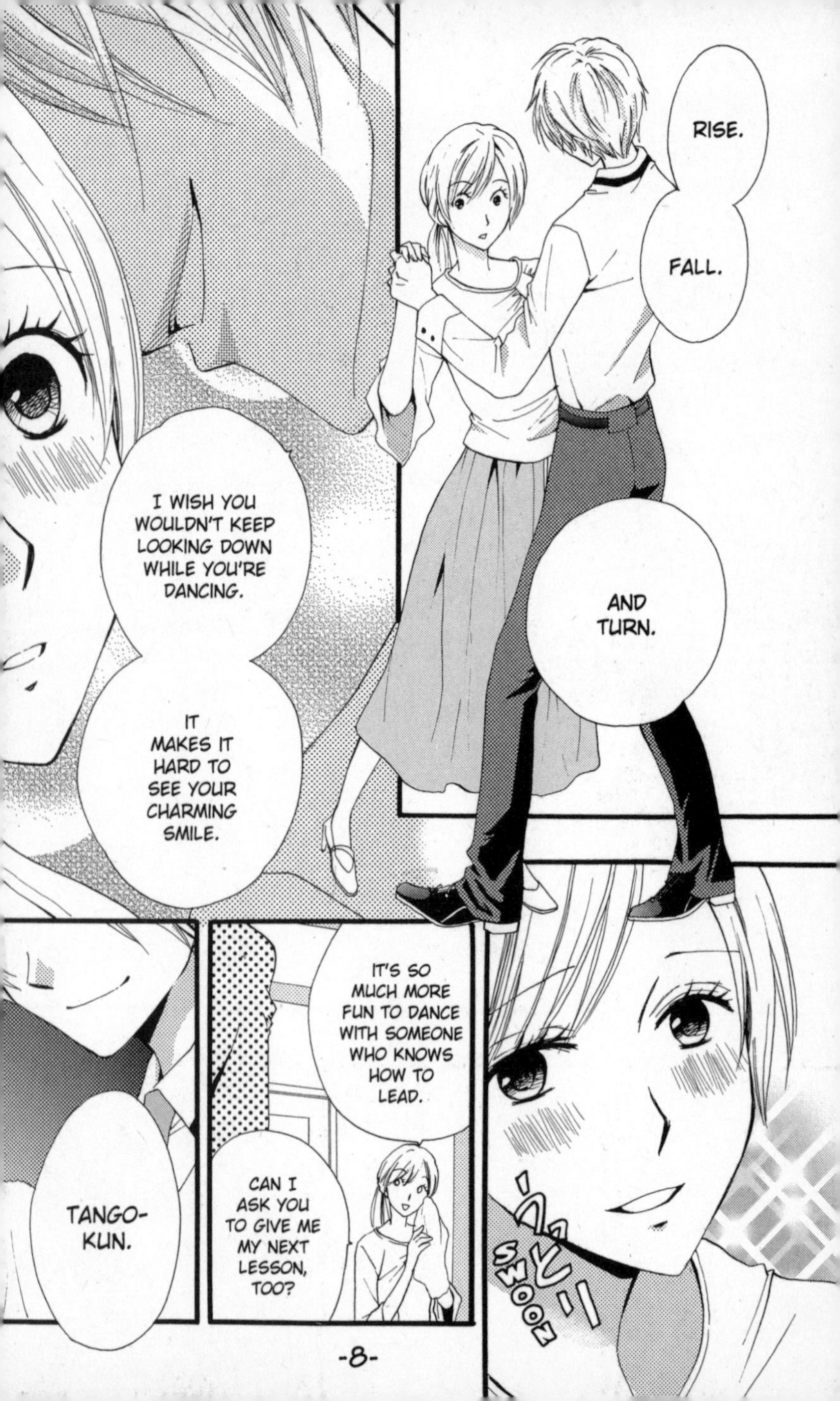
RISE.
FALL.
AND TURN.
I WISH YOU WOULDN'T KEEP LOOKING DOWN WHILE YOU'RE DANCING.
IT MAKES IT HARD TO SEE YOUR CHARMING SMILE.
SWOON
IT'S SO MUCH MORE FUN TO DANCE WITH SOMEONE WHO KNOWS HOW TO LEAD.
CAN I ASK YOU TO GIVE ME MY NEXT LESSON, TOO?
TANGO-KUN.

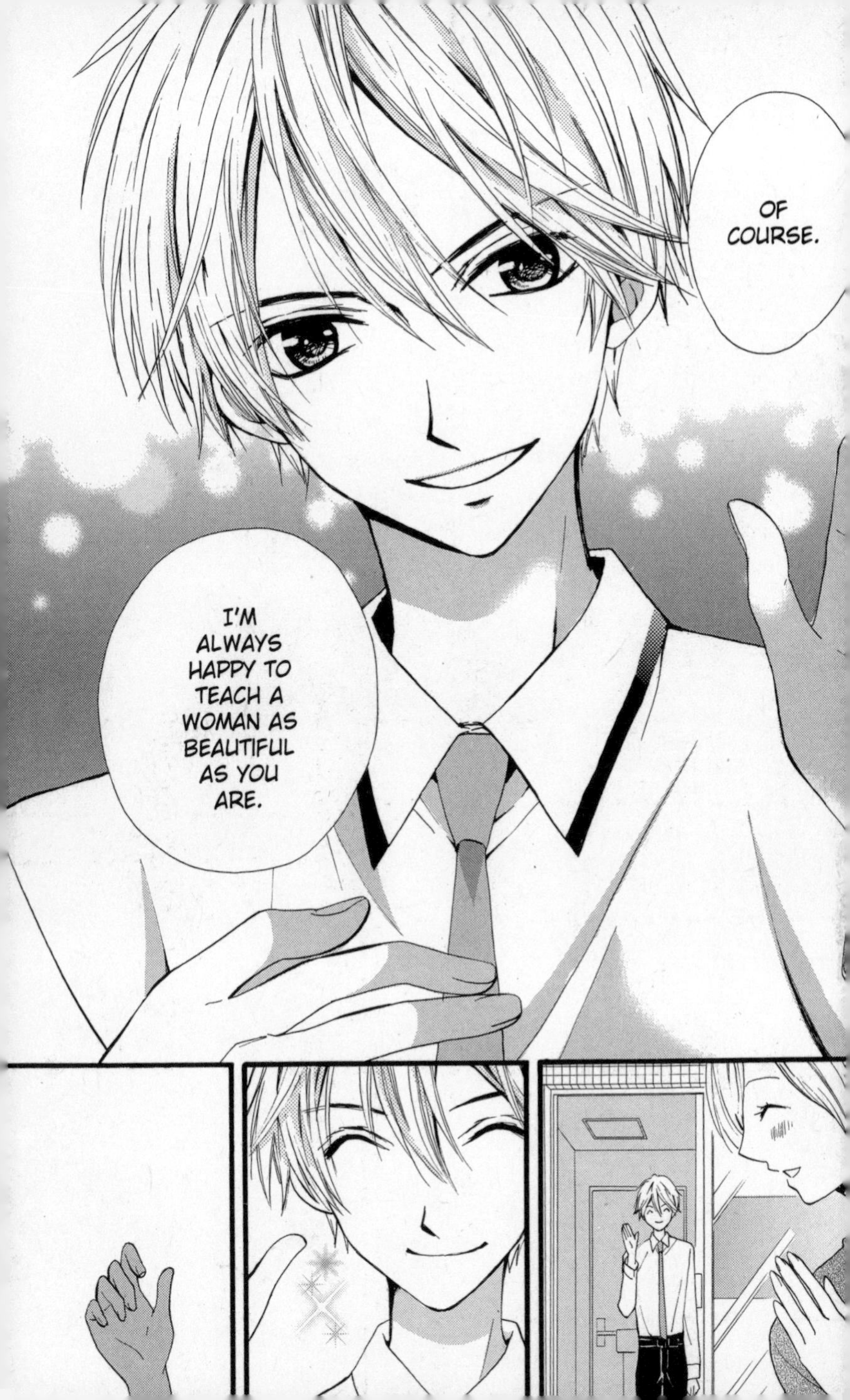
OF COURSE.
I'M ALWAYS HAPPY TO TEACH A WOMAN AS BEAUTIFUL AS YOU ARE.

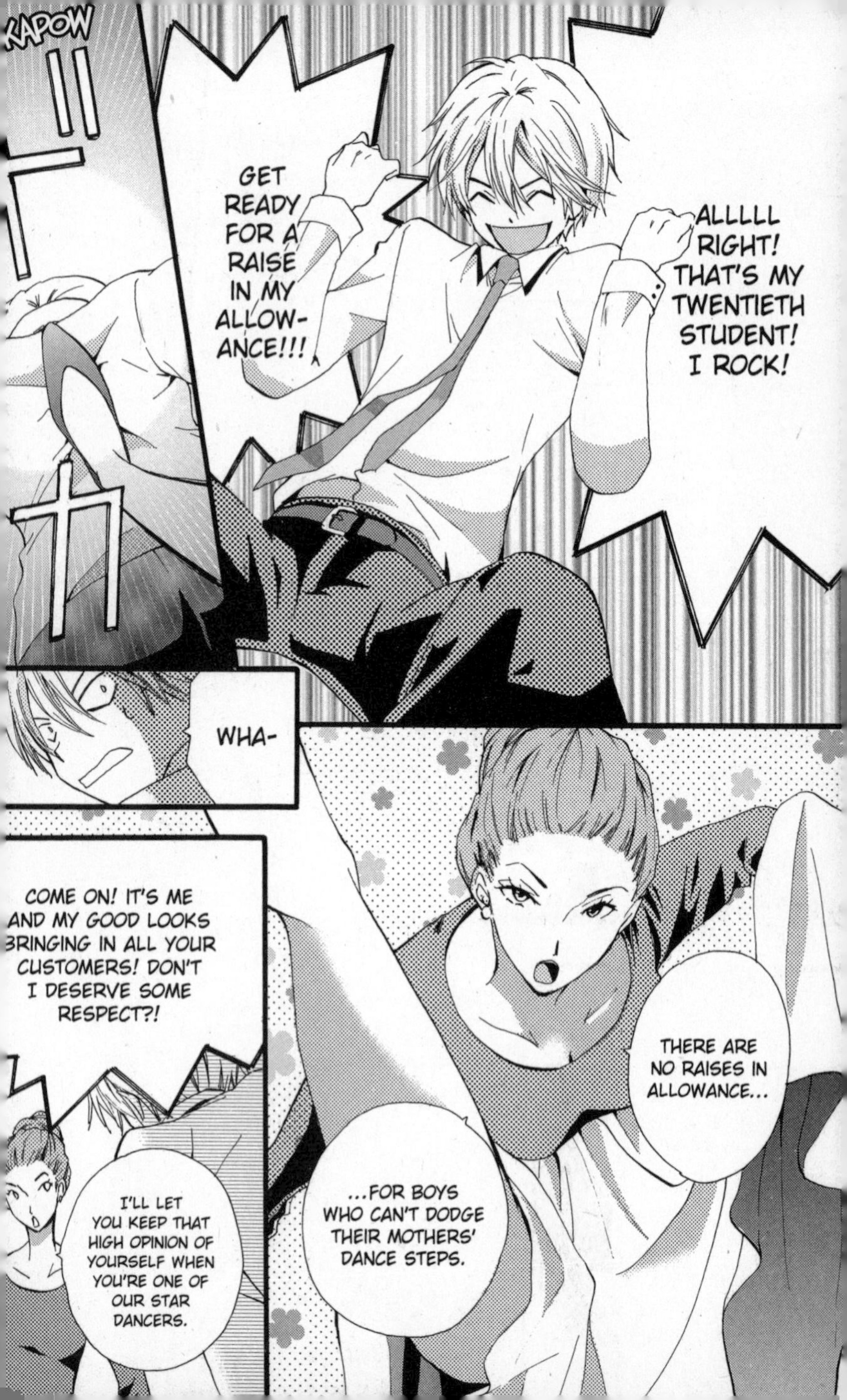
ALLLLL RIGHT! THAT'S MY TWENTIETH STUDENT! I ROCK!
GET READY FOR A RAISE IN MY ALLOW-ANCE!!!
KAPOW
THERE ARE NO RAISES IN ALLOWANCE...
...FOR BOYS WHO CAN'T DODGE THEIR MOTHERS' DANCE STEPS.
WHA-
COME ON! IT'S ME AND MY GOOD LOOKS BRINGING IN ALL YOUR CUSTOMERS! DON'T I DESERVE SOME RESPECT?!
I'LL LET YOU KEEP THAT HIGH OPINION OF YOURSELF WHEN YOU'RE ONE OF OUR STAR DANCERS.

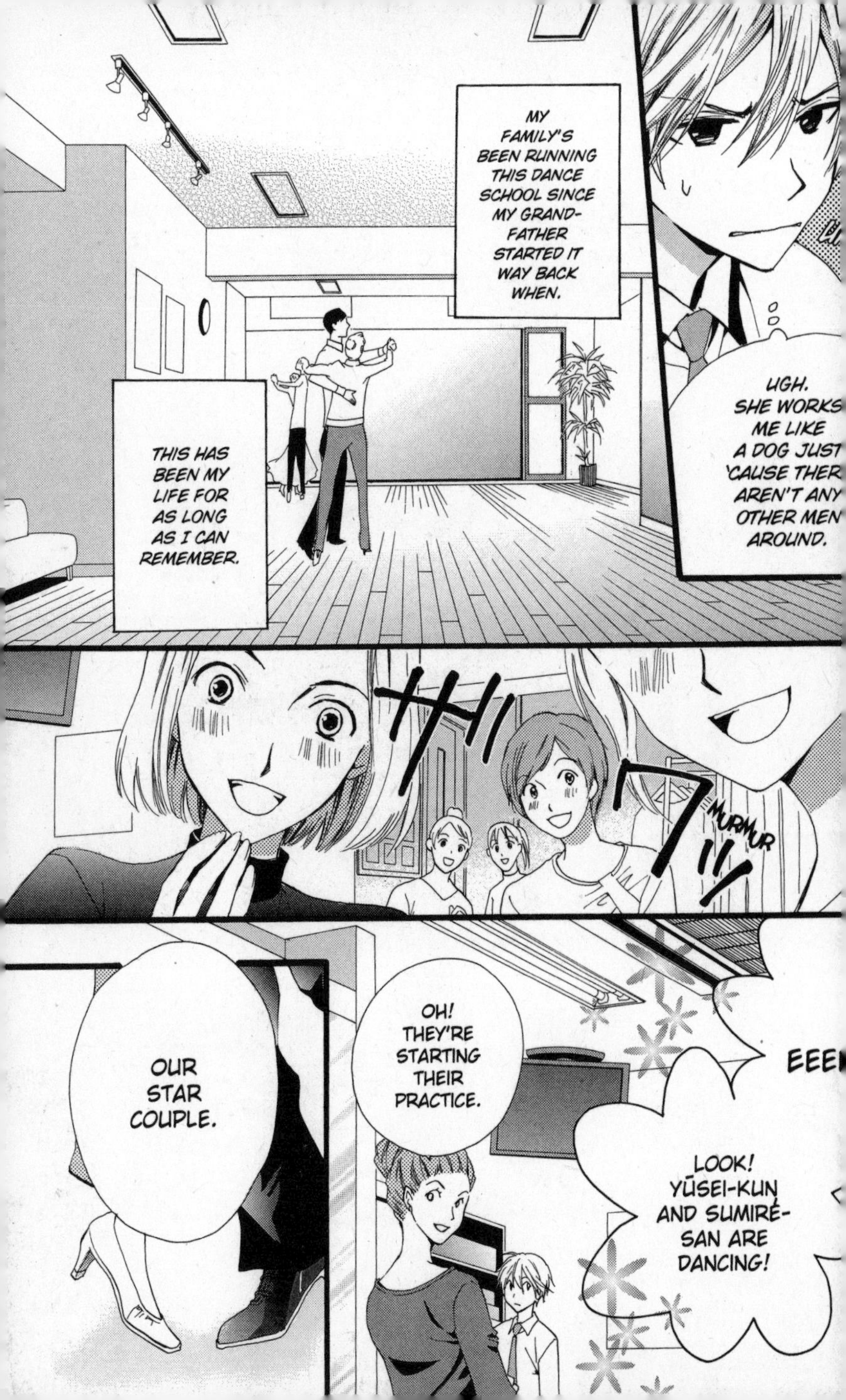
MY FAMILY'S BEEN RUNNING THIS DANCE SCHOOL SINCE MY GRAND-FATHER STARTED IT WAY BACK WHEN.
THIS HAS BEEN MY LIFE FOR AS LONG AS I CAN REMEMBER.
UGH. SHE WORKS ME LIKE A DOG JUST 'CAUSE THER AREN'T ANY OTHER MEN AROUND.
MURMUR
EEE
LOOK! YŪSEI-KUN AND SUMIRÉ-SAN ARE DANCING!
OH! THEY'RE STARTING THEIR PRACTICE.
OUR STAR COUPLE.

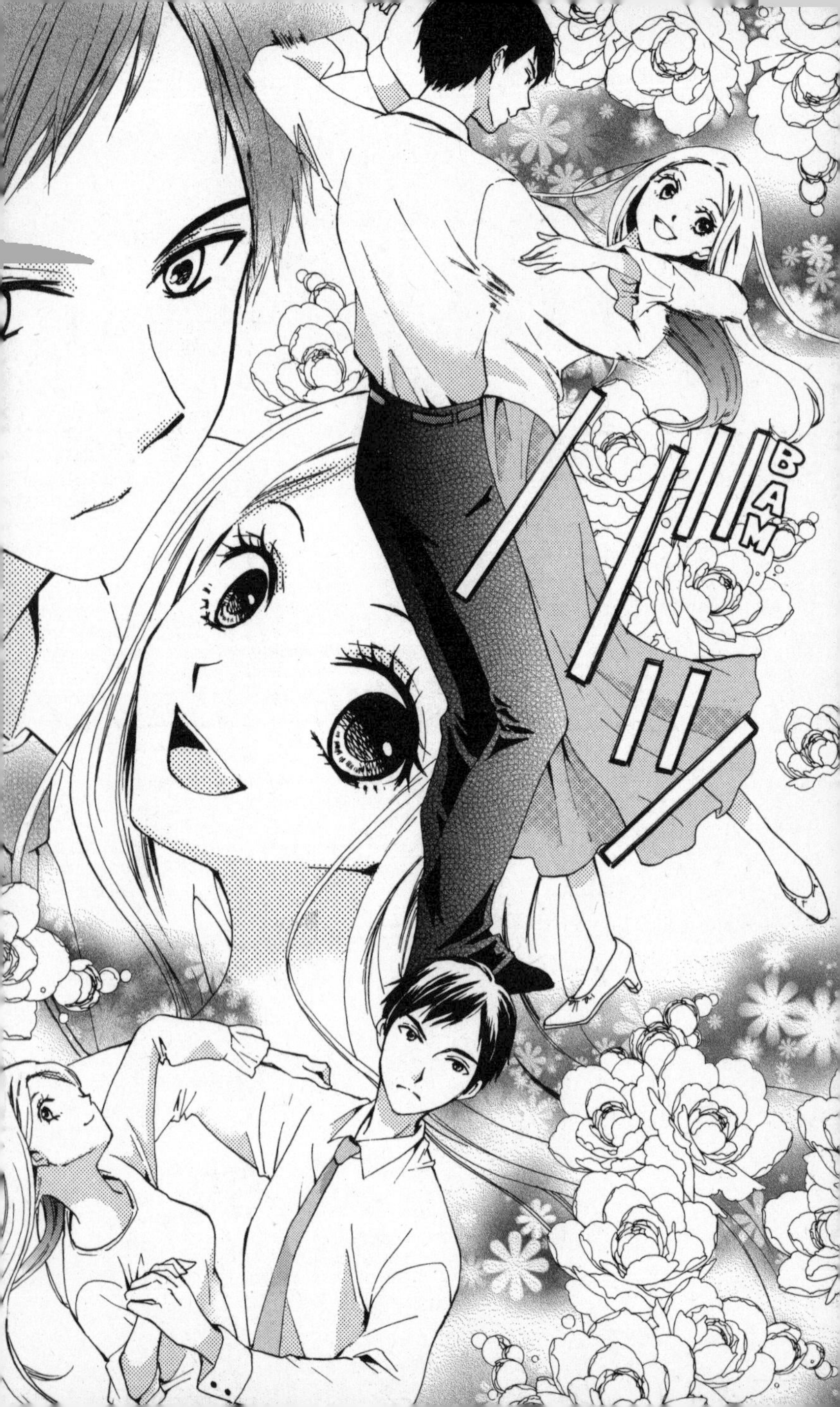
BAM

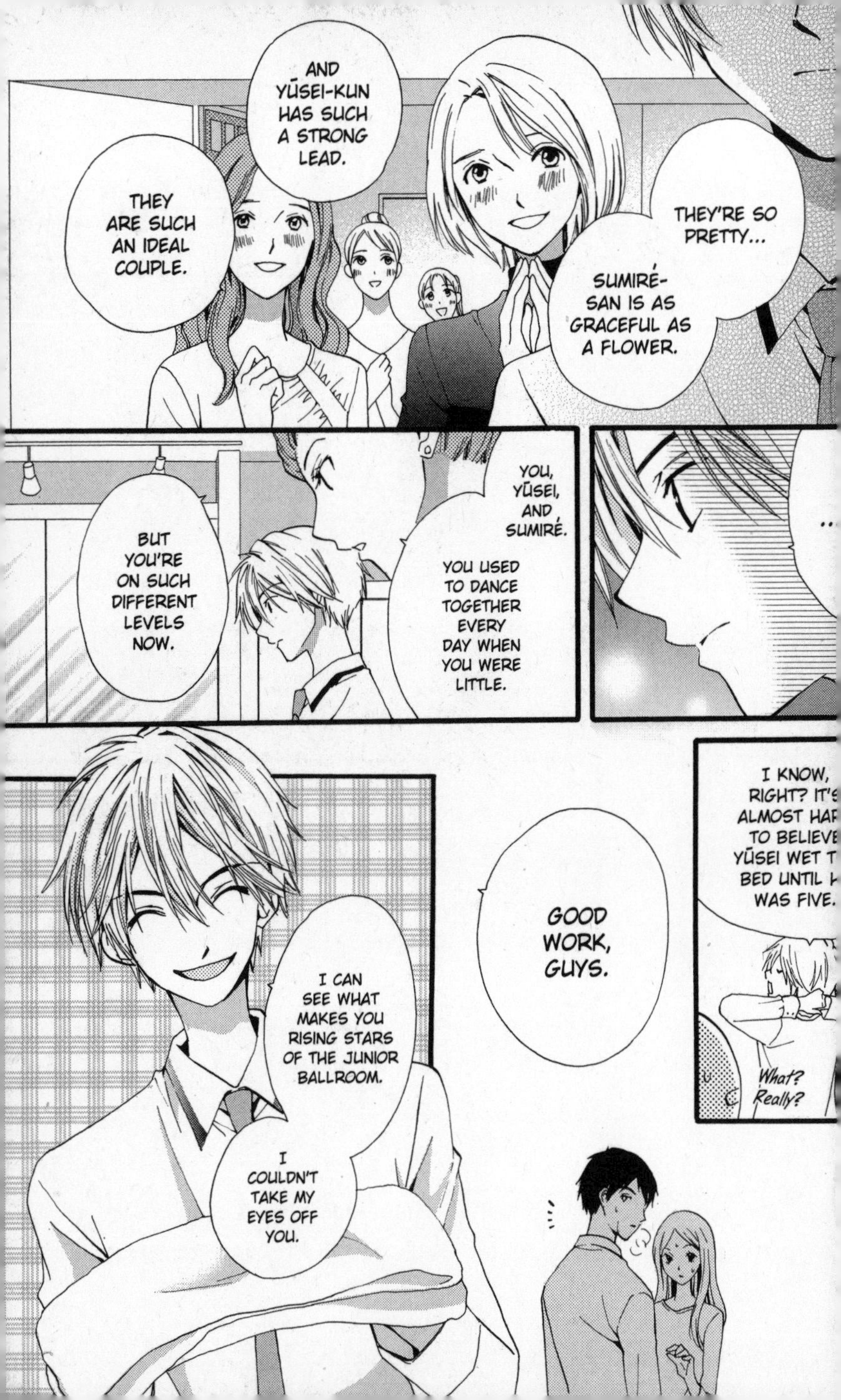
THEY'RE SO PRETTY...
SUMIRÉ-SAN IS AS GRACEFUL AS A FLOWER.
AND YŪSEI-KUN HAS SUCH A STRONG LEAD.
THEY ARE SUCH AN IDEAL COUPLE.
...
YOU, YŪSEI, AND SUMIRÉ.
YOU USED TO DANCE TOGETHER EVERY DAY WHEN YOU WERE LITTLE.
BUT YOU'RE ON SUCH DIFFERENT LEVELS NOW.
I KNOW, RIGHT? IT'S ALMOST HAR TO BELIEVE YŪSEI WET T BED UNTIL H WAS FIVE.
What? Really?
GOOD WORK, GUYS.
I CAN SEE WHAT MAKES YOU RISING STARS OF THE JUNIOR BALLROOM.
I COULDN'T TAKE MY EYES OFF YOU.

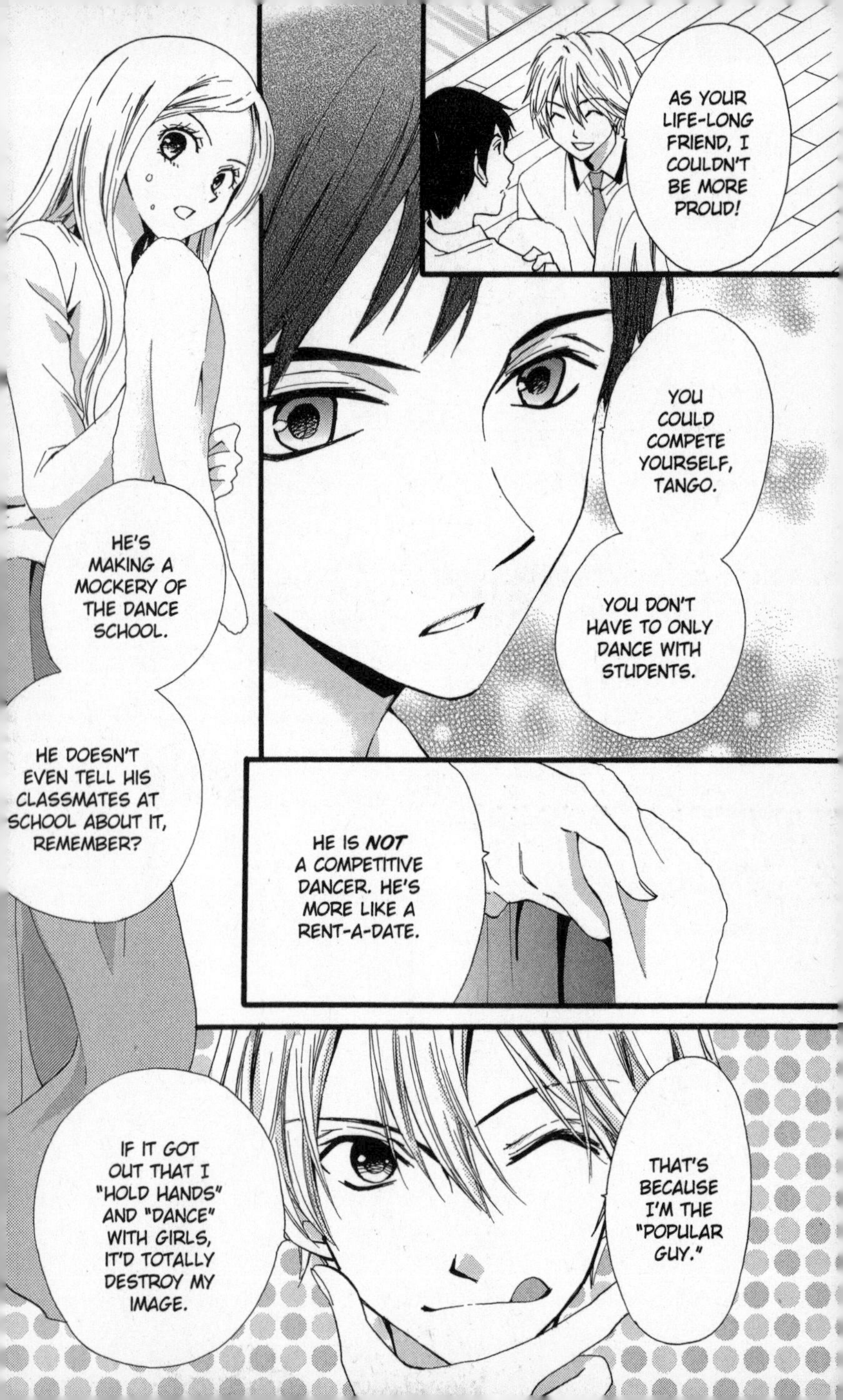
AS YOUR LIFE-LONG FRIEND, I COULDN'T BE MORE PROUD!
YOU COULD COMPETE YOURSELF, TANGO.
YOU DON'T HAVE TO ONLY DANCE WITH STUDENTS.
HE IS *NOT* A COMPETITIVE DANCER. HE'S MORE LIKE A RENT-A-DATE.
HE'S MAKING A MOCKERY OF THE DANCE SCHOOL.
HE DOESN'T EVEN TELL HIS CLASSMATES AT SCHOOL ABOUT IT, REMEMBER?
THAT'S BECAUSE I'M THE "POPULAR GUY."
IF IT GOT OUT THAT I "HOLD HANDS" AND "DANCE" WITH GIRLS, IT'D TOTALLY DESTROY MY IMAGE.

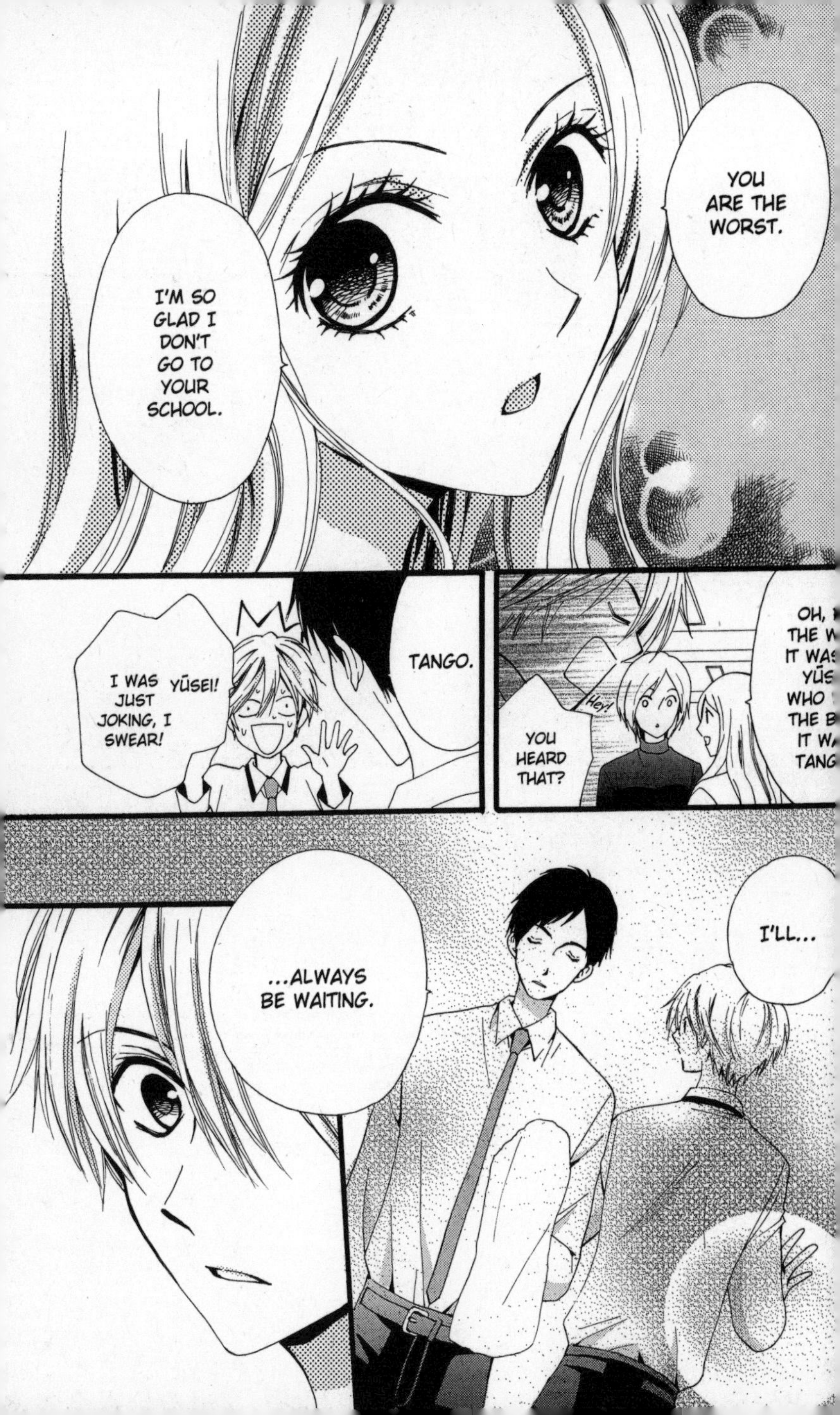
YOU ARE THE WORST.
I'M SO GLAD I DON'T GO TO YOUR SCHOOL.
OH, THE W IT WAS YŪS WHO THE B IT WA TANG
Hey!
YOU HEARD THAT?
TANGO.
YŪSEI!
I WAS JUST JOKING, I SWEAR!
I'LL...
...ALWAYS BE WAITING.

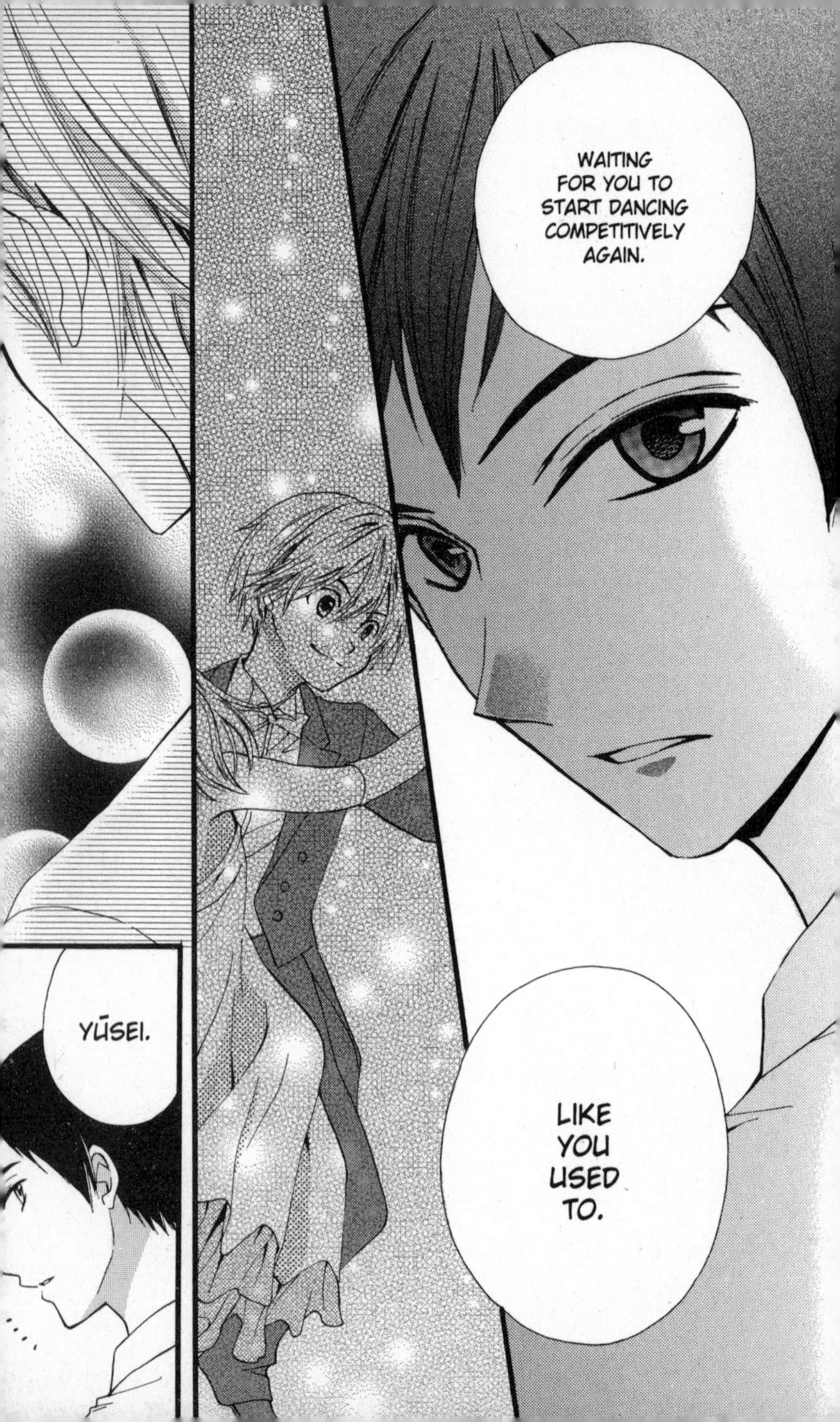
WAITING FOR YOU TO START DANCING COMPETITIVELY AGAIN.
LIKE YOU USED TO.
YŪSEI.
...

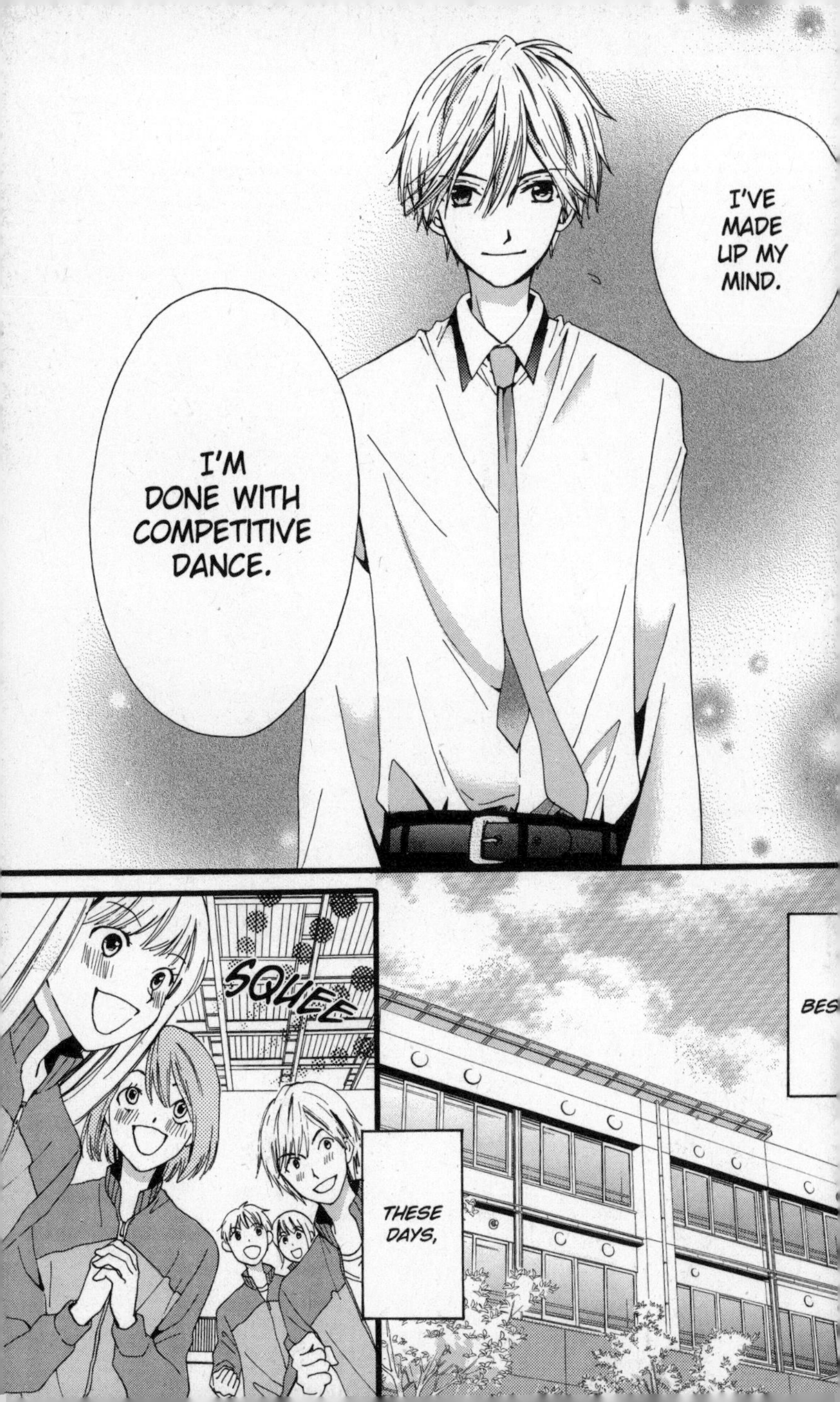
I'VE MADE UP MY MIND.
I'M DONE WITH COMPETITIVE DANCE.
BES
THESE DAYS,
SQUEE

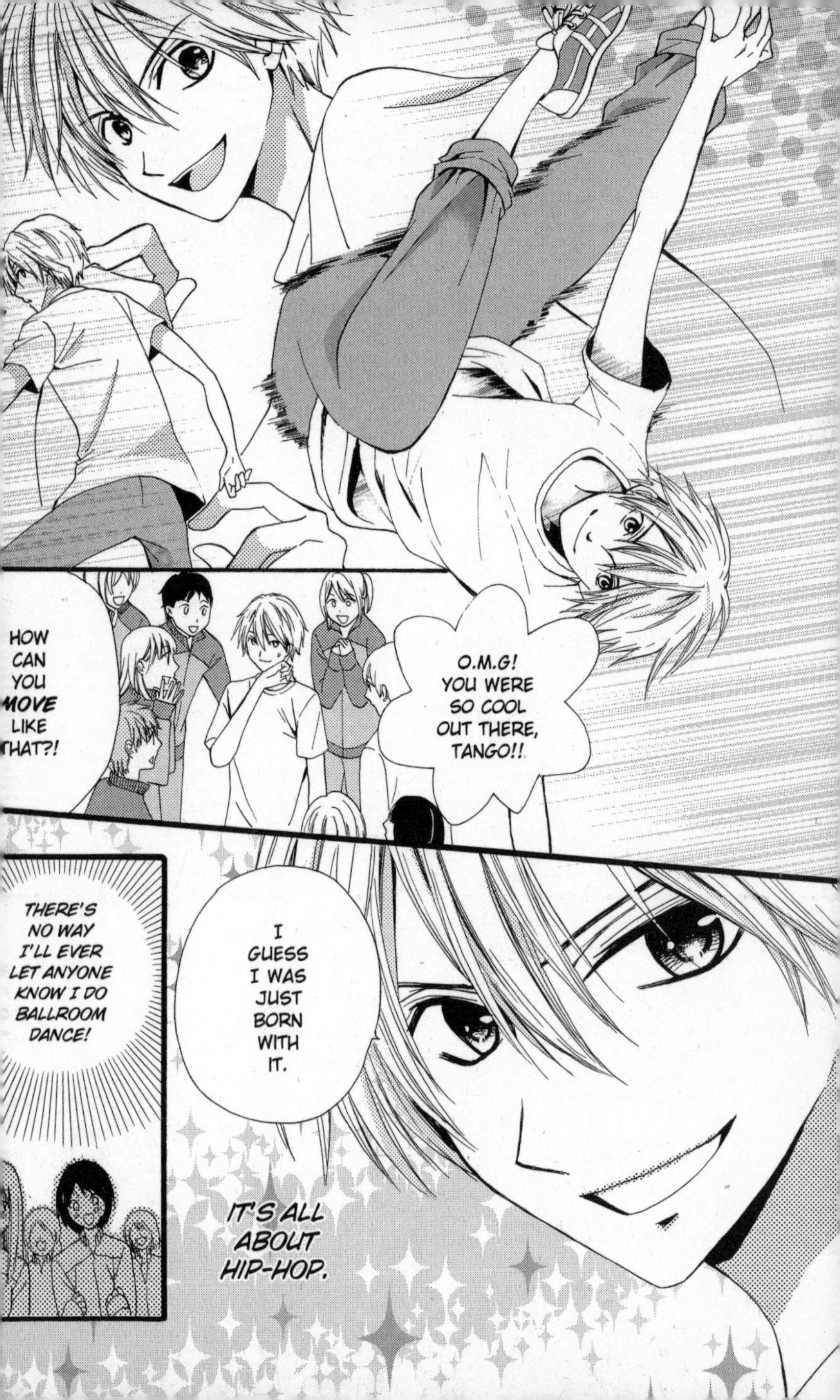
O.M.G! YOU WERE SO COOL OUT THERE, TANGO!!
HOW CAN YOU MOVE LIKE THAT?!
I GUESS I WAS JUST BORN WITH IT.
IT'S ALL ABOUT HIP-HOP.
THERE'S NO WAY I'LL EVER LET ANYONE KNOW I DO BALLROOM DANCE!

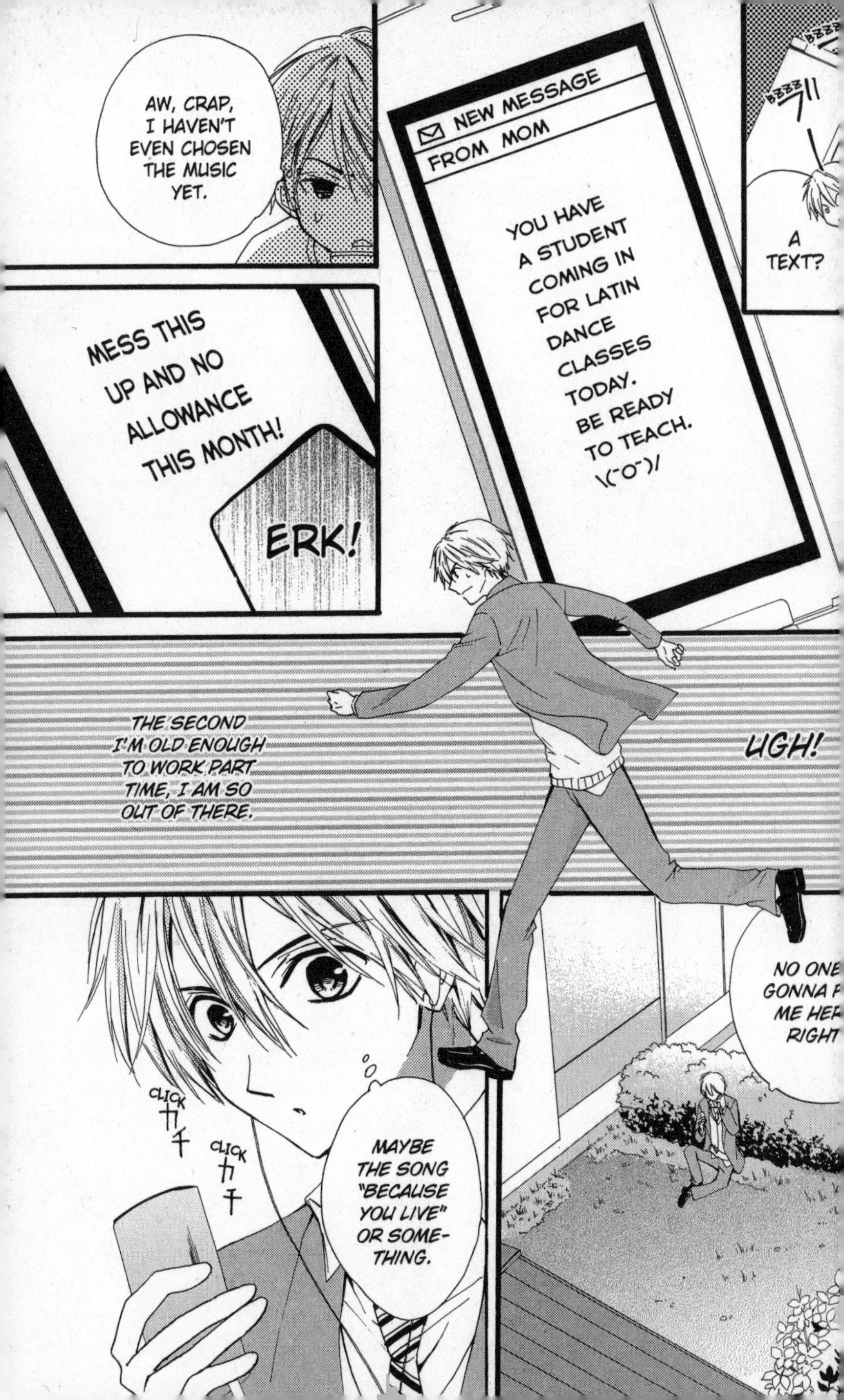
BZZZ
BZZZ
A TEXT?
NEW MESSAGE
FROM MOM
YOU HAVE A STUDENT COMING IN FOR LATIN DANCE CLASSES TODAY. BE READY TO TEACH. \(¯O¯)/
AW, CRAP, I HAVEN'T EVEN CHOSEN THE MUSIC YET.
MESS THIS UP AND NO ALLOWANCE THIS MONTH!
ERK!
UGH!
THE SECOND I'M OLD ENOUGH TO WORK PART TIME, I AM SO OUT OF THERE.
NO ONE GONNA F ME HER RIGHT
MAYBE THE SONG "BECAUSE YOU LIVE" OR SOME-THING.
CLICK
CLICK

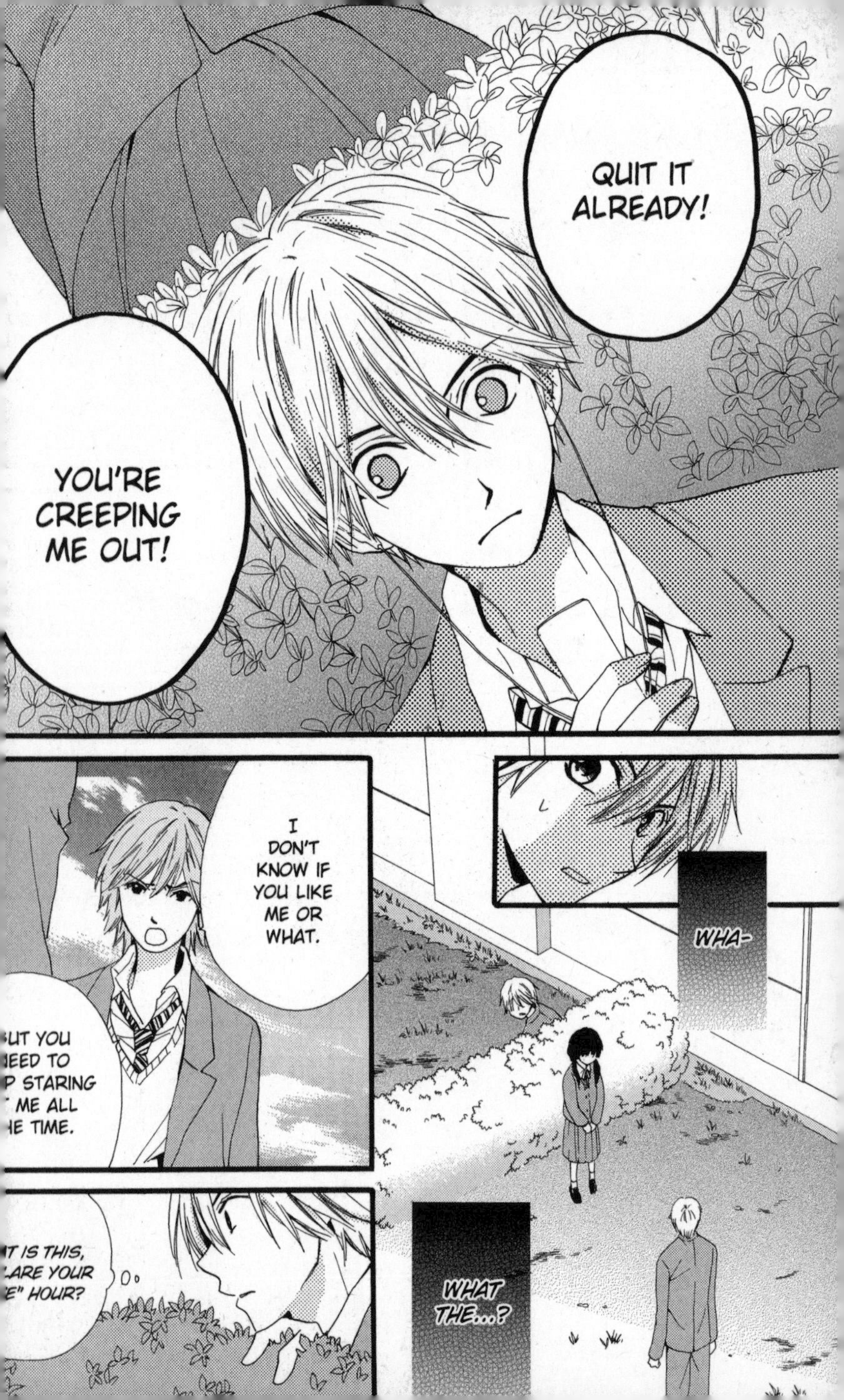

QUIT IT ALREADY!
YOU'RE CREEPING ME OUT!
WHA-
WHAT THE...?
I DON'T KNOW IF YOU LIKE ME OR WHAT.
UT YOU EED TO P STARING ME ALL HE TIME.
T IS THIS, ARE YOUR E" HOUR?

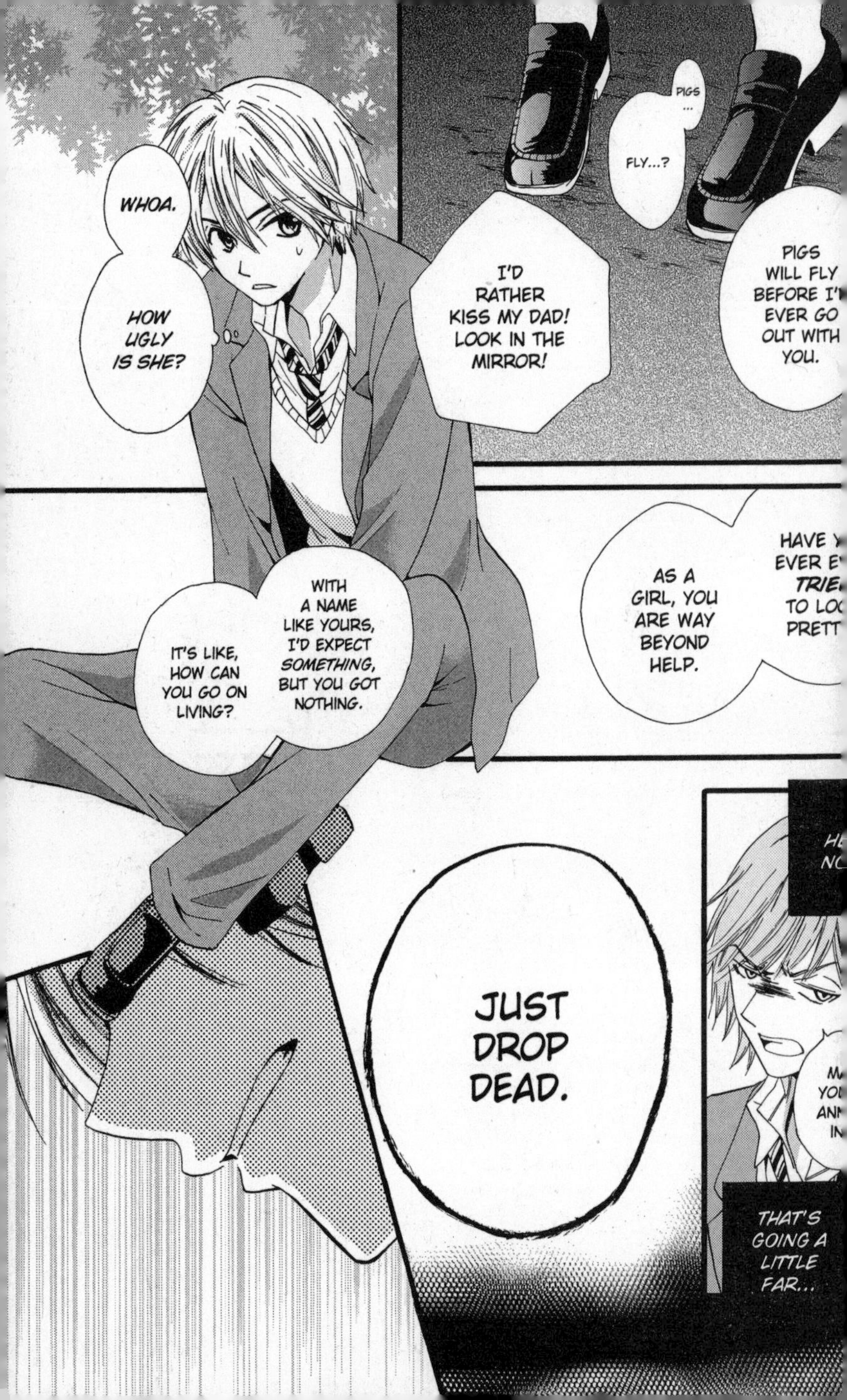
PIGS WILL FLY BEFORE I'
EVER GO OUT WITH YOU.
PIGS ...
FLY...?
I'D RATHER KISS MY DAD! LOOK IN THE MIRROR!
WHOA.
HOW UGLY IS SHE?
HAVE Y EVER E TRIE TO LO PRETT
AS A GIRL, YOU ARE WAY BEYOND HELP.
WITH A NAME LIKE YOURS, I'D EXPECT SOMETHING, BUT YOU GOT NOTHING.
IT'S LIKE, HOW CAN YOU GO ON LIVING?
THAT'S GOING A LITTLE FAR...
JUST DROP DEAD.

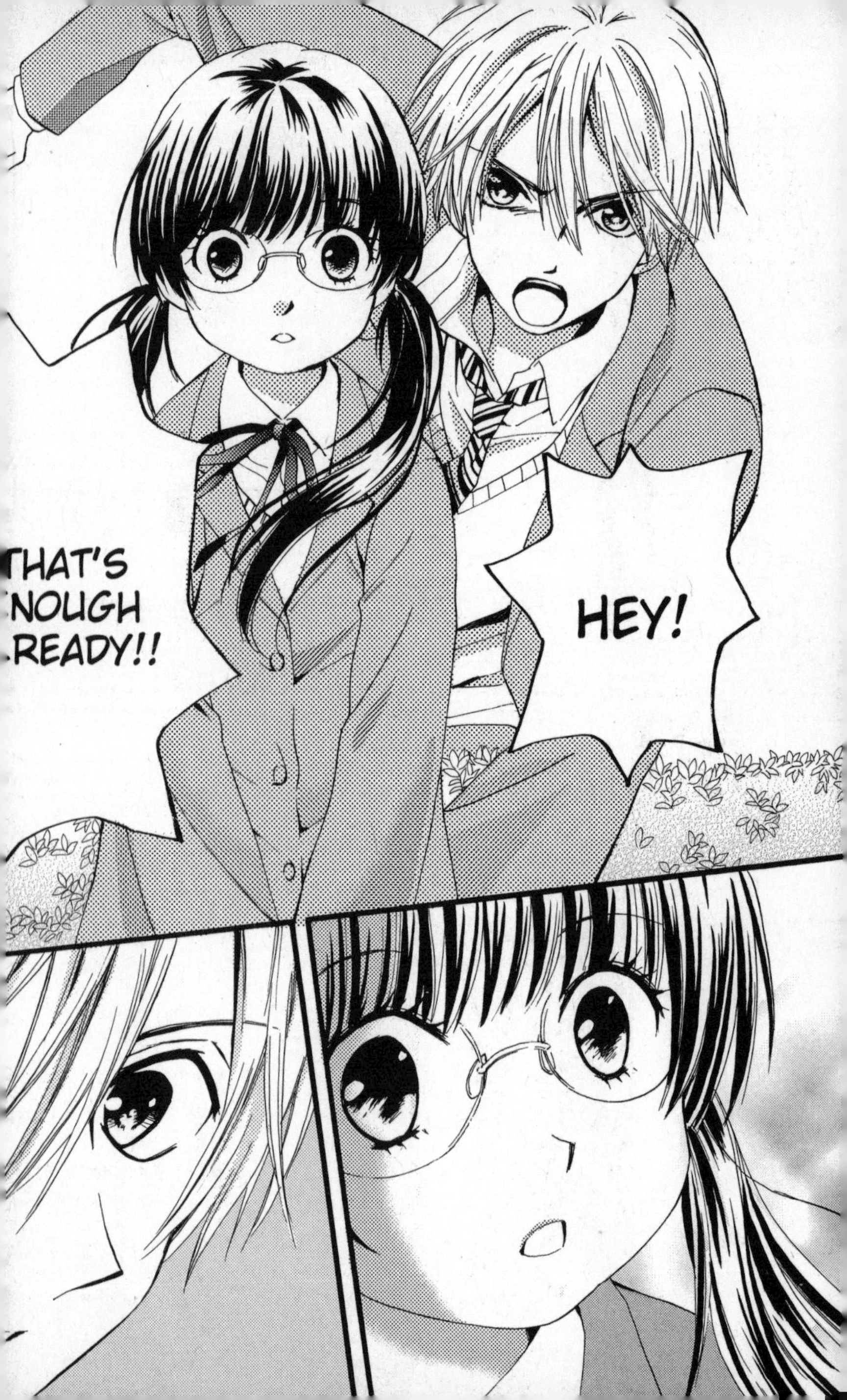
HEY!
THAT'S NOUGH READY!!

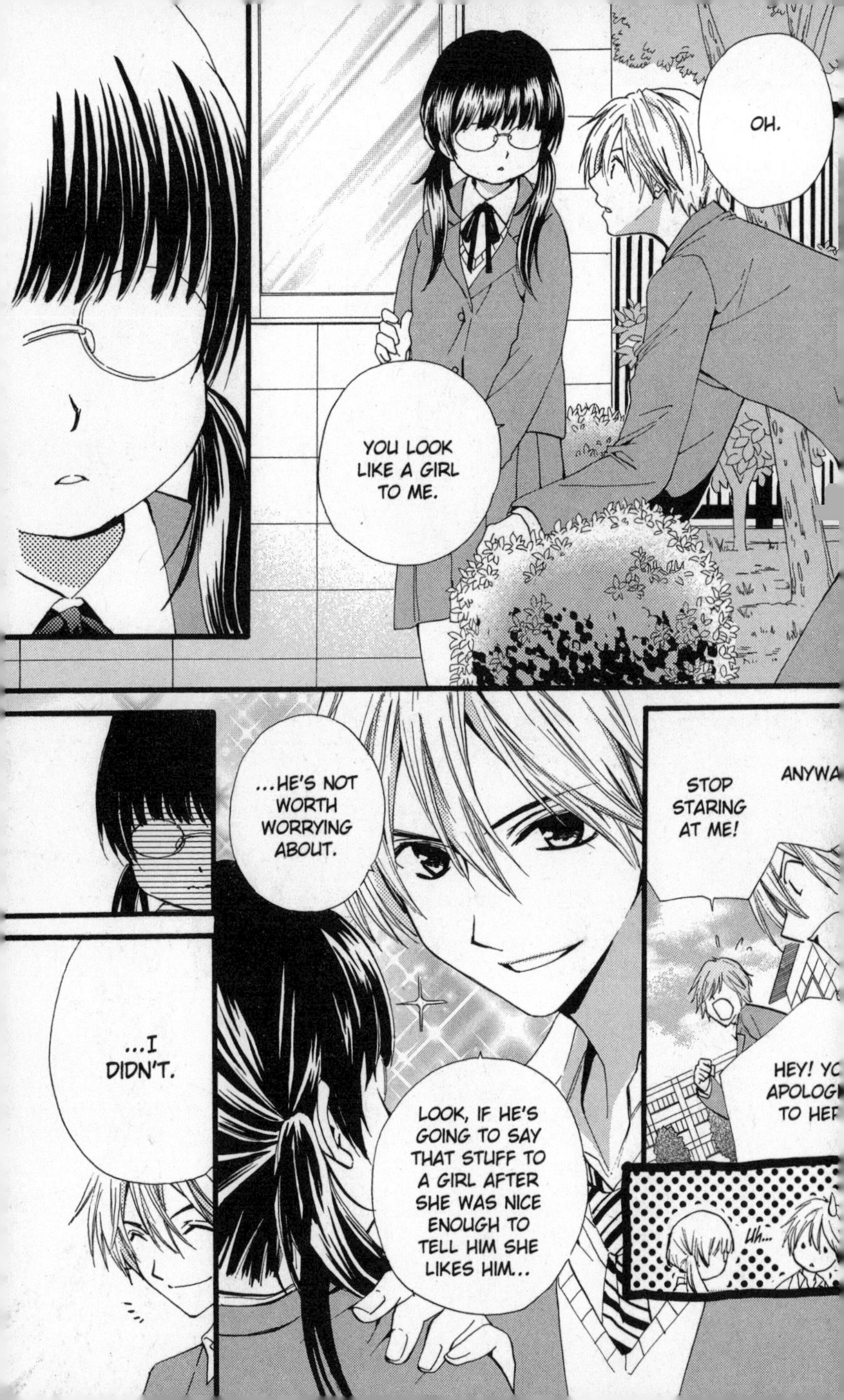

OH.
YOU LOOK LIKE A GIRL TO ME.
ANYWA
STOP STARING AT ME!
HEY! YO APOLOG TO HEF
Uh...
LOOK, IF HE'S GOING TO SAY THAT STUFF TO A GIRL AFTER SHE WAS NICE ENOUGH TO TELL HIM SHE LIKES HIM...
...HE'S NOT WORTH WORRYING ABOUT.
...I DIDN'T.

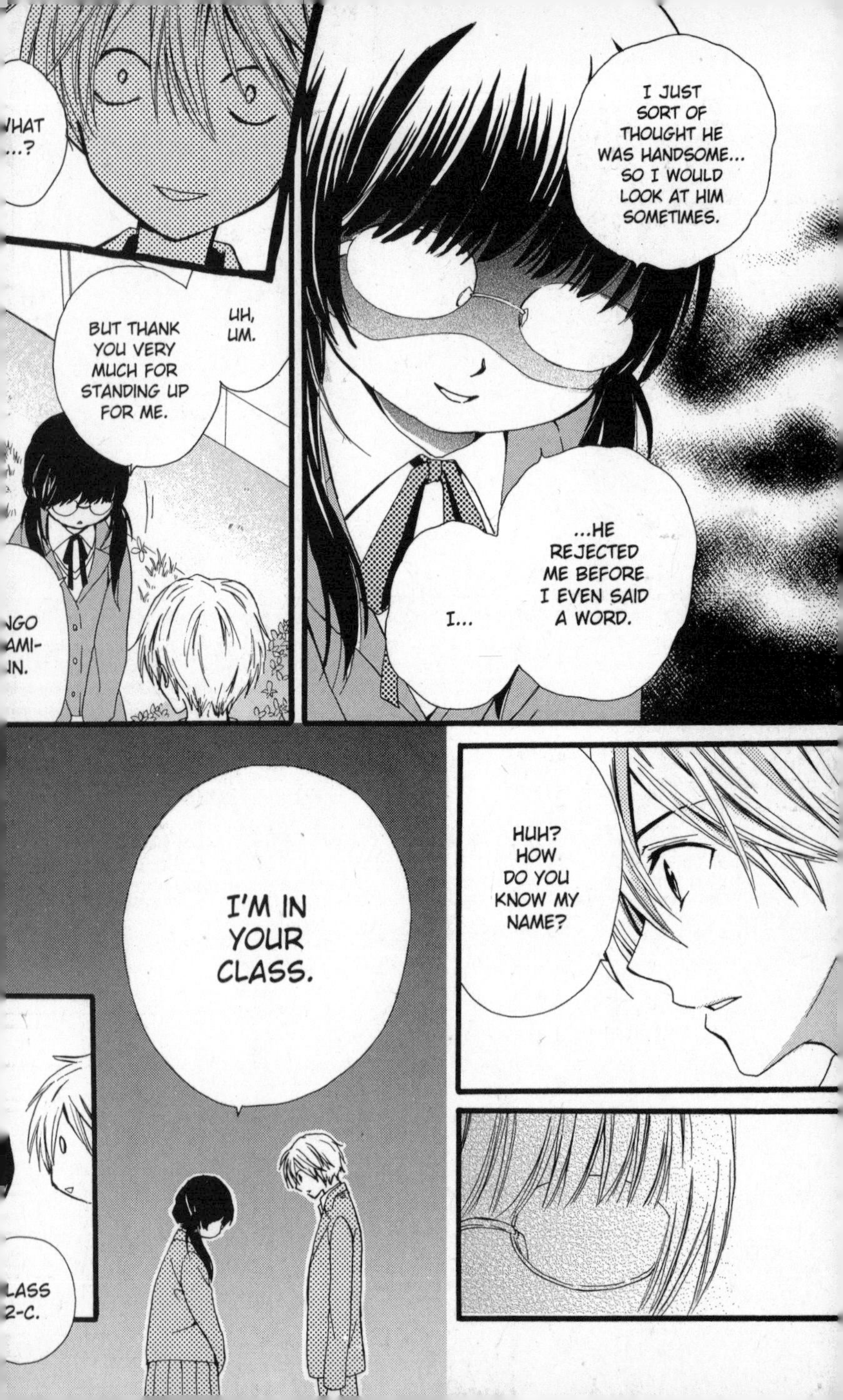
I JUST SORT OF THOUGHT HE WAS HANDSOME... SO I WOULD LOOK AT HIM SOMETIMES.
I...
...HE REJECTED ME BEFORE I EVEN SAID A WORD.
HAT ...?
UH, UM.
BUT THANK YOU VERY MUCH FOR STANDING UP FOR ME.
NGO AMI- IN.
HUH? HOW DO YOU KNOW MY NAME?
I'M IN YOUR CLASS.
LASS 2-C.

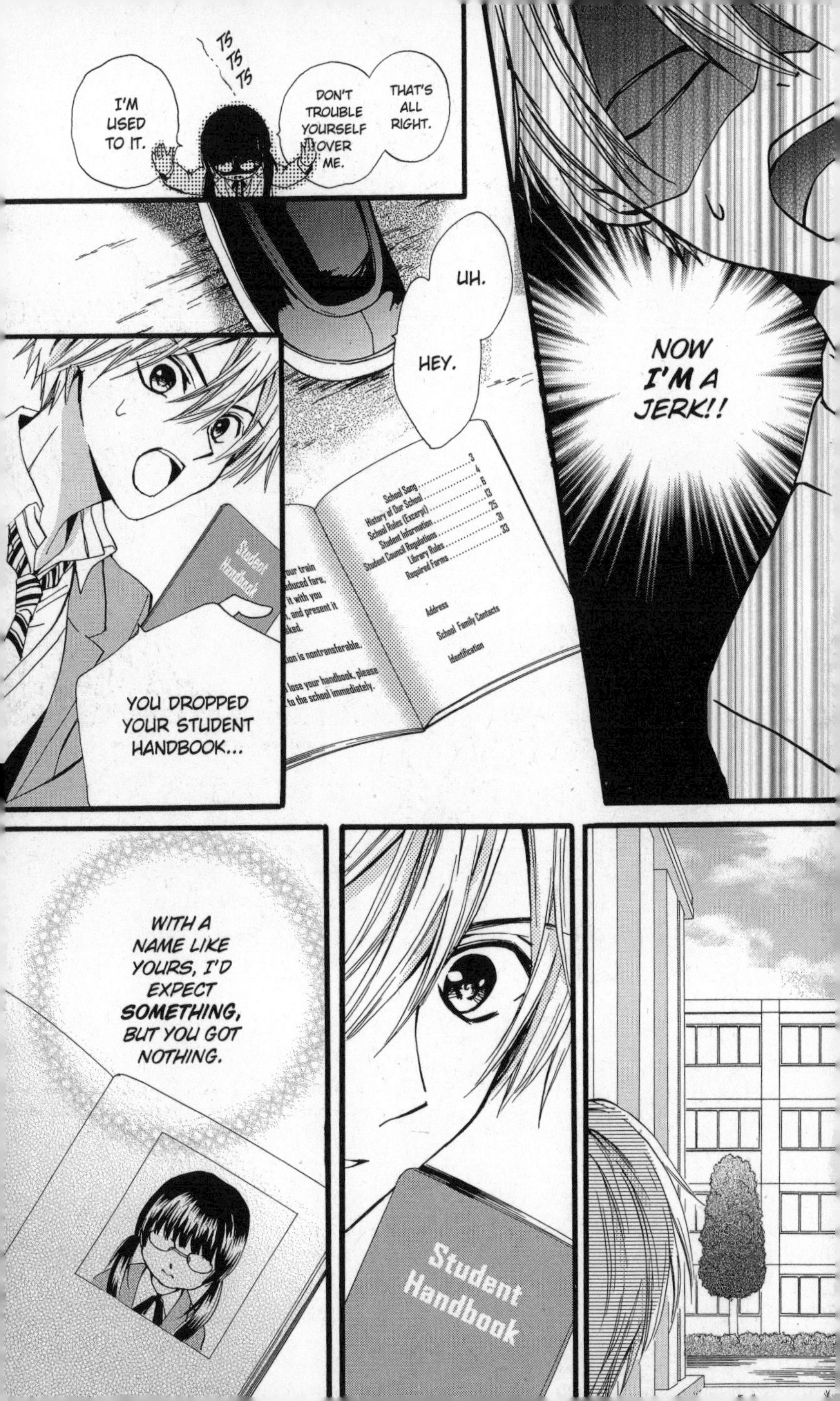
NOW I'M A JERK!!
THAT'S ALL RIGHT.
DON'T TROUBLE YOURSELF OVER ME.
TS TS TS
I'M USED TO IT.
UH.
HEY.
School Song 3
History of Our School 4
School Rules (Excerpt) 6
Student Information 13
Student Council Regulations 25
Library Rules 31
Required Forms 33
Address
School Family Contacts
Identification
Student Handbook
YOU DROPPED YOUR STUDENT HANDBOOK...
Student Handbook
WITH A NAME LIKE YOURS, I'D EXPECT SOMETHING, BUT YOU GOT NOTHING.

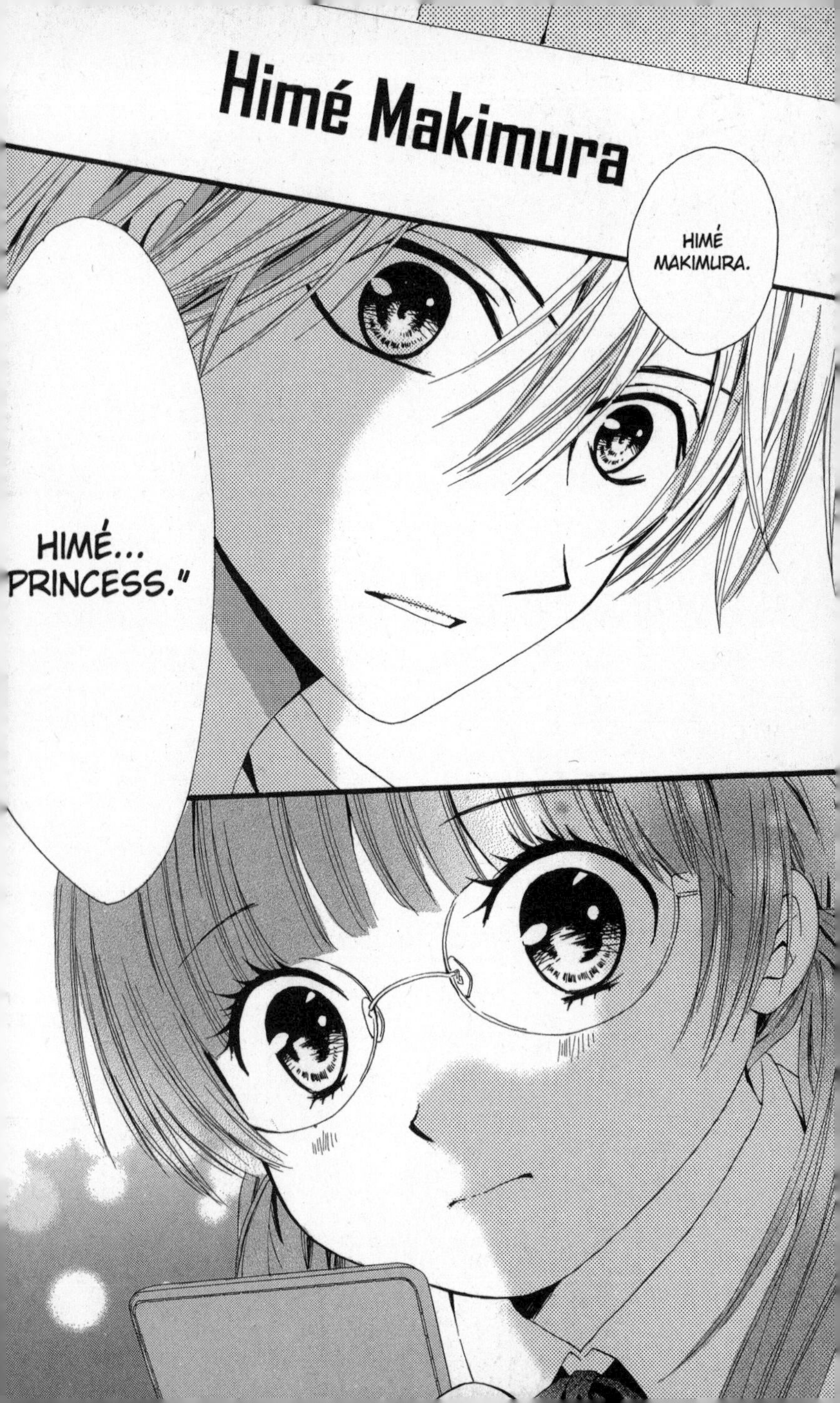
Himé Makimura
HIMÉ MAKIMURA.
HIMÉ... PRINCESS."

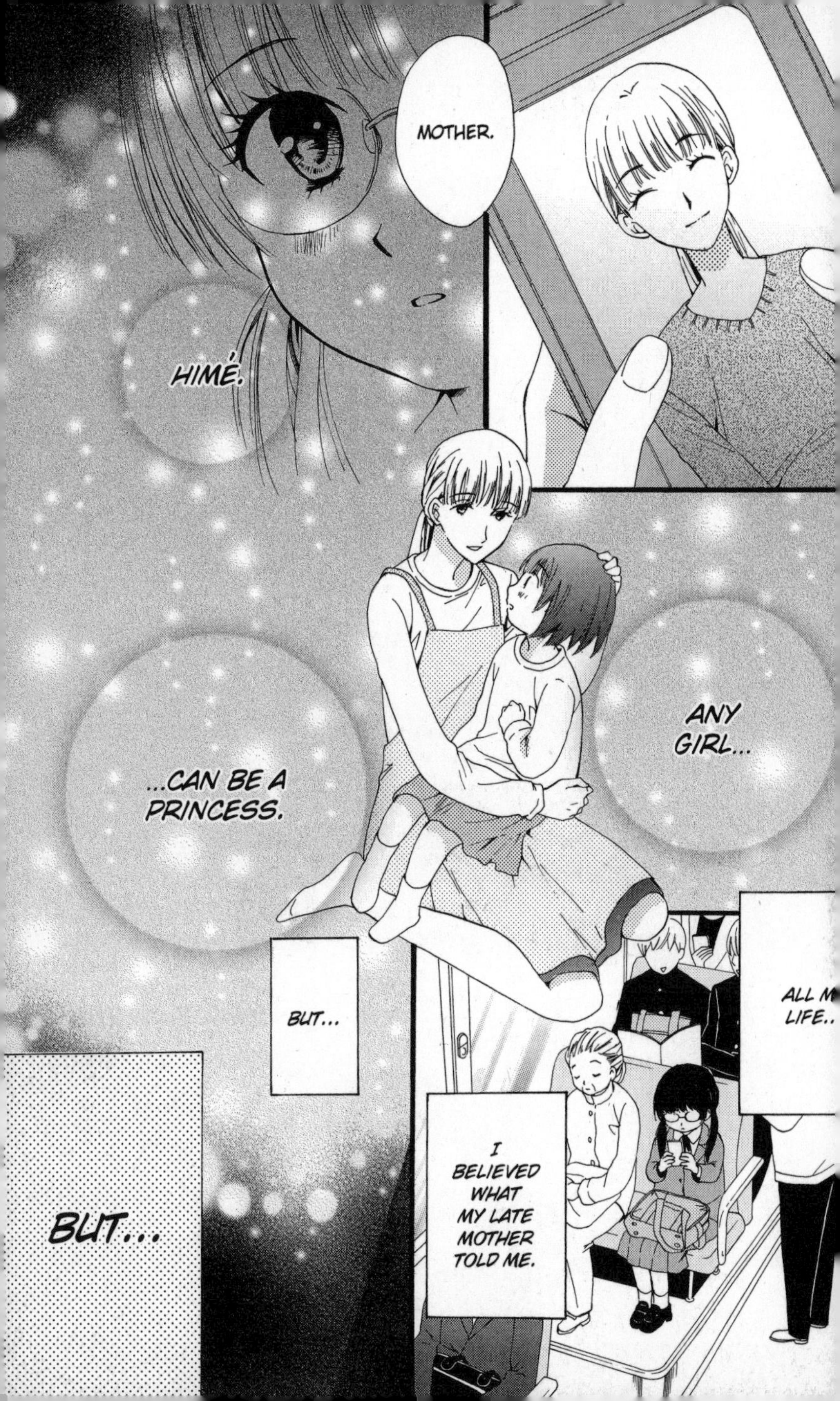
MOTHER.
HIMÉ.
ANY GIRL...
...CAN BE A PRINCESS.
ALL M
LIFE..
I BELIEVED WHAT MY LATE MOTHER TOLD ME.
BUT...
BUT...

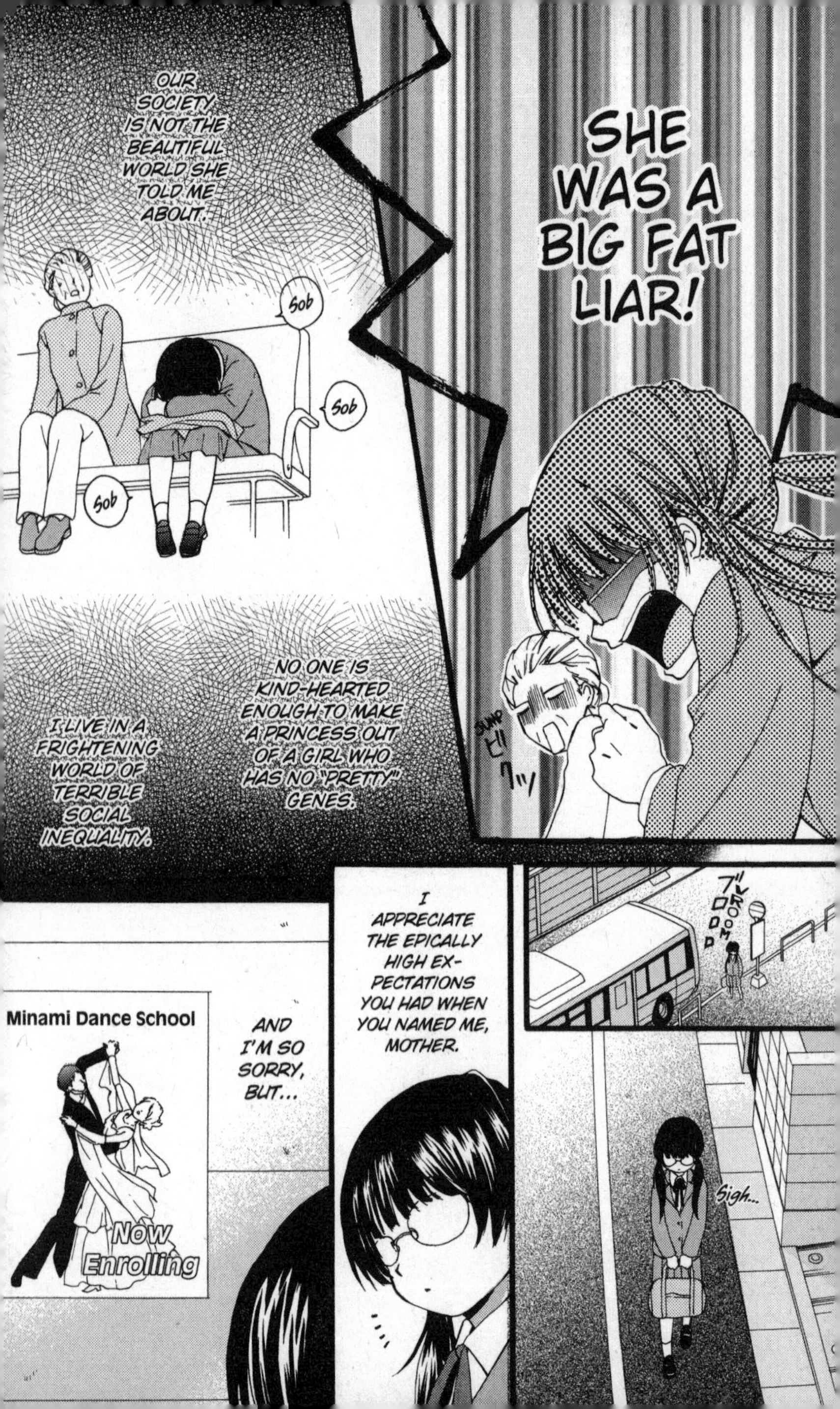
SHE WAS A BIG FAT LIAR!
SLUMP
OUR SOCIETY IS NOT THE BEAUTIFUL WORLD SHE TOLD ME ABOUT.
Sob
Sob
Sob
NO ONE IS KIND-HEARTED ENOUGH TO MAKE A PRINCESS OUT OF A GIRL WHO HAS NO "PRETTY" GENES.
I LIVE IN A FRIGHTENING WORLD OF TERRIBLE SOCIAL INEQUALITY.
VROOOM
Sigh...
I APPRECIATE THE EPICALLY HIGH EX-PECTATIONS YOU HAD WHEN YOU NAMED ME, MOTHER.
AND I'M SO SORRY, BUT...
Minami Dance School
Now Enrolling

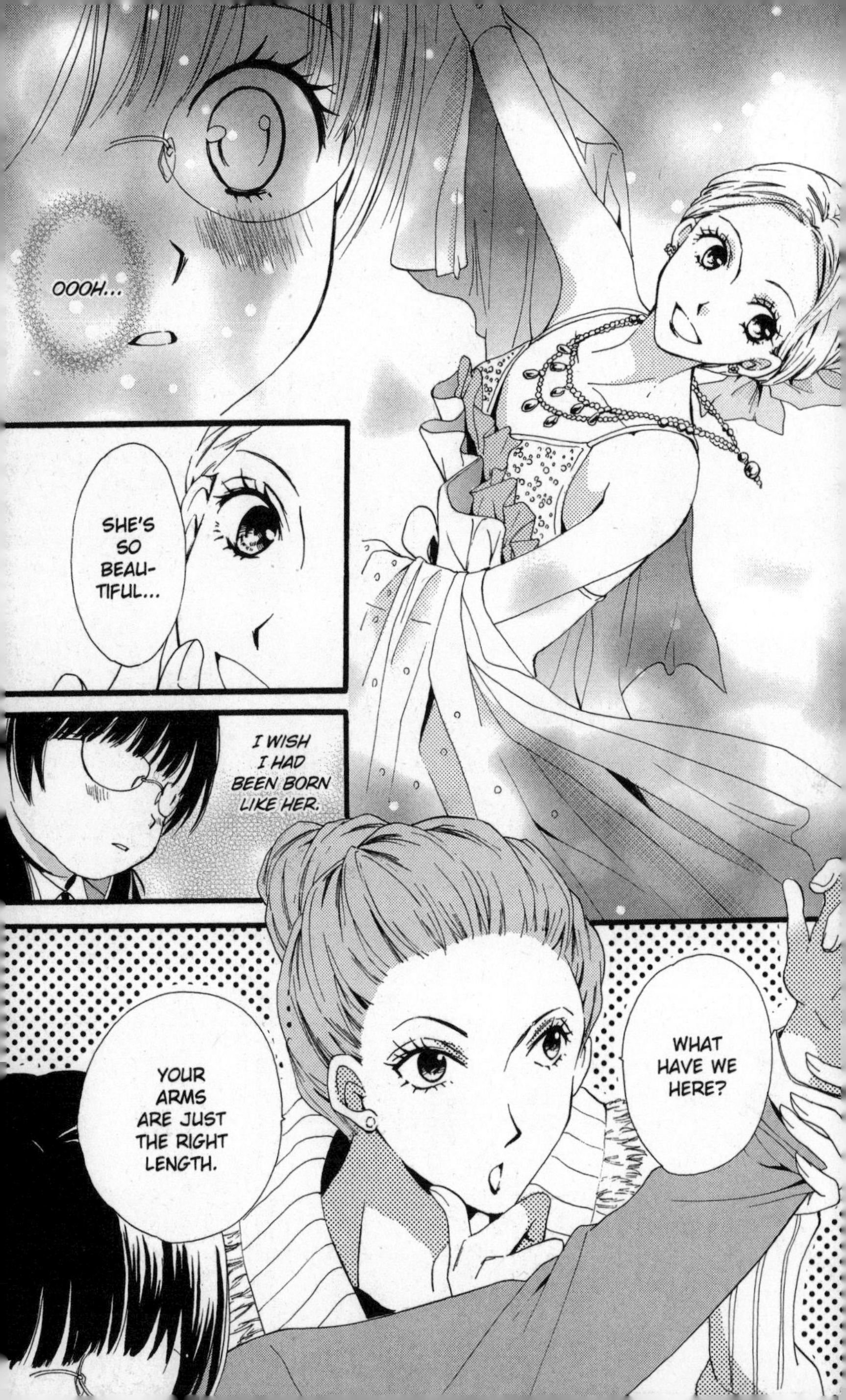
OOOH...
SHE'S SO BEAUTIFUL...
I WISH I HAD BEEN BORN LIKE HER.
WHAT HAVE WE HERE?
YOUR ARMS ARE JUST THE RIGHT LENGTH.

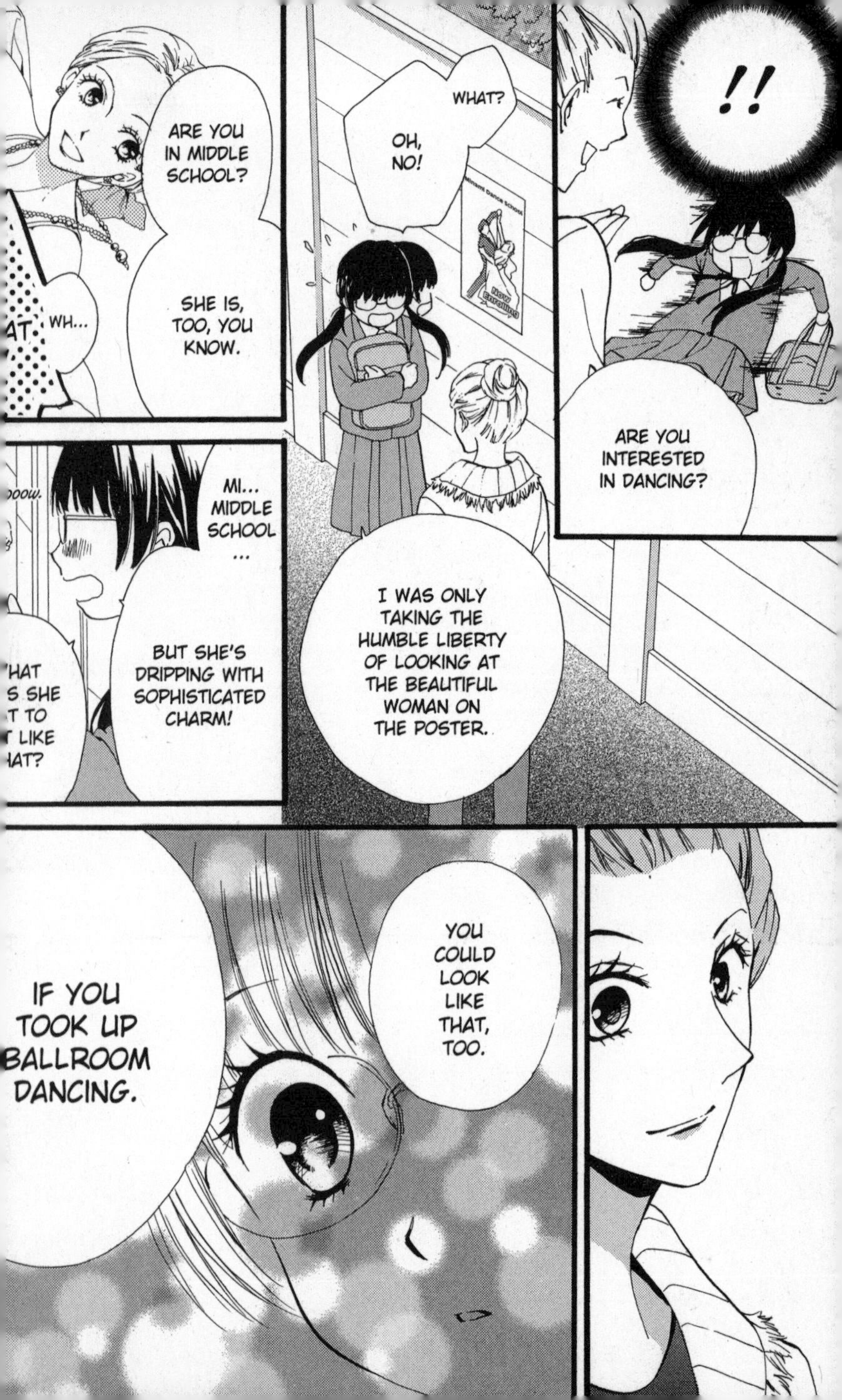
!!
ARE YOU INTERESTED IN DANCING?
WHAT?
OH, NO!
Minami Dance School
New Enrolling
I WAS ONLY TAKING THE HUMBLE LIBERTY OF LOOKING AT THE BEAUTIFUL WOMAN ON THE POSTER.
ARE YOU IN MIDDLE SCHOOL?
SHE IS, TOO, YOU KNOW.
WH...
MI... MIDDLE SCHOOL ...
BUT SHE'S DRIPPING WITH SOPHISTICATED CHARM!
YOU COULD LOOK LIKE THAT, TOO.
IF YOU TOOK UP BALLROOM DANCING.

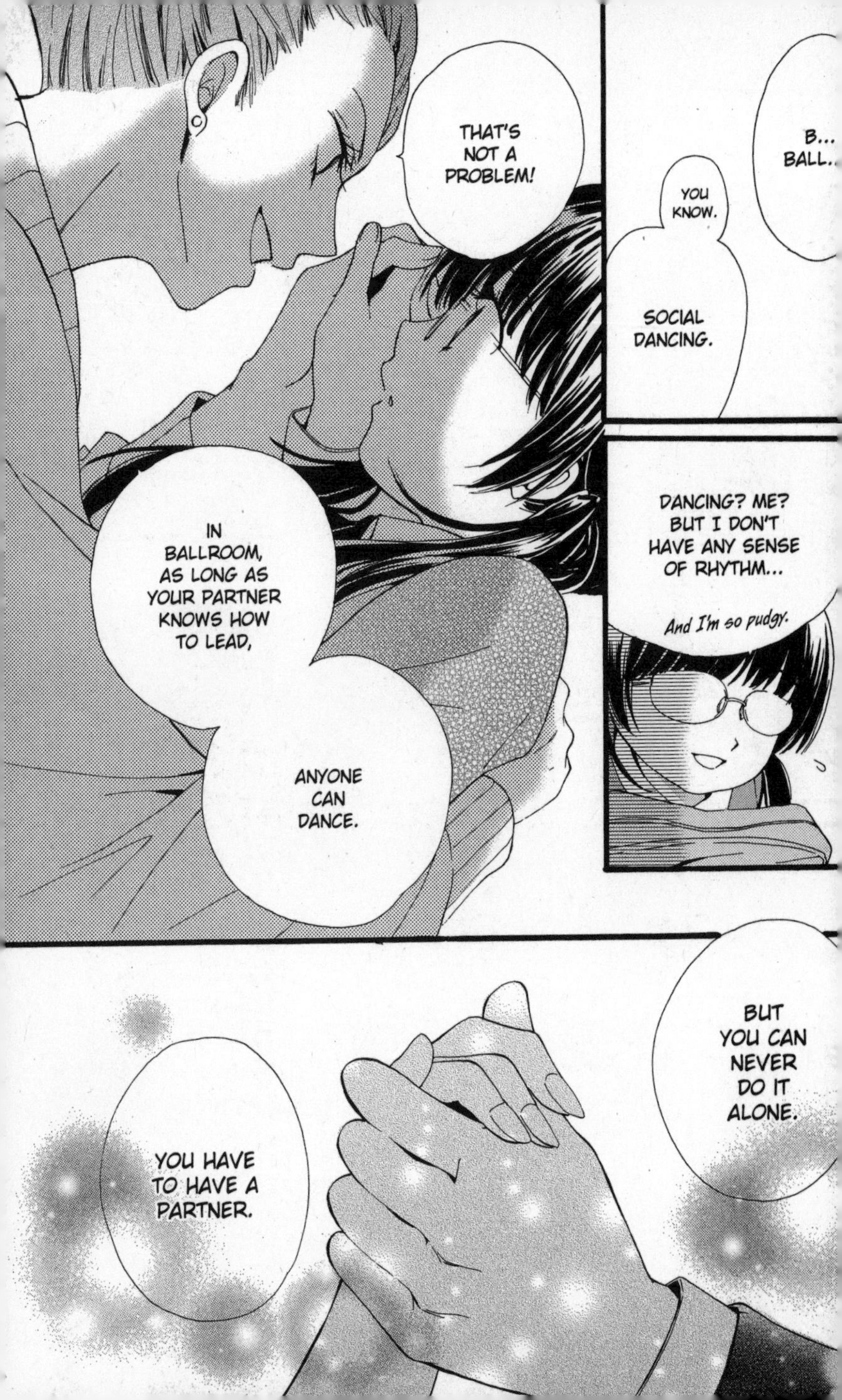
B... BALL...
YOU KNOW.
SOCIAL DANCING.
DANCING? ME? BUT I DON'T HAVE ANY SENSE OF RHYTHM...
And I'm so pudgy.
THAT'S NOT A PROBLEM!
IN BALLROOM, AS LONG AS YOUR PARTNER KNOWS HOW TO LEAD,
ANYONE CAN DANCE.
BUT YOU CAN NEVER DO IT ALONE.
YOU HAVE TO HAVE A PARTNER.

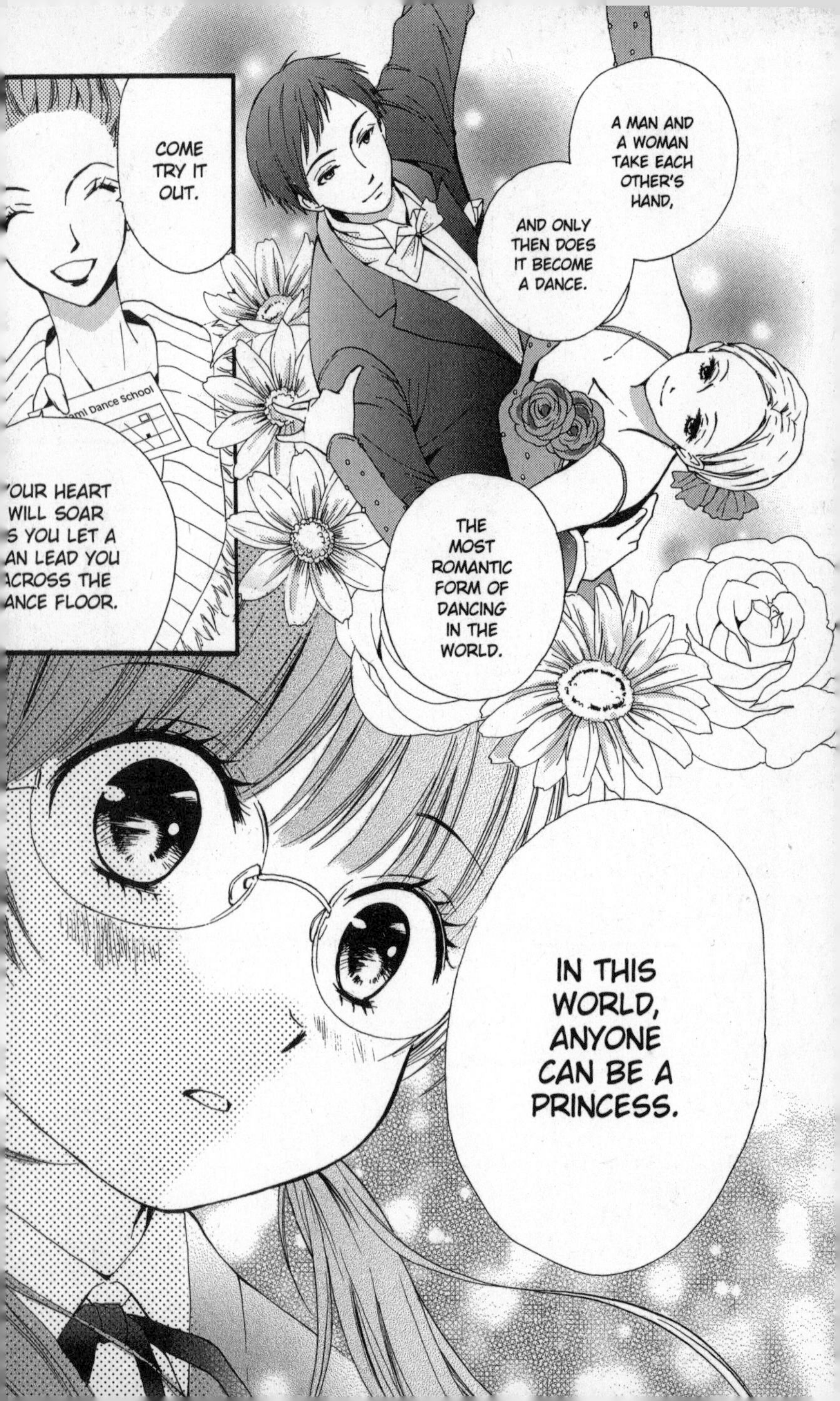
A MAN AND A WOMAN TAKE EACH OTHER'S HAND,
AND ONLY THEN DOES IT BECOME A DANCE.
THE MOST ROMANTIC FORM OF DANCING IN THE WORLD.
COME TRY IT OUT.
OUR HEART WILL SOAR S YOU LET A AN LEAD YOU ACROSS THE ANCE FLOOR.
IN THIS WORLD, ANYONE CAN BE A PRINCESS.

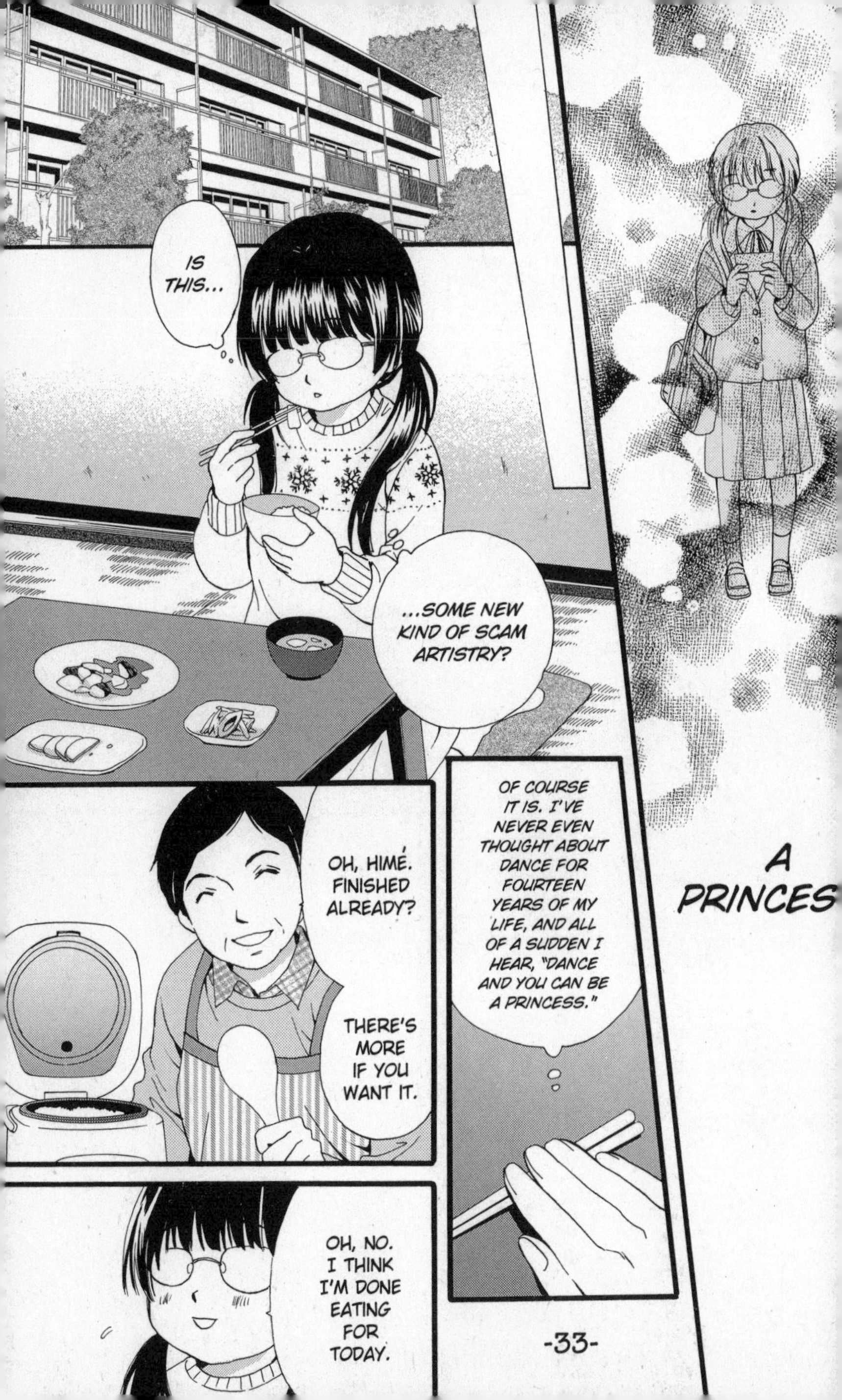
A PRINCES
IS THIS...
...SOME NEW KIND OF SCAM ARTISTRY?
OF COURSE IT IS. I'VE NEVER EVEN THOUGHT ABOUT DANCE FOR FOURTEEN YEARS OF MY LIFE, AND ALL OF A SUDDEN I HEAR, "DANCE AND YOU CAN BE A PRINCESS."
OH, HIMÉ. FINISHED ALREADY?
THERE'S MORE IF YOU WANT IT.
OH, NO. I THINK I'M DONE EATING FOR TODAY.

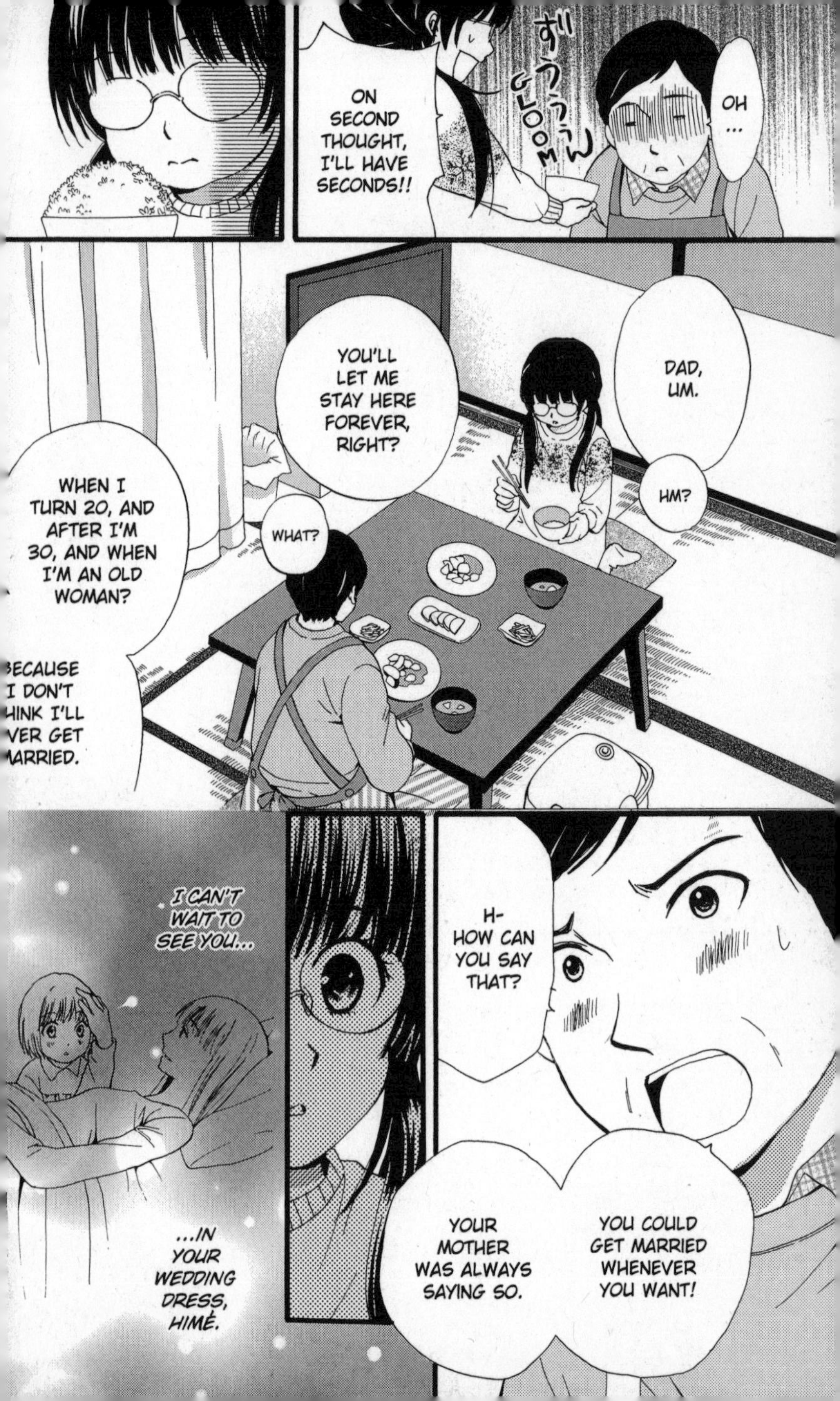
ずううん
GLOOM
OH ...
ON SECOND THOUGHT, I'LL HAVE SECONDS!!
DAD, UM.
HM?
YOU'LL LET ME STAY HERE FOREVER, RIGHT?
WHAT?
WHEN I TURN 20, AND AFTER I'M 30, AND WHEN I'M AN OLD WOMAN?
ECAUSE I DON'T HINK I'LL VER GET ARRIED.
H- HOW CAN YOU SAY THAT?
YOU COULD GET MARRIED WHENEVER YOU WANT!
YOUR MOTHER WAS ALWAYS SAYING SO.
I CAN'T WAIT TO SEE YOU...
...IN YOUR WEDDING DRESS, HIME.

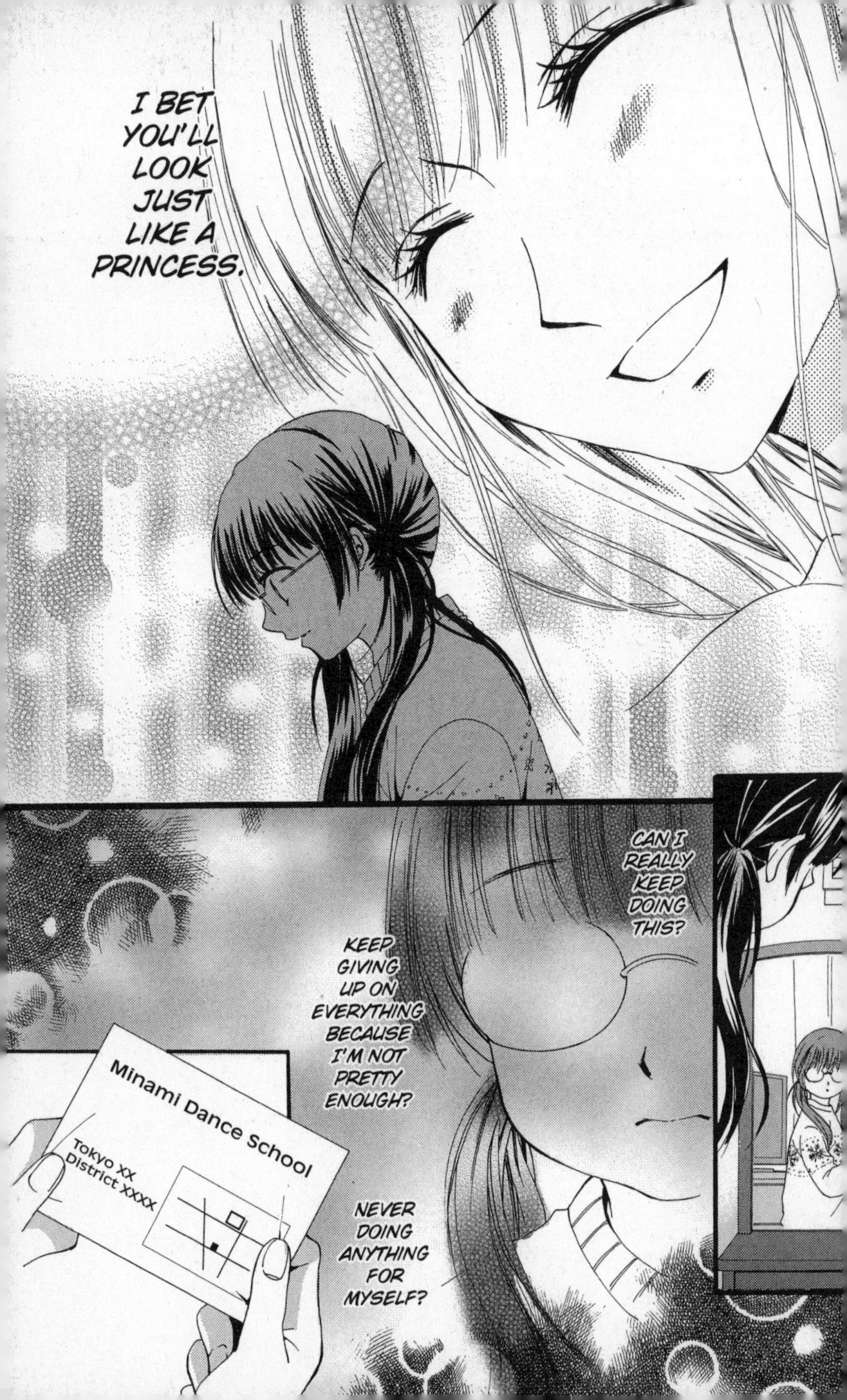
I BET YOU'LL LOOK JUST LIKE A PRINCESS.
CAN I REALLY KEEP DOING THIS?
KEEP GIVING UP ON EVERYTHING BECAUSE I'M NOT PRETTY ENOUGH?
NEVER DOING ANYTHING FOR MYSELF?
Minami Dance School
Tokyo XX
District XXXX

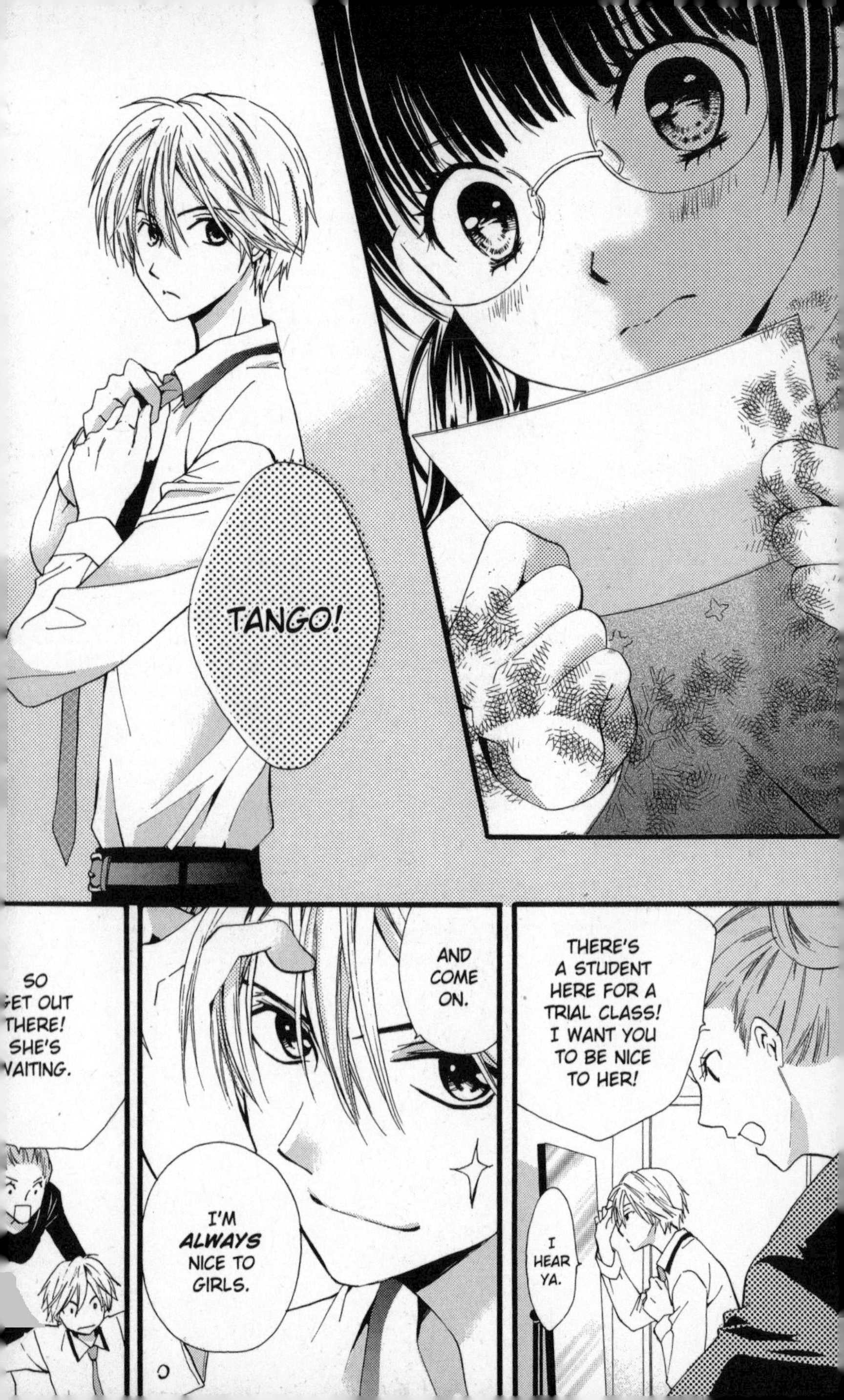
TANGO!
THERE'S A STUDENT HERE FOR A TRIAL CLASS! I WANT YOU TO BE NICE TO HER!
I HEAR YA.
AND COME ON.
I'M *ALWAYS* NICE TO GIRLS.
SO GET OUT THERE! SHE'S WAITING.

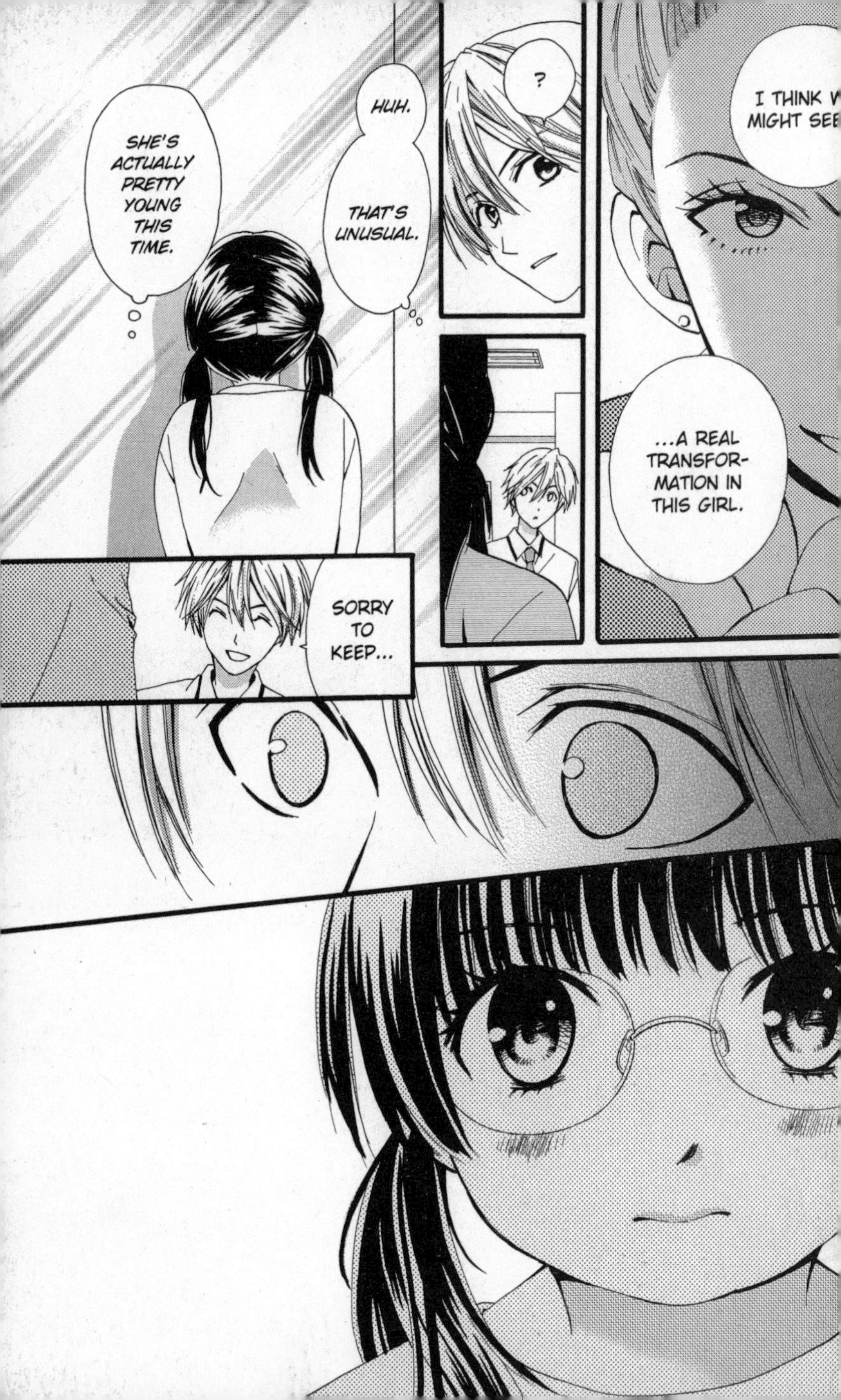
I THINK W
MIGHT SEE
...A REAL TRANSFORMATION IN THIS GIRL.
?
HUH.
THAT'S UNUSUAL.
SHE'S ACTUALLY PRETTY YOUNG THIS TIME.
SORRY TO KEEP...

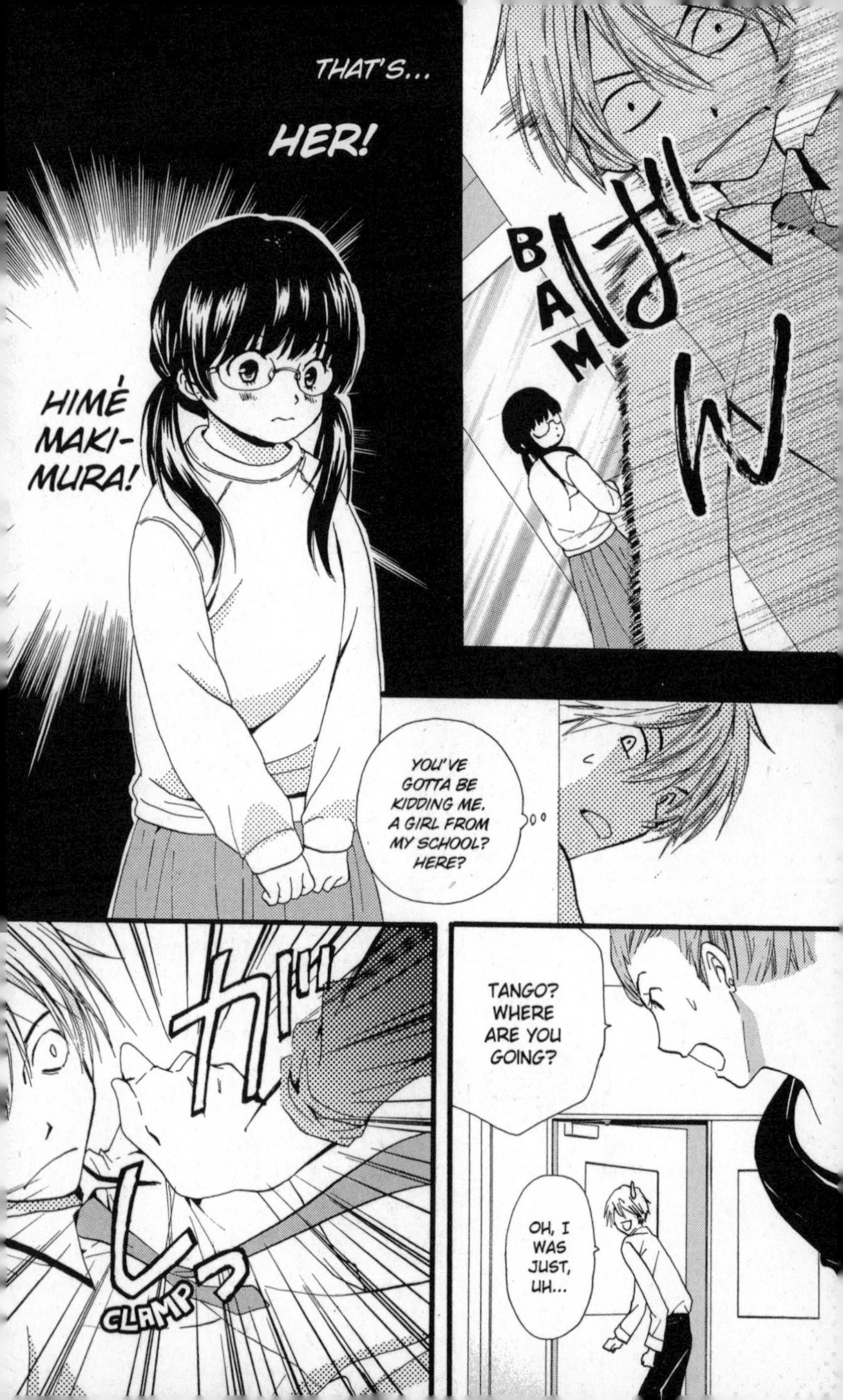
BAM
YOU'VE GOTTA BE KIDDING ME. A GIRL FROM MY SCHOOL? HERE?
THAT'S...
HER!
HIME MAKIMURA!
TANGO? WHERE ARE YOU GOING?
OH, I WAS JUST, UH...
CLAMP

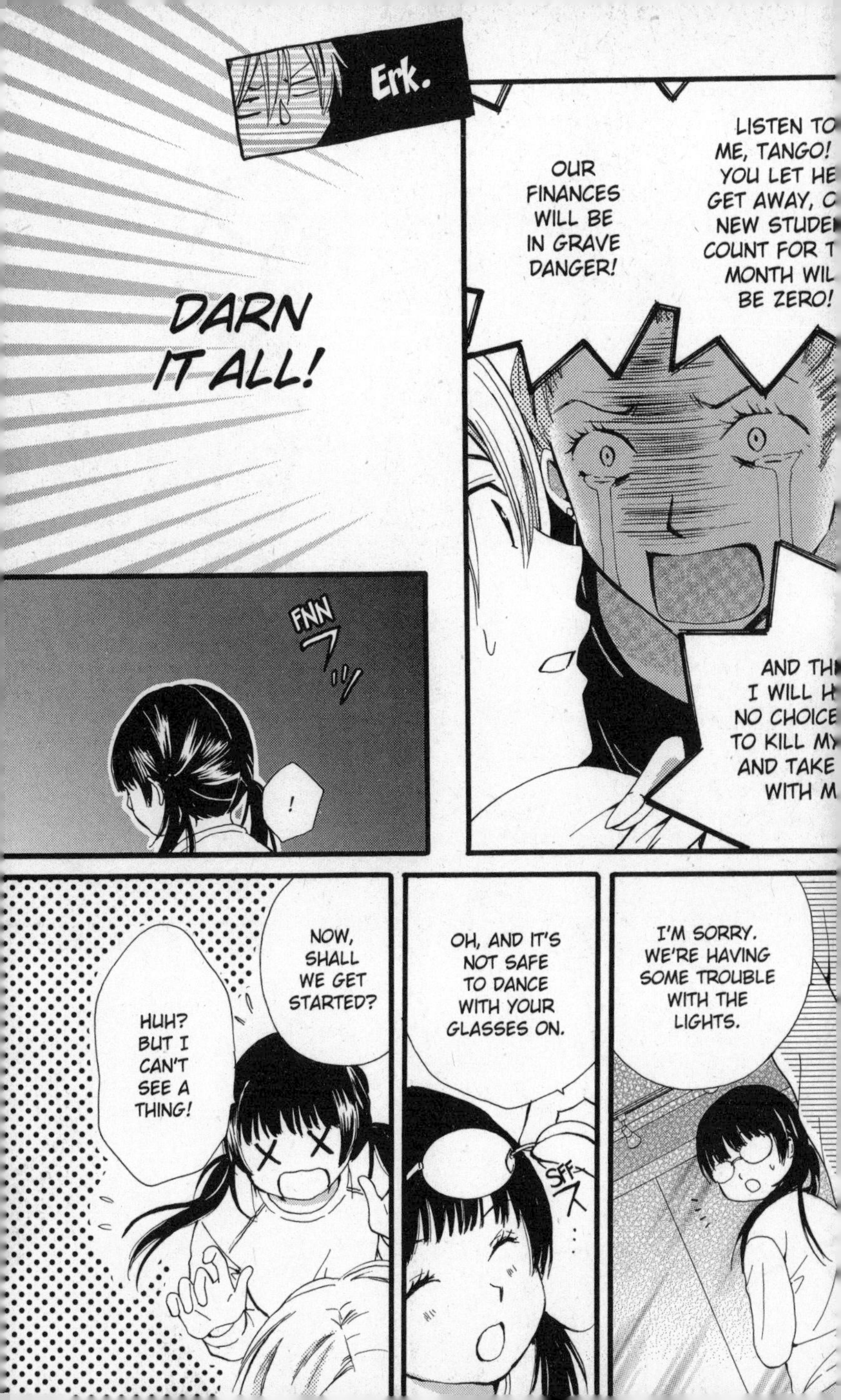
LISTEN TO ME, TANGO! YOU LET HE GET AWAY, C NEW STUDE COUNT FOR T MONTH WIL BE ZERO!
OUR FINANCES WILL BE IN GRAVE DANGER!
AND TH I WILL H NO CHOICE TO KILL MY AND TAKE WITH M
Erk.
DARN IT ALL!
FNN
!
I'M SORRY. WE'RE HAVING SOME TROUBLE WITH THE LIGHTS.
OH, AND IT'S NOT SAFE TO DANCE WITH YOUR GLASSES ON.
SFF
NOW, SHALL WE GET STARTED?
HUH? BUT I CAN'T SEE A THING!

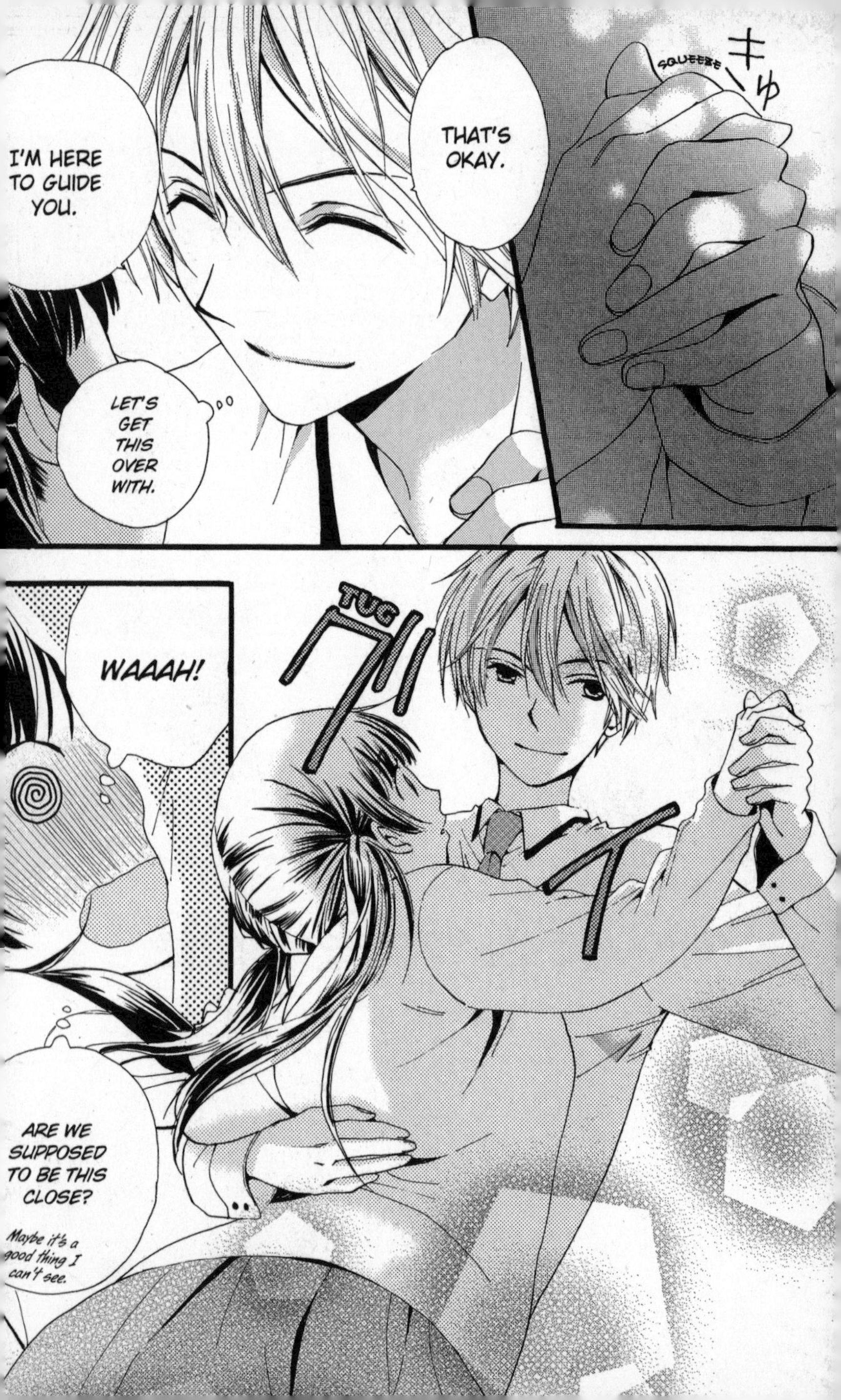
SQUEEZE
キュ
THAT'S OKAY.
I'M HERE TO GUIDE YOU.
LET'S GET THIS OVER WITH.
TUG
グイ
WAAAH!
ARE WE SUPPOSED TO BE THIS CLOSE?
Maybe it's a good thing I can't see.

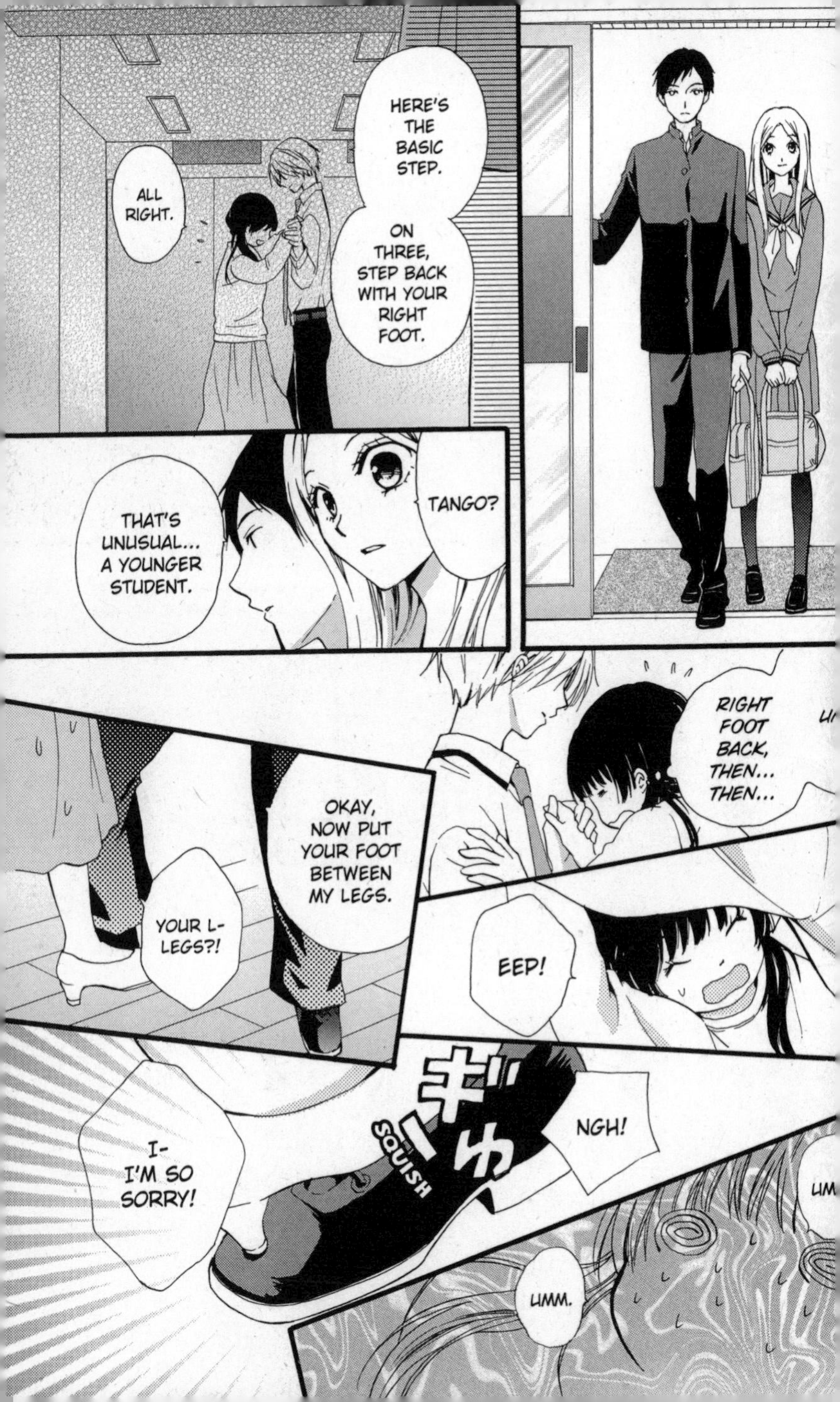
HERE'S THE BASIC STEP.
ON THREE, STEP BACK WITH YOUR RIGHT FOOT.
ALL RIGHT.
TANGO?
THAT'S UNUSUAL... A YOUNGER STUDENT.
RIGHT FOOT BACK, THEN... THEN...
OKAY, NOW PUT YOUR FOOT BETWEEN MY LEGS.
YOUR L- LEGS?!
EEP!
ぎゅ
SQUISH
NGH!
I- I'M SO SORRY!
UM
UMM.

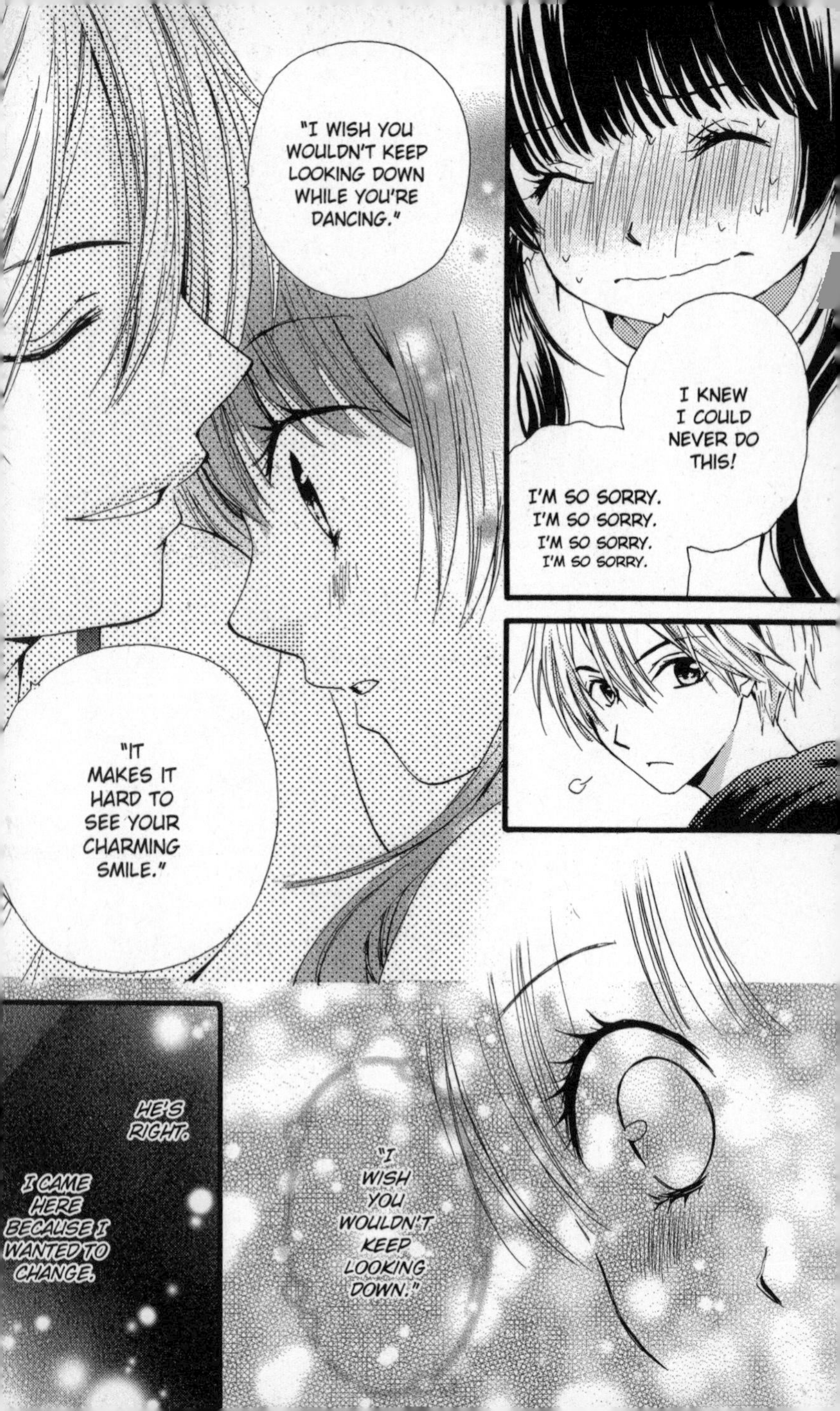
I KNEW I COULD NEVER DO THIS!
I'M SO SORRY. I'M SO SORRY. I'M SO SORRY. I'M SO SORRY.
"I WISH YOU WOULDN'T KEEP LOOKING DOWN WHILE YOU'RE DANCING."
"IT MAKES IT HARD TO SEE YOUR CHARMING SMILE."
"I WISH YOU WOULDN'T KEEP LOOKING DOWN."
HE'S RIGHT.
I CAME HERE BECAUSE I WANTED TO CHANGE.

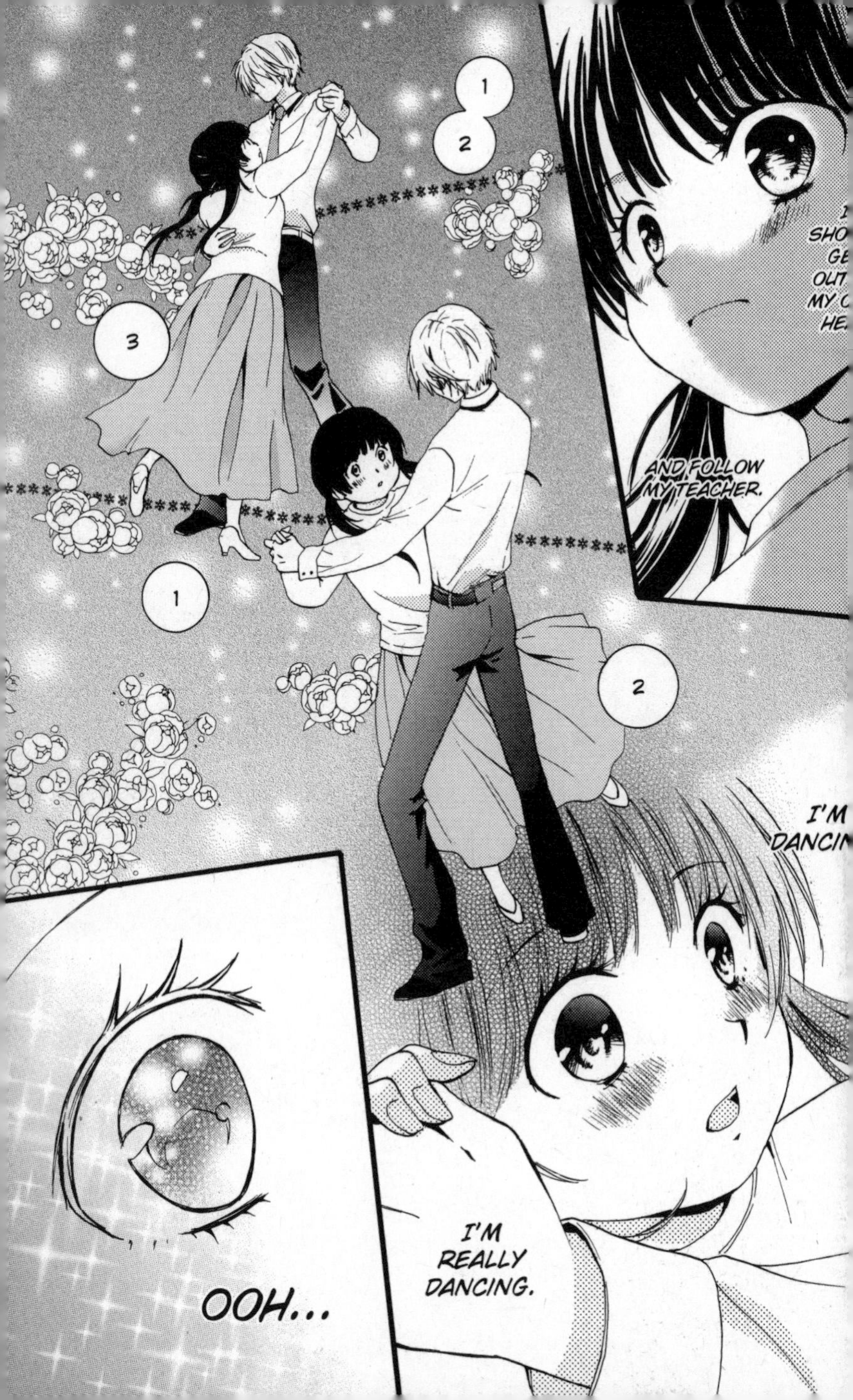

I SHO GE OUT MY C HE
AND FOLLOW MY TEACHER.
1
2
3
1
2
I'M DANCIN
I'M REALLY DANCING.
OOH...

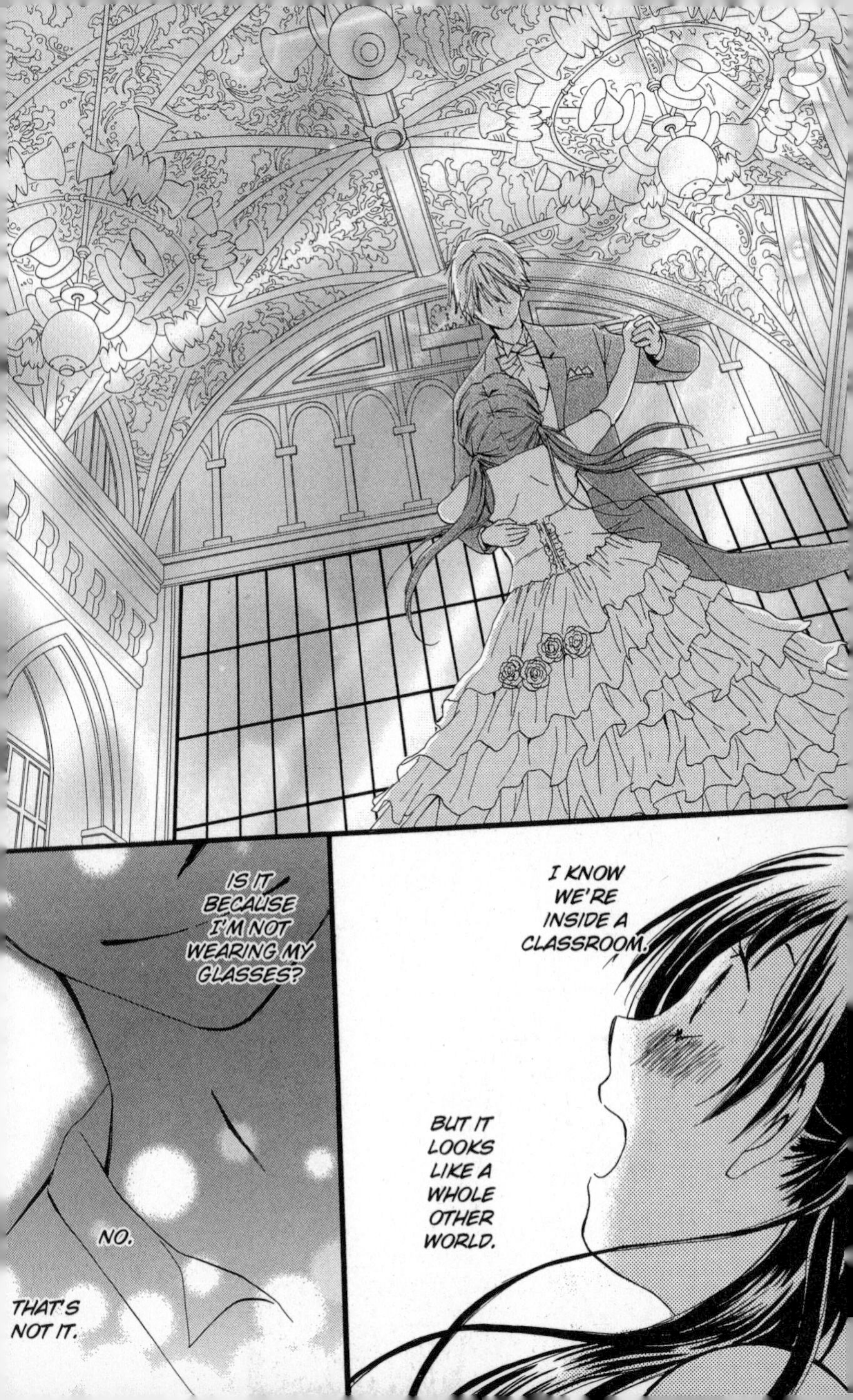
I KNOW WE'RE INSIDE A CLASSROOM.
BUT IT LOOKS LIKE A WHOLE OTHER WORLD.
IS IT BECAUSE I'M NOT WEARING MY GLASSES?
NO.
THAT'S NOT IT.

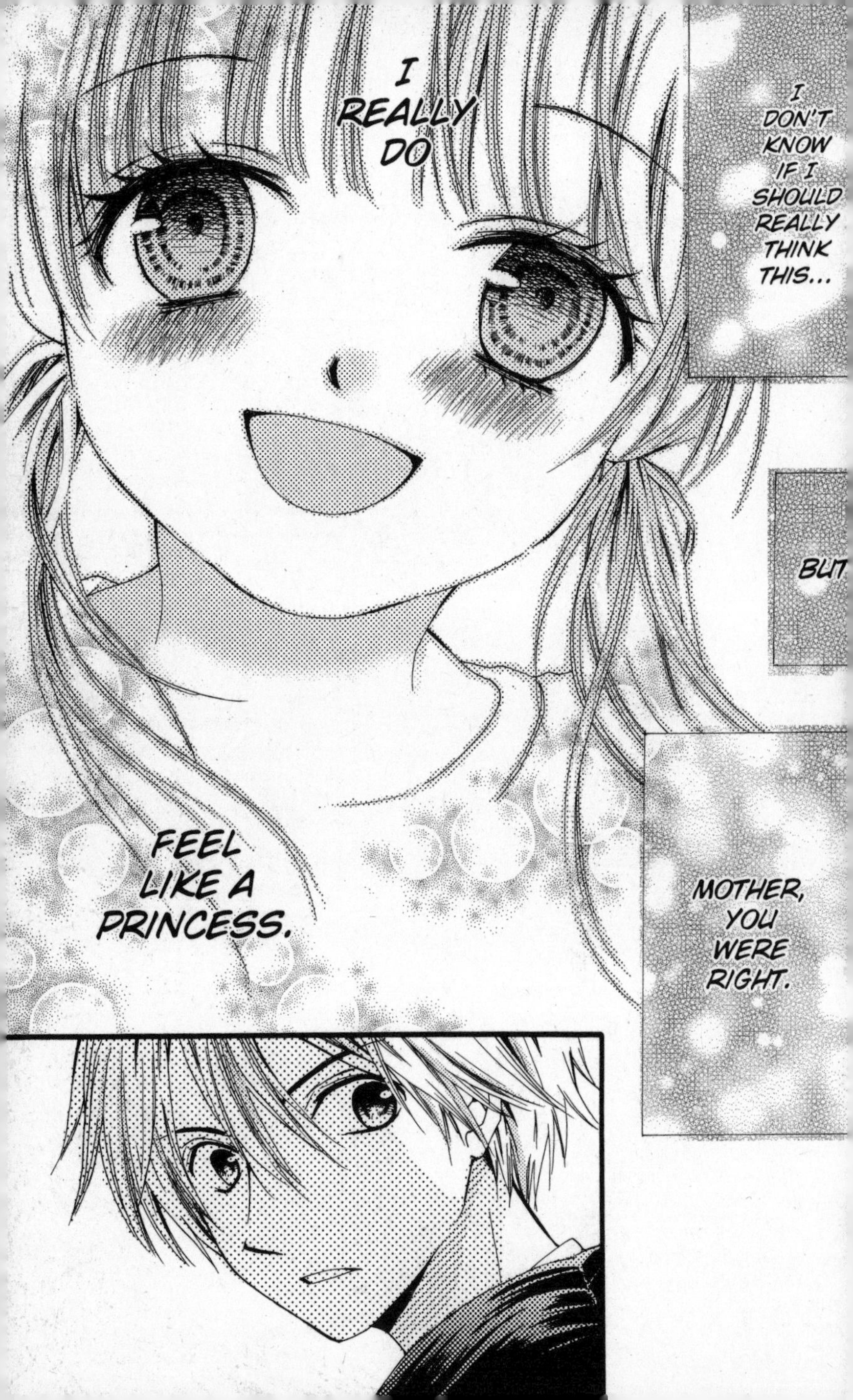
I DON'T KNOW IF I SHOULD REALLY THINK THIS...
BUT
MOTHER, YOU WERE RIGHT.
I REALLY DO
FEEL LIKE A PRINCESS.

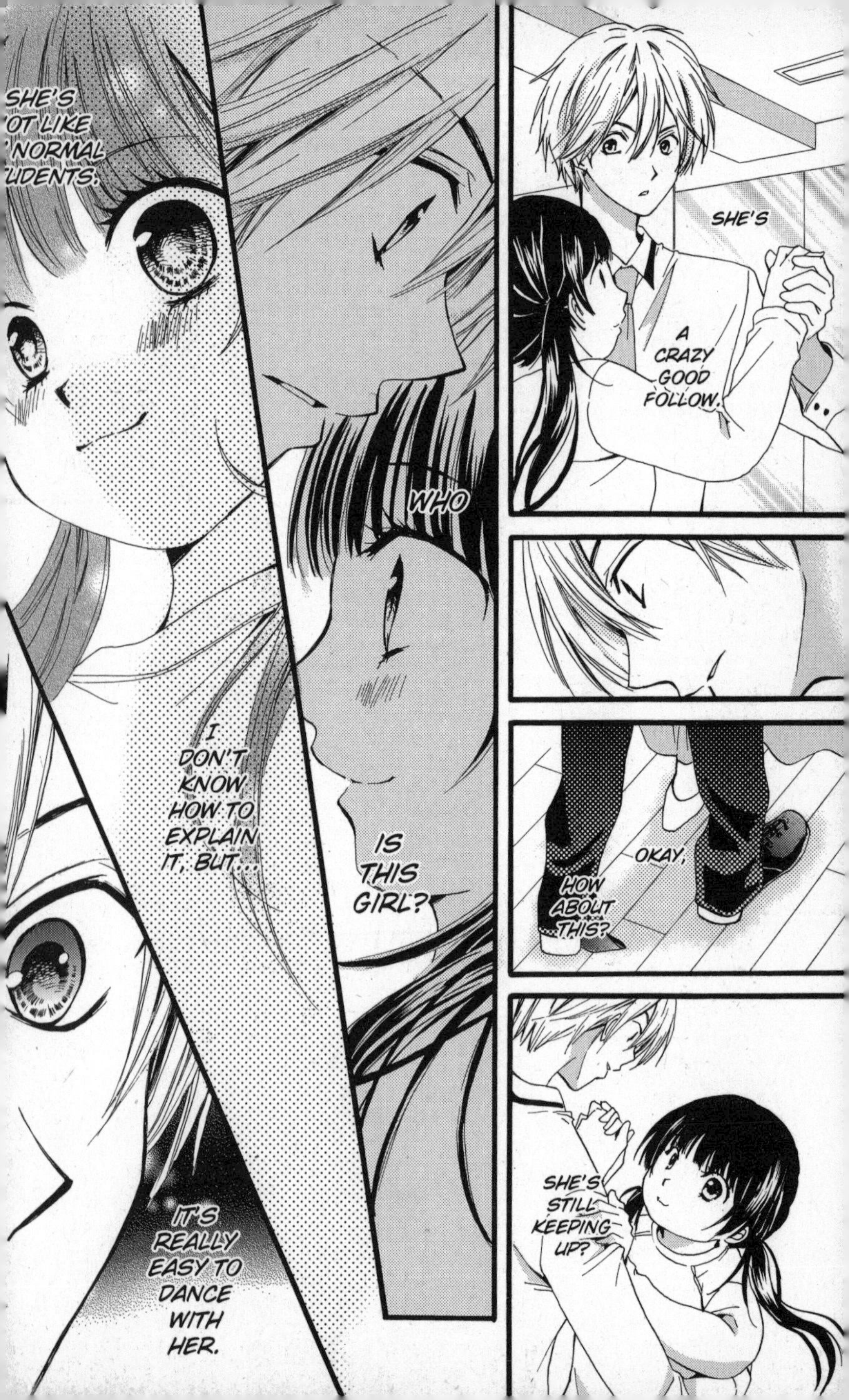
SHE'S
A CRAZY GOOD FOLLOW.
OKAY,
HOW ABOUT THIS?
SHE'S STILL KEEPING UP?
WHO
IS THIS GIRL?
SHE'S OT LIKE NORMAL UDENTS.
I DON'T KNOW HOW TO EXPLAIN IT, BUT...
IT'S REALLY EASY TO DANCE WITH HER.

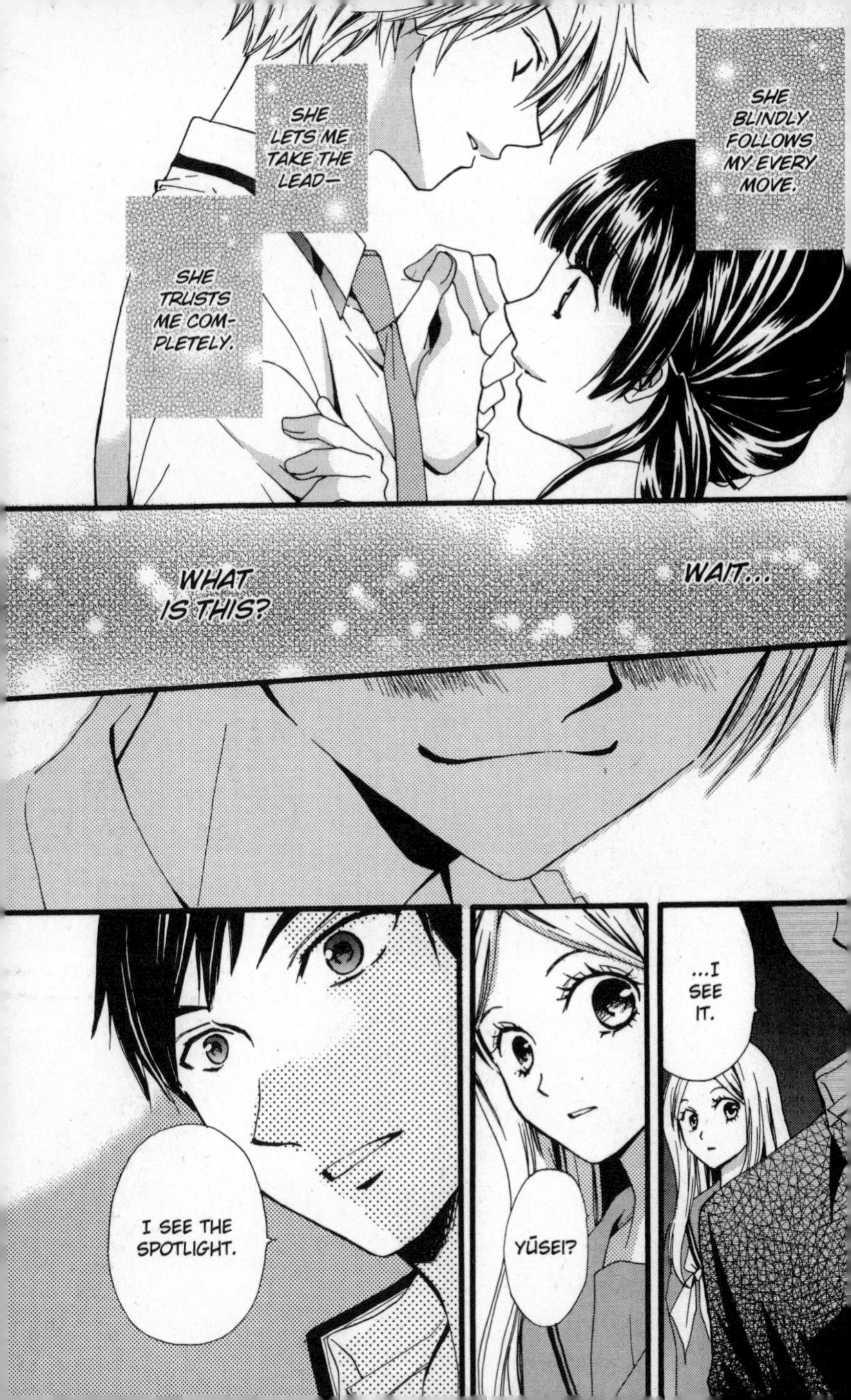
SHE BLINDLY FOLLOWS MY EVERY MOVE.
SHE LETS ME TAKE THE LEAD—
SHE TRUSTS ME COMPLETELY.
WAIT...
WHAT IS THIS?
...I SEE IT.
YŪSEI?
I SEE THE SPOTLIGHT.

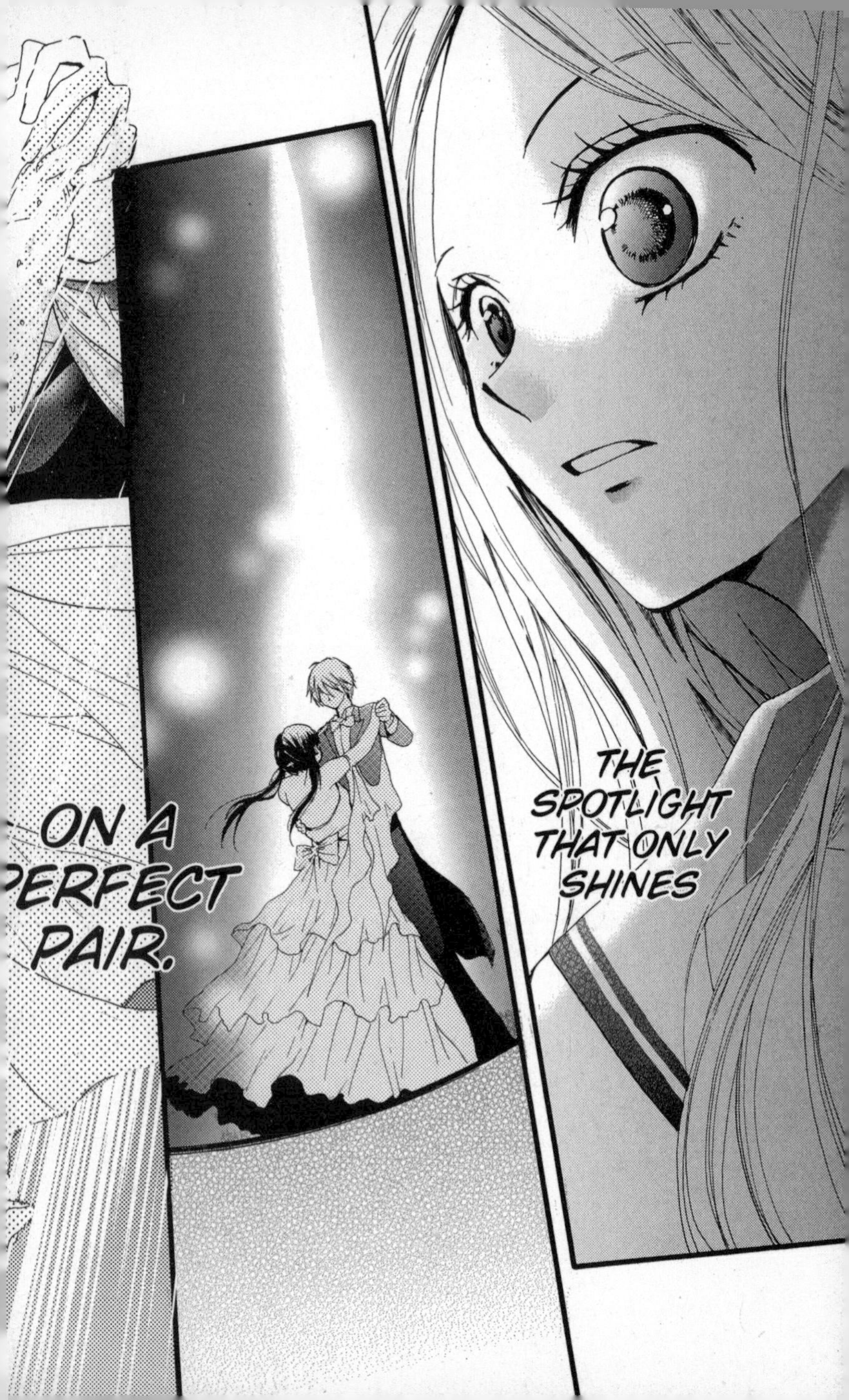
THE SPOTLIGHT THAT ONLY SHINES
ON A PERFECT PAIR.

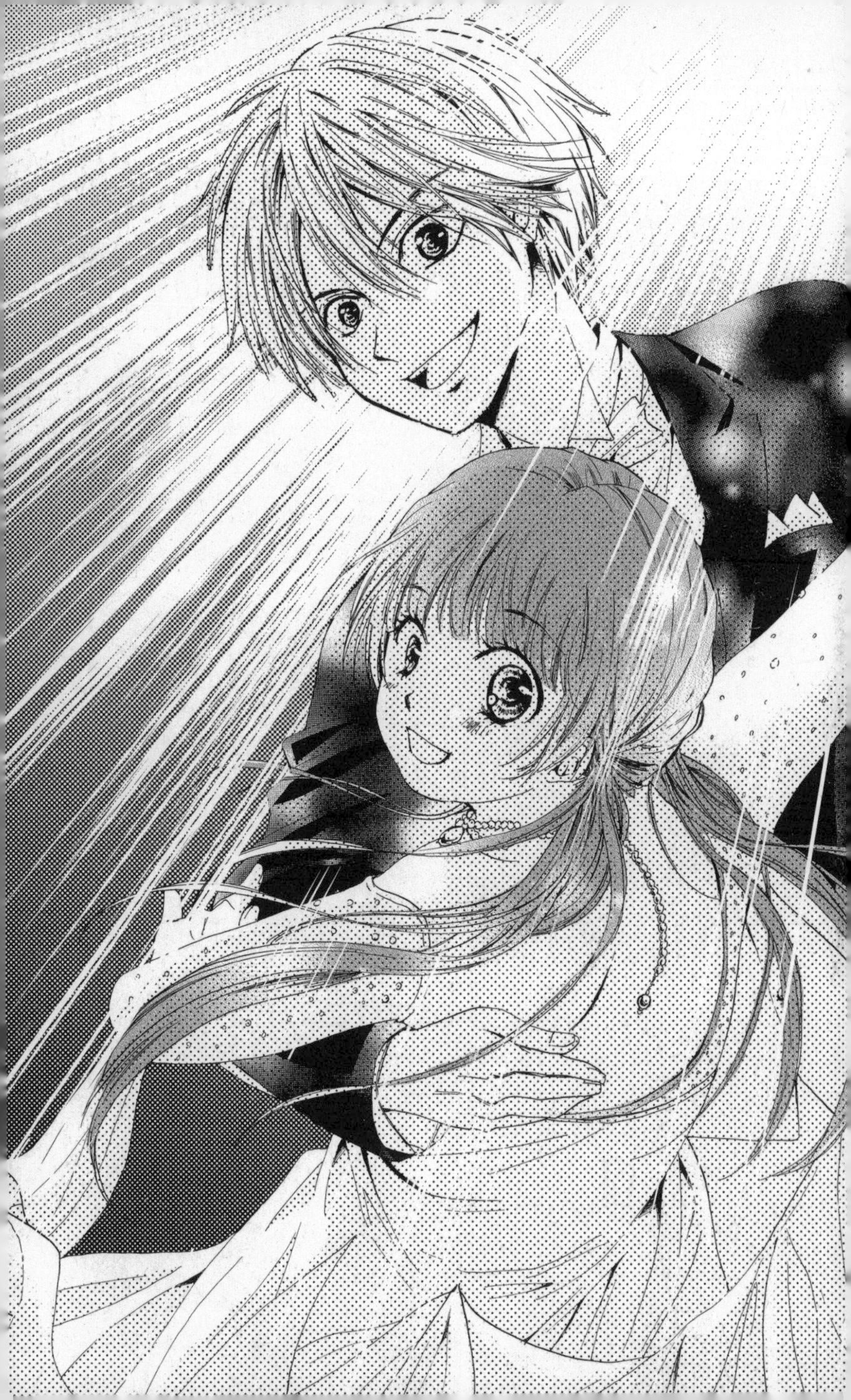

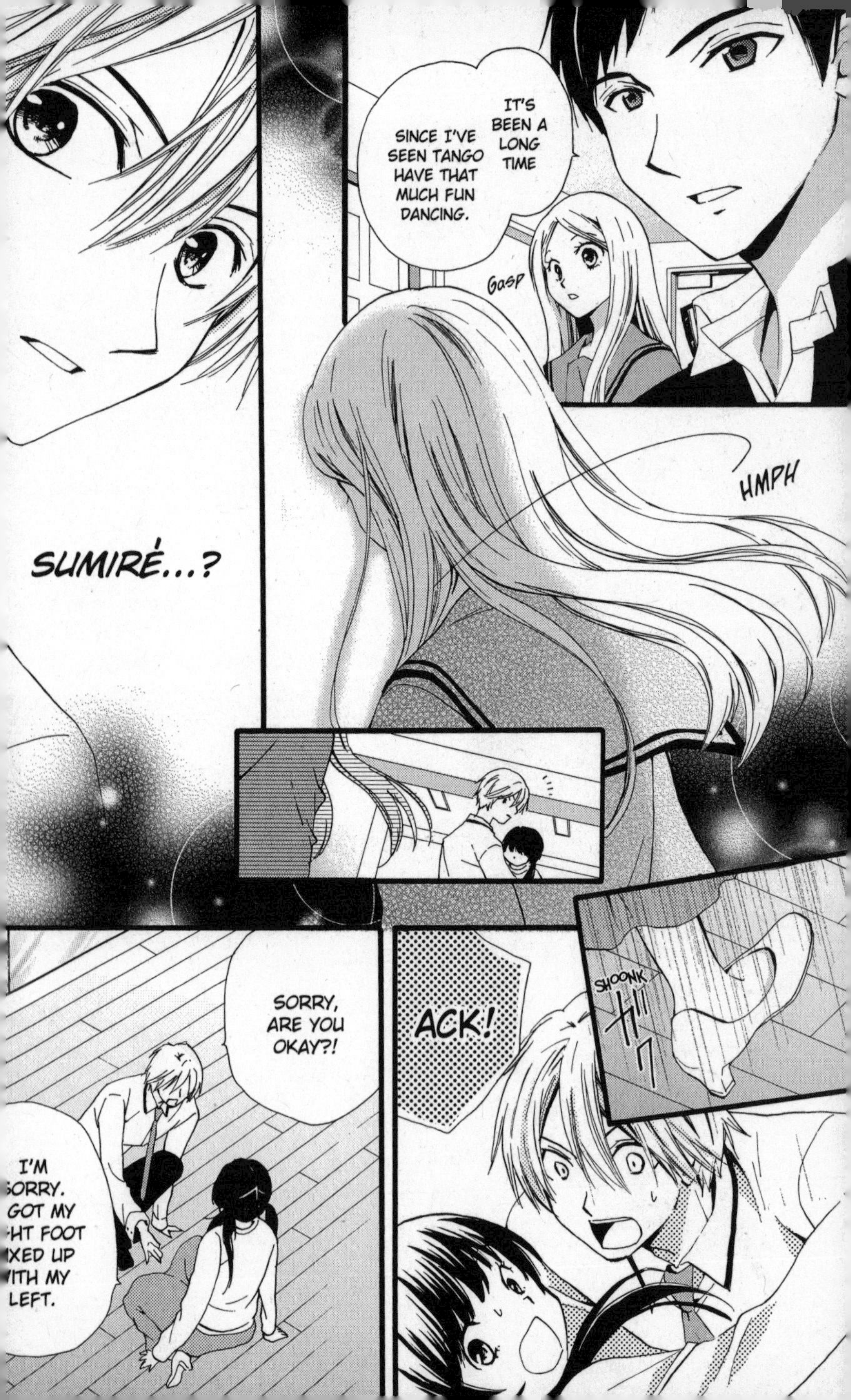
IT'S BEEN A LONG TIME
SINCE I'VE SEEN TANGO HAVE THAT MUCH FUN DANCING.
Gasp
HMPH
SUMIRÉ...?
SHOONK
ACK!
SORRY, ARE YOU OKAY?!
I'M SORRY. GOT MY HT FOOT XED UP WITH MY LEFT.

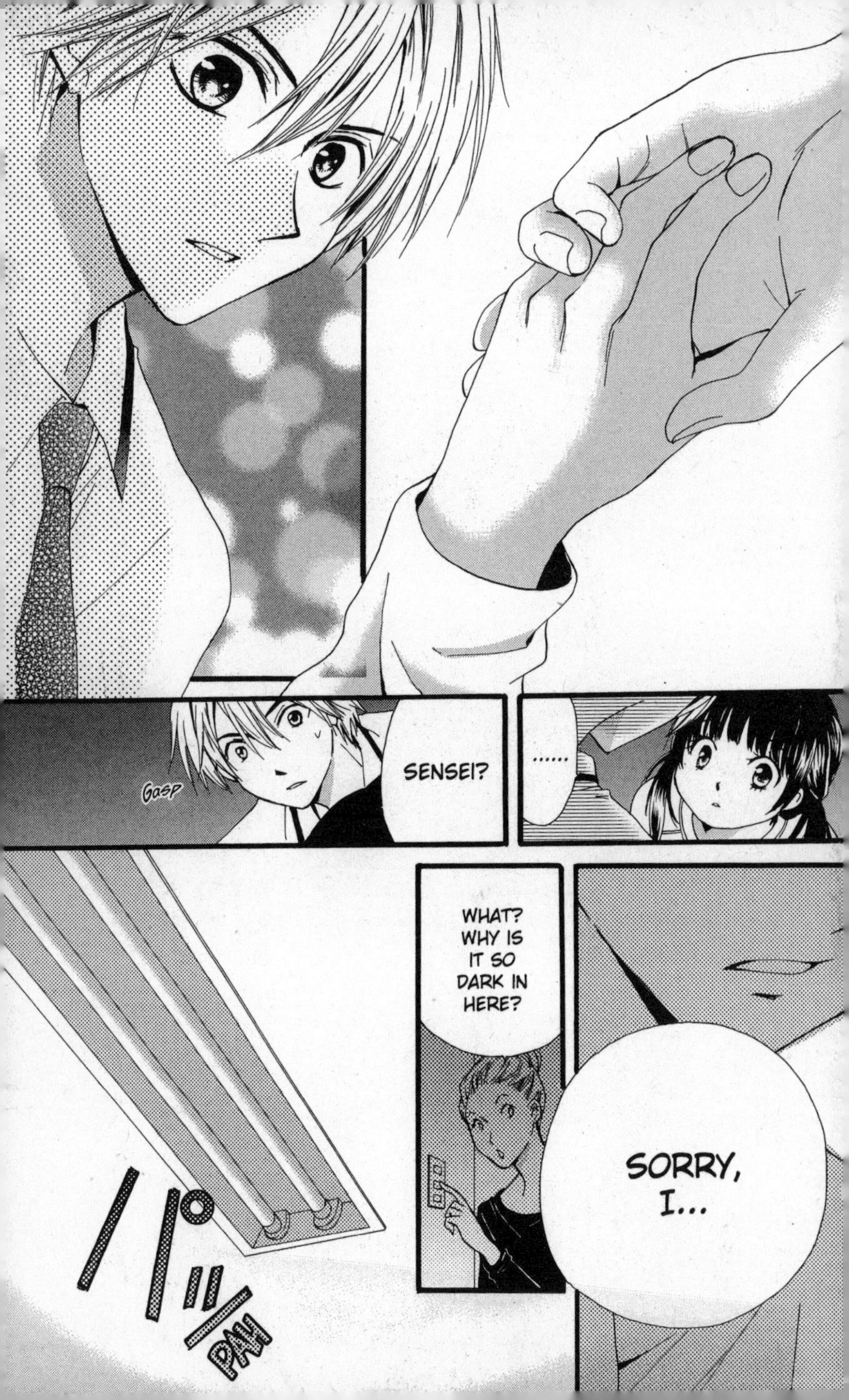
......
SENSEI?
Gasp
SORRY, I...
WHAT? WHY IS IT SO DARK IN HERE?
PAH

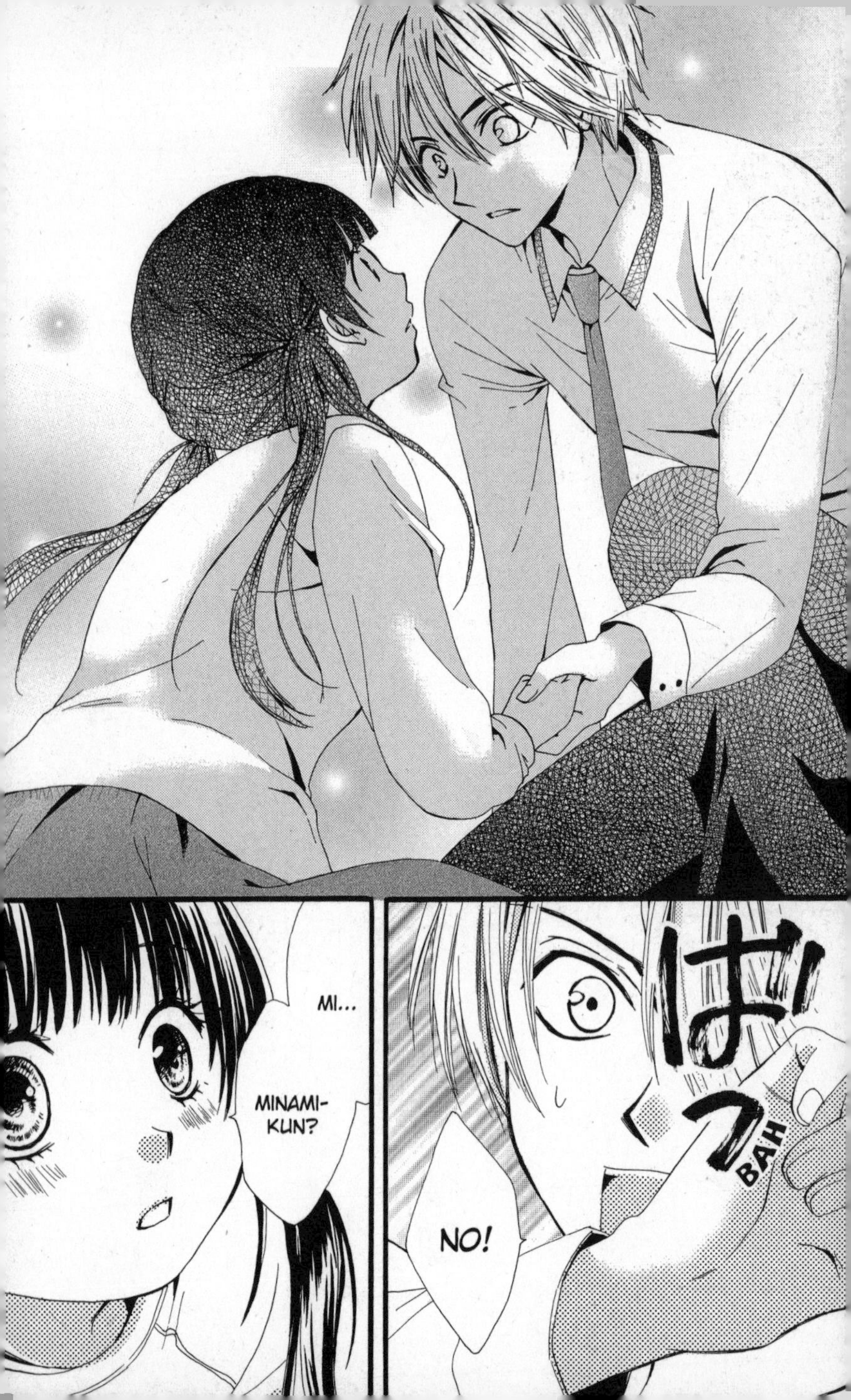
はっ
BAH
NO!
MI...
MINAMI-KUN?

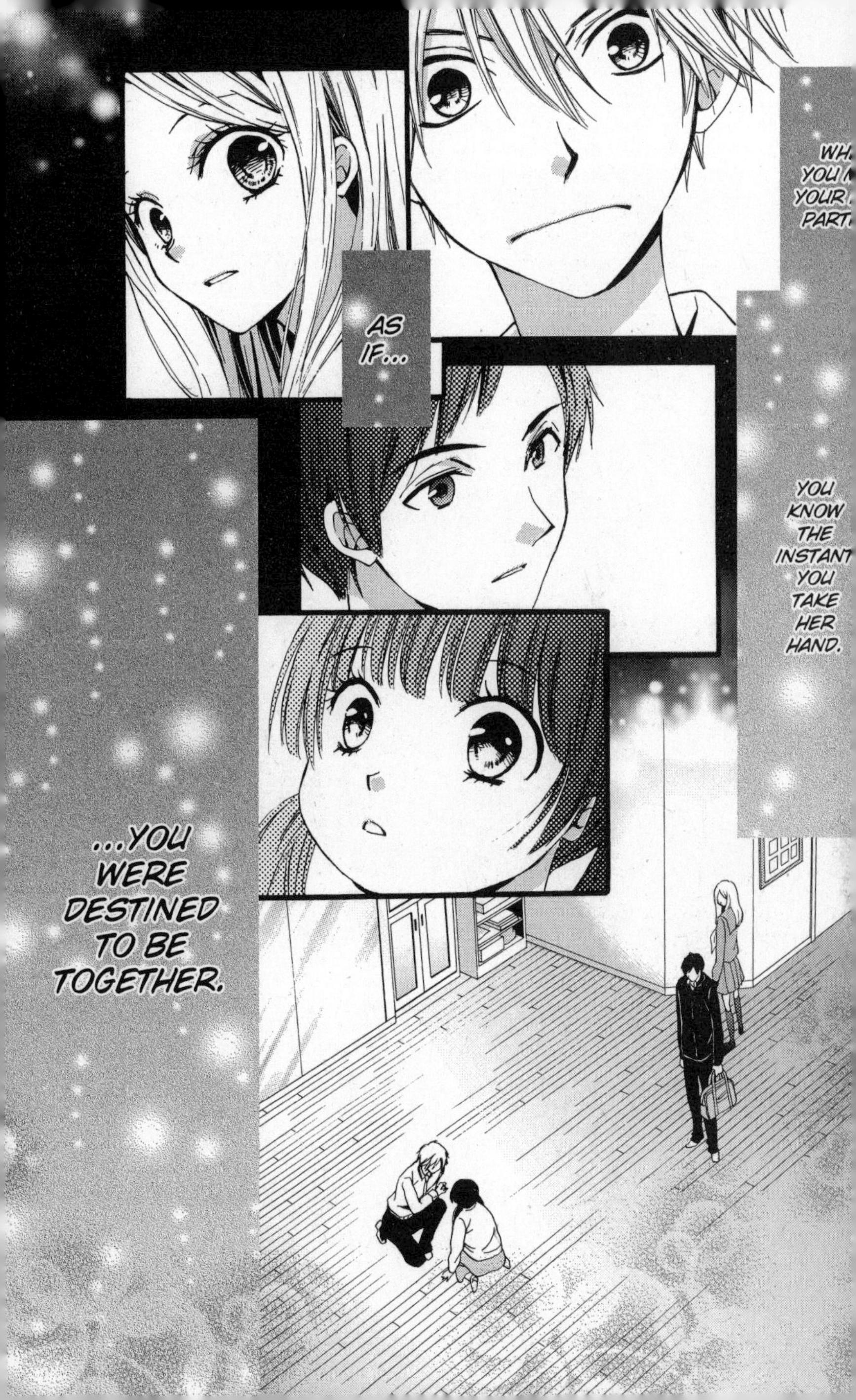
WH
YOU M
YOUR
PART
YOU KNOW THE INSTANT YOU TAKE HER HAND.
AS IF...
...YOU WERE DESTINED TO BE TOGETHER.

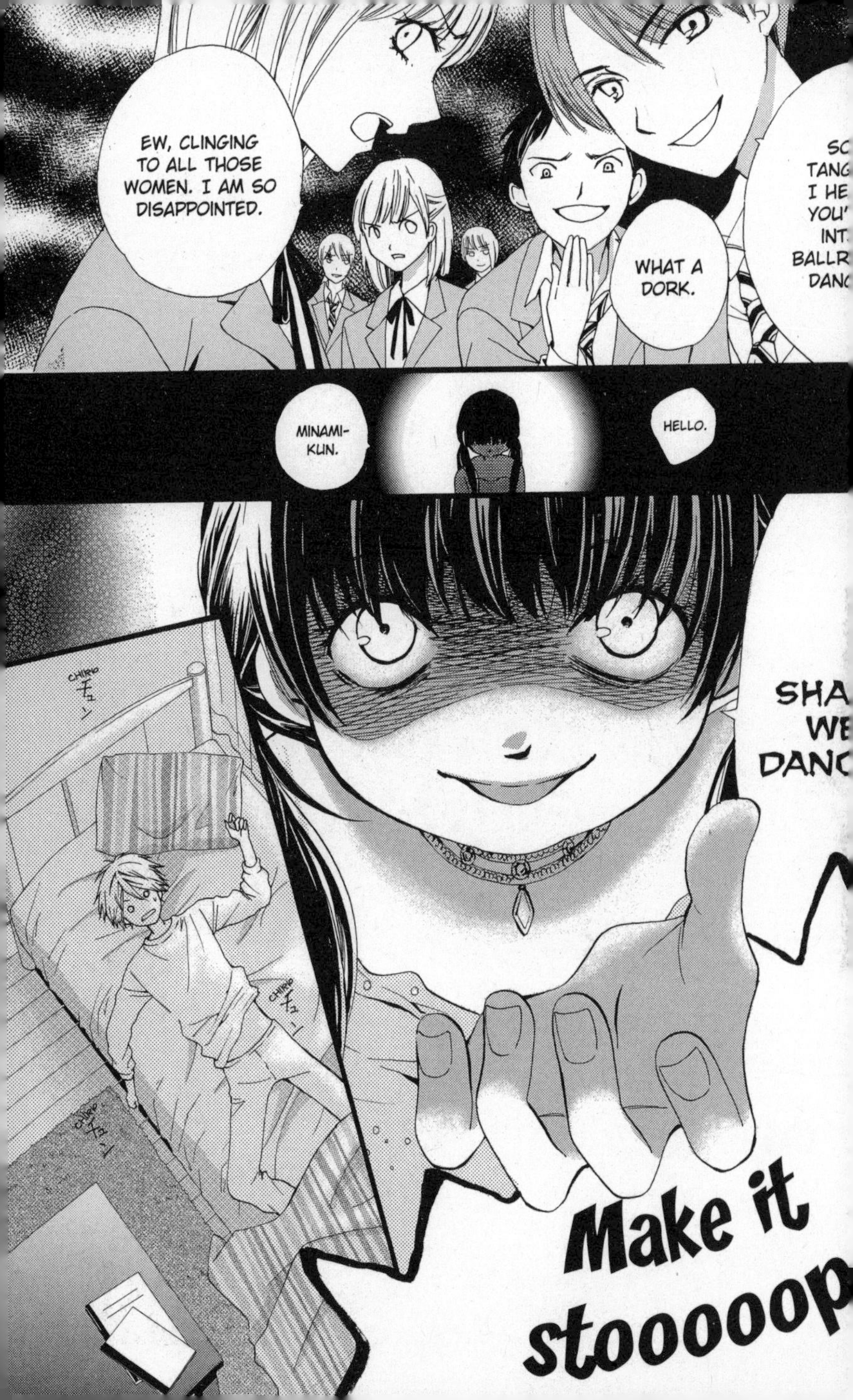
SC TANG I HE YOU' INT. BALLR DANC
WHAT A DORK.
EW, CLINGING TO ALL THOSE WOMEN. I AM SO DISAPPOINTED.
HELLO.
MINAMI-KUN.
SHA WE DANC
CHIRP
CHIRP
CHIRP
Make it stoooooop

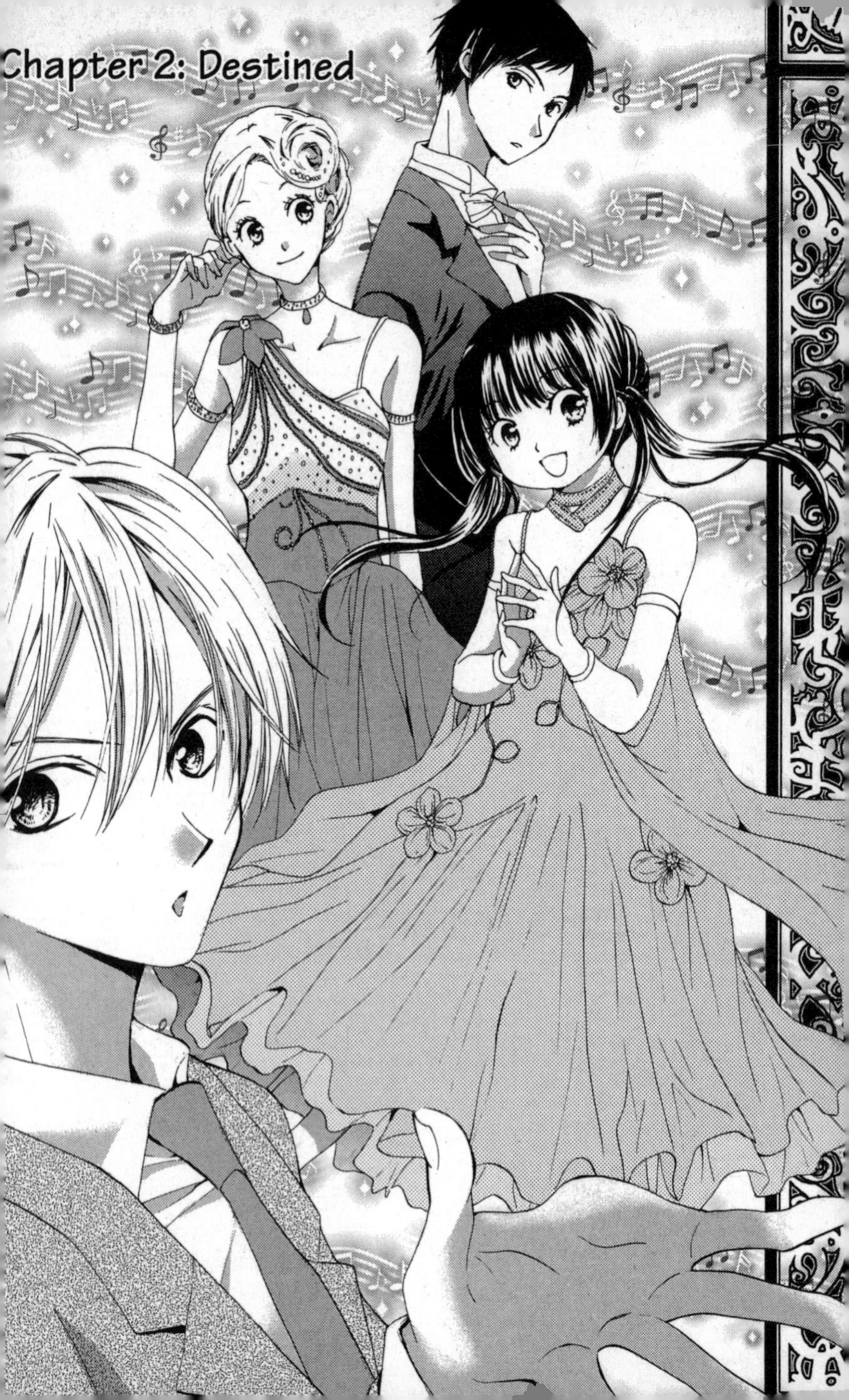
Chapter 2: Destined

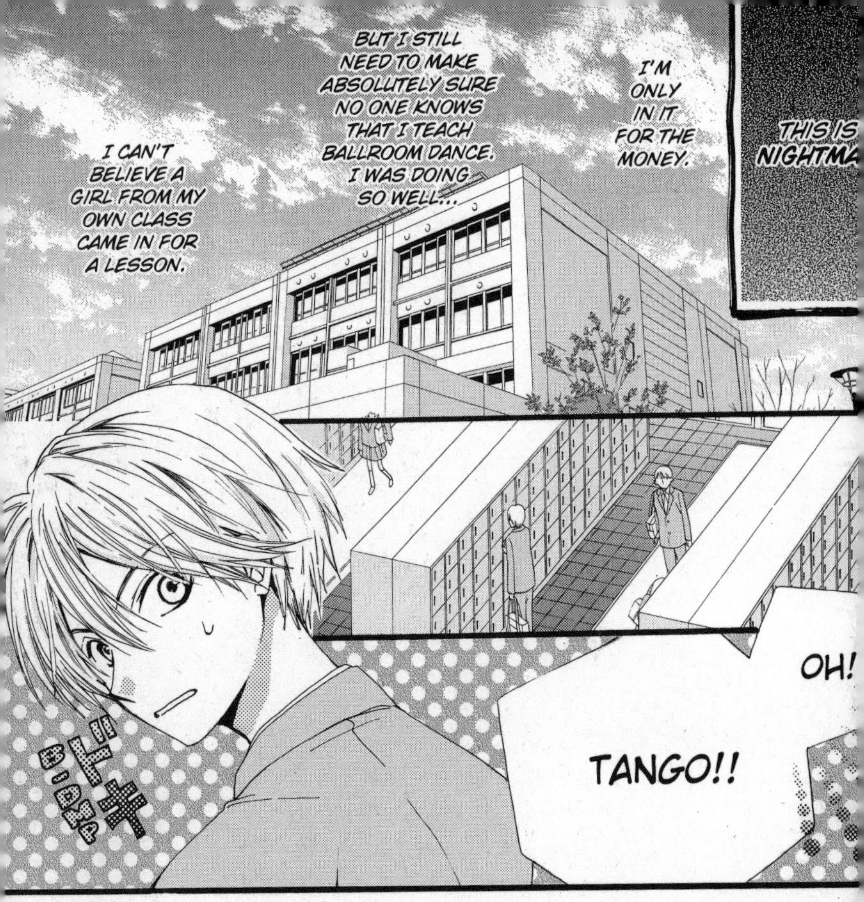
THIS IS NIGHTMA
I'M ONLY IN IT FOR THE MONEY.
BUT I STILL NEED TO MAKE ABSOLUTELY SURE NO ONE KNOWS THAT I TEACH BALLROOM DANCE. I WAS DOING SO WELL...
I CAN'T BELIEVE A GIRL FROM MY OWN CLASS CAME IN FOR A LESSON.
OH!
TANGO!!
ドキ
B-DMP

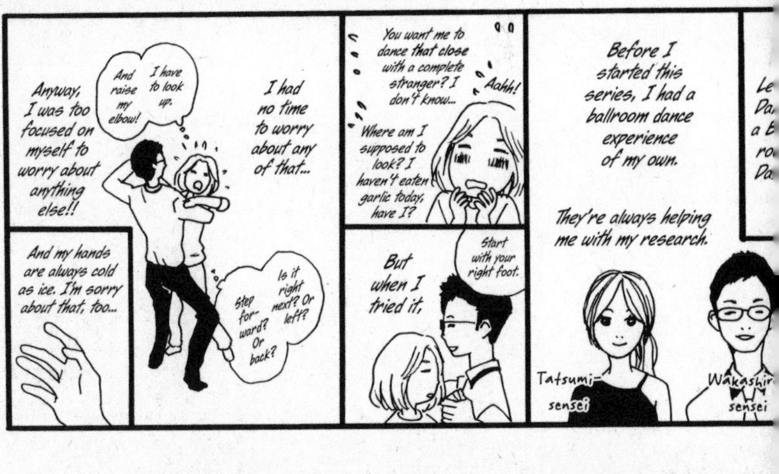
Before I started this series, I had a ballroom dance experience of my own.
They're always helping me with my research.
Wakashir sensei
Tatsumi-sensei
You want me to dance that close with a complete stranger? I don't know...
Aahh!
Where am I supposed to look? I haven't eaten garlic today, have I?
But when I tried it,
Start with your right foot.
I had no time to worry about any of that...
I have to look up.
And raise my elbow!
Anyway, I was too focused on myself to worry about anything else!!
Is it right next? Or left?
Step for-ward? Or back?
And my hands are always cold as ice. I'm sorry about that, too...

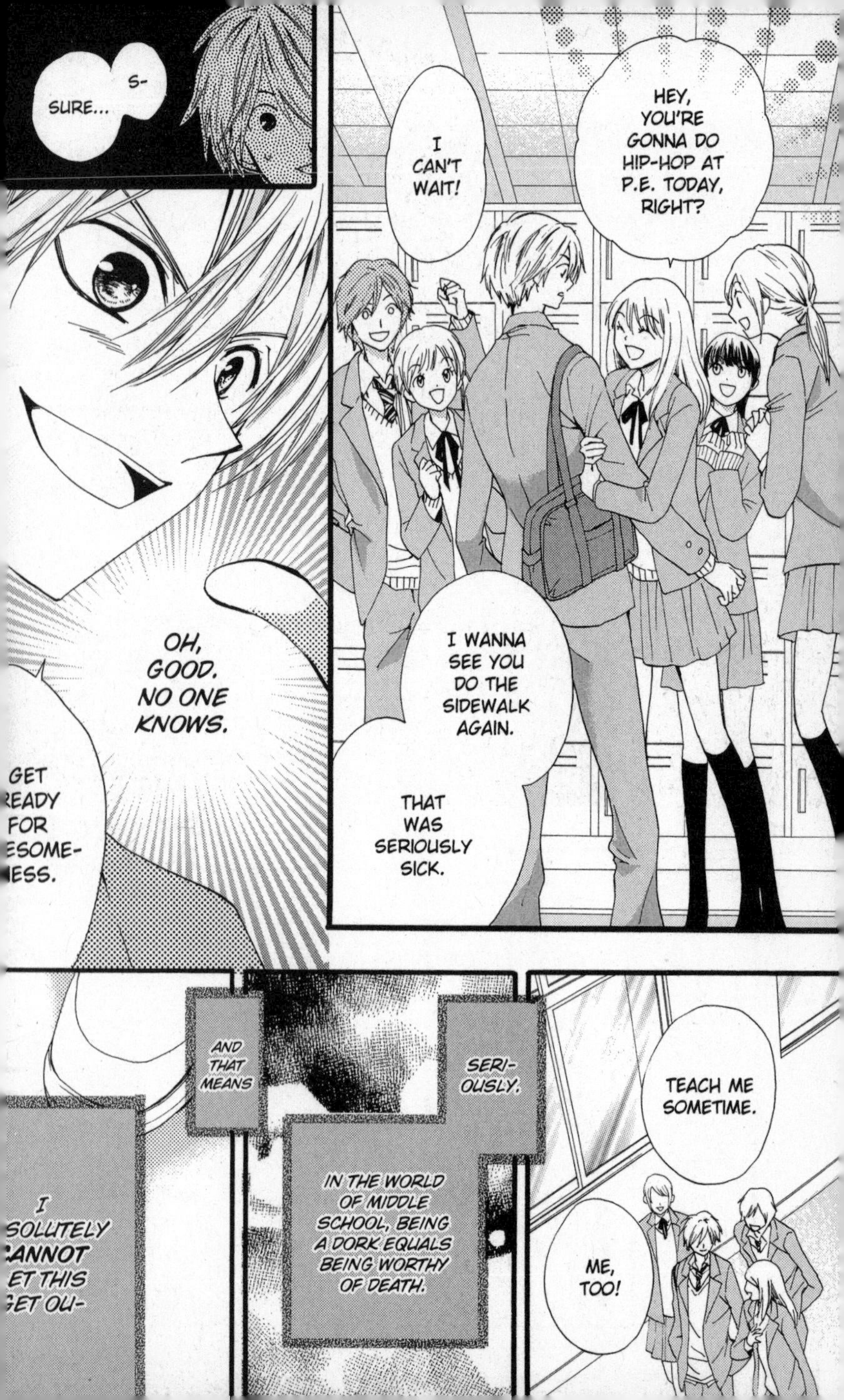
HEY, YOU'RE GONNA DO HIP-HOP AT P.E. TODAY, RIGHT?
I CAN'T WAIT!
I WANNA SEE YOU DO THE SIDEWALK AGAIN.
THAT WAS SERIOUSLY SICK.
S- SURE...
OH, GOOD. NO ONE KNOWS.
GET READY FOR ESOME-NESS.
TEACH ME SOMETIME.
ME, TOO!
SERI-OUSLY.
AND THAT MEANS
IN THE WORLD OF MIDDLE SCHOOL, BEING A DORK EQUALS BEING WORTHY OF DEATH.
I SOLUTELY CANNOT ET THIS GET OU-

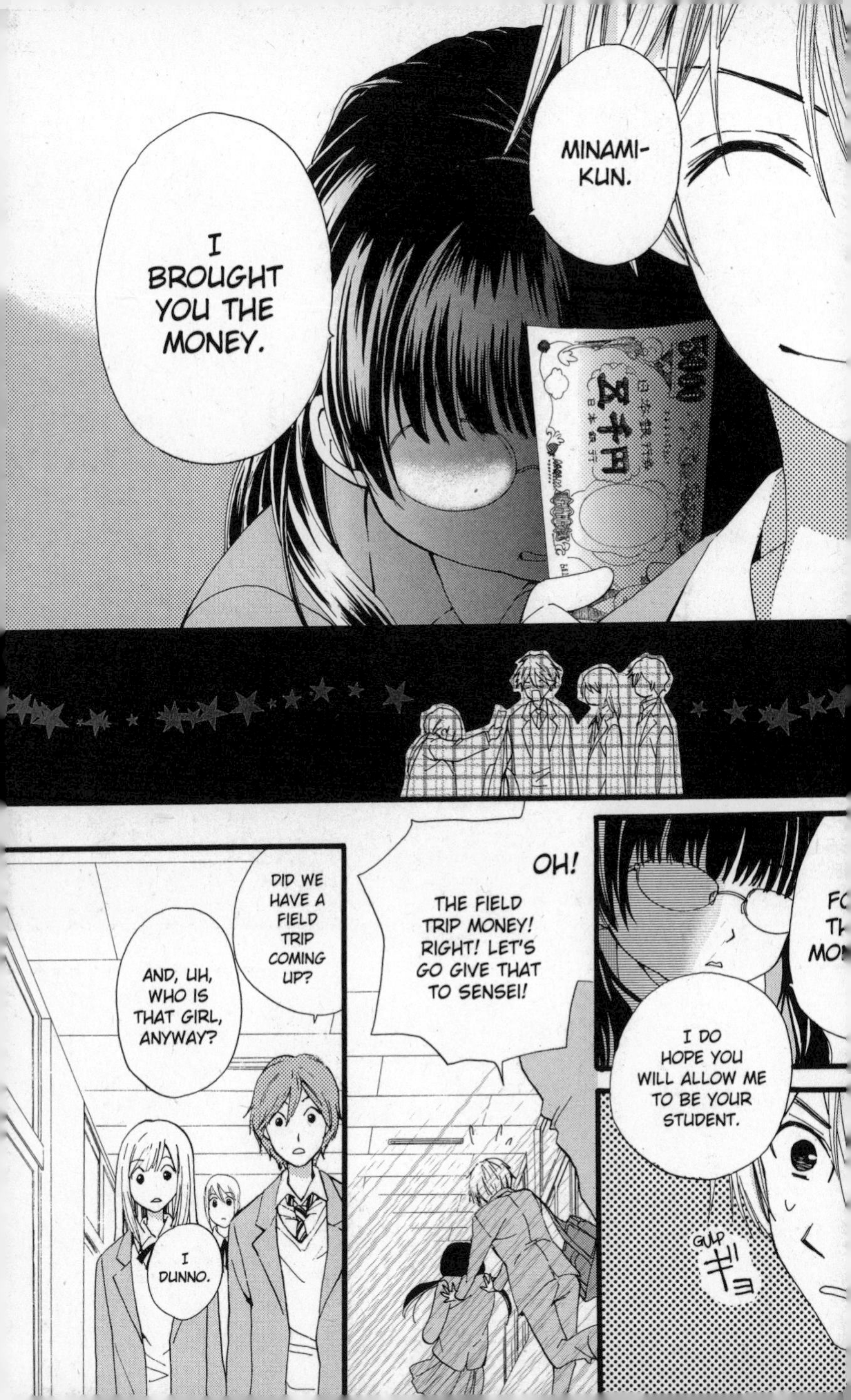
MINAMI-KUN.
I BROUGHT YOU THE MONEY.
五千円
I DO HOPE YOU WILL ALLOW ME TO BE YOUR STUDENT.
GULP
ギョ
OH!
THE FIELD TRIP MONEY! RIGHT! LET'S GO GIVE THAT TO SENSEI!
DID WE HAVE A FIELD TRIP COMING UP?
AND, UH, WHO IS THAT GIRL, ANYWAY?
I DUNNO.

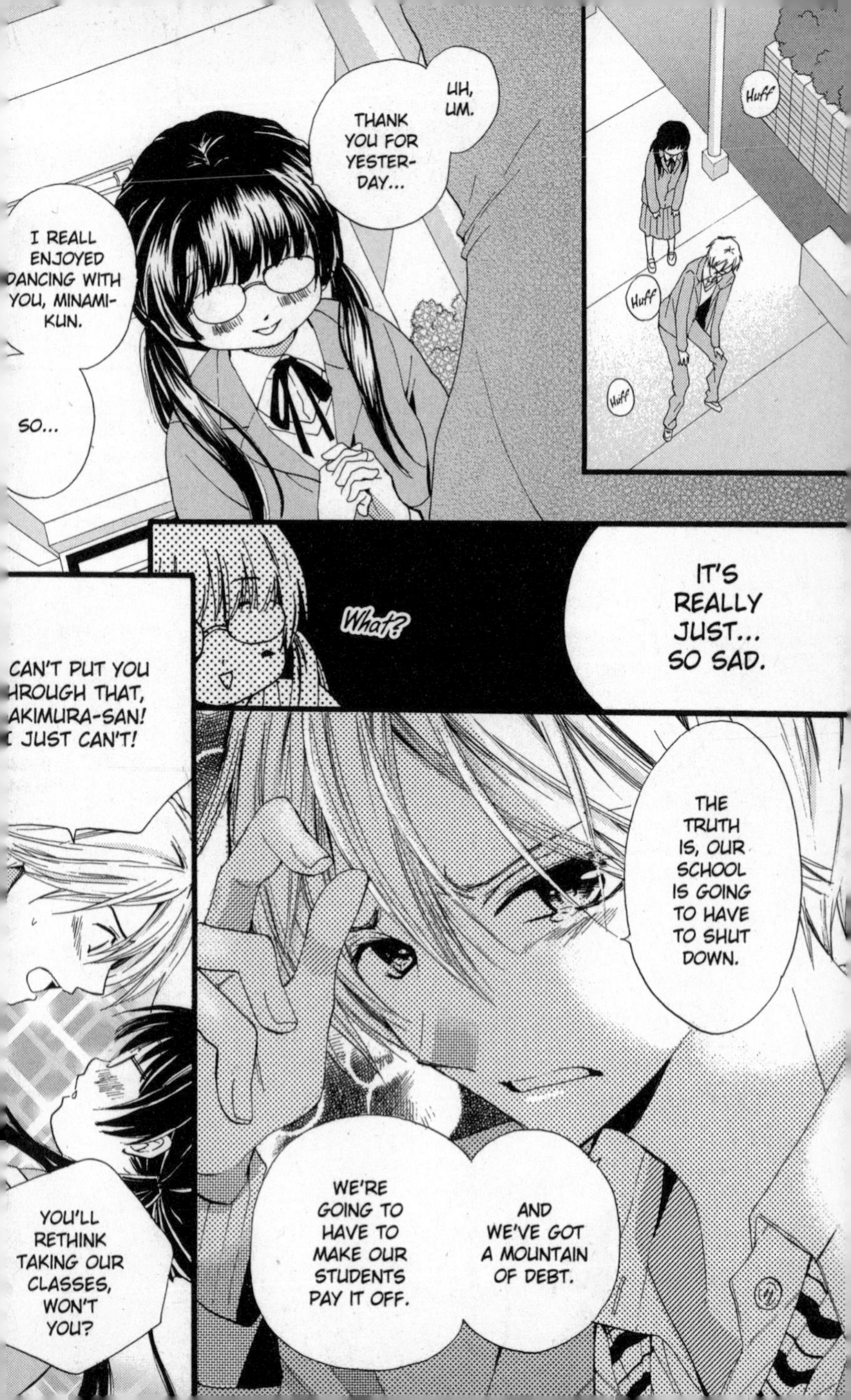
Huff
Huff
Huff
UH, UM.
THANK YOU FOR YESTER-DAY...
I REALL ENJOYED DANCING WITH YOU, MINAMI-KUN.
SO...
IT'S REALLY JUST... SO SAD.
What?
THE TRUTH IS, OUR SCHOOL IS GOING TO HAVE TO SHUT DOWN.
AND WE'VE GOT A MOUNTAIN OF DEBT.
WE'RE GOING TO HAVE TO MAKE OUR STUDENTS PAY IT OFF.
CAN'T PUT YOU HROUGH THAT, AKIMURA-SAN! I JUST CAN'T!
YOU'LL RETHINK TAKING OUR CLASSES, WON'T YOU?

THAT WAS CLOSE.

IT HURTS ME TO BREAK MY STUDENT RECRUITMENT STREAK.

BUT IF I'M GOING TO TAKE MY SECRET TO THE GRAVE, THEN I MUST NEVER SPEAK TO HER AGAIN.

Minami Dance School

Minami Dance Sch

WELL I'M SA FOR NC ANYWA

I'M HOME!

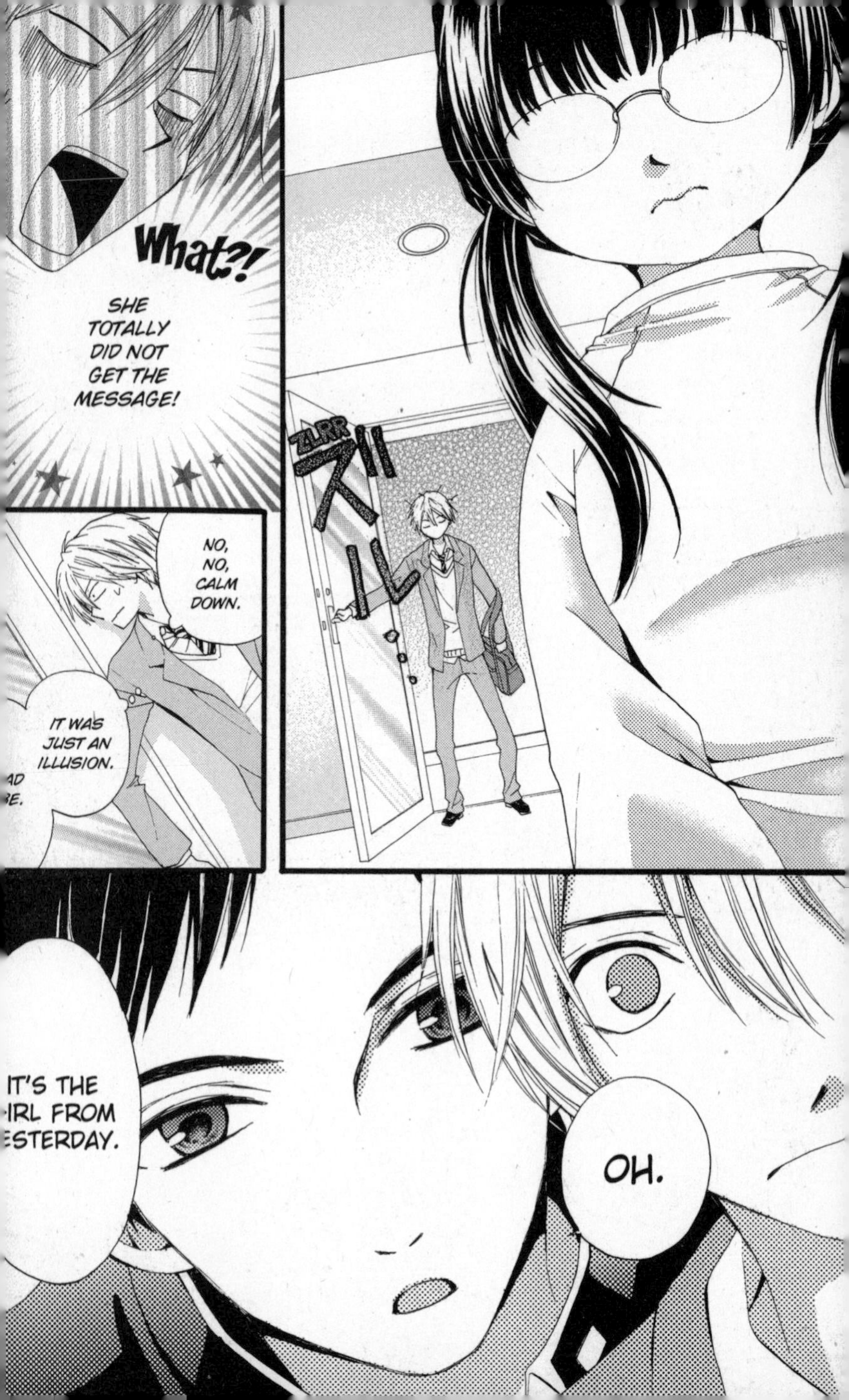
ZLRR
What?!
SHE TOTALLY DID NOT GET THE MESSAGE!
NO, NO, CALM DOWN.
IT WAS JUST AN ILLUSION.
OH.
IT'S THE
IRL FROM
ESTERDAY.

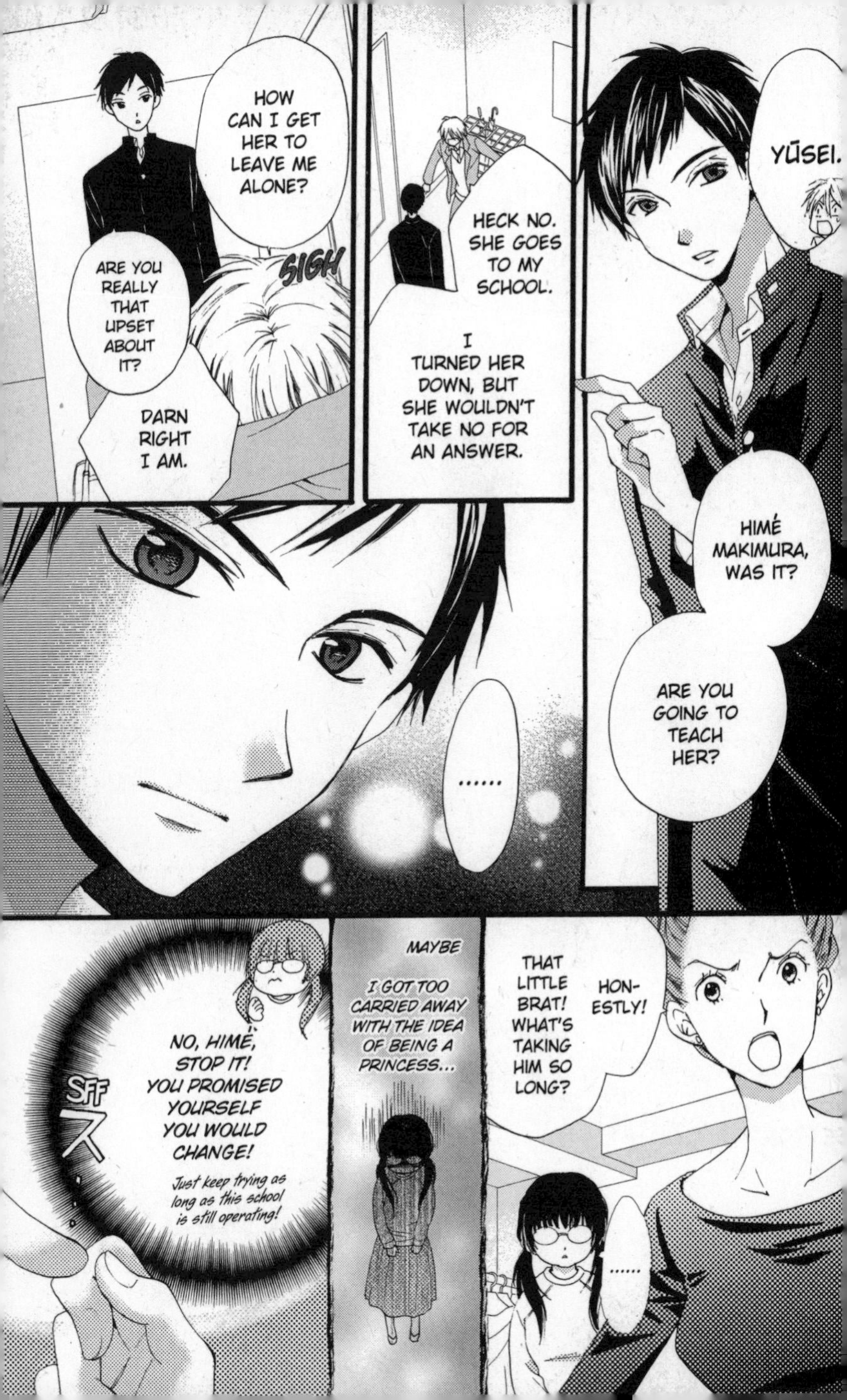
YŪSEI.
HIMÉ MAKIMURA, WAS IT?
ARE YOU GOING TO TEACH HER?
HECK NO. SHE GOES TO MY SCHOOL.
I TURNED HER DOWN, BUT SHE WOULDN'T TAKE NO FOR AN ANSWER.
HOW CAN I GET HER TO LEAVE ME ALONE?
SIGH
ARE YOU REALLY THAT UPSET ABOUT IT?
DARN RIGHT I AM.
......
HON-ESTLY!
THAT LITTLE BRAT! WHAT'S TAKING HIM SO LONG?
......
MAYBE
I GOT TOO CARRIED AWAY WITH THE IDEA OF BEING A PRINCESS...
NO, HIMÉ, STOP IT! YOU PROMISED YOURSELF YOU WOULD CHANGE!
Just keep trying as long as this school is still operating!
SFF
ス

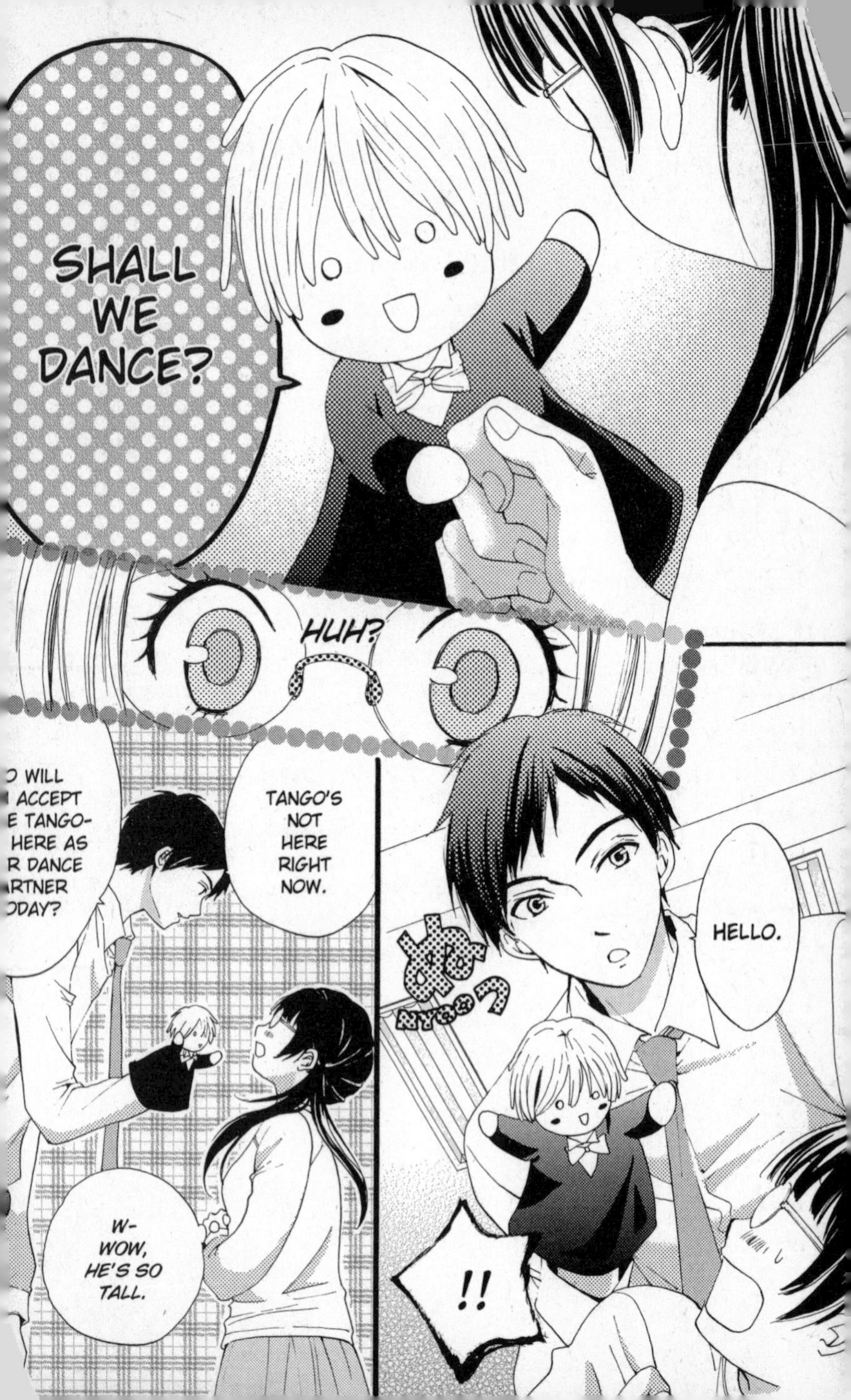
SHALL WE DANCE?
HUH?
HELLO.
!!
TANGO'S NOT HERE RIGHT NOW.
O WILL ACCEPT E TANGO-HERE AS R DANCE RTNER ODAY?
W-WOW, HE'S SO TALL.

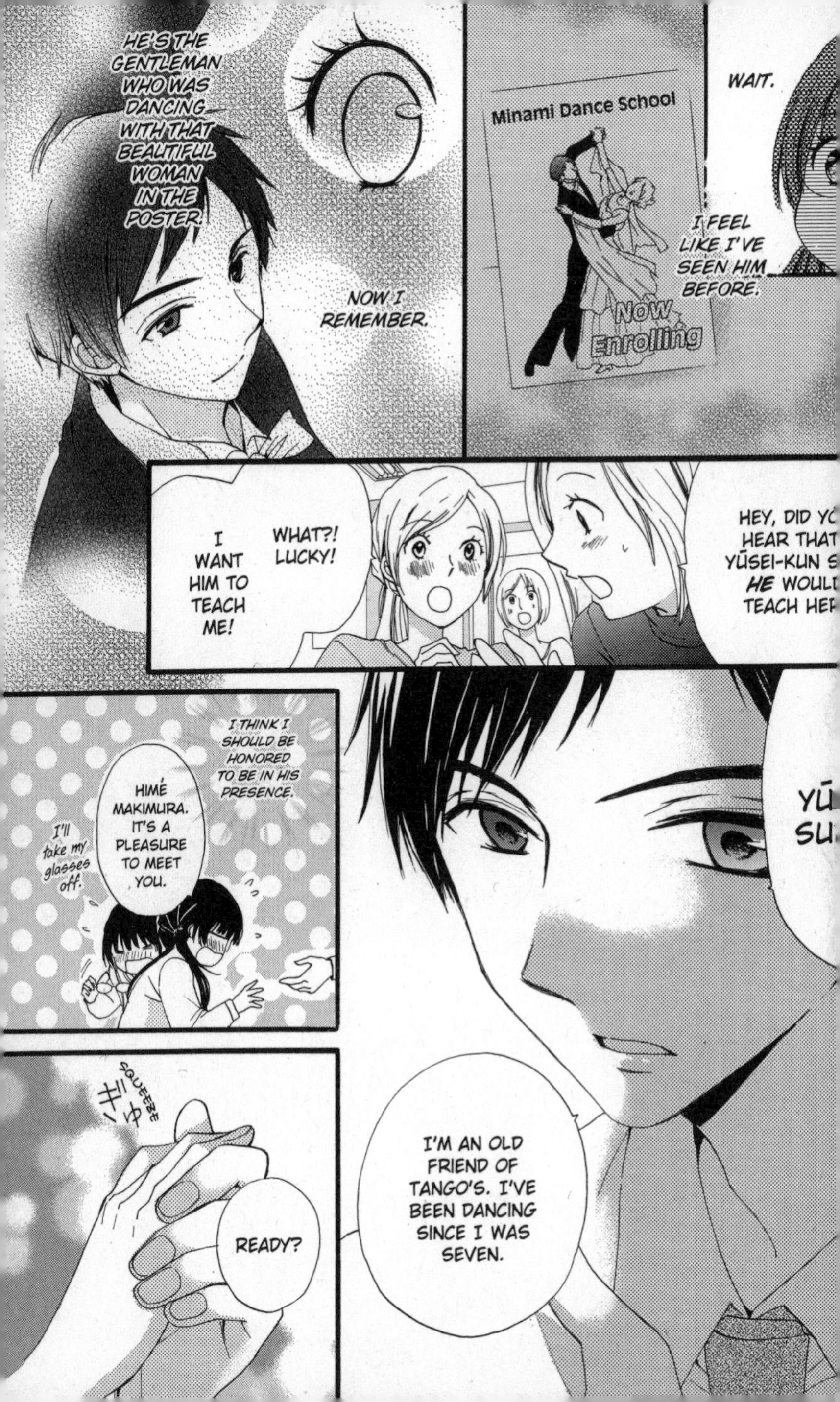
WAIT.
Minami Dance School
Now Enrolling
I FEEL LIKE I'VE SEEN HIM BEFORE.
NOW I REMEMBER.
HE'S THE GENTLEMAN WHO WAS DANCING WITH THAT BEAUTIFUL WOMAN IN THE POSTER.
HEY, DID YO HEAR THAT YŪSEI-KUN S *HE* WOULD TEACH HE
WHAT?! LUCKY!
I WANT HIM TO TEACH ME!
YŪ SU
I'M AN OLD FRIEND OF TANGO'S. I'VE BEEN DANCING SINCE I WAS SEVEN.
I THINK I SHOULD BE HONORED TO BE IN HIS PRESENCE.
HIMÉ MAKIMURA. IT'S A PLEASURE TO MEET YOU.
I'll take my glasses off.
SQUEEEE
READY?

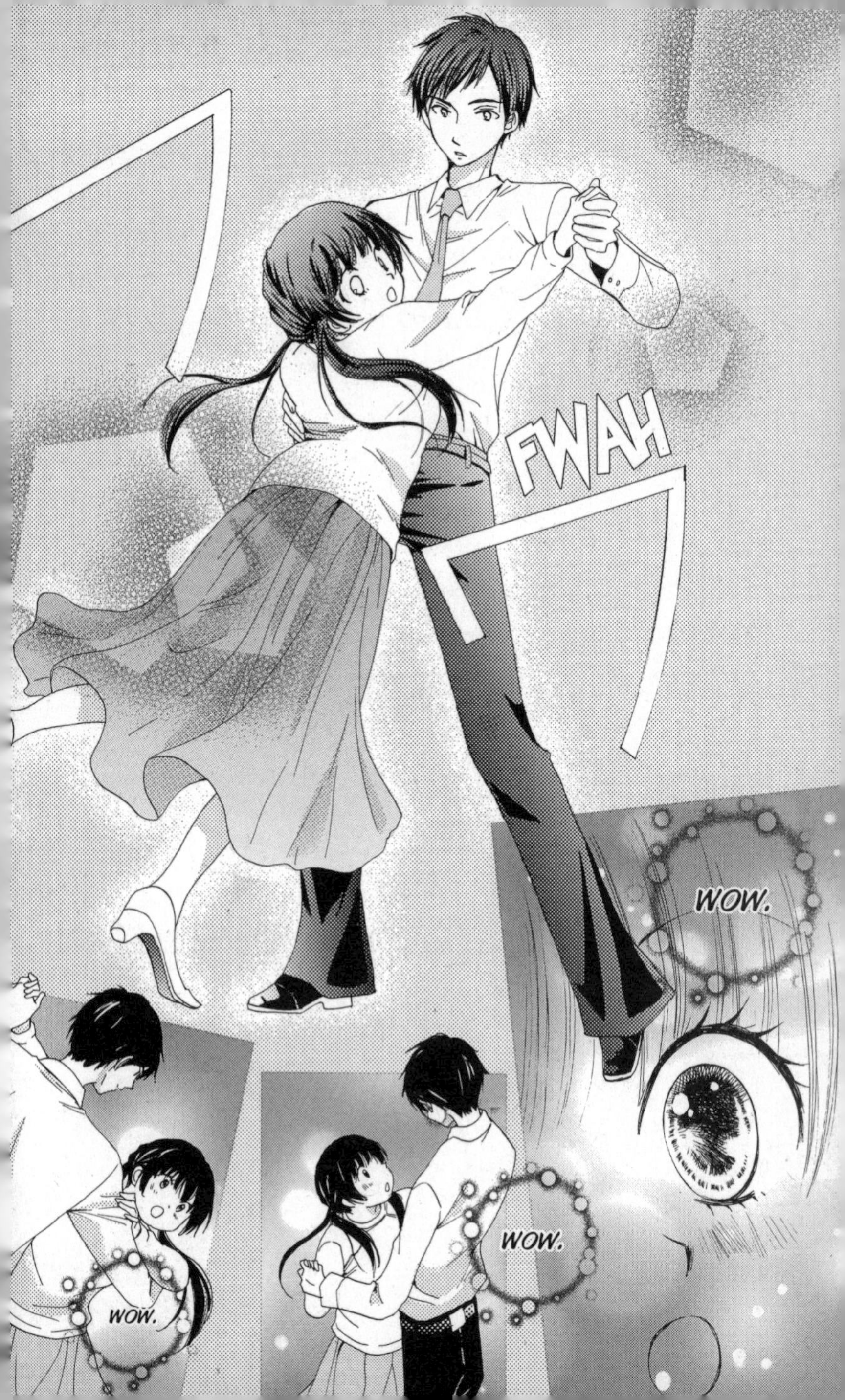
FWAH
WOW.
WOW.
WOW.

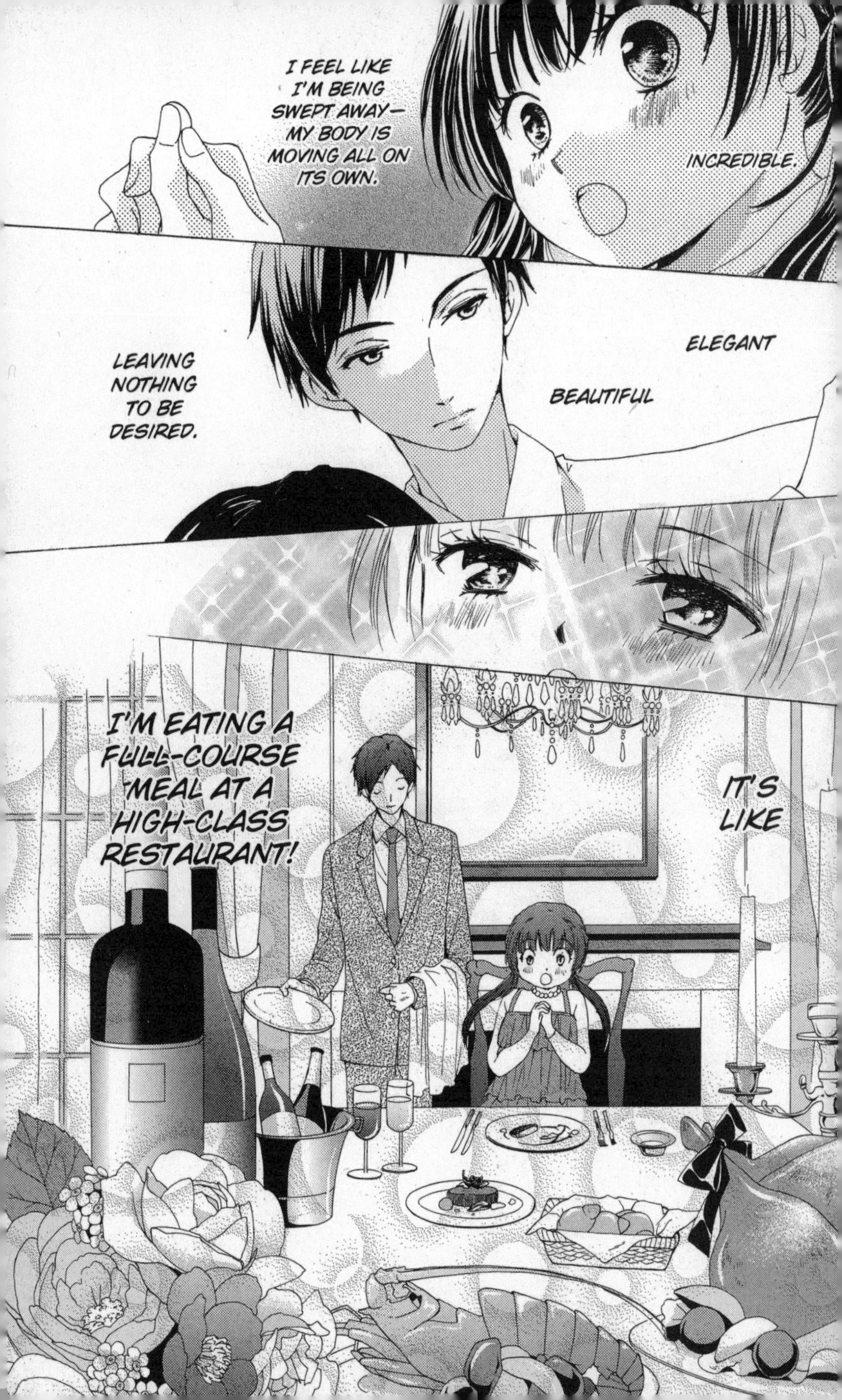
INCREDIBLE.
I FEEL LIKE I'M BEING SWEPT AWAY—MY BODY IS MOVING ALL ON ITS OWN.
ELEGANT
BEAUTIFUL
LEAVING NOTHING TO BE DESIRED.
IT'S LIKE
I'M EATING A FULL-COURSE MEAL AT A HIGH-CLASS RESTAURANT!

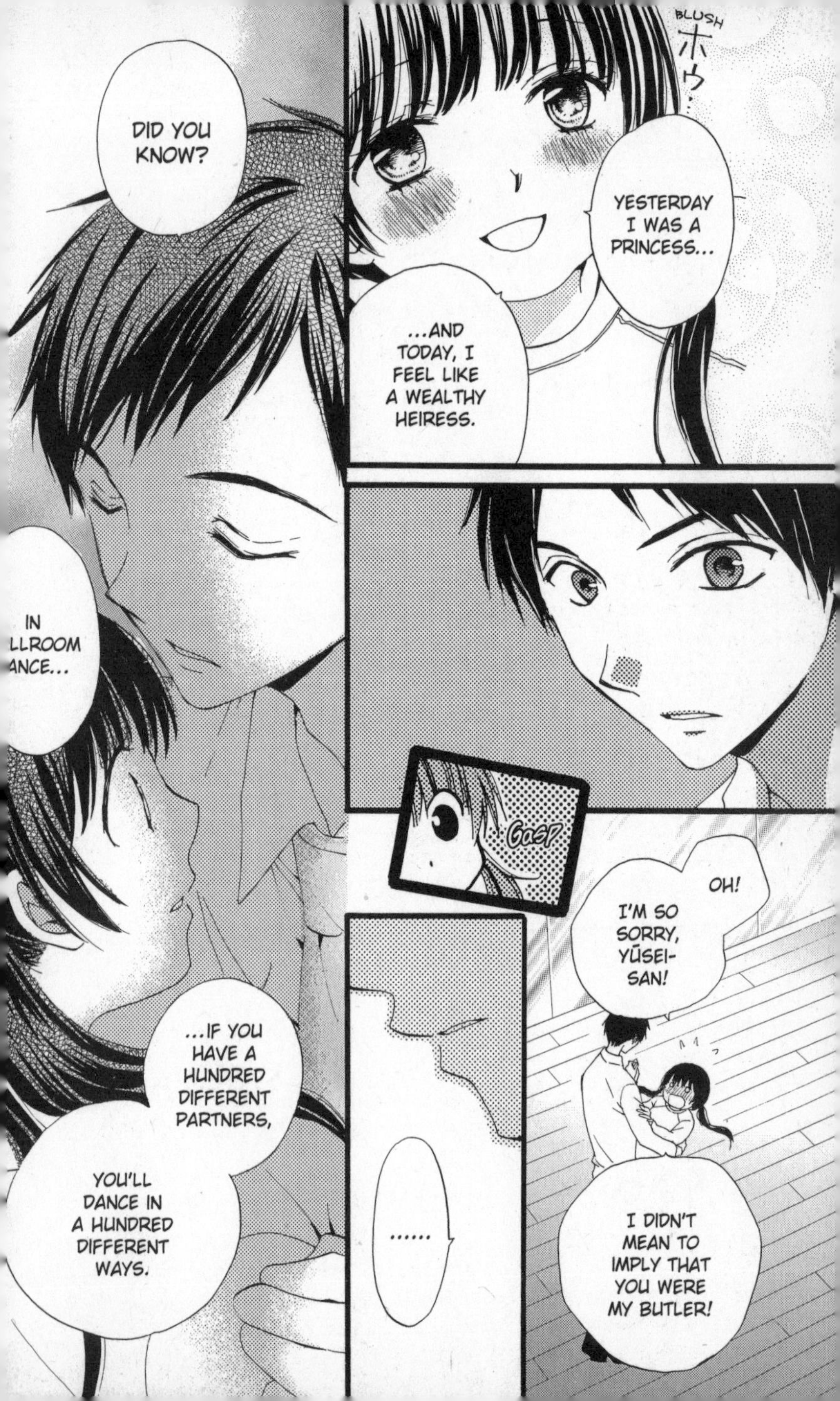
BLUSH
ホウ
YESTERDAY I WAS A PRINCESS...
...AND TODAY, I FEEL LIKE A WEALTHY HEIRESS.
GASP
OH!
I'M SO SORRY, YŪSEI-SAN!
I DIDN'T MEAN TO IMPLY THAT YOU WERE MY BUTLER!
......
DID YOU KNOW?
IN LLROOM ANCE...
...IF YOU HAVE A HUNDRED DIFFERENT PARTNERS,
YOU'LL DANCE IN A HUNDRED DIFFERENT WAYS.

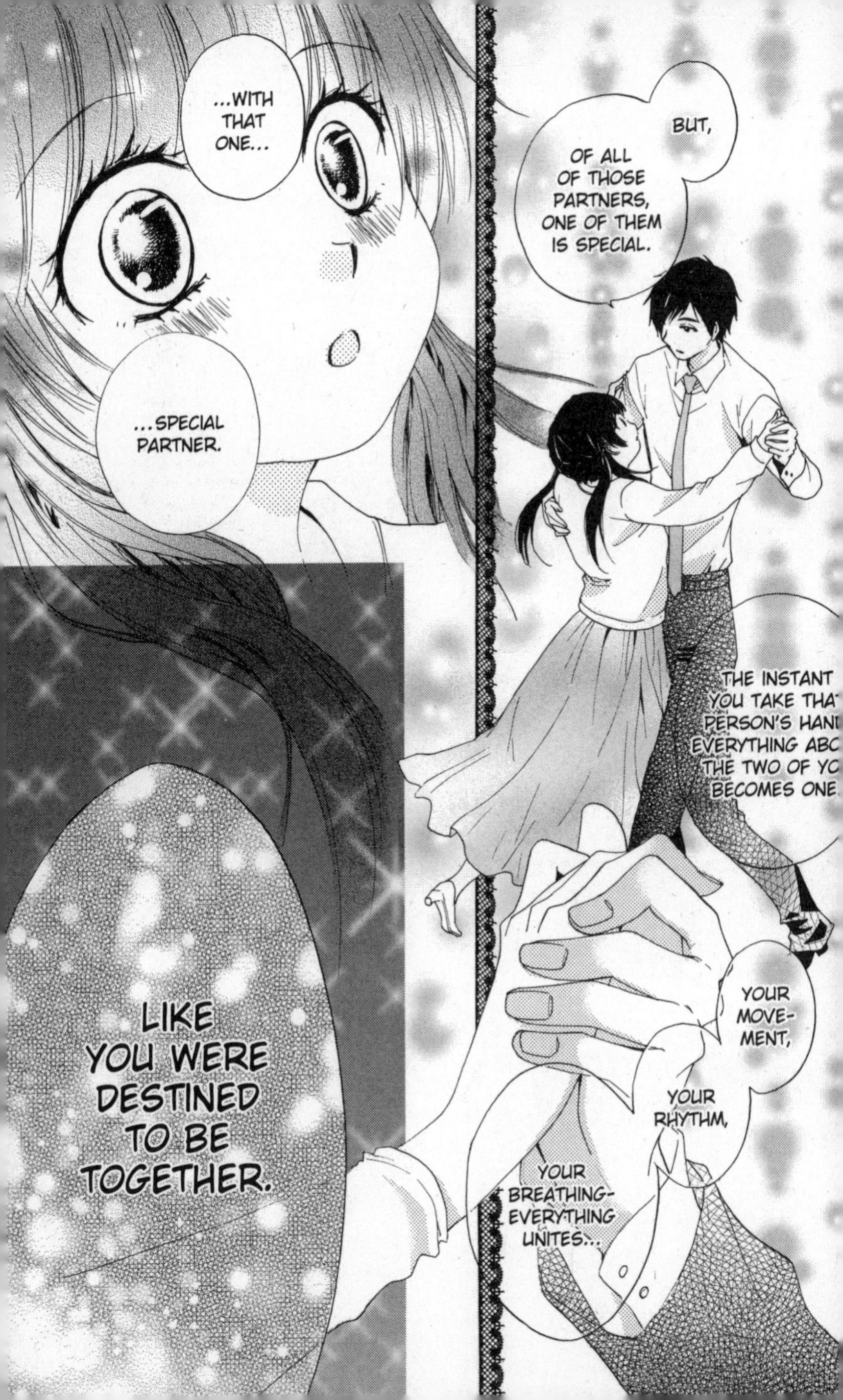
BUT,
OF ALL OF THOSE PARTNERS, ONE OF THEM IS SPECIAL.
THE INSTANT YOU TAKE THA PERSON'S HAN EVERYTHING AB THE TWO OF Y BECOMES ONE.
YOUR MOVE-MENT,
YOUR RHYTHM,
YOUR BREATHING-EVERYTHING UNITES...
...WITH THAT ONE...
...SPECIAL PARTNER.
LIKE YOU WERE DESTINED TO BE TOGETHER.

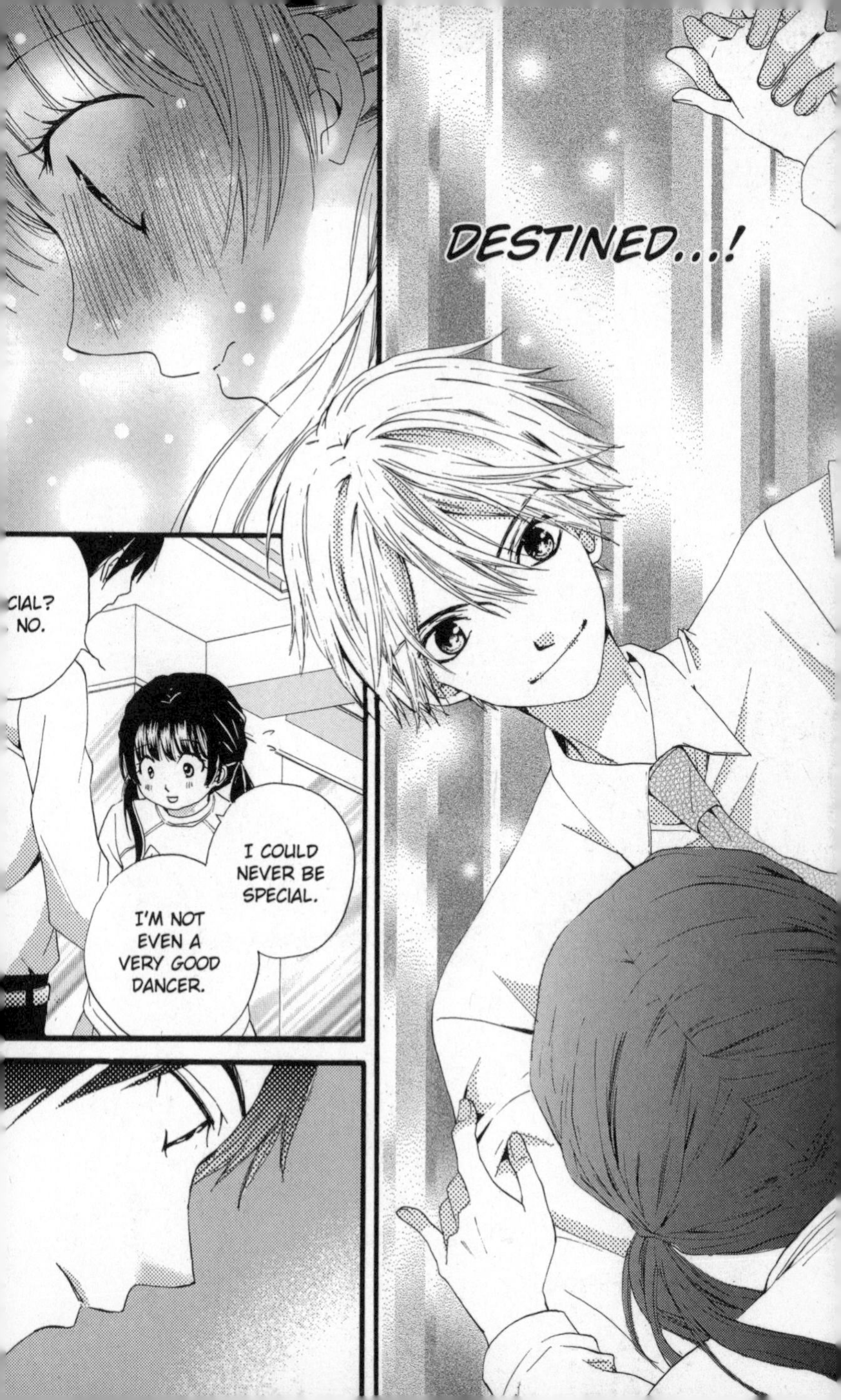
DESTINED...!
CIAL? NO.
I COULD NEVER BE SPECIAL.
I'M NOT EVEN A VERY GOOD DANCER.

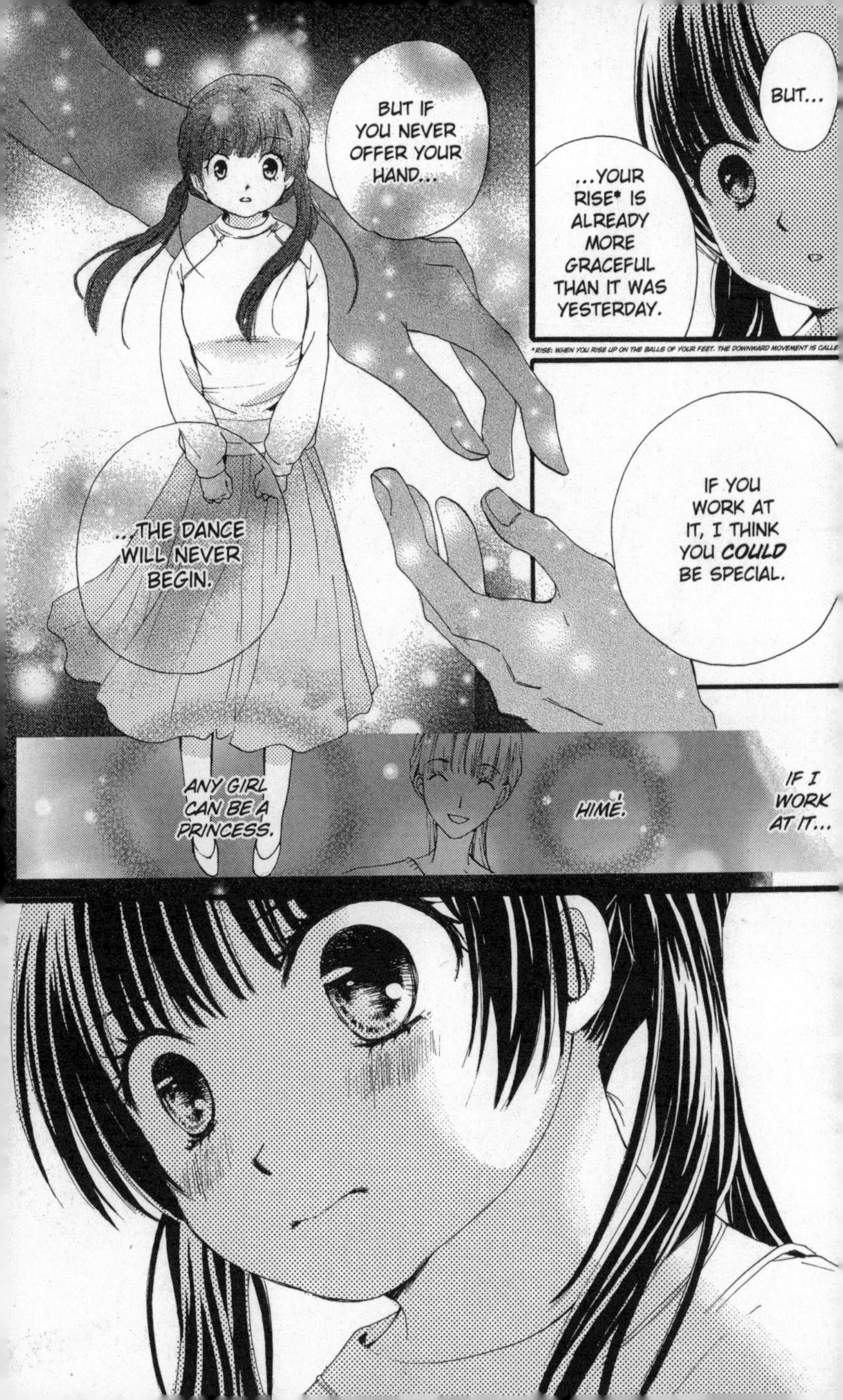
BUT...
...YOUR RISE* IS ALREADY MORE GRACEFUL THAN IT WAS YESTERDAY.
IF YOU WORK AT IT, I THINK YOU **COULD** BE SPECIAL.
BUT IF YOU NEVER OFFER YOUR HAND...
...THE DANCE WILL NEVER BEGIN.
IF I WORK AT IT...
HIME.
ANY GIRL CAN BE A PRINCESS.

*RISE: WHEN YOU RISE UP ON THE BALLS OF YOUR FEET. THE DOWNWARD MOVEMENT IS CALLE

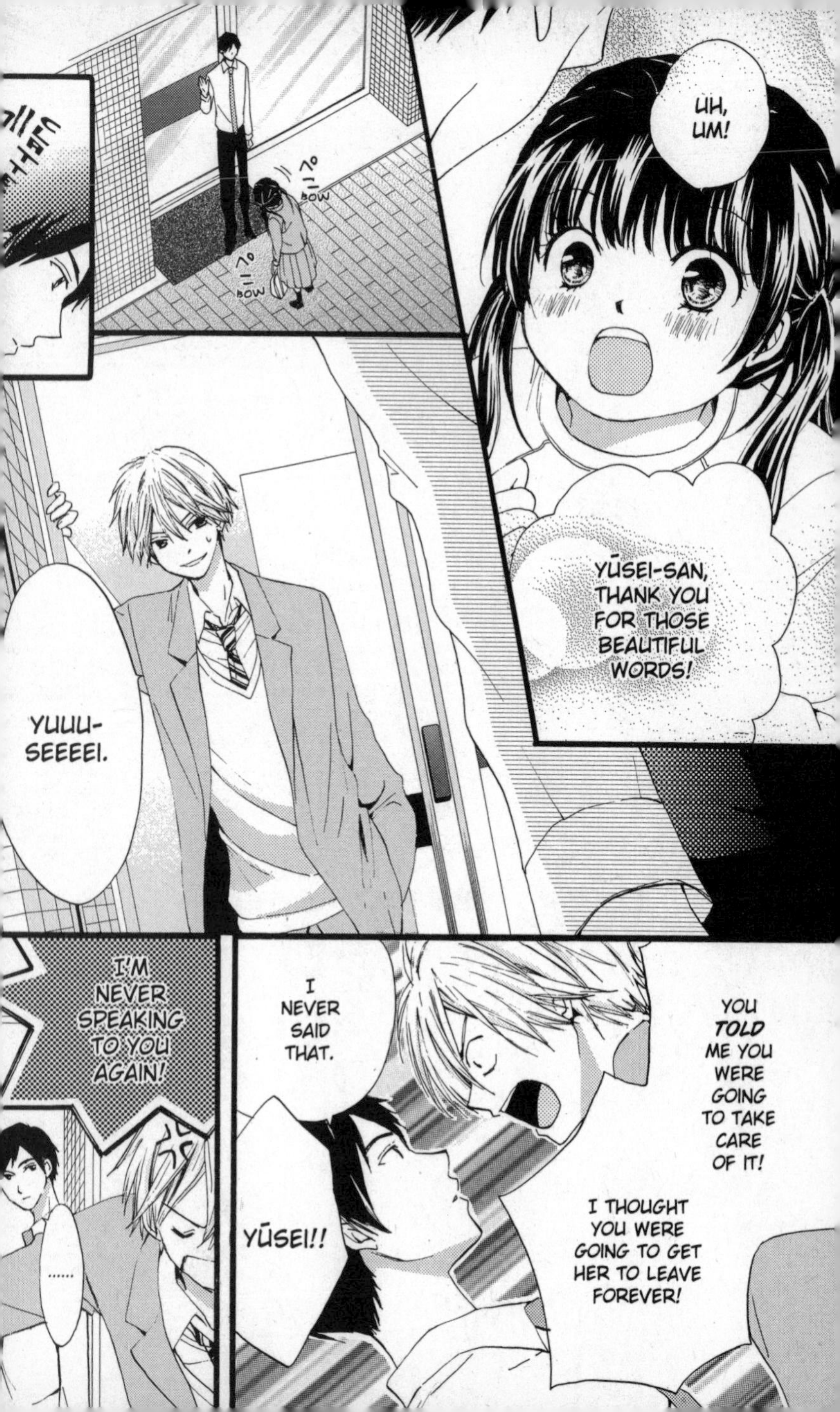
UH, UM!
YŪSEI-SAN, THANK YOU FOR THOSE BEAUTIFUL WORDS!
BOW
BOW
YUUU-SEEEEI.
YOU TOLD ME YOU WERE GOING TO TAKE CARE OF IT!
I NEVER SAID THAT.
I THOUGHT YOU WERE GOING TO GET HER TO LEAVE FOREVER!
YŪSEI!!
I'M NEVER SPEAKING TO YOU AGAIN!
......

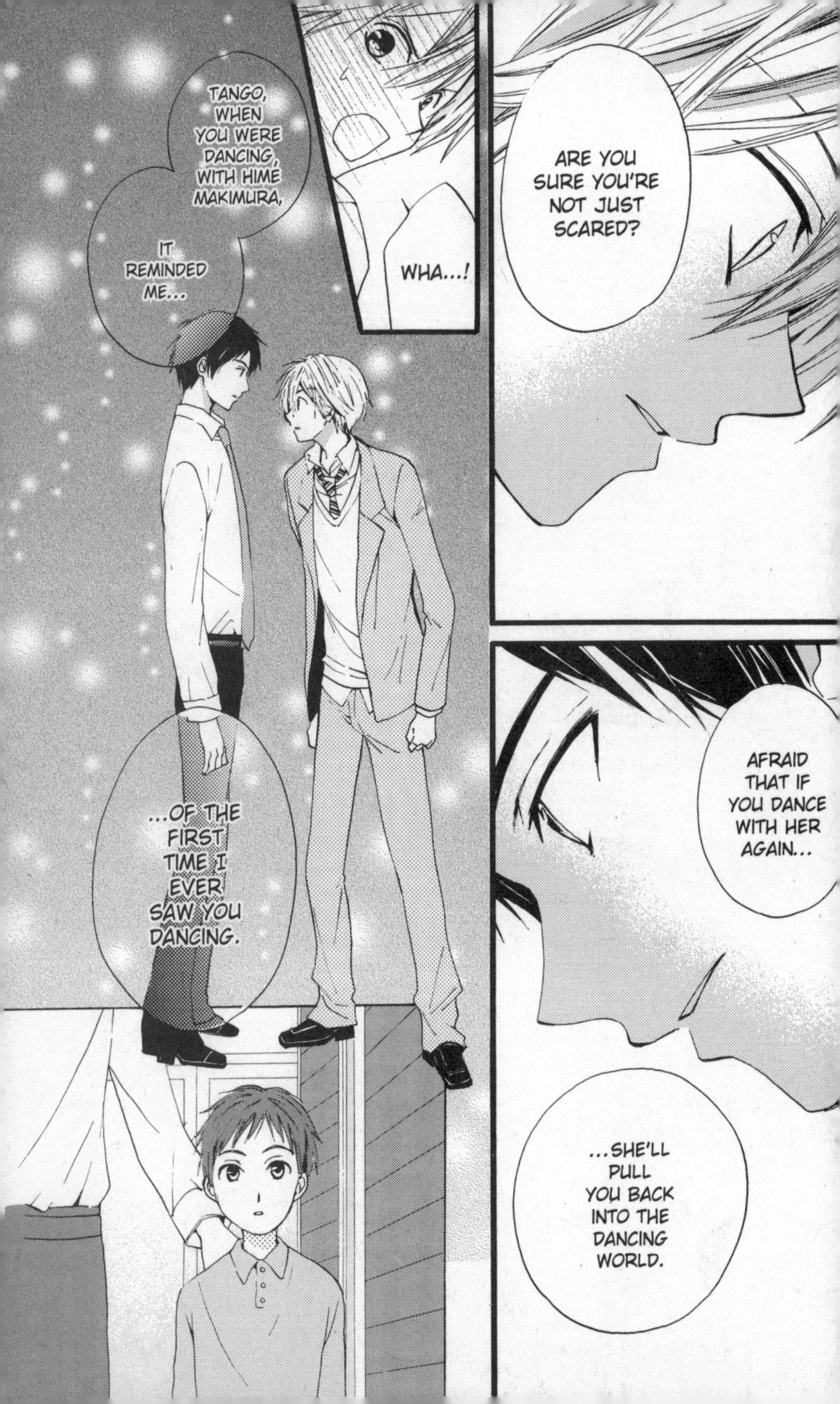
ARE YOU SURE YOU'RE NOT JUST SCARED?
WHA...!
AFRAID THAT IF YOU DANCE WITH HER AGAIN...
...SHE'LL PULL YOU BACK INTO THE DANCING WORLD.
TANGO, WHEN YOU WERE DANCING, WITH HIME MAKIMURA,
IT REMINDED ME...
...OF THE FIRST TIME I EVER SAW YOU DANCING.

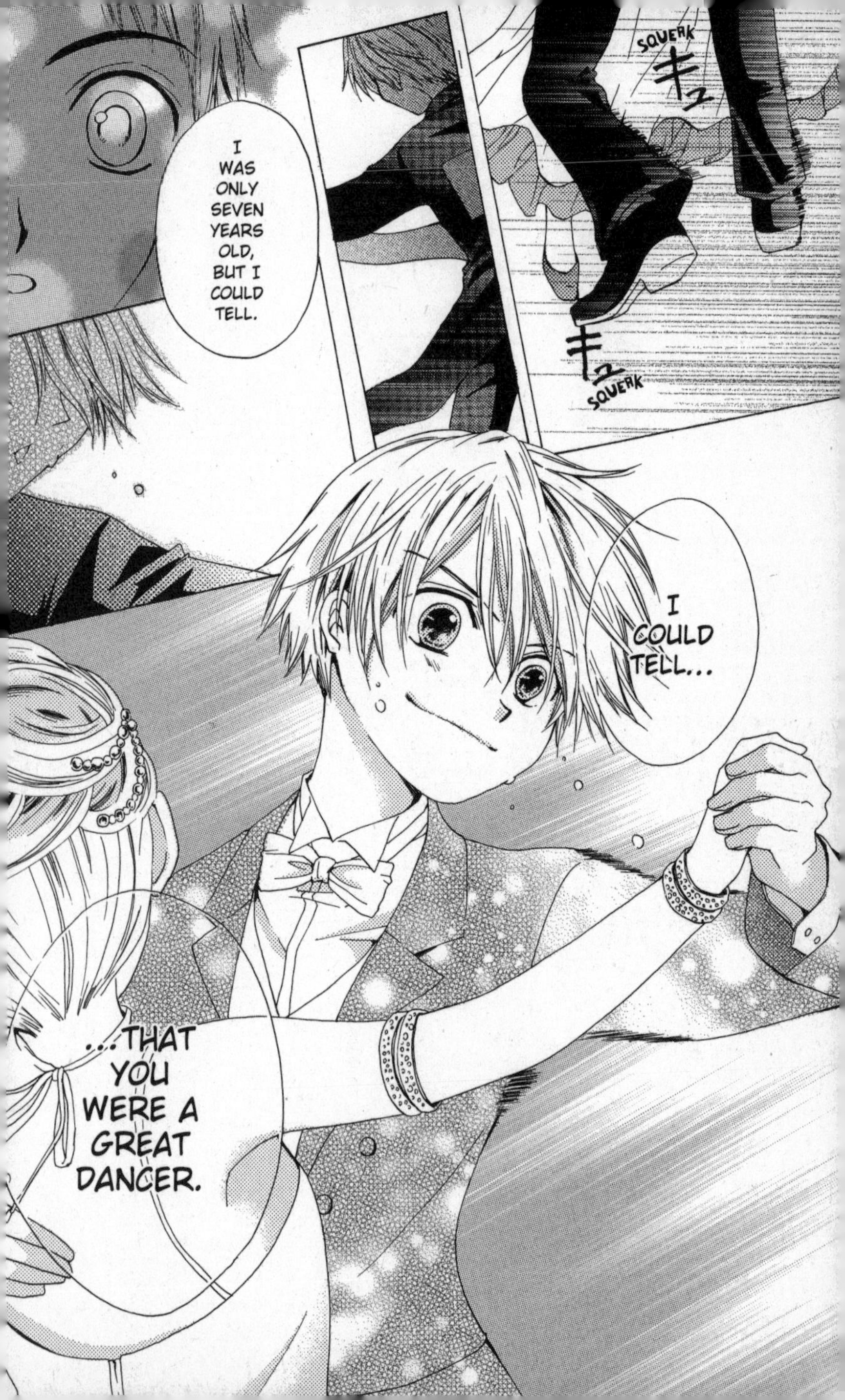

SQUEAK キュ
キュ SQUEAK
I WAS ONLY SEVEN YEARS OLD, BUT I COULD TELL.
I COULD TELL...
...THAT YOU WERE A GREAT DANCER.

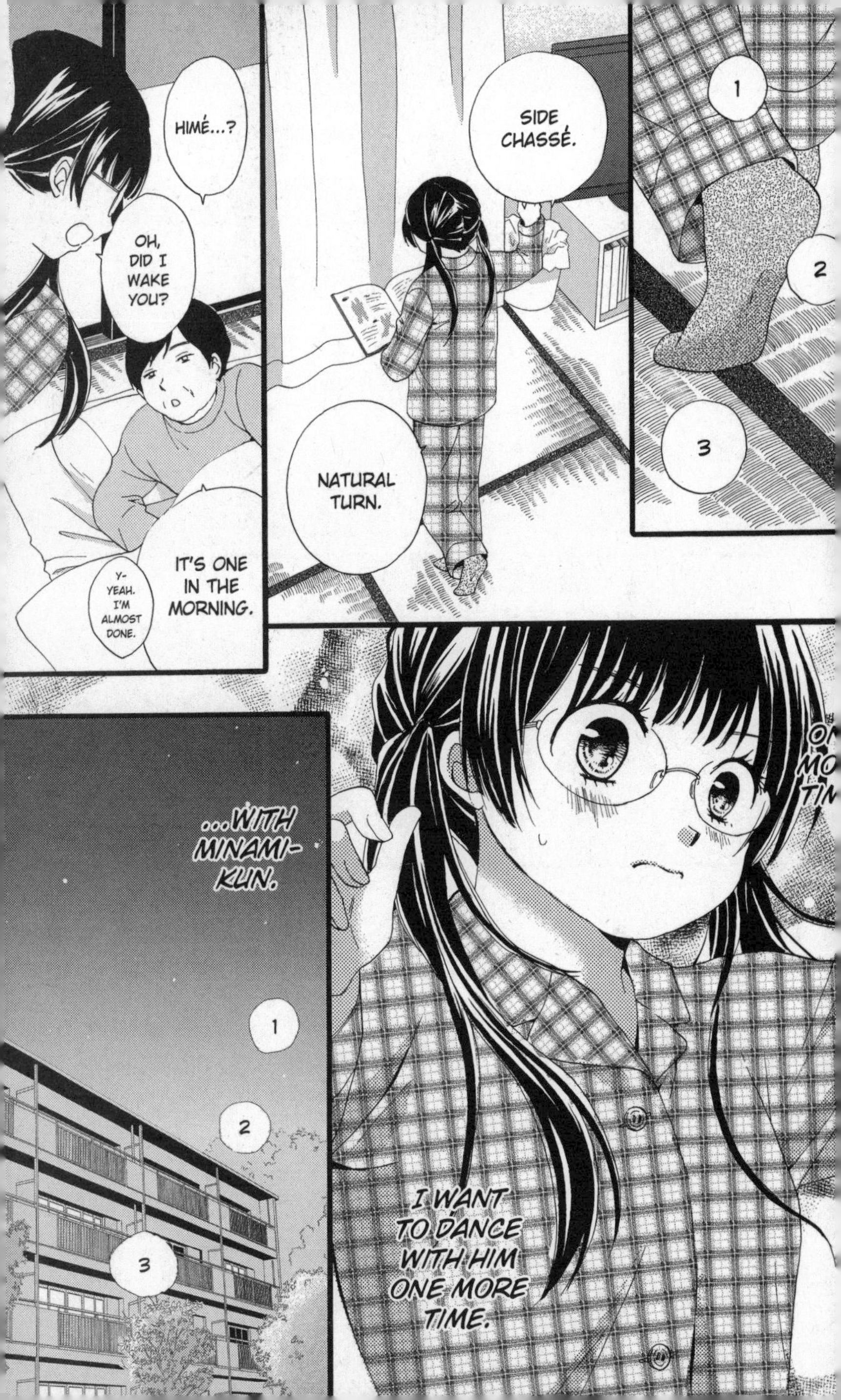
1
2
3
SIDE CHASSÉ.
NATURAL TURN.
HIMÉ...?
OH, DID I WAKE YOU?
IT'S ONE IN THE MORNING.
Y-YEAH. I'M ALMOST DONE.
I WANT TO DANCE WITH HIM ONE MORE TIME.
...WITH MINAMI-KUN.
1
2
3

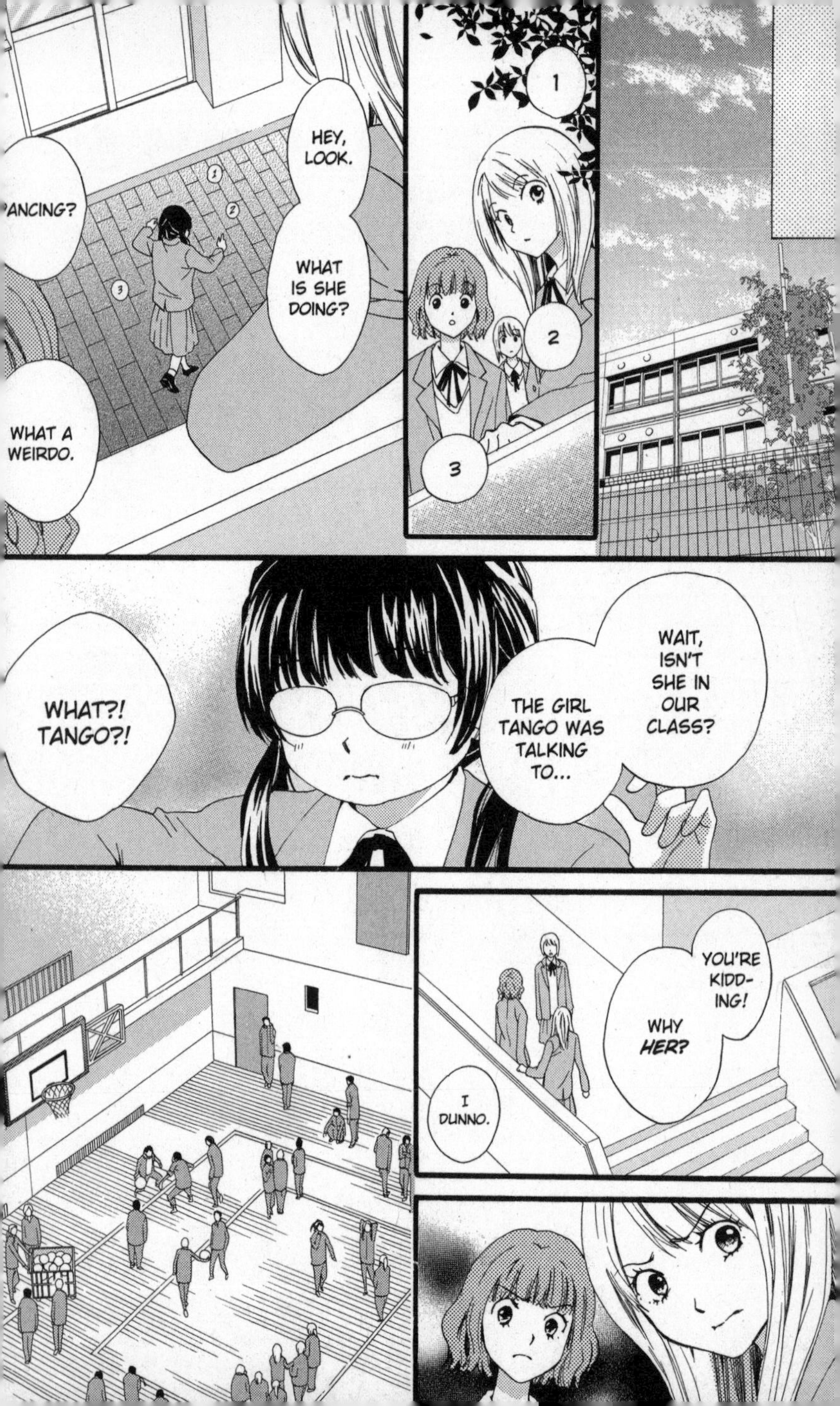
1
2
3
HEY, LOOK.
WHAT IS SHE DOING?
1
2
3
ANCING?
WHAT A WEIRDO.
WAIT, ISN'T SHE IN OUR CLASS?
THE GIRL TANGO WAS TALKING TO...
WHAT?! TANGO?!
YOU'RE KIDD-ING!
WHY *HER*?
I DUNNO.

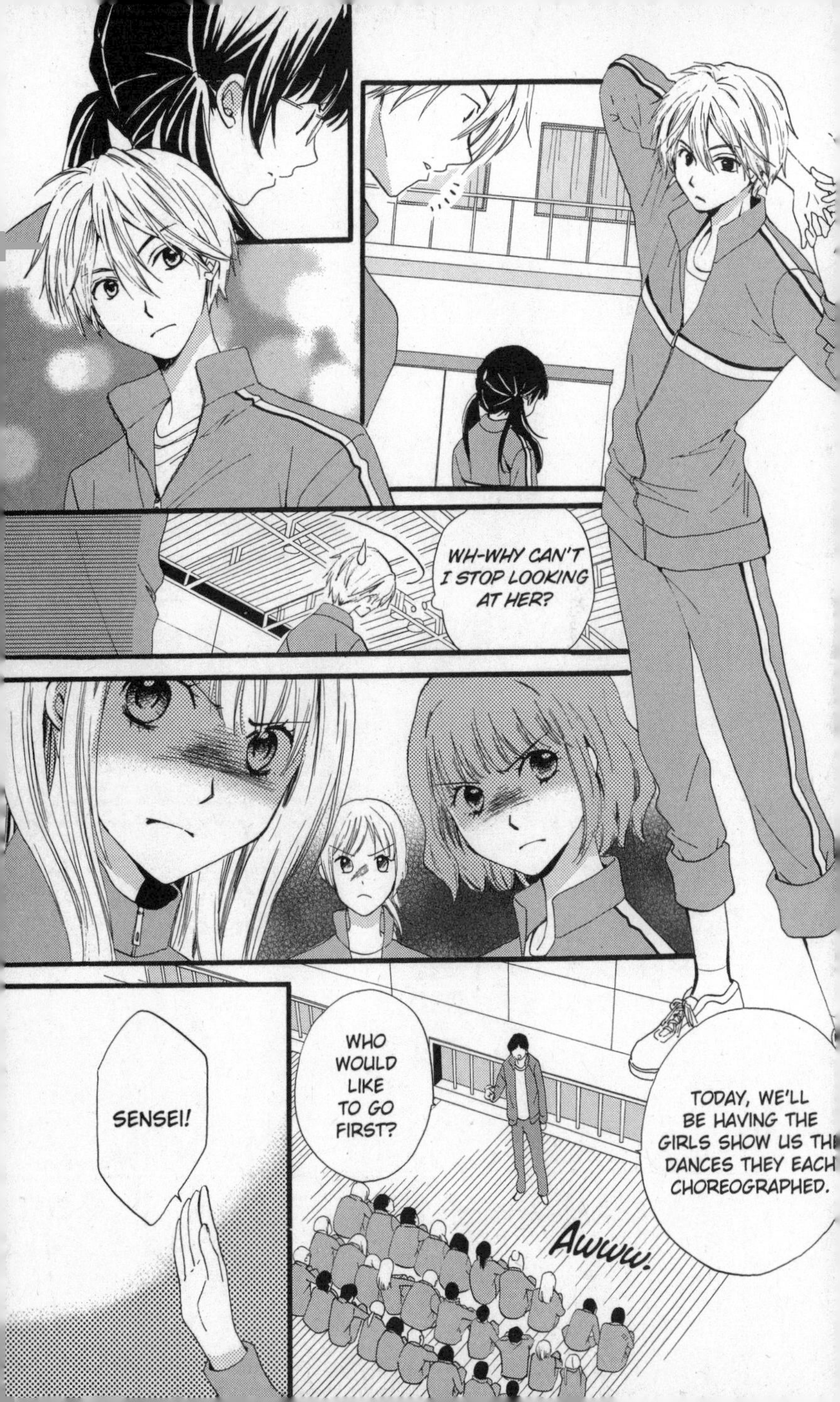
WH-WHY CAN'T I STOP LOOKING AT HER?
TODAY, WE'LL BE HAVING THE GIRLS SHOW US THE DANCES THEY EACH CHOREOGRAPHED.
Awww.
WHO WOULD LIKE TO GO FIRST?
SENSEI!

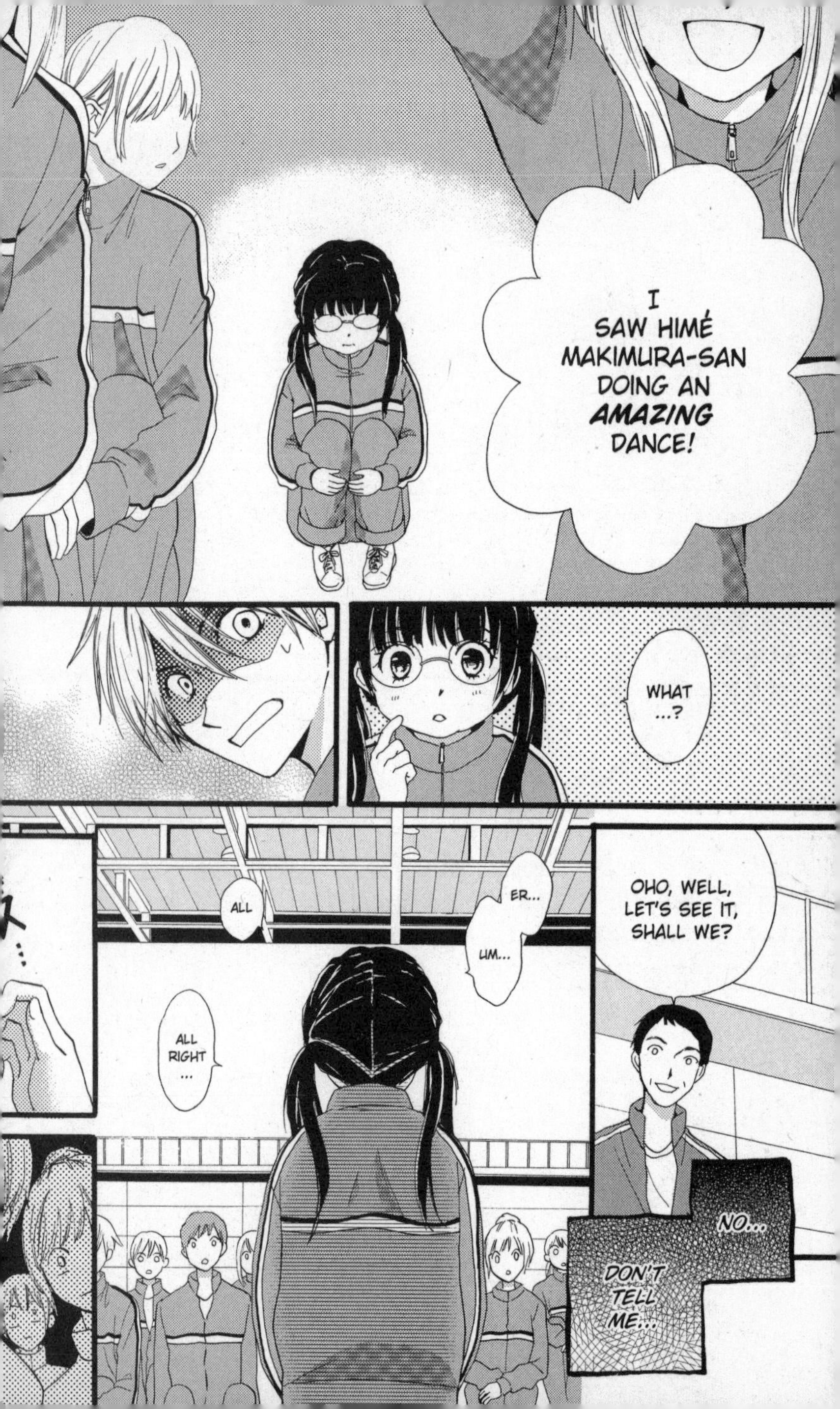
I SAW HIMÉ MAKIMURA-SAN DOING AN AMAZING DANCE!
WHAT ...?
OHO, WELL, LET'S SEE IT, SHALL WE?
ER... UM...
ALL
ALL RIGHT ...
NO... DON'T TELL ME...

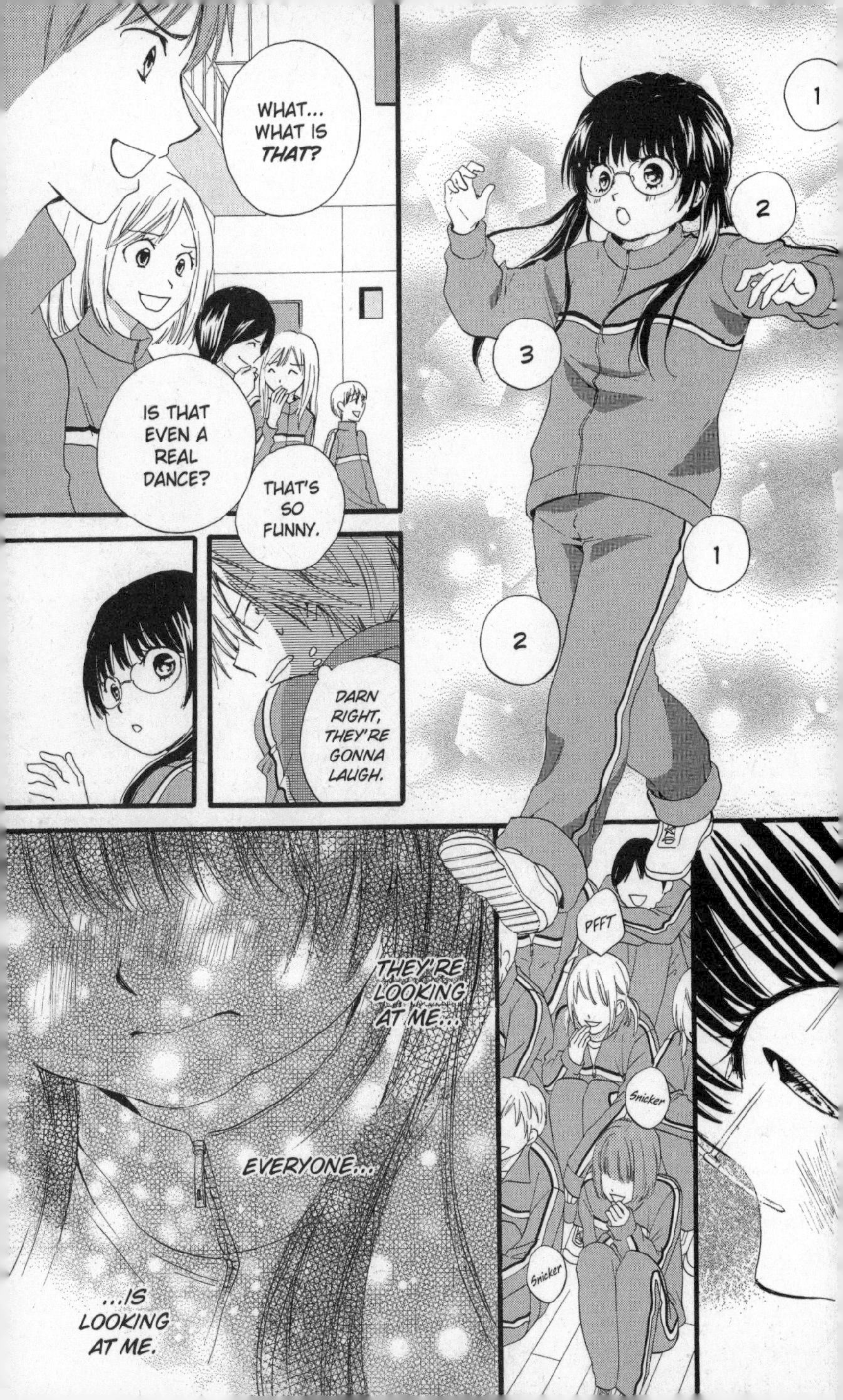

1
2
3
1
2
WHAT... WHAT IS *THAT?*
IS THAT EVEN A REAL DANCE?
THAT'S SO FUNNY.
DARN RIGHT, THEY'RE GONNA LAUGH.
PFFT
Snicker
Snicker
THEY'RE LOOKING AT ME...
EVERYONE...
...IS LOOKING AT ME.

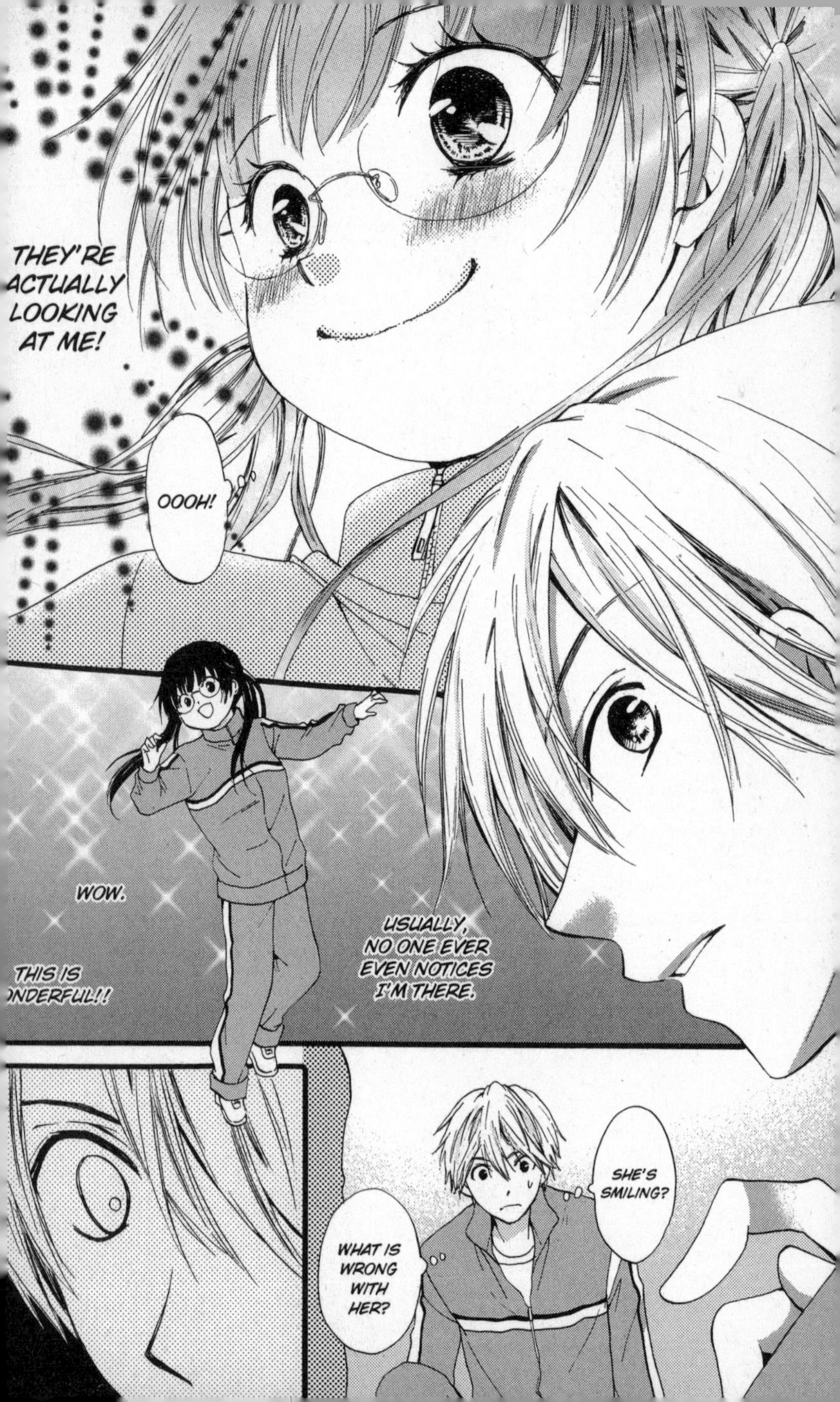
THEY'RE ACTUALLY LOOKING AT ME!
OOOH!
USUALLY, NO ONE EVER EVEN NOTICES I'M THERE.
WOW.
THIS IS ONDERFUL!!
SHE'S SMILING?
WHAT IS WRONG WITH HER?

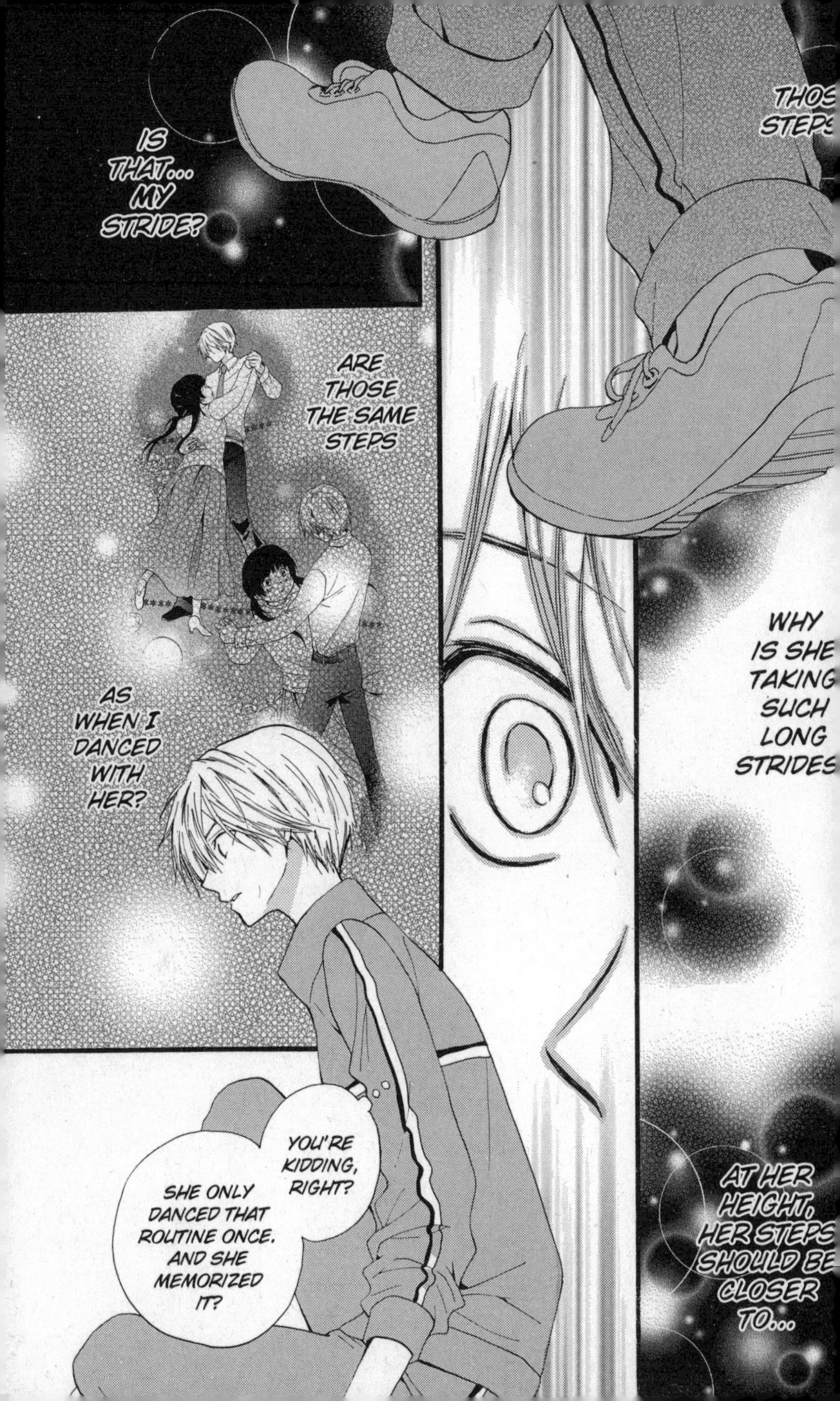
THOS STEPS
WHY IS SHE TAKING SUCH LONG STRIDES
AT HER HEIGHT, HER STEPS SHOULD BE CLOSER TO...
IS THAT... MY STRIDE?
ARE THOSE THE SAME STEPS
AS WHEN I DANCED WITH HER?
YOU'RE KIDDING, RIGHT?
SHE ONLY DANCED THAT ROUTINE ONCE. AND SHE MEMORIZED IT?

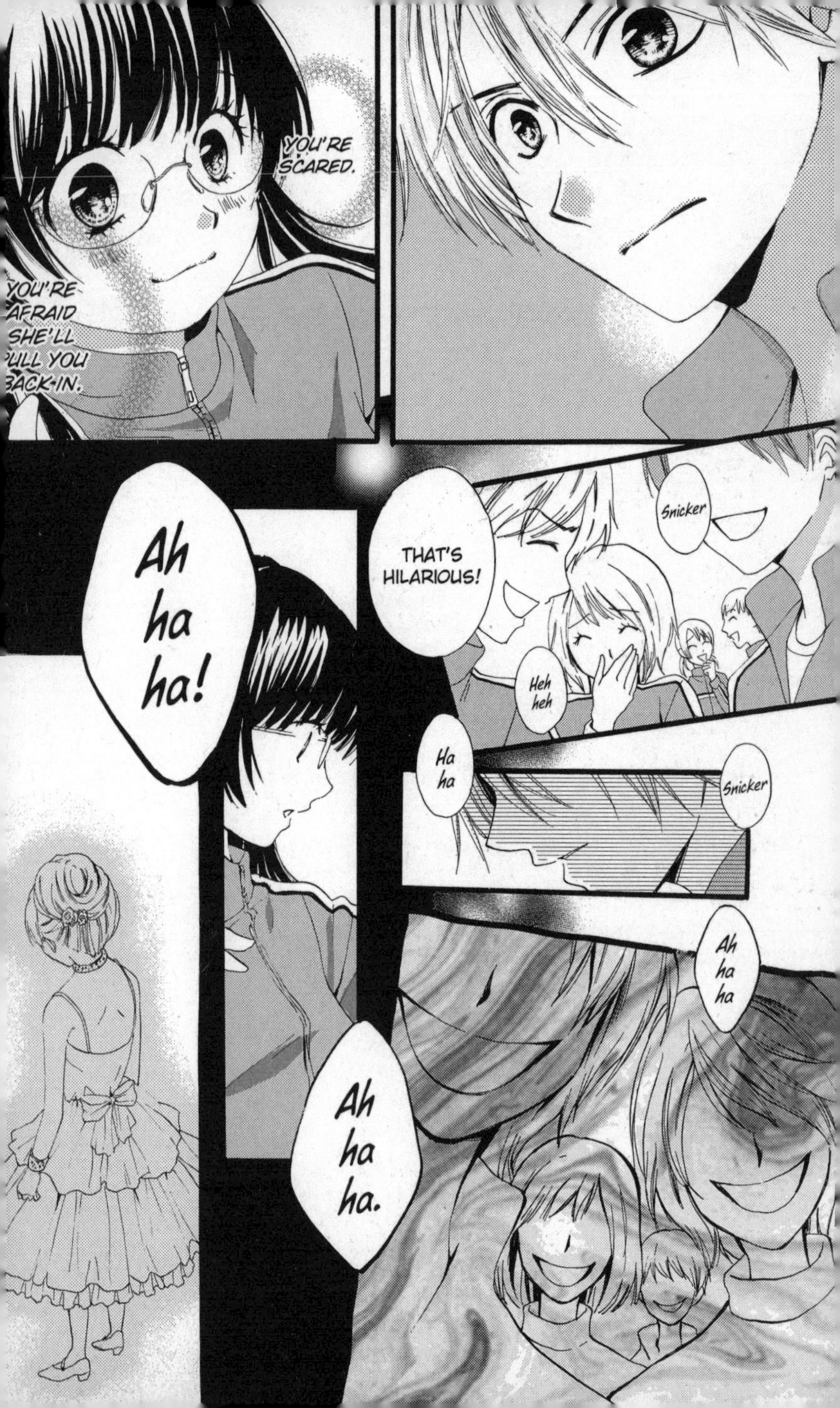
YOU'RE SCARED.
YOU'RE AFRAID SHE'LL PULL YOU BACK IN.
Snicker
THAT'S HILARIOUS!
Heh heh
Snicker
Ha ha
Ah ha ha
Ah ha ha.
Ah ha ha!

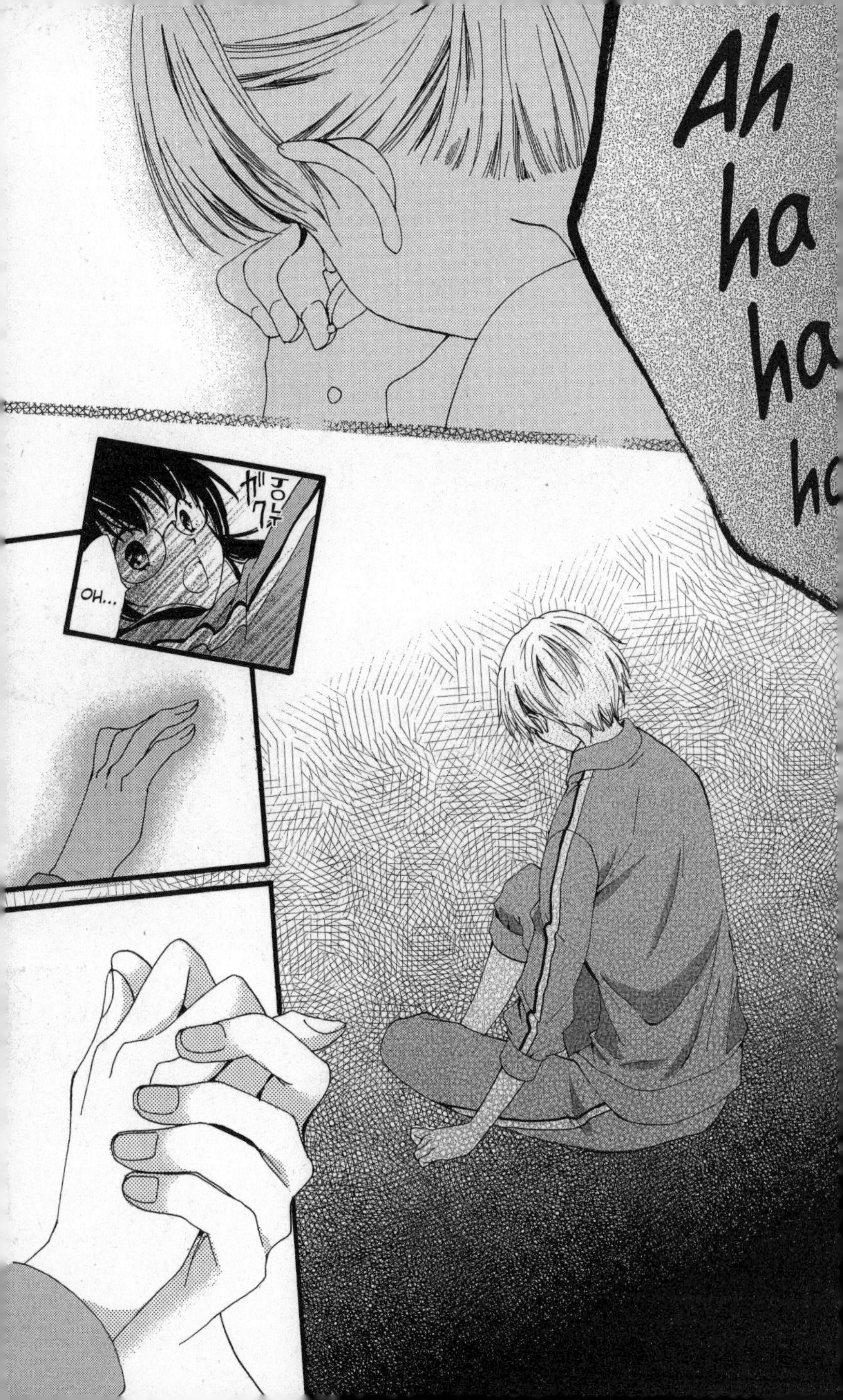
Ah ha ha ha
ガクッ
JOLT
OH...

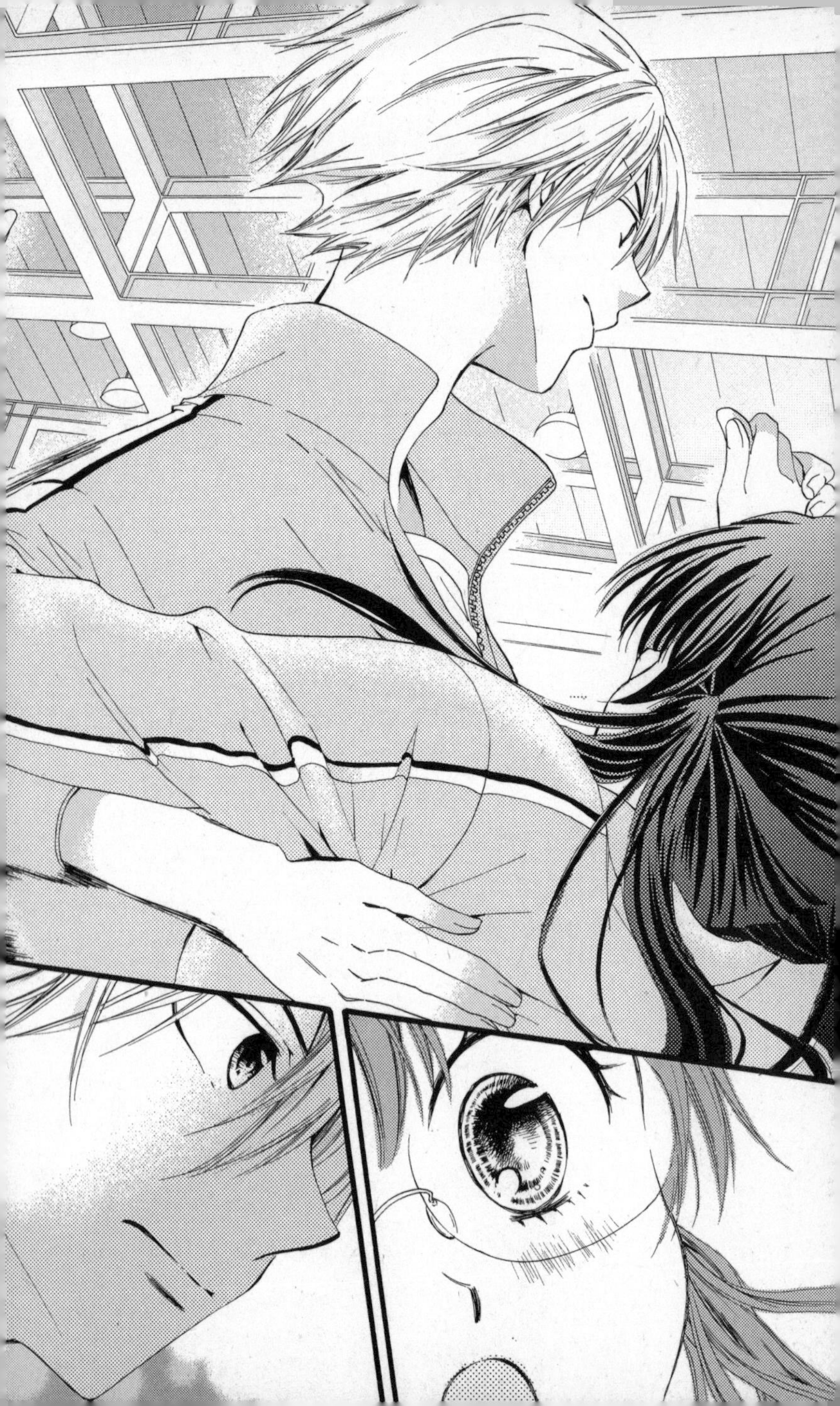

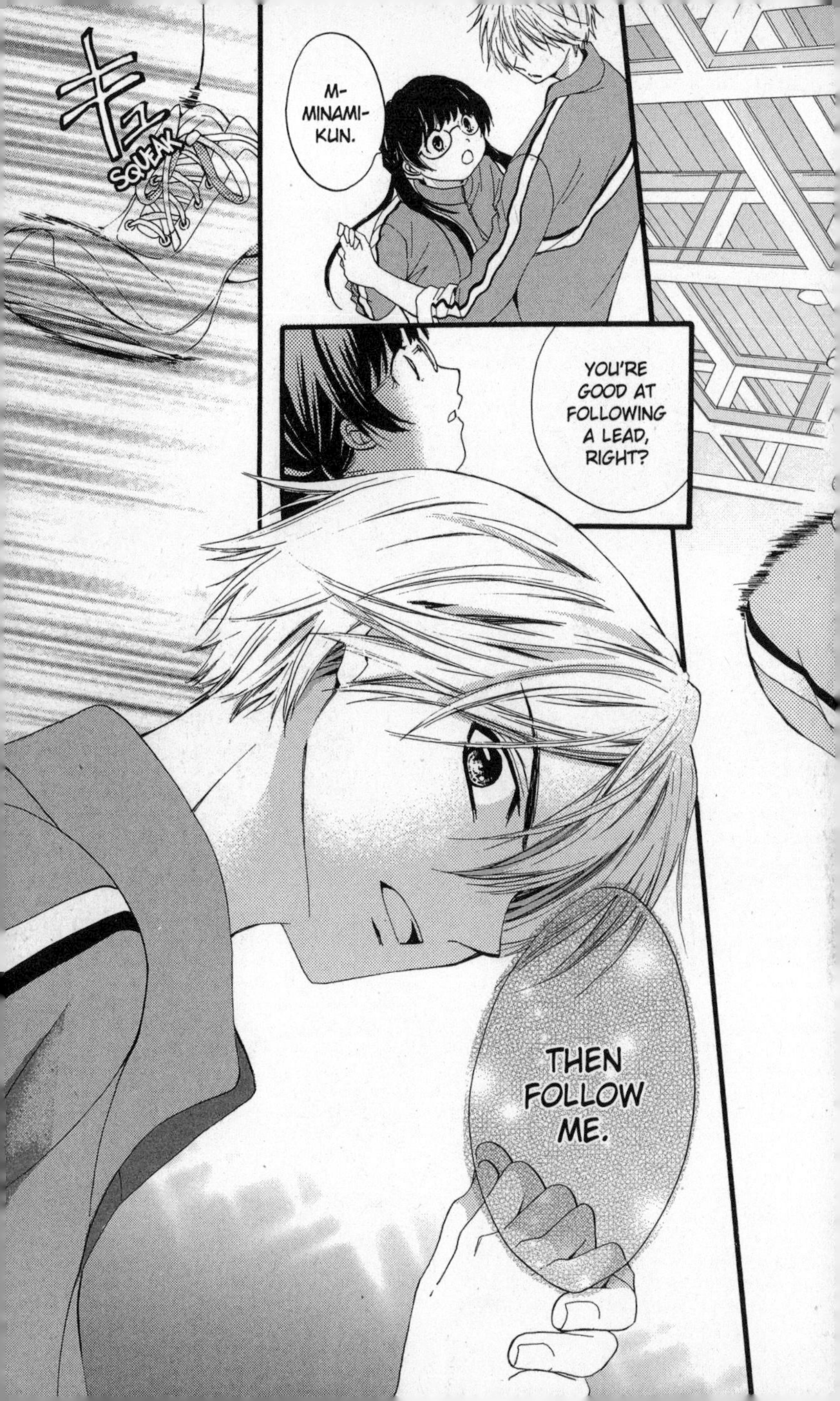
M-MINAMI-KUN.
YOU'RE GOOD AT FOLLOWING A LEAD, RIGHT?
キュ
SQUEAK
THEN FOLLOW ME.

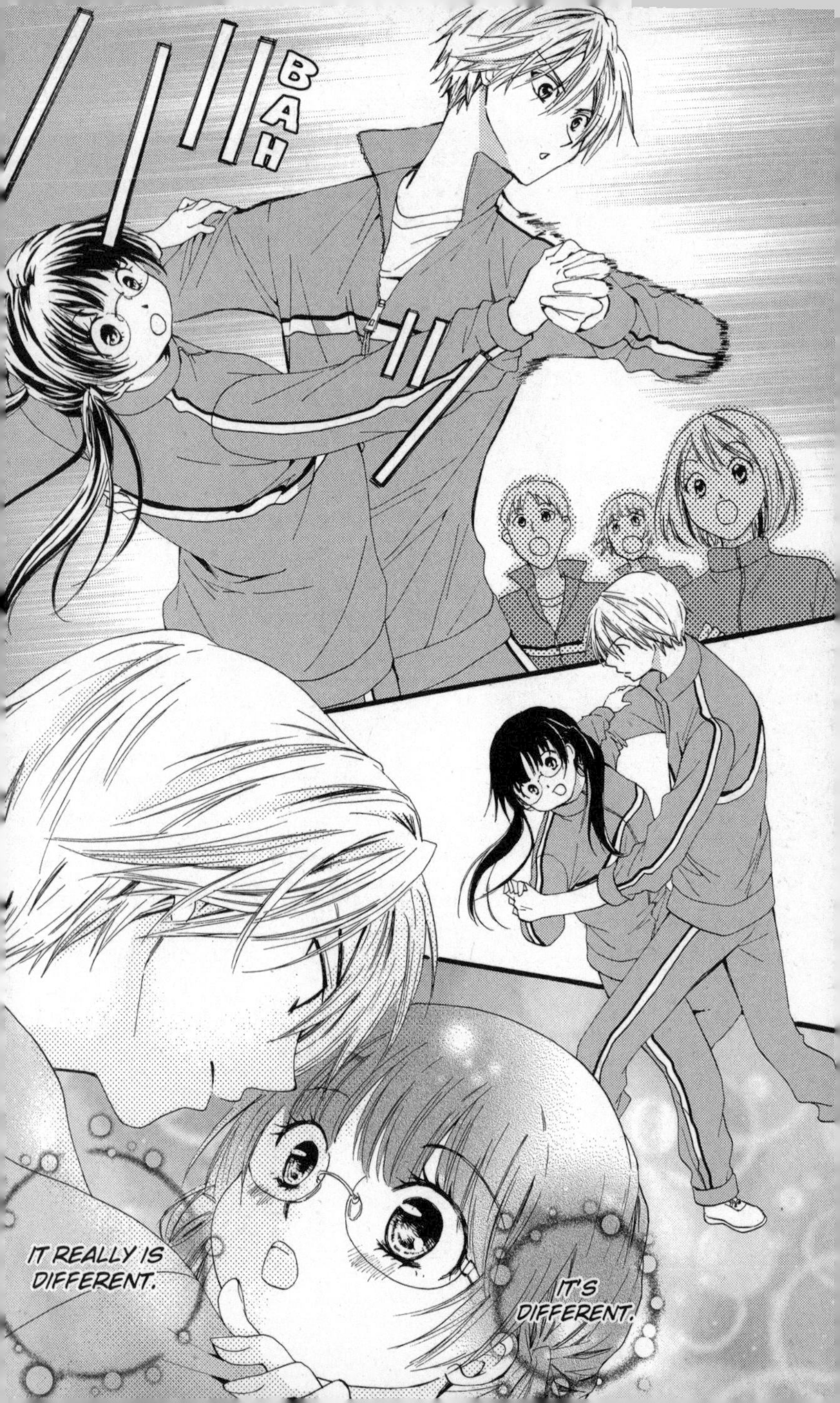
BAH
IT'S DIFFERENT.
IT REALLY IS DIFFERENT.

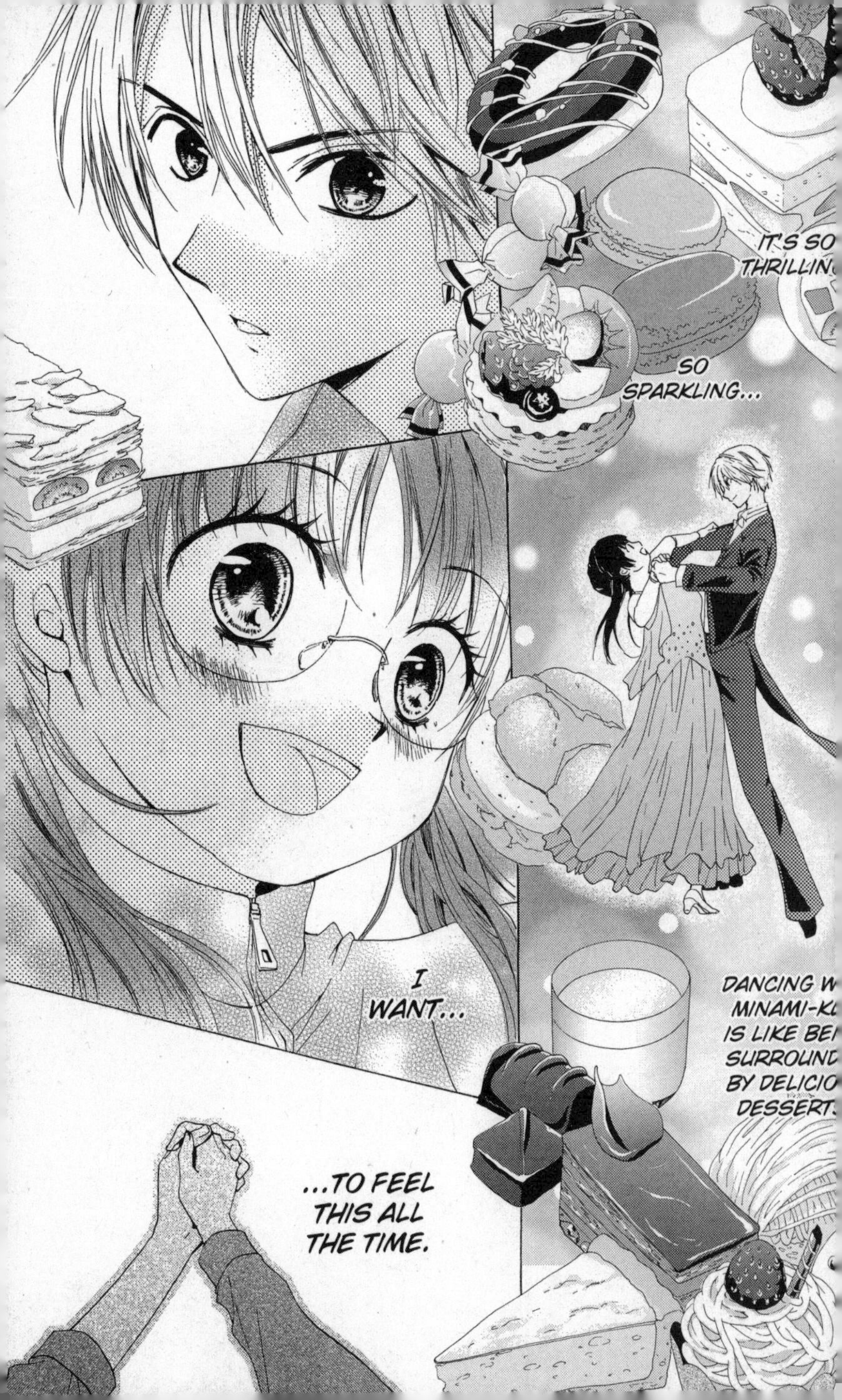
IT'S SO
THRILLIN
SO
SPARKLING...
DANCING W
MINAMI-K
IS LIKE BE
SURROUND
BY DELICIO
DESSERT
I
WANT...
...TO FEEL
THIS ALL
THE TIME.

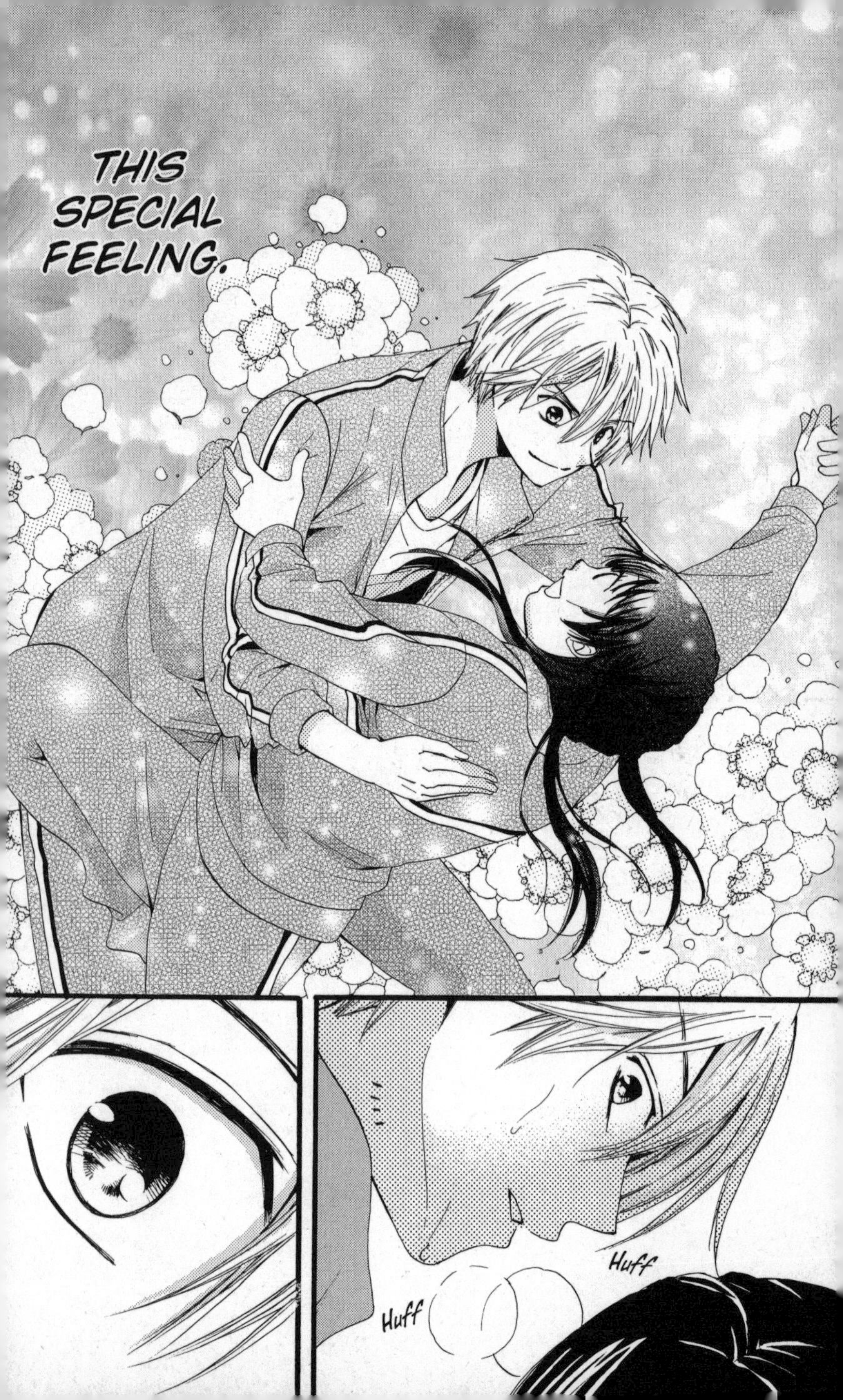
THIS SPECIAL FEELING.
Huff
Huff

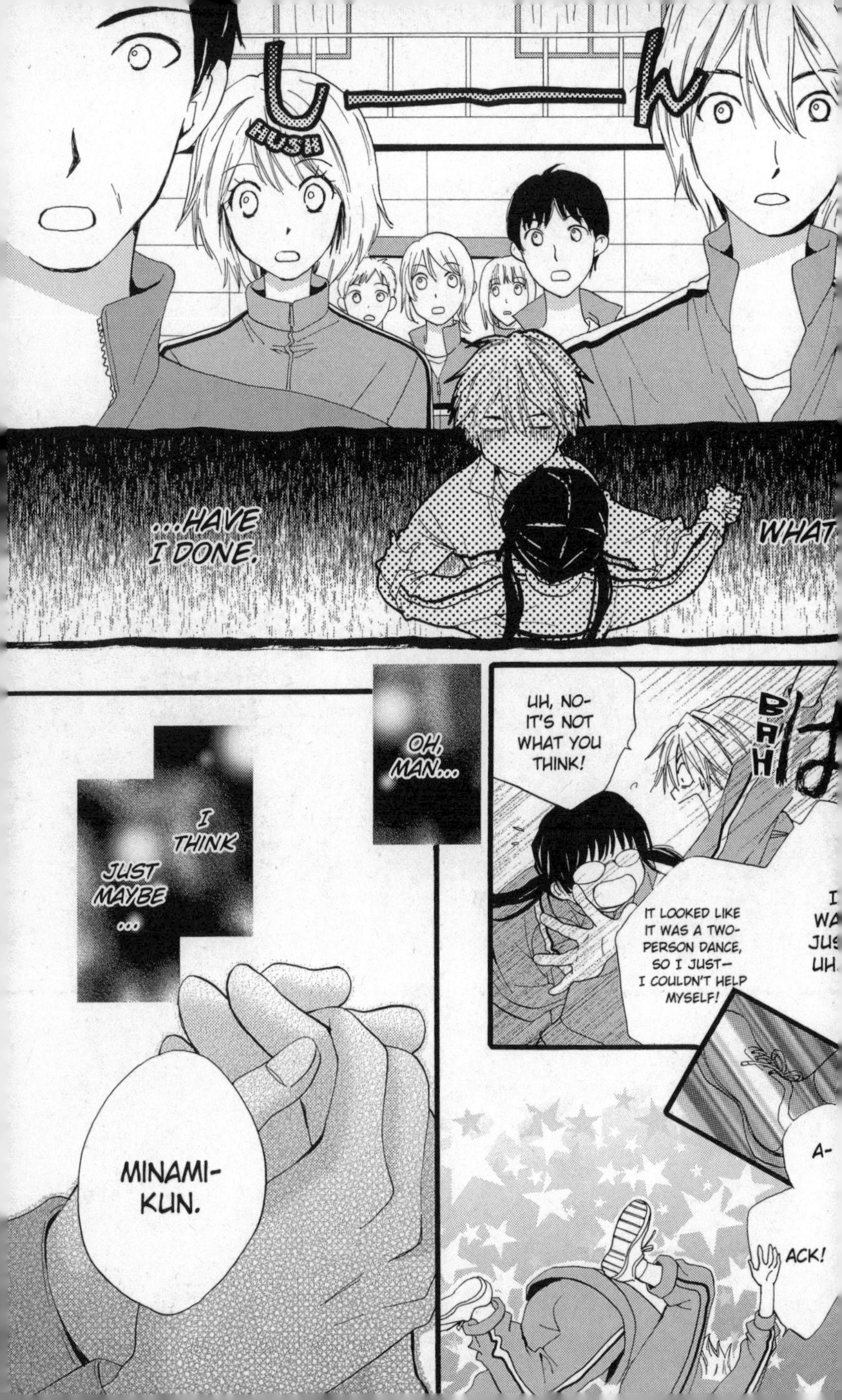
HUSH
WHAT
...HAVE I DONE.
UH, NO- IT'S NOT WHAT YOU THINK!
BAH
IT LOOKED LIKE IT WAS A TWO-PERSON DANCE, SO I JUST— I COULDN'T HELP MYSELF!
A-
ACK!
OH, MAN...
I THINK
JUST MAYBE...
MINAMI-KUN.

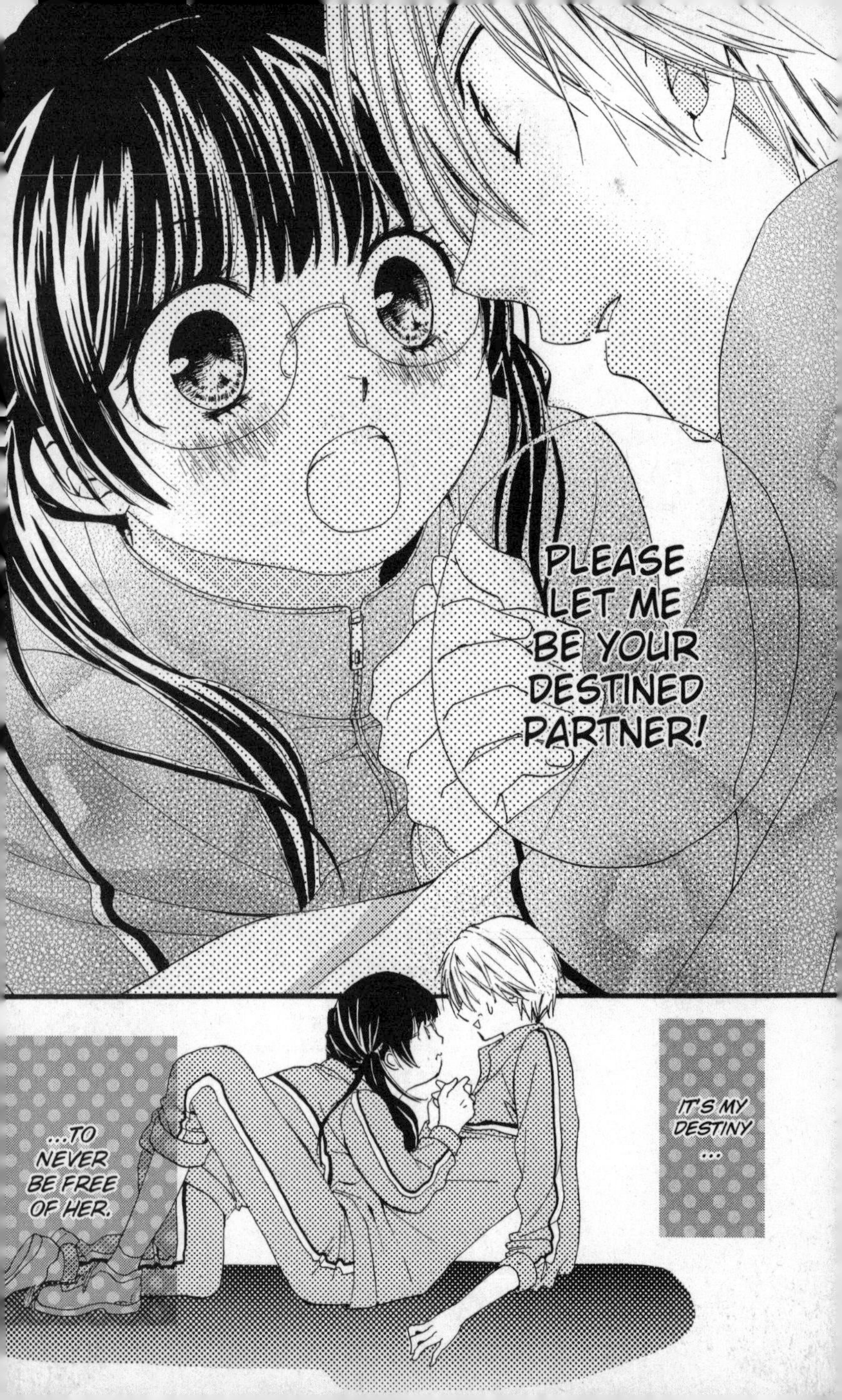
PLEASE LET ME BE YOUR DESTINED PARTNER!
IT'S MY DESTINY ...
...TO NEVER BE FREE OF HER.

Chapter 3

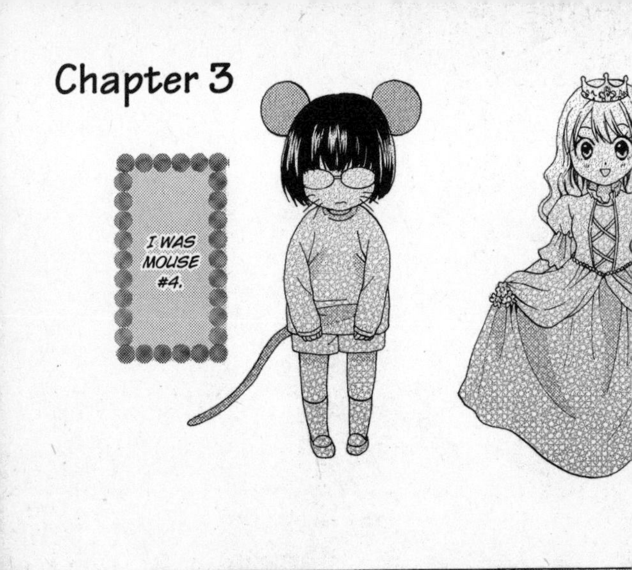
I WAS MOUSE #4.

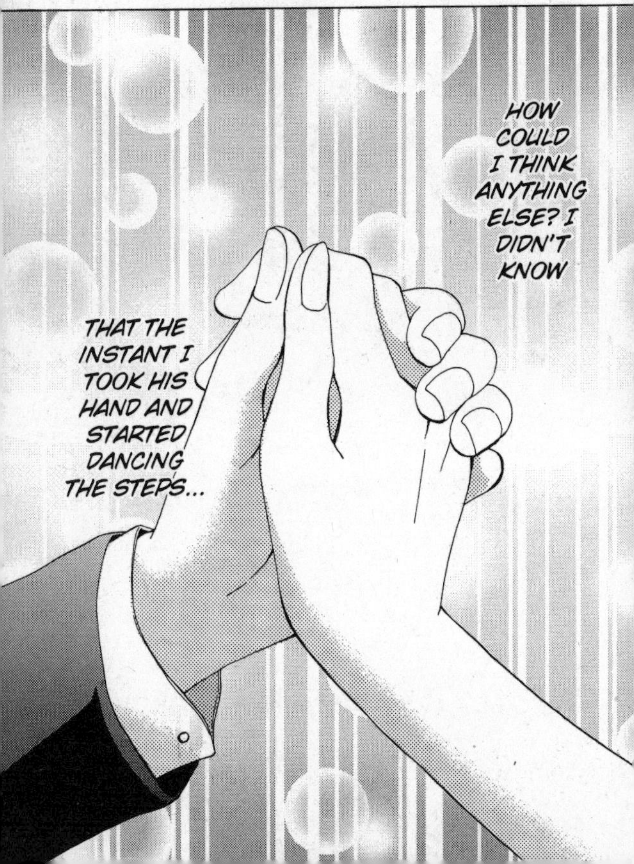
HOW COULD I THINK ANYTHING ELSE? I DIDN'T KNOW
THAT THE INSTANT I TOOK HIS HAND AND STARTED DANCING THE STEPS...

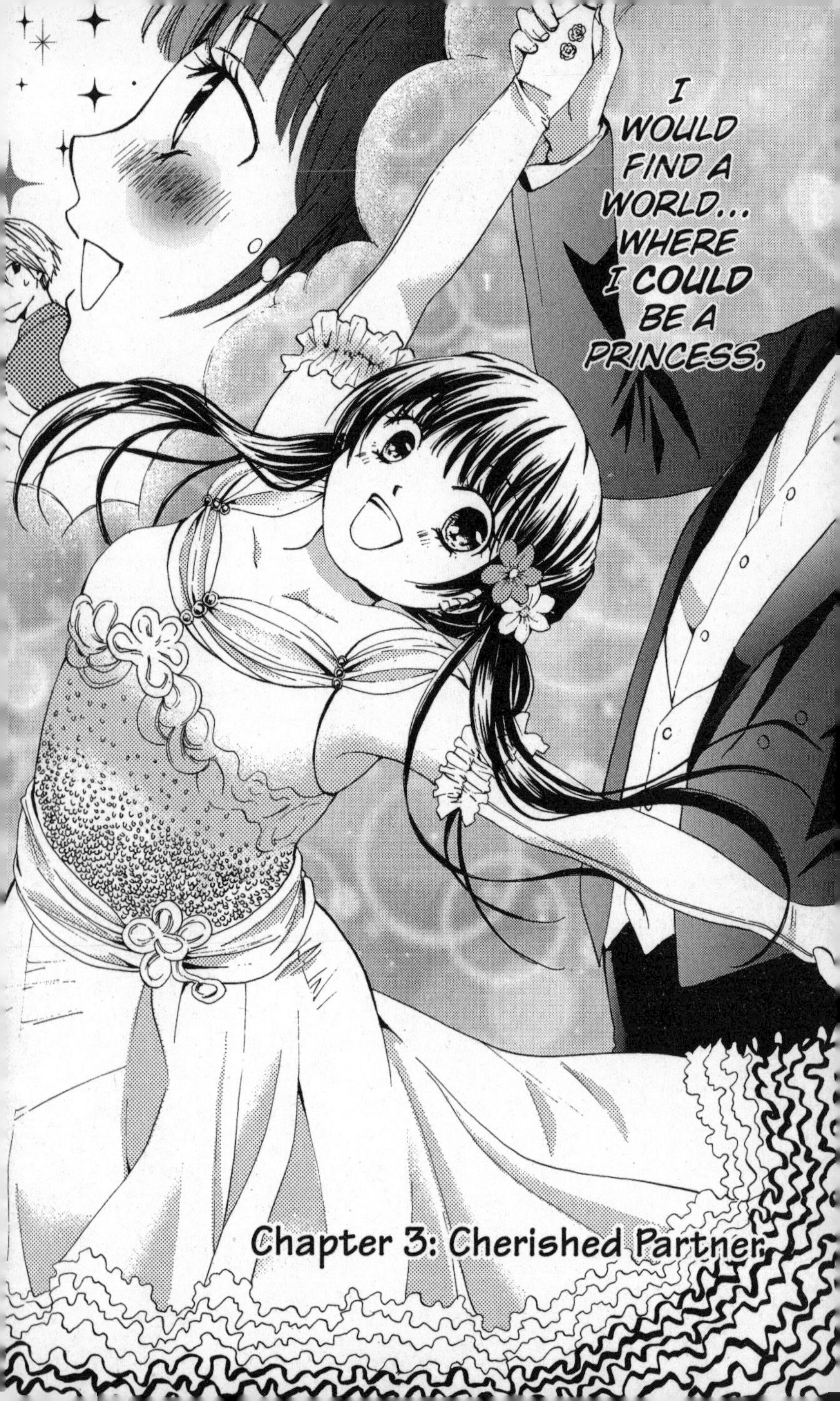
I WOULD FIND A WORLD... WHERE I COULD BE A PRINCESS.
Chapter 3: Cherished Partner

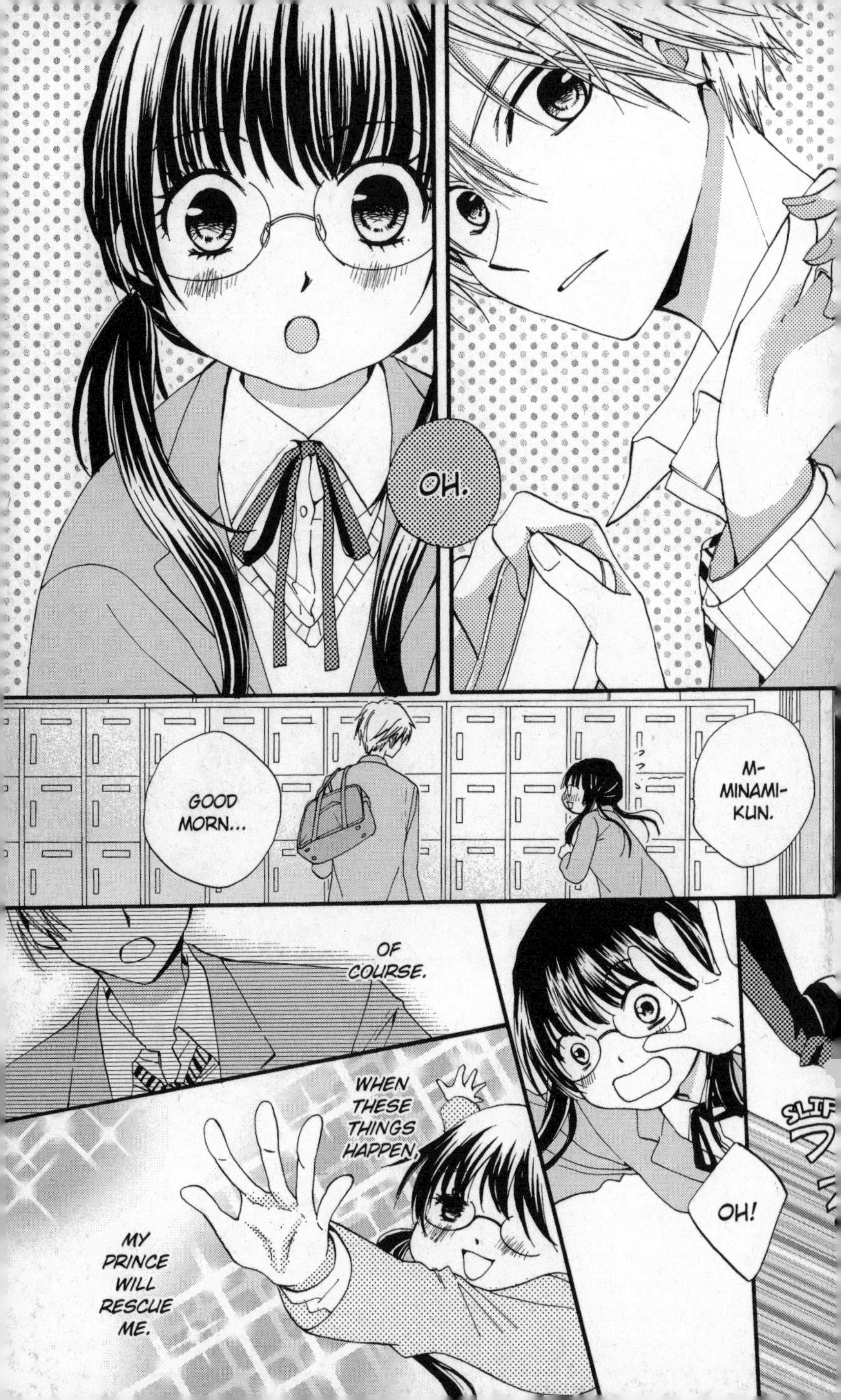
OH.
M-MINAMI-KUN.
GOOD MORN...
OH!
OF COURSE.
WHEN THESE THINGS HAPPEN,
MY PRINCE WILL RESCUE ME.

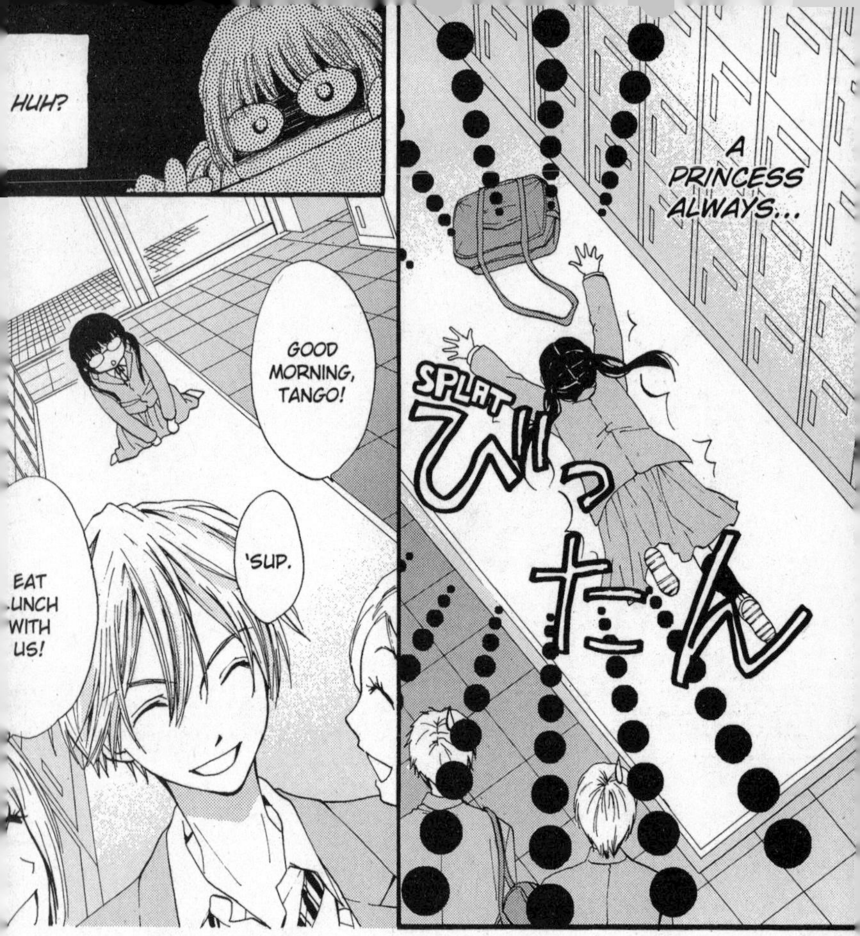
A PRINCESS ALWAYS...
SPLAT
ひったーん
HUH?
GOOD MORNING, TANGO!
'SUP.
EAT LUNCH WITH US!

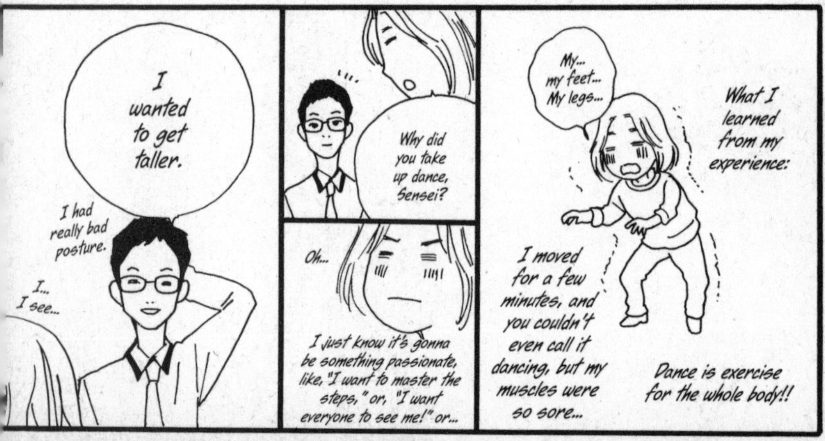
What I learned from my experience:
My... my feet... My legs...
I moved for a few minutes, and you couldn't even call it dancing, but my muscles were so sore...
Dance is exercise for the whole body!!
Why did you take up dance, Sensei?
Oh...
I just know it's gonna be something passionate, like, "I want to master the steps," or, "I want everyone to see me!" or...
I wanted to get taller.
I had really bad posture.
I... I see...

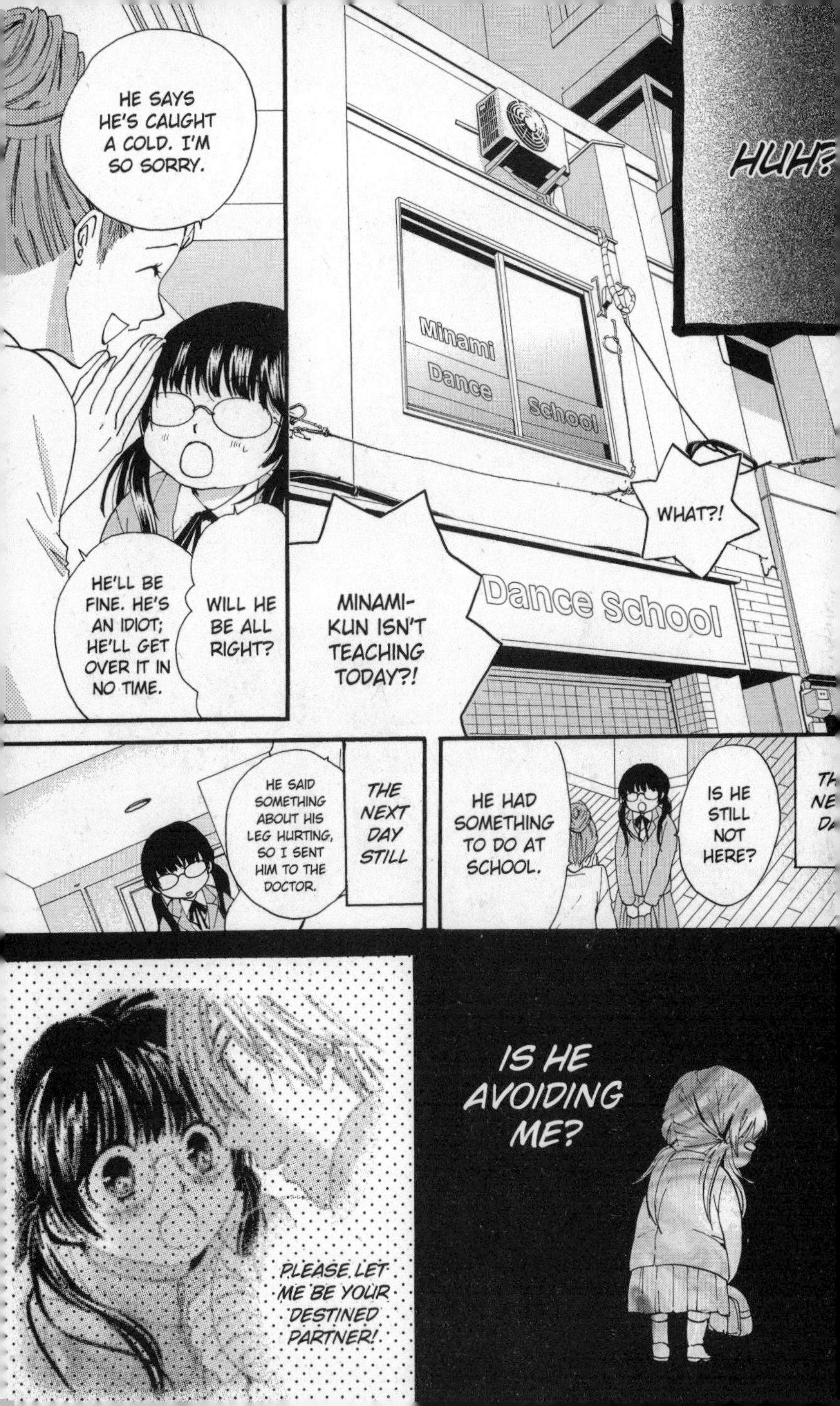
HUH?
Minami Dance School
WHAT?!
Dance School
MINAMI-KUN ISN'T TEACHING TODAY?!
HE SAYS HE'S CAUGHT A COLD. I'M SO SORRY.
WILL HE BE ALL RIGHT?
HE'LL BE FINE. HE'S AN IDIOT; HE'LL GET OVER IT IN NO TIME.
IS HE STILL NOT HERE?
HE HAD SOMETHING TO DO AT SCHOOL.
THE NEXT DAY STILL
HE SAID SOMETHING ABOUT HIS LEG HURTING, SO I SENT HIM TO THE DOCTOR.
IS HE AVOIDING ME?
PLEASE LET ME BE YOUR DESTINED PARTNER!

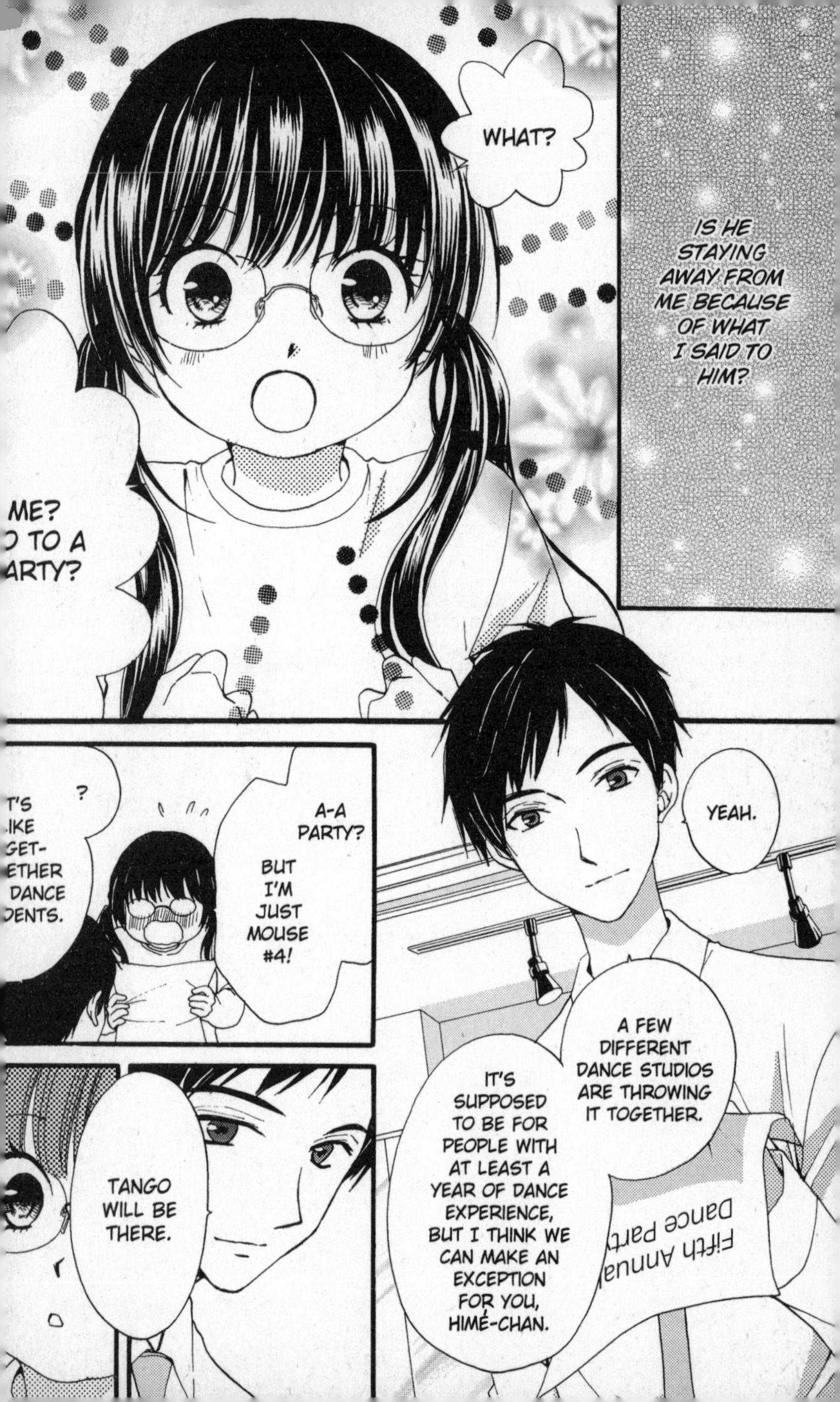
IS HE STAYING AWAY FROM ME BECAUSE OF WHAT I SAID TO HIM?
WHAT?
ME? TO A ARTY?
YEAH.
A FEW DIFFERENT DANCE STUDIOS ARE THROWING IT TOGETHER.
IT'S SUPPOSED TO BE FOR PEOPLE WITH AT LEAST A YEAR OF DANCE EXPERIENCE, BUT I THINK WE CAN MAKE AN EXCEPTION FOR YOU, HIMÉ-CHAN.
Fifth Annual Dance Part
A-A PARTY?
BUT I'M JUST MOUSE #4!
?
T'S IKE GET- ETHER DANCE DENTS.
TANGO WILL BE THERE.

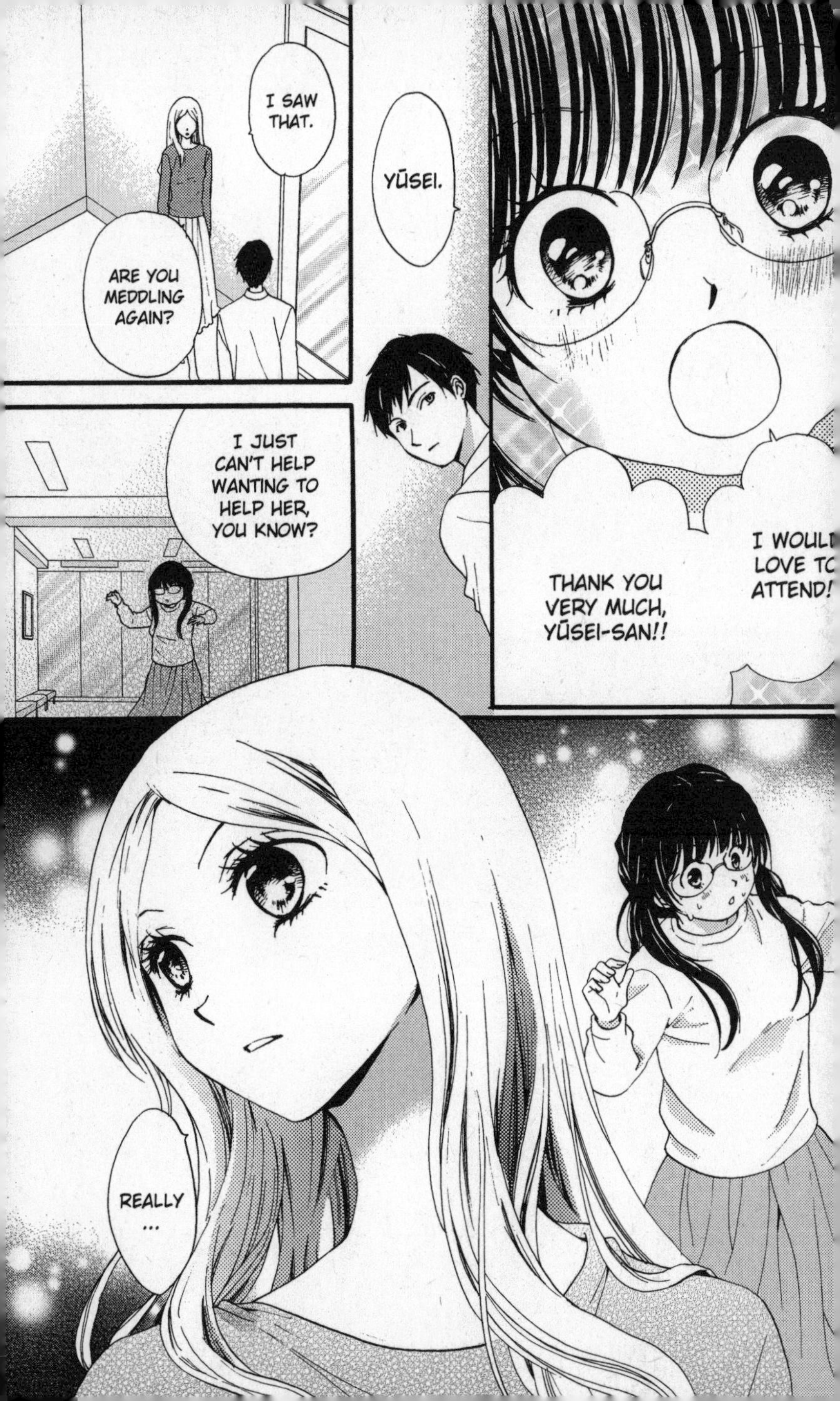
I WOULD LOVE TO ATTEND!
THANK YOU VERY MUCH, YŪSEI-SAN!!
YŪSEI.
I SAW THAT.
ARE YOU MEDDLING AGAIN?
I JUST CAN'T HELP WANTING TO HELP HER, YOU KNOW?
REALLY ...

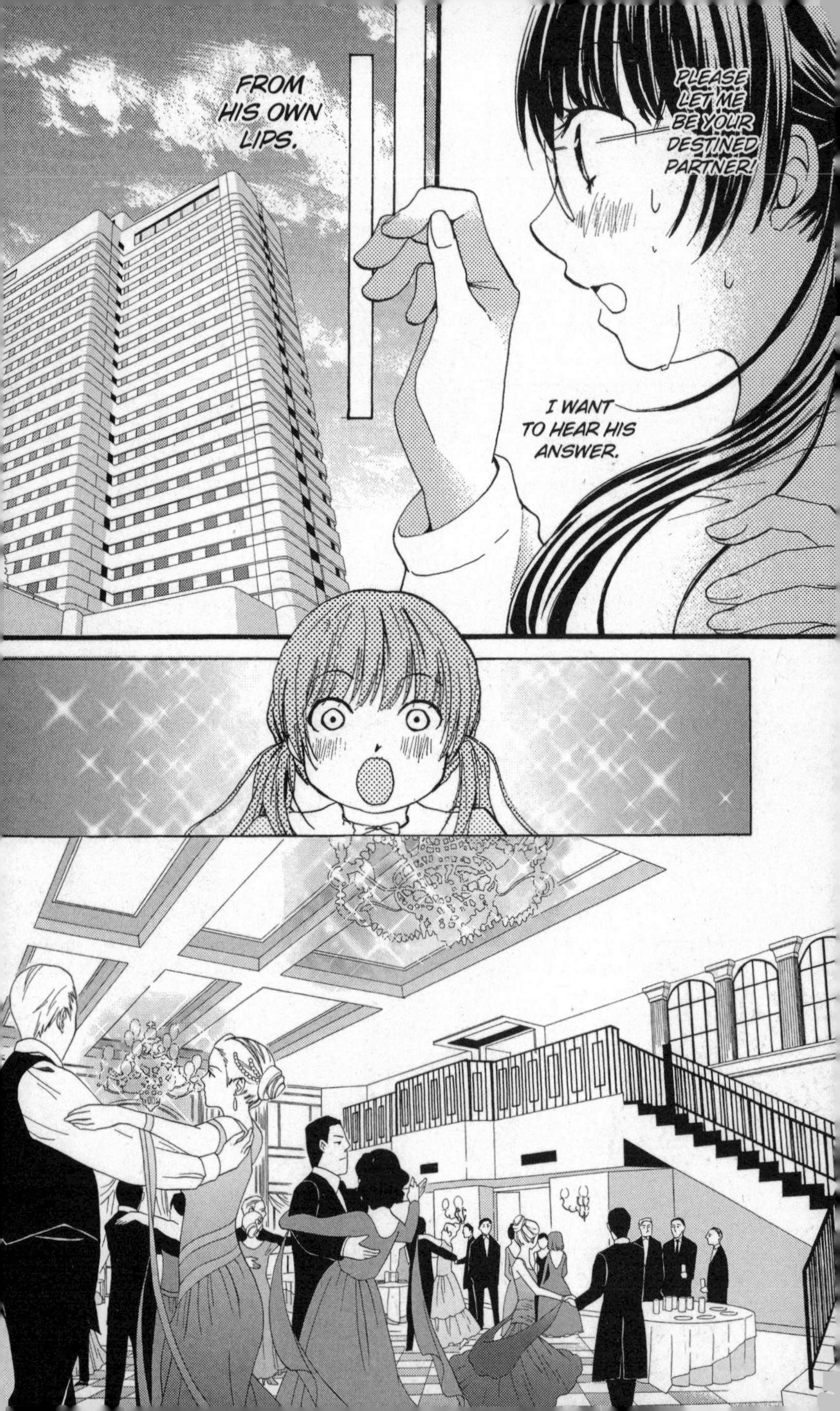
PLEASE LET ME BE YOUR DESTINED PARTNER!
I WANT TO HEAR HIS ANSWER.
FROM HIS OWN LIPS.

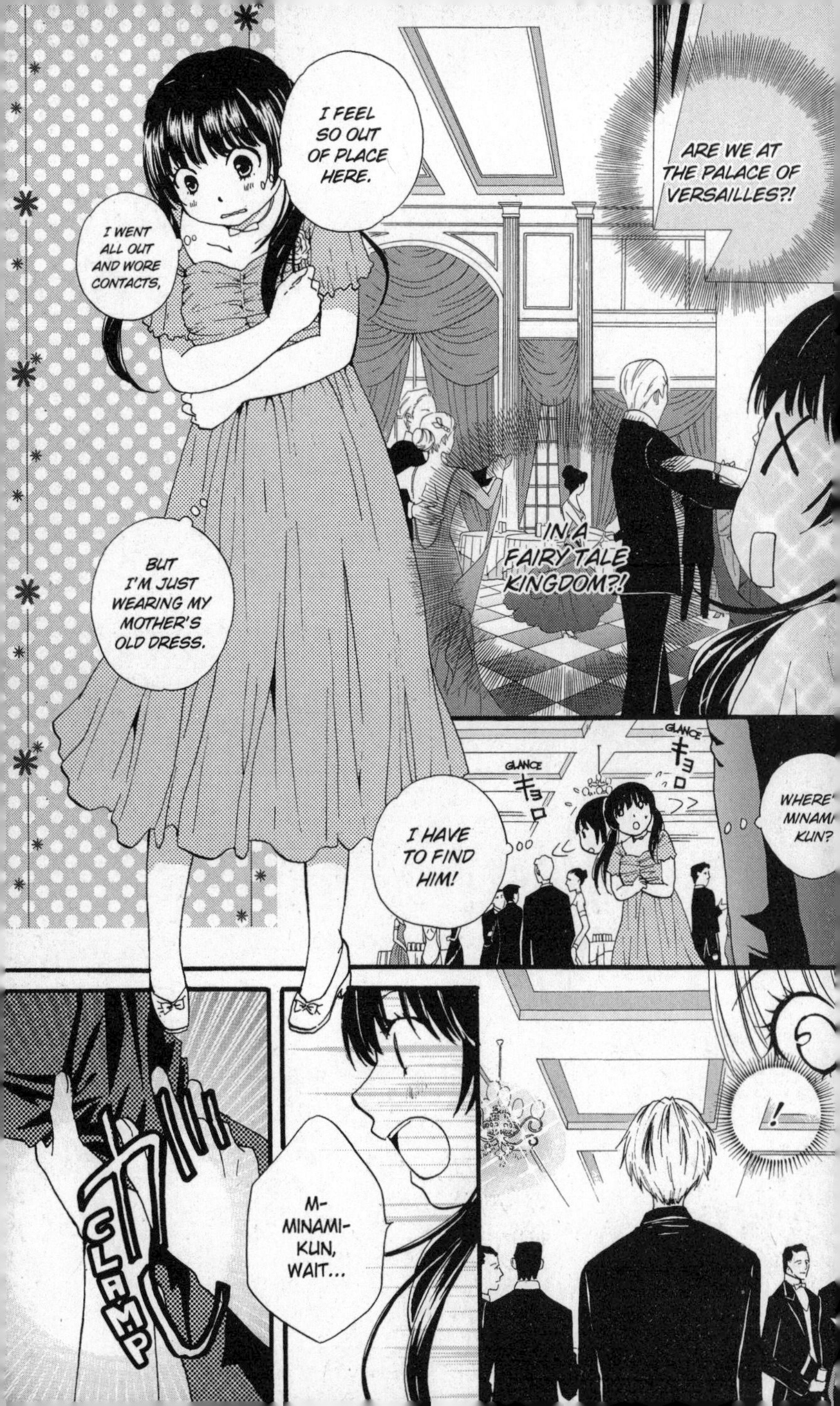
ARE WE AT THE PALACE OF VERSAILLES?!
IN A FAIRY TALE KINGDOM?!
WHERE' MINAMI KUN?
GLANCE
キョロ
GLANCE
キョロ
I HAVE TO FIND HIM!
I FEEL SO OUT OF PLACE HERE.
I WENT ALL OUT AND WORE CONTACTS,
BUT I'M JUST WEARING MY MOTHER'S OLD DRESS.
!
M-MINAMI-KUN, WAIT...
CLAMP

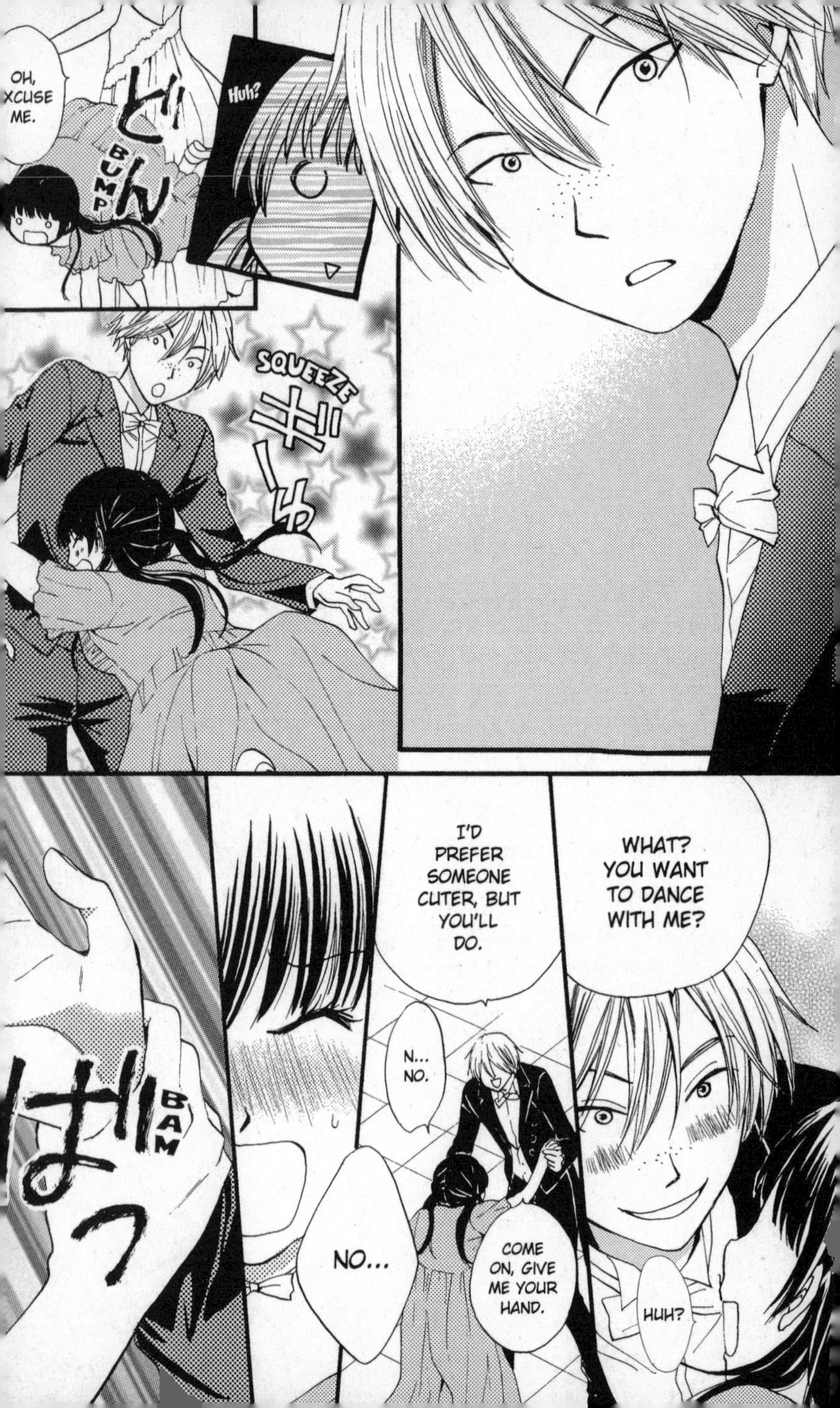
Huh?
OH, XCUSE ME.
どん
BUMP
SQUEEZE
ぎゅ
WHAT? YOU WANT TO DANCE WITH ME?
HUH?
I'D PREFER SOMEONE CUTER, BUT YOU'LL DO.
N... NO.
COME ON, GIVE ME YOUR HAND.
NO...
はっ
BAM

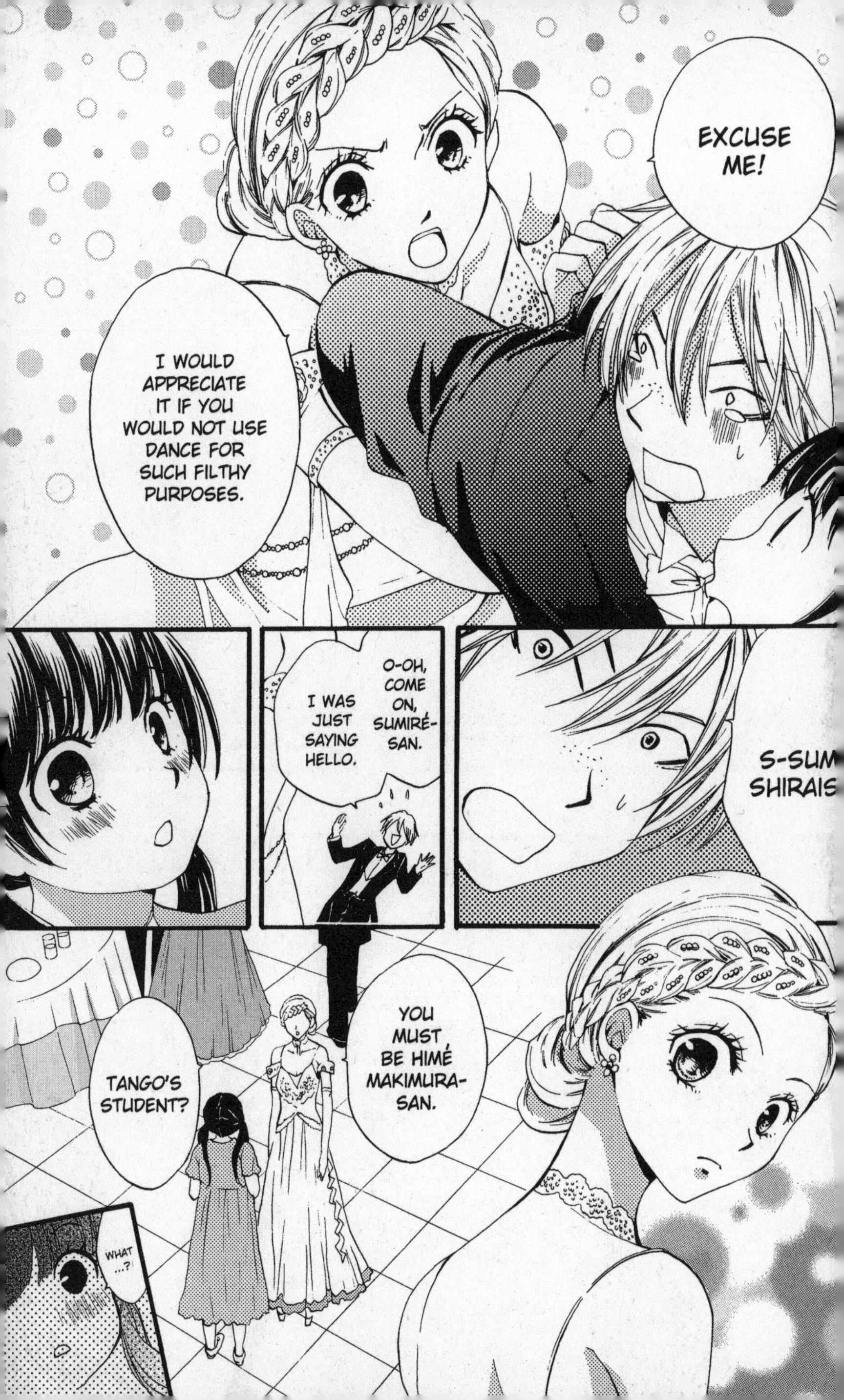
EXCUSE ME!
I WOULD APPRECIATE IT IF YOU WOULD NOT USE DANCE FOR SUCH FILTHY PURPOSES.
S-SUM
SHIRAIS
O-OH, COME ON, SUMIRÉ-SAN.
I WAS JUST SAYING HELLO.
YOU MUST BE HIMÉ MAKIMURA-SAN.
TANGO'S STUDENT?
WHAT ...?

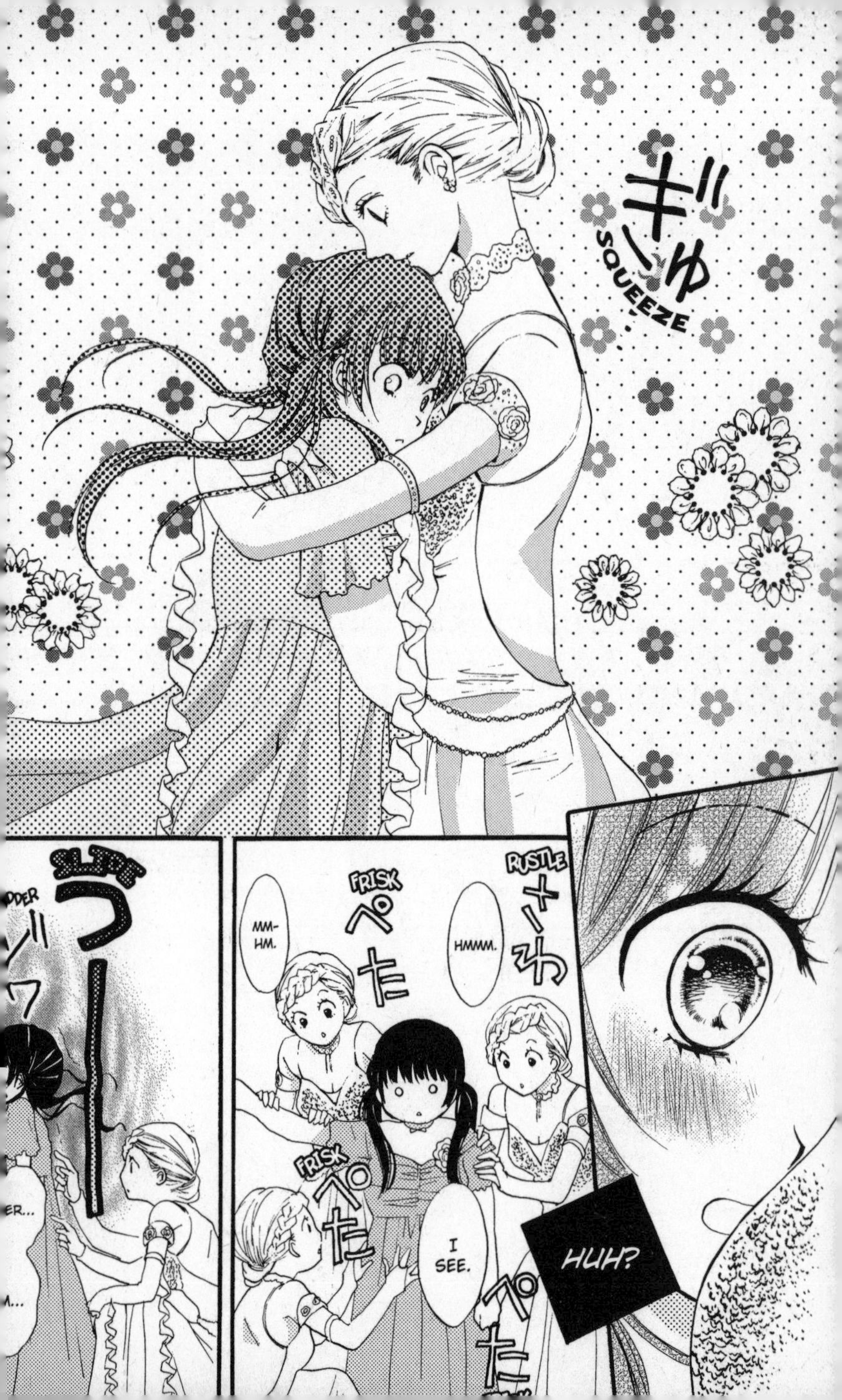
ぎゅ
SQUEEZE
HUH?
さわ
RUSTLE
HMMM.
ぺた
FRISK
MM-HM.
ぺた
FRISK
I SEE.
ぺた
SLIP

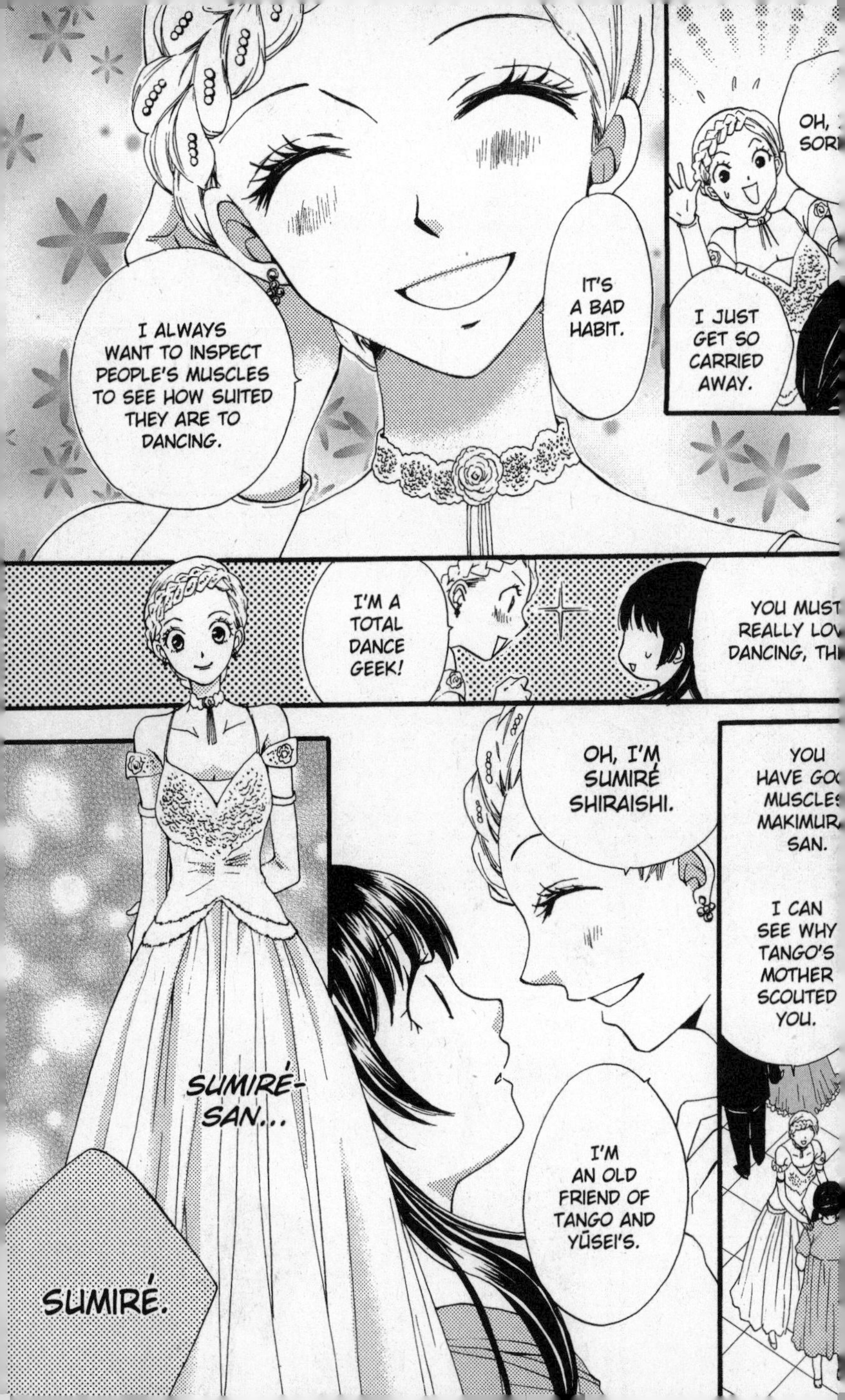
OH, SOR
I JUST GET SO CARRIED AWAY.
IT'S A BAD HABIT.
I ALWAYS WANT TO INSPECT PEOPLE'S MUSCLES TO SEE HOW SUITED THEY ARE TO DANCING.
YOU MUST REALLY LOV DANCING, TH
I'M A TOTAL DANCE GEEK!
YOU HAVE GO MUSCLE MAKIMUR SAN.
I CAN SEE WHY TANGO'S MOTHER SCOUTED YOU.
OH, I'M SUMIRÉ SHIRAISHI.
I'M AN OLD FRIEND OF TANGO AND YŪSEI'S.
SUMIRÉ-SAN...
SUMIRÉ.

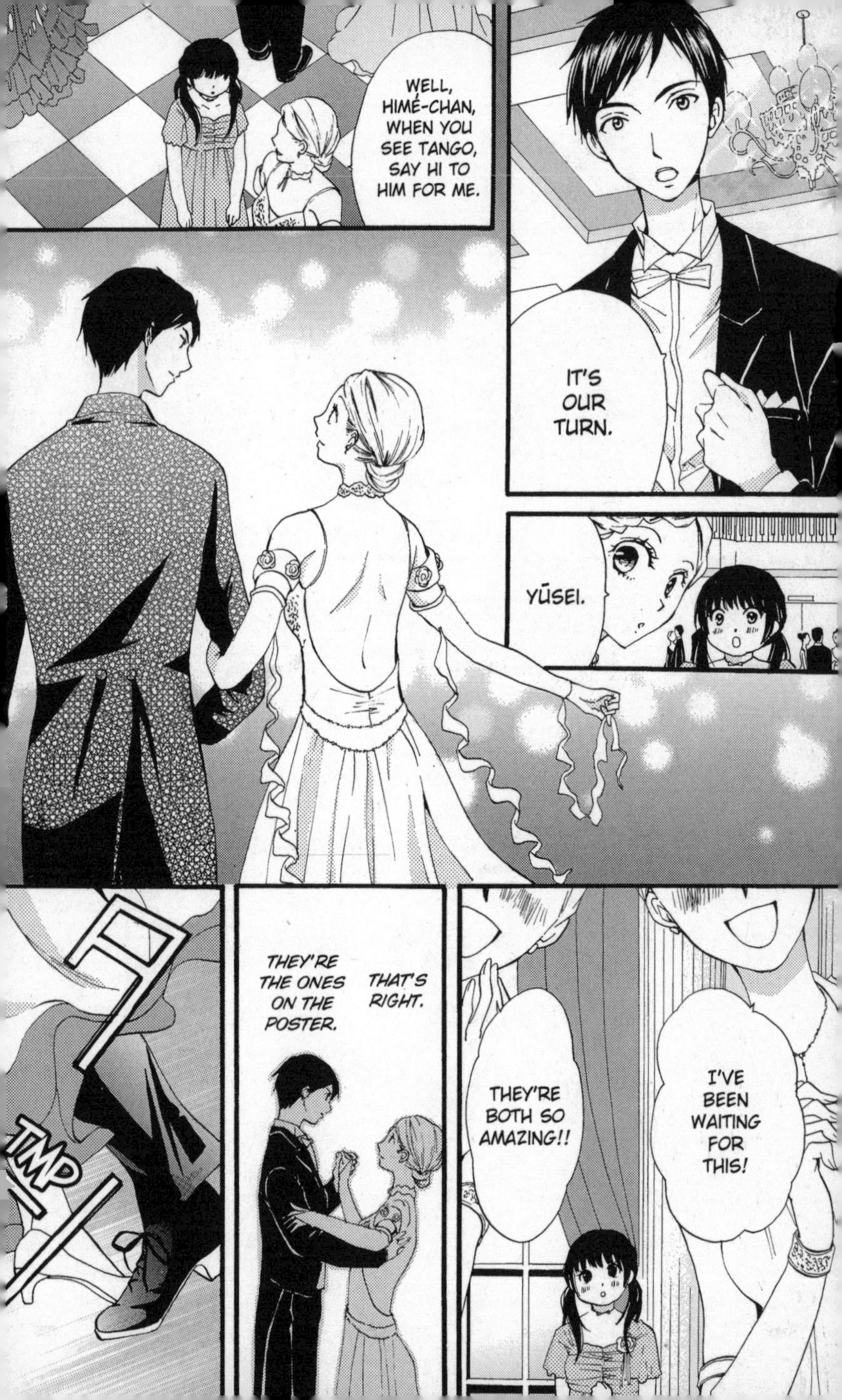
IT'S OUR TURN.
WELL, HIMÉ-CHAN, WHEN YOU SEE TANGO, SAY HI TO HIM FOR ME.
YŪSEI.
I'VE BEEN WAITING FOR THIS!
THEY'RE BOTH SO AMAZING!!
THAT'S RIGHT.
THEY'RE THE ONES ON THE POSTER.
TMP

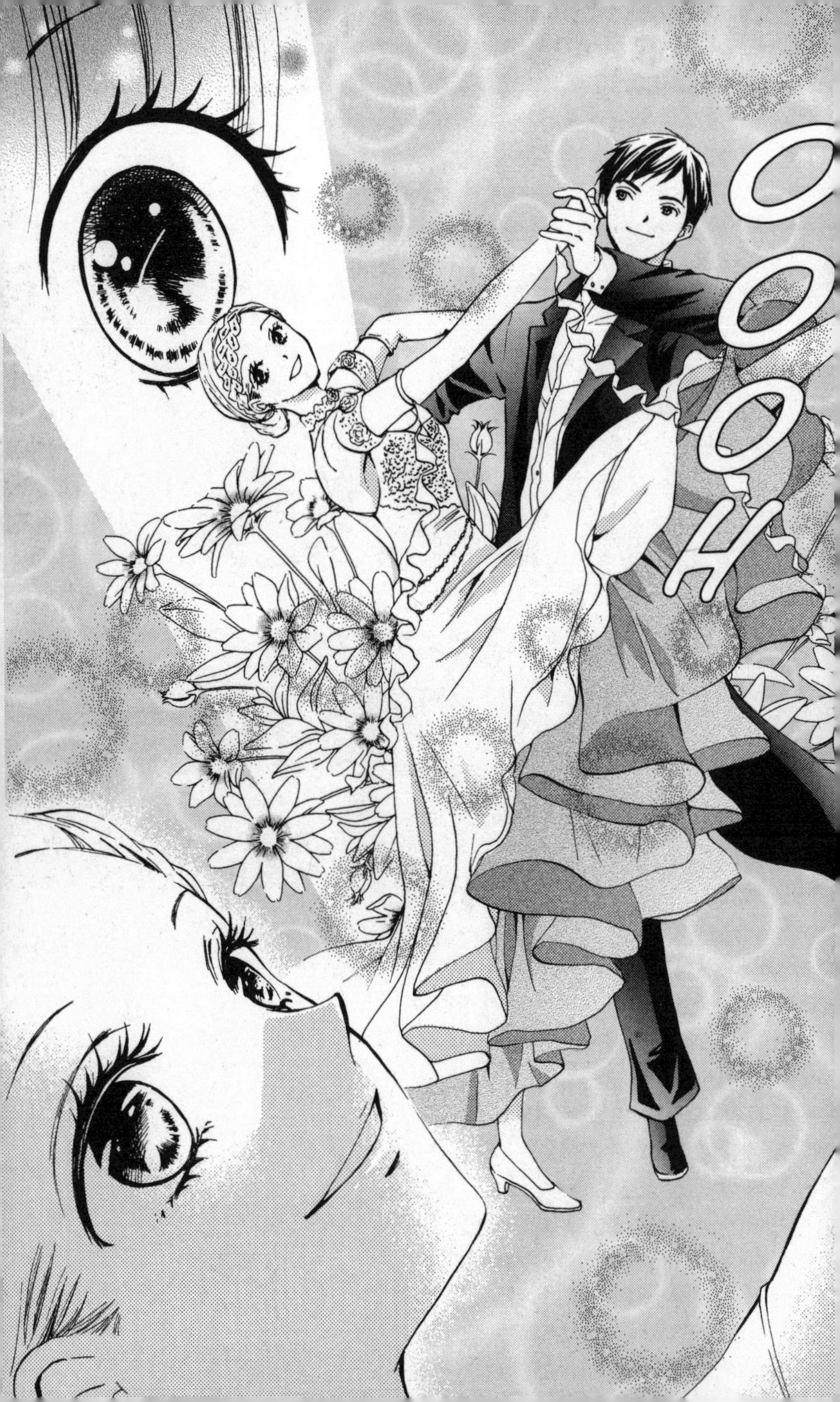
OOOOH

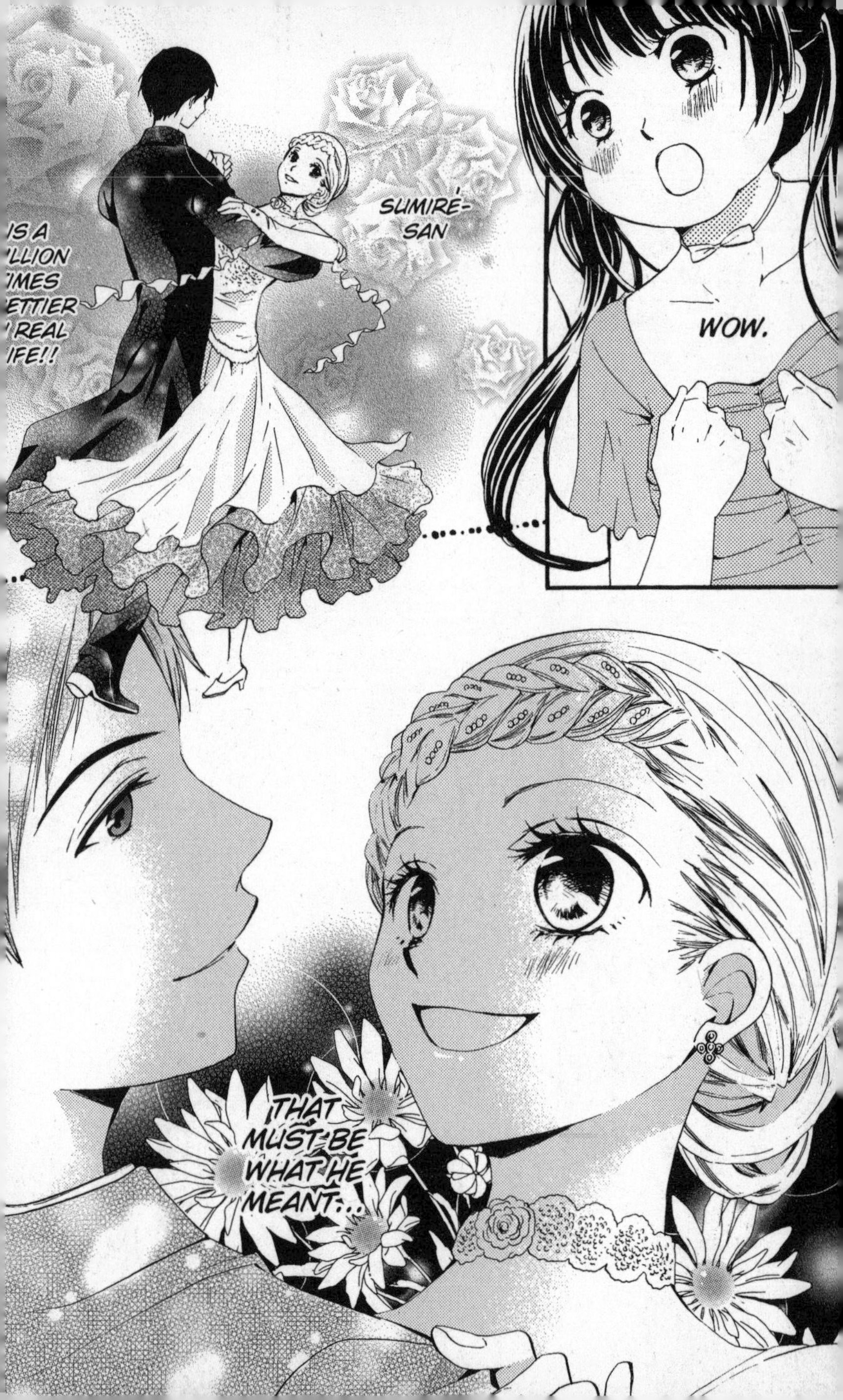
WOW.
SUMIRE-SAN
IS A LLION IMES ETTIER REAL IFE!!
THAT MUST BE WHAT HE MEANT...

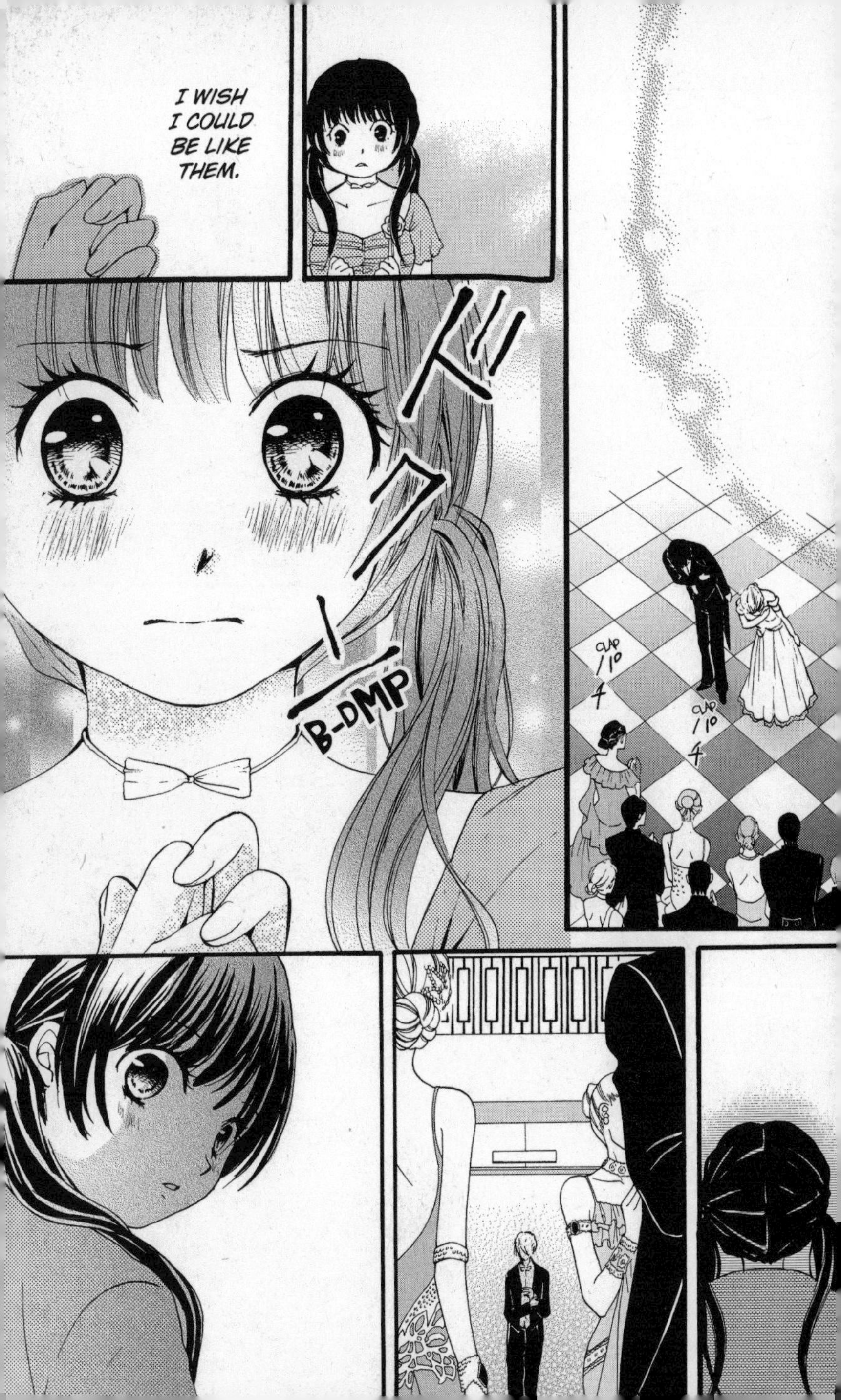
CLAP
CLAP
I WISH I COULD BE LIKE THEM.
B-DMP

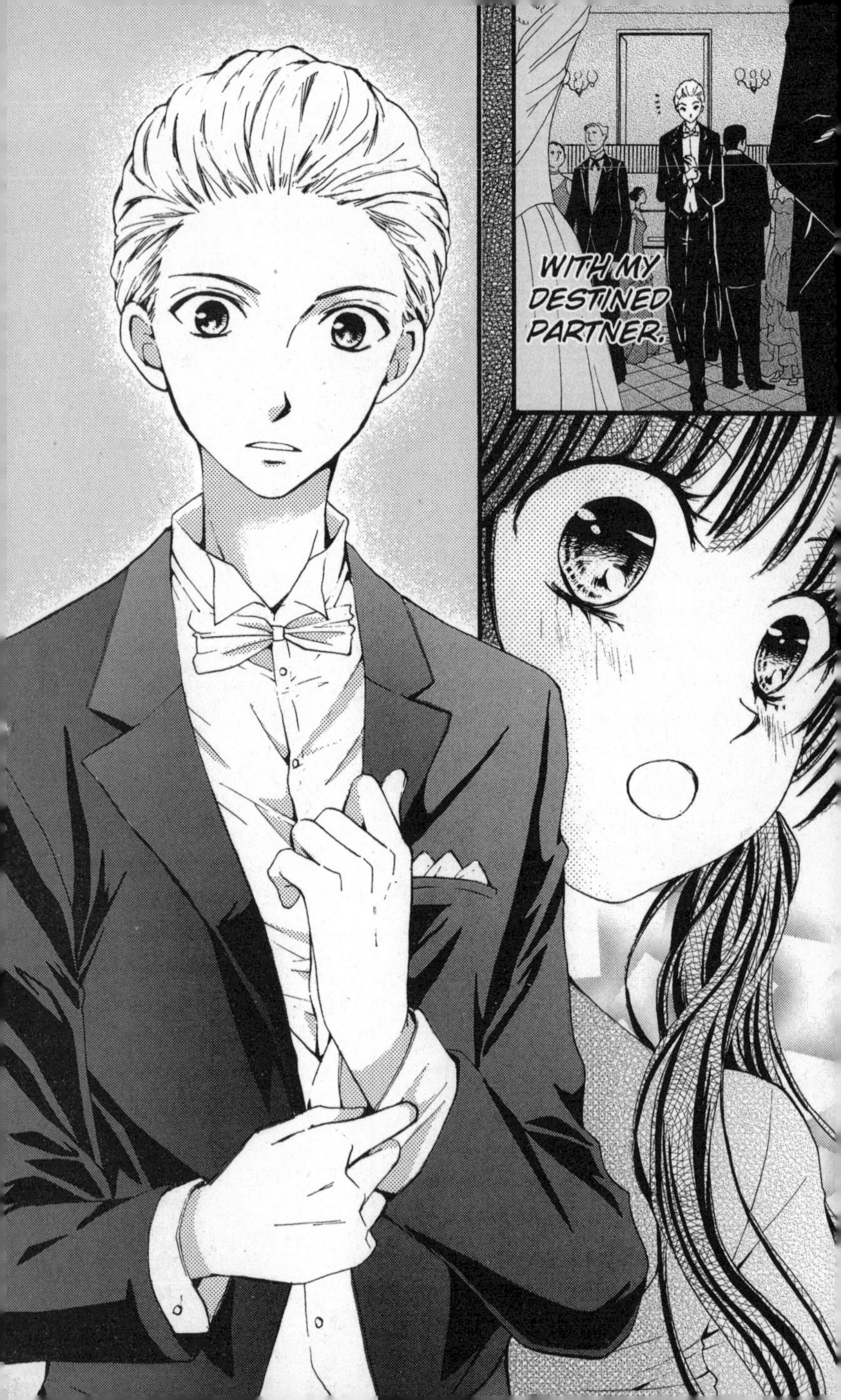
WITH MY DESTINED PARTNER.

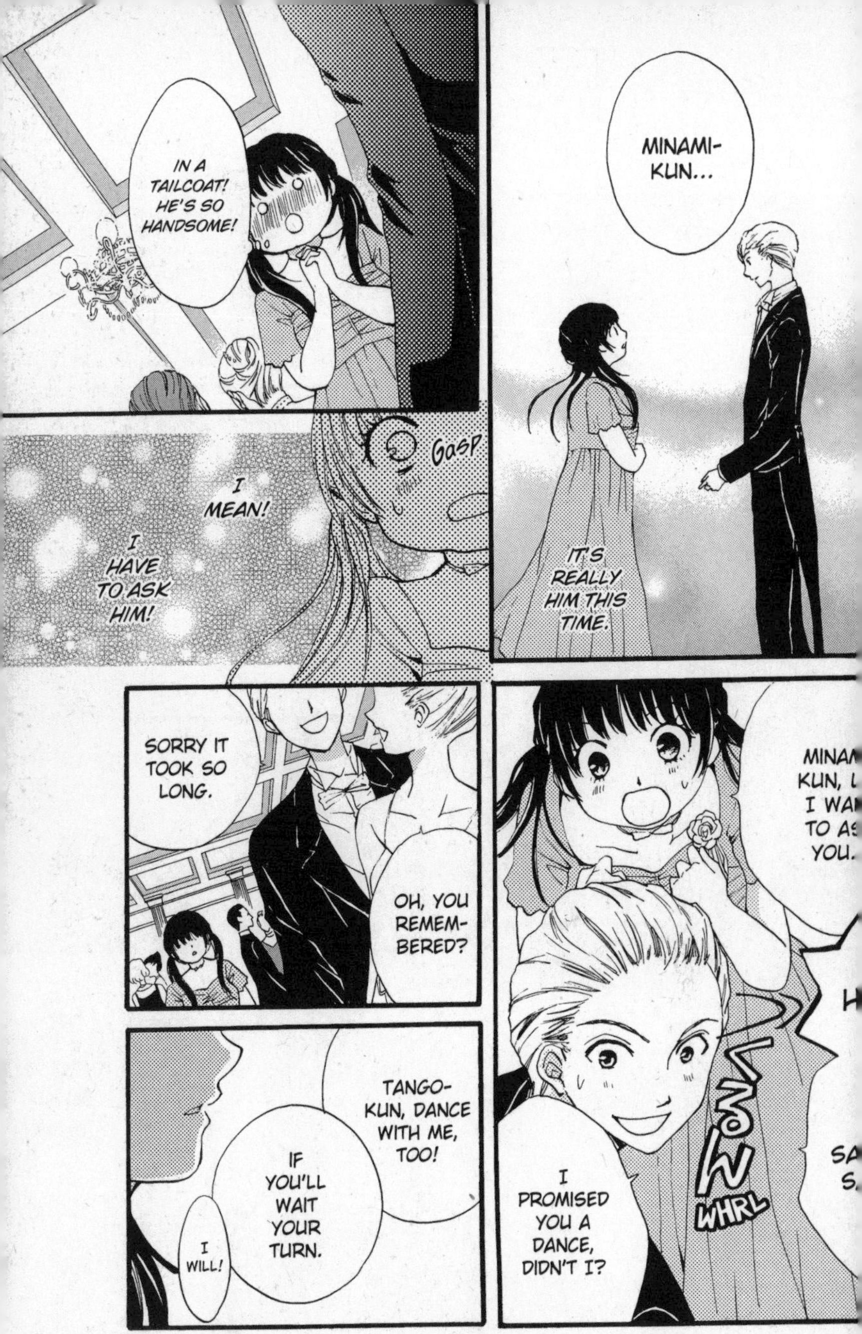
MINAMI-KUN...
IT'S REALLY HIM THIS TIME.
IN A TAILCOAT! HE'S SO HANDSOME!
Gasp
I MEAN!
I HAVE TO ASK HIM!
MINAM KUN, I WAN TO AS YOU.
WHRL
I PROMISED YOU A DANCE, DIDN'T I?
SORRY IT TOOK SO LONG.
OH, YOU REMEMBERED?
TANGO-KUN, DANCE WITH ME, TOO!
IF YOU'LL WAIT YOUR TURN.
I WILL!

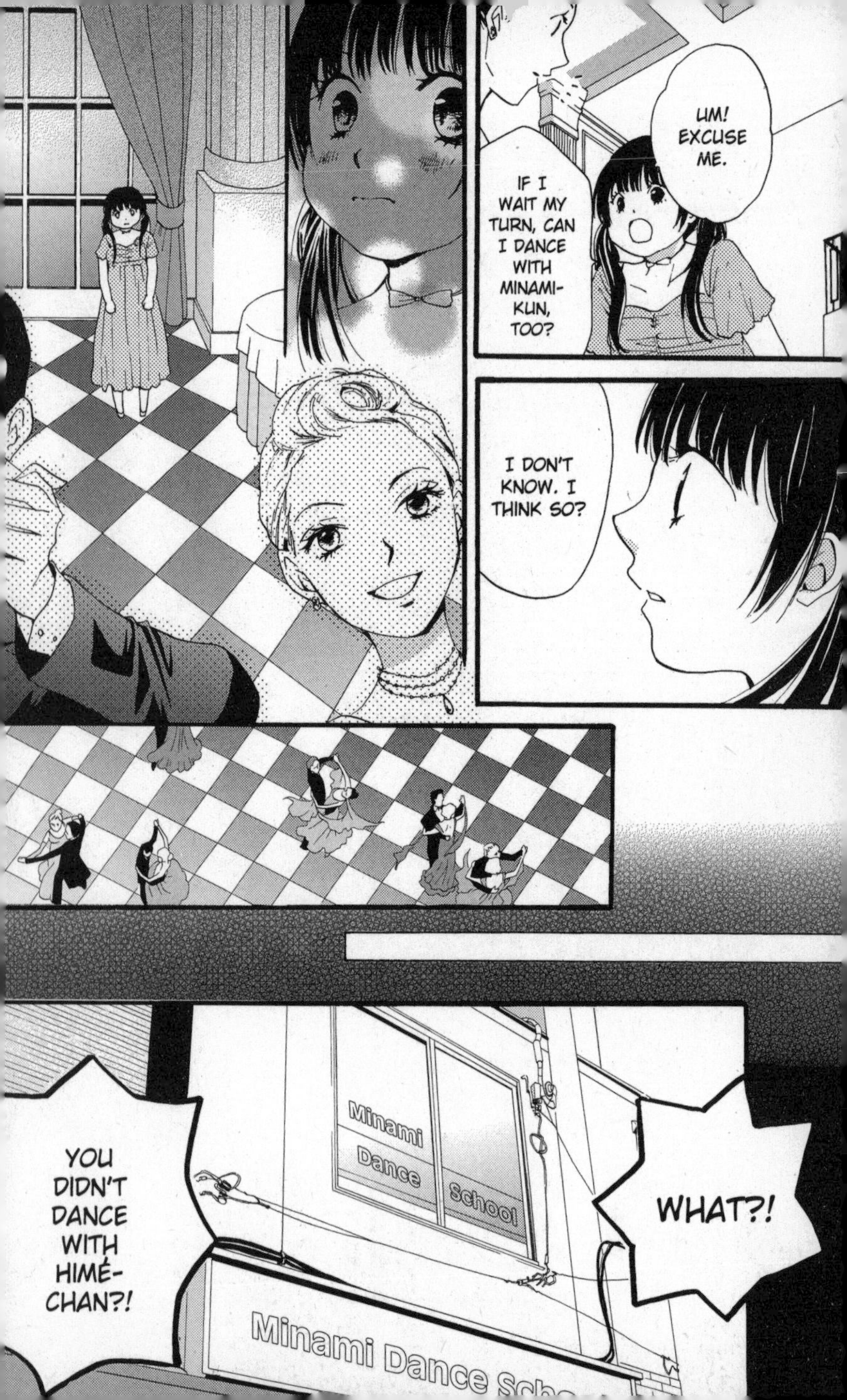
UM! EXCUSE ME.
IF I WAIT MY TURN, CAN I DANCE WITH MINAMI-KUN, TOO?
I DON'T KNOW. I THINK SO?
WHAT?!
Minami Dance School
YOU DIDN'T DANCE WITH HIMÉ-CHAN?!

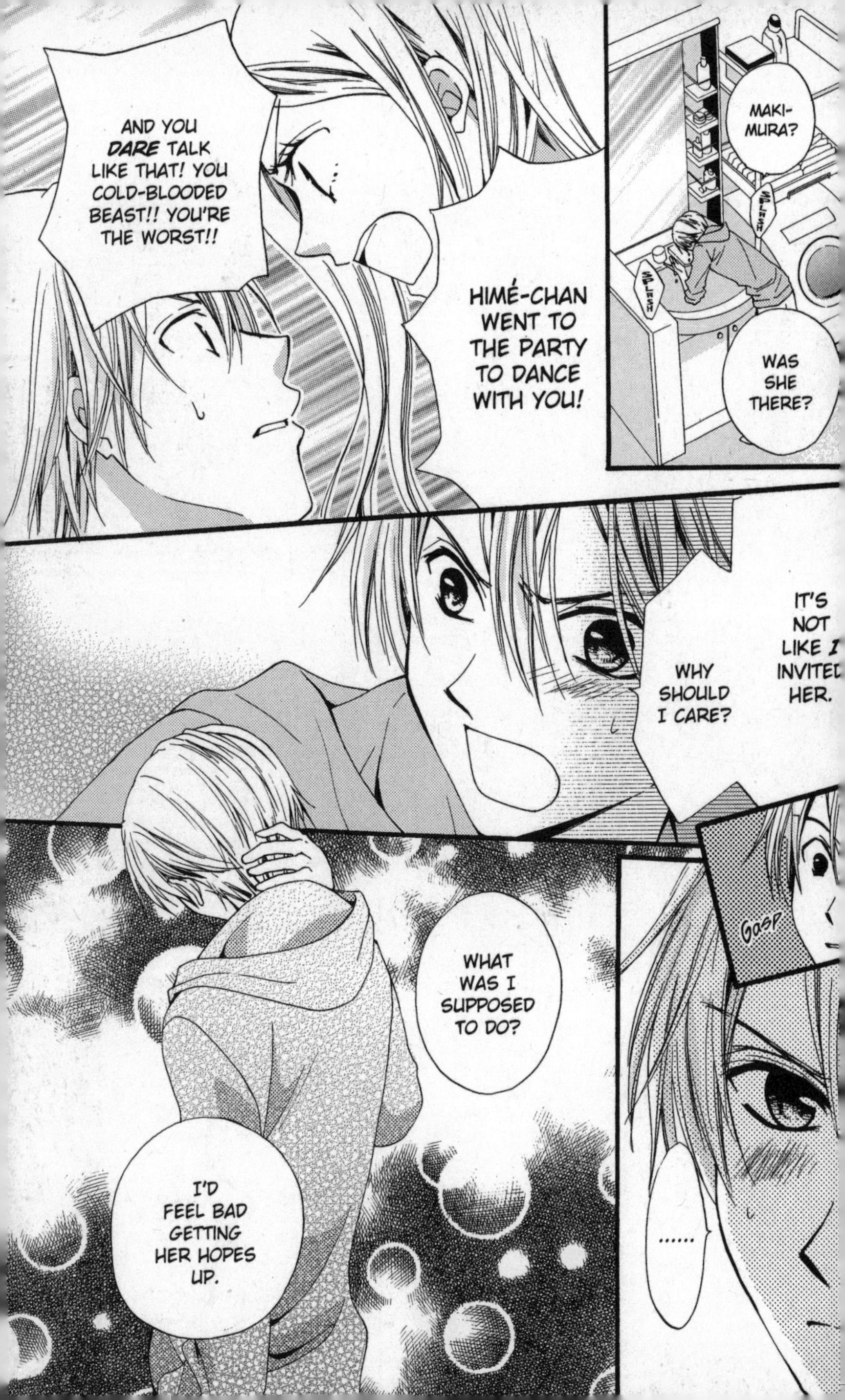
MAKI-MURA?
SPLASH
SPLASH
WAS SHE THERE?
HIMÉ-CHAN WENT TO THE PARTY TO DANCE WITH YOU!
AND YOU DARE TALK LIKE THAT! YOU COLD-BLOODED BEAST!! YOU'RE THE WORST!!
IT'S NOT LIKE I INVITED HER.
WHY SHOULD I CARE?
Gasp
......
WHAT WAS I SUPPOSED TO DO?
I'D FEEL BAD GETTING HER HOPES UP.

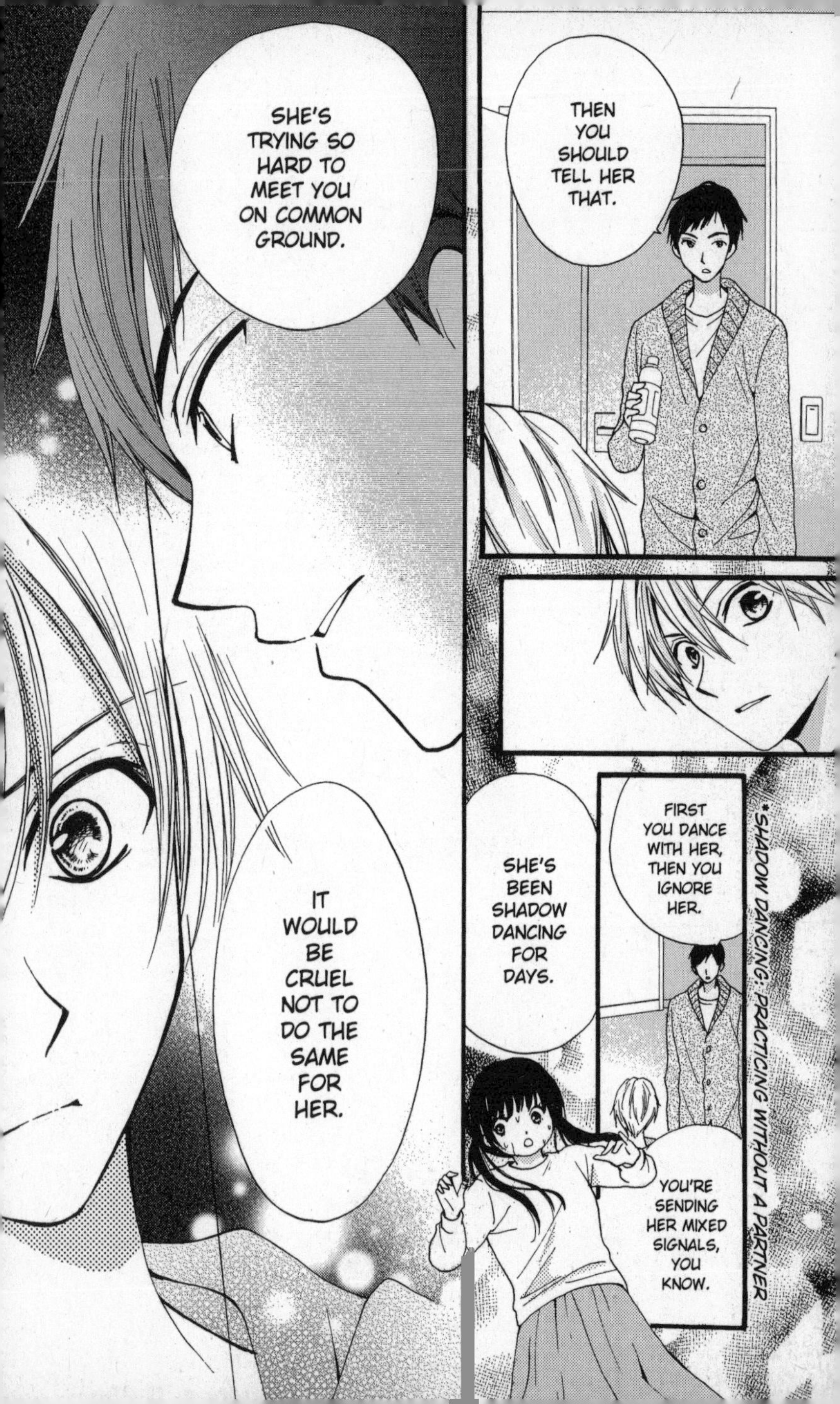
THEN YOU SHOULD TELL HER THAT.
FIRST YOU DANCE WITH HER, THEN YOU IGNORE HER.
SHE'S BEEN SHADOW DANCING FOR DAYS.
YOU'RE SENDING HER MIXED SIGNALS, YOU KNOW.
*SHADOW DANCING: PRACTICING WITHOUT A PARTNER
SHE'S TRYING SO HARD TO MEET YOU ON COMMON GROUND.
IT WOULD BE CRUEL NOT TO DO THE SAME FOR HER.

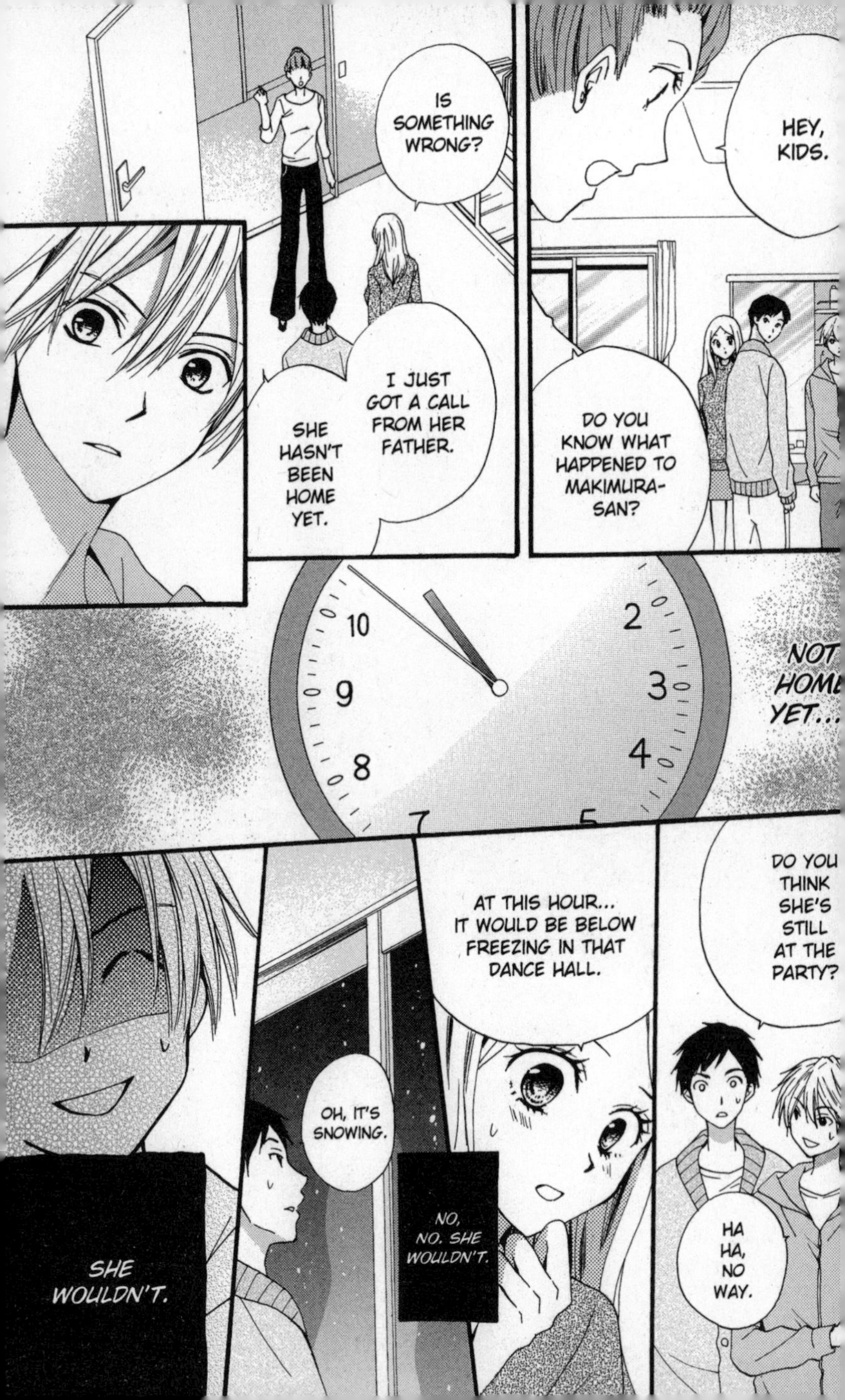
HEY, KIDS.
DO YOU KNOW WHAT HAPPENED TO MAKIMURA-SAN?
IS SOMETHING WRONG?
I JUST GOT A CALL FROM HER FATHER.
SHE HASN'T BEEN HOME YET.
NOT HOME YET...
DO YOU THINK SHE'S STILL AT THE PARTY?
HA HA, NO WAY.
AT THIS HOUR... IT WOULD BE BELOW FREEZING IN THAT DANCE HALL.
NO, NO. SHE WOULDN'T.
OH, IT'S SNOWING.
SHE WOULDN'T.

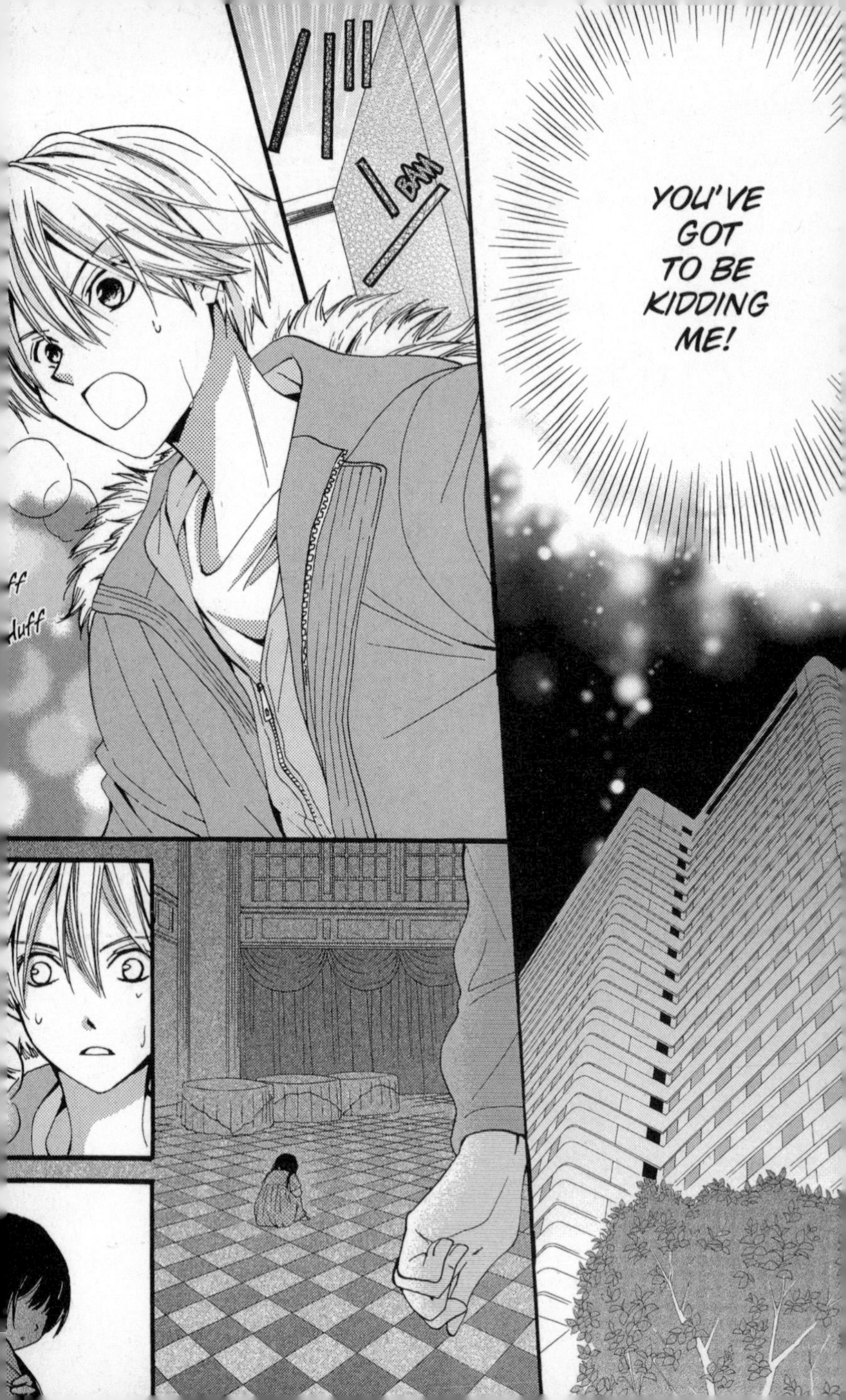
YOU'VE GOT TO BE KIDDING ME!
BAM
ff
duff

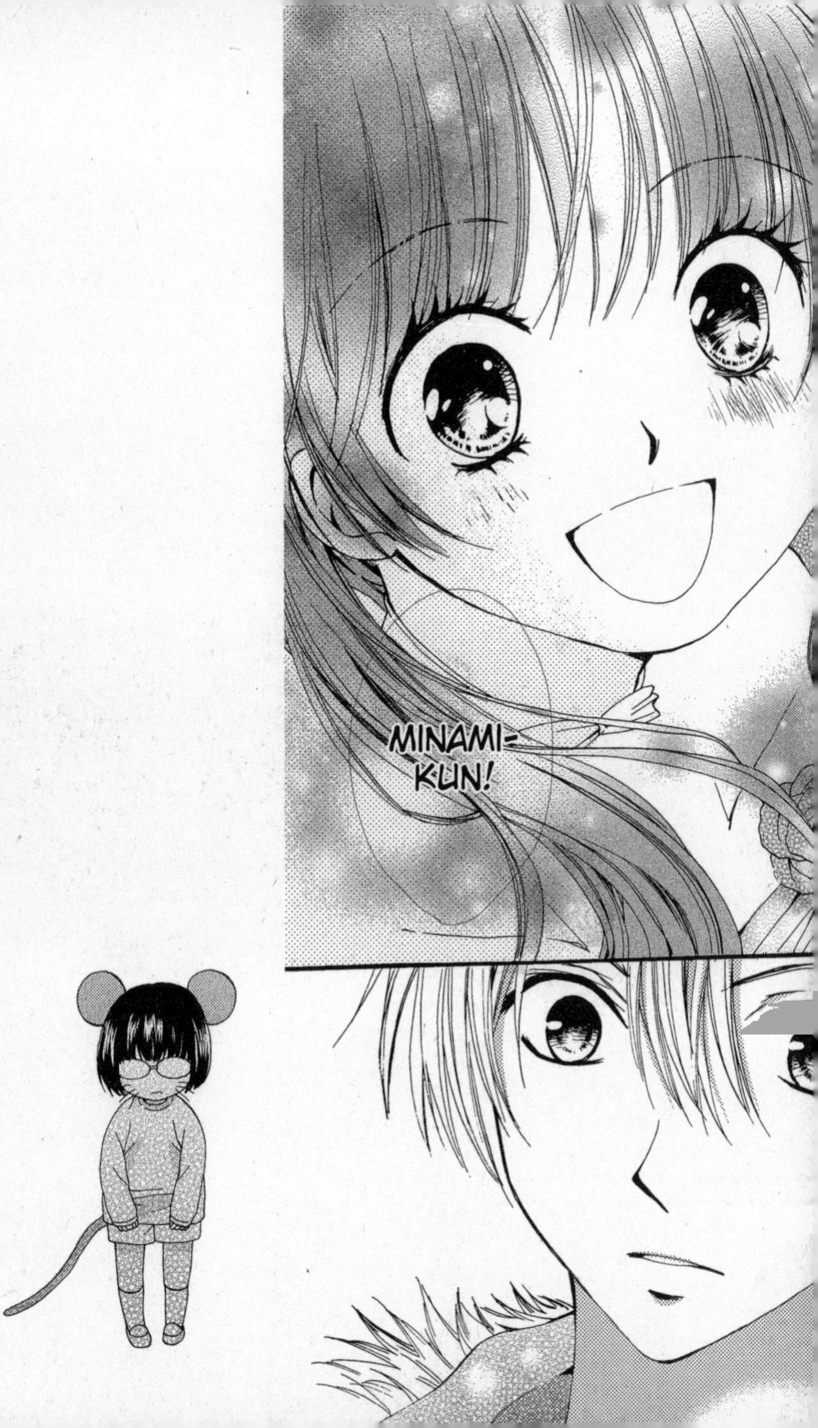
MINAMI-
KUN!

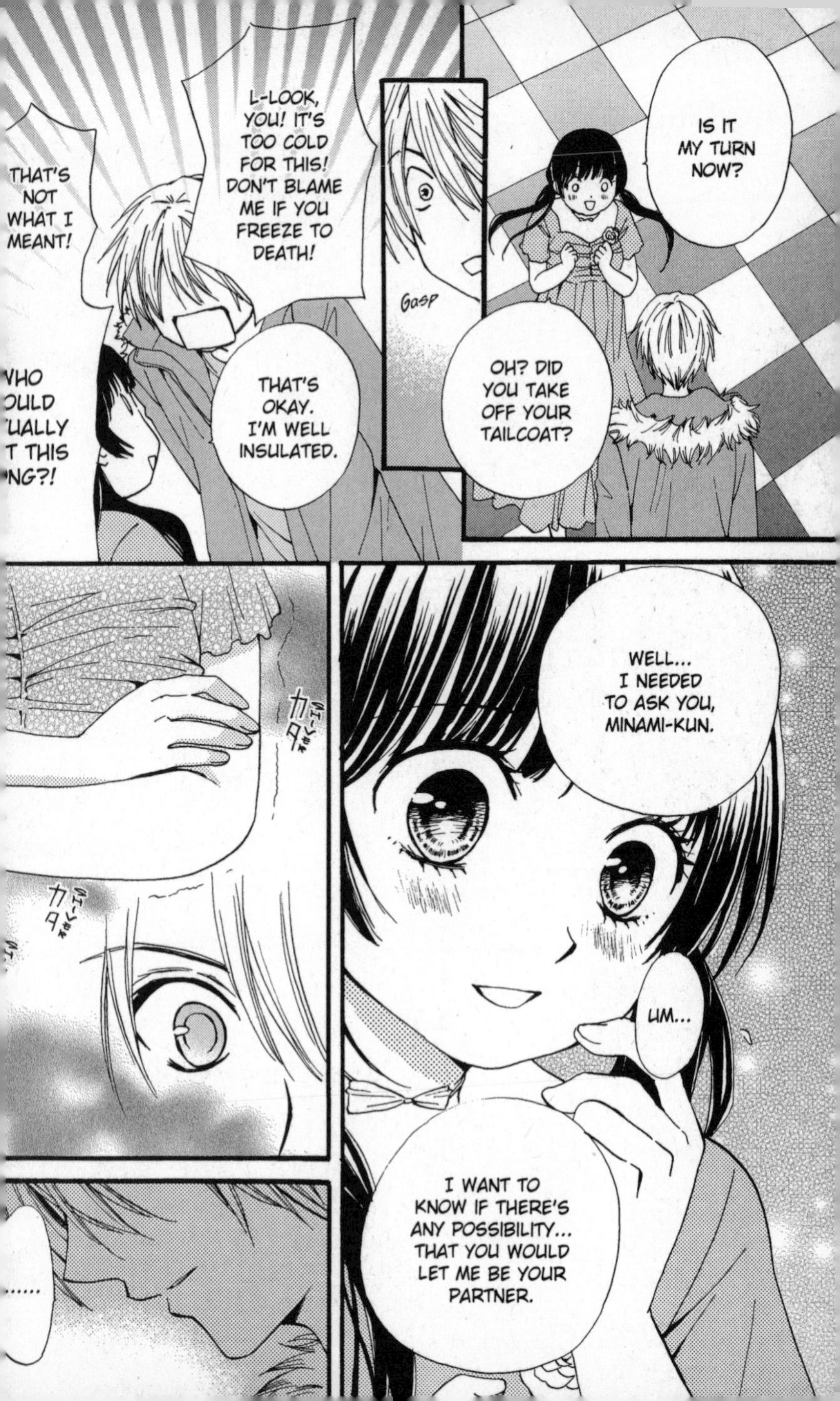
IS IT MY TURN NOW?
OH? DID YOU TAKE OFF YOUR TAILCOAT?
Gasp
L-LOOK, YOU! IT'S TOO COLD FOR THIS! DON'T BLAME ME IF YOU FREEZE TO DEATH!
THAT'S OKAY. I'M WELL INSULATED.
THAT'S NOT WHAT I MEANT!
WELL... I NEEDED TO ASK YOU, MINAMI-KUN.
UM...
I WANT TO KNOW IF THERE'S ANY POSSIBILITY... THAT YOU WOULD LET ME BE YOUR PARTNER.
......

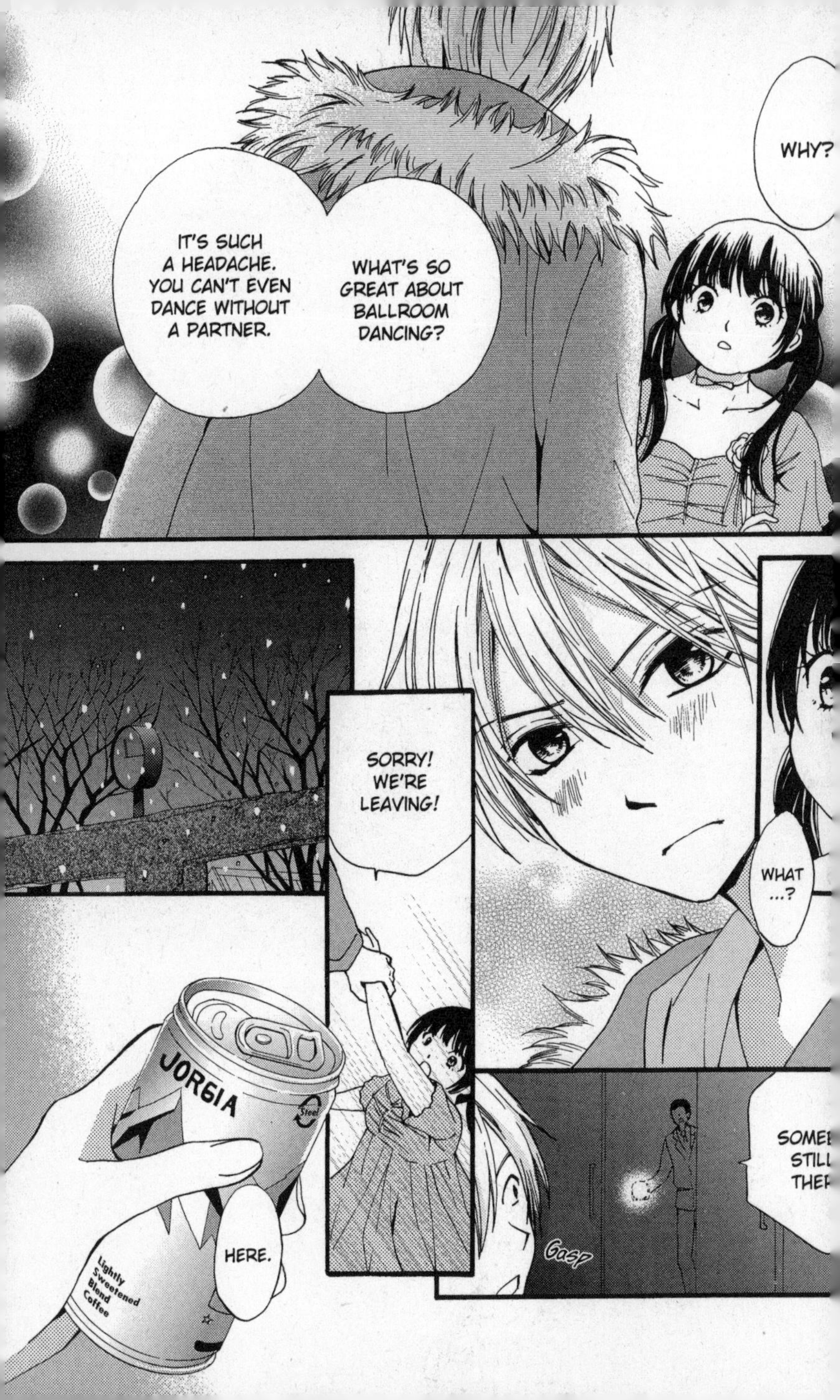
WHY?
WHAT'S SO GREAT ABOUT BALLROOM DANCING?
IT'S SUCH A HEADACHE. YOU CAN'T EVEN DANCE WITHOUT A PARTNER.
WHAT ...?
SORRY! WE'RE LEAVING!
SOME
STILL
THE
Gasp
JORGIA
Steel
HERE.
Lightly Sweetened Blend Coffee

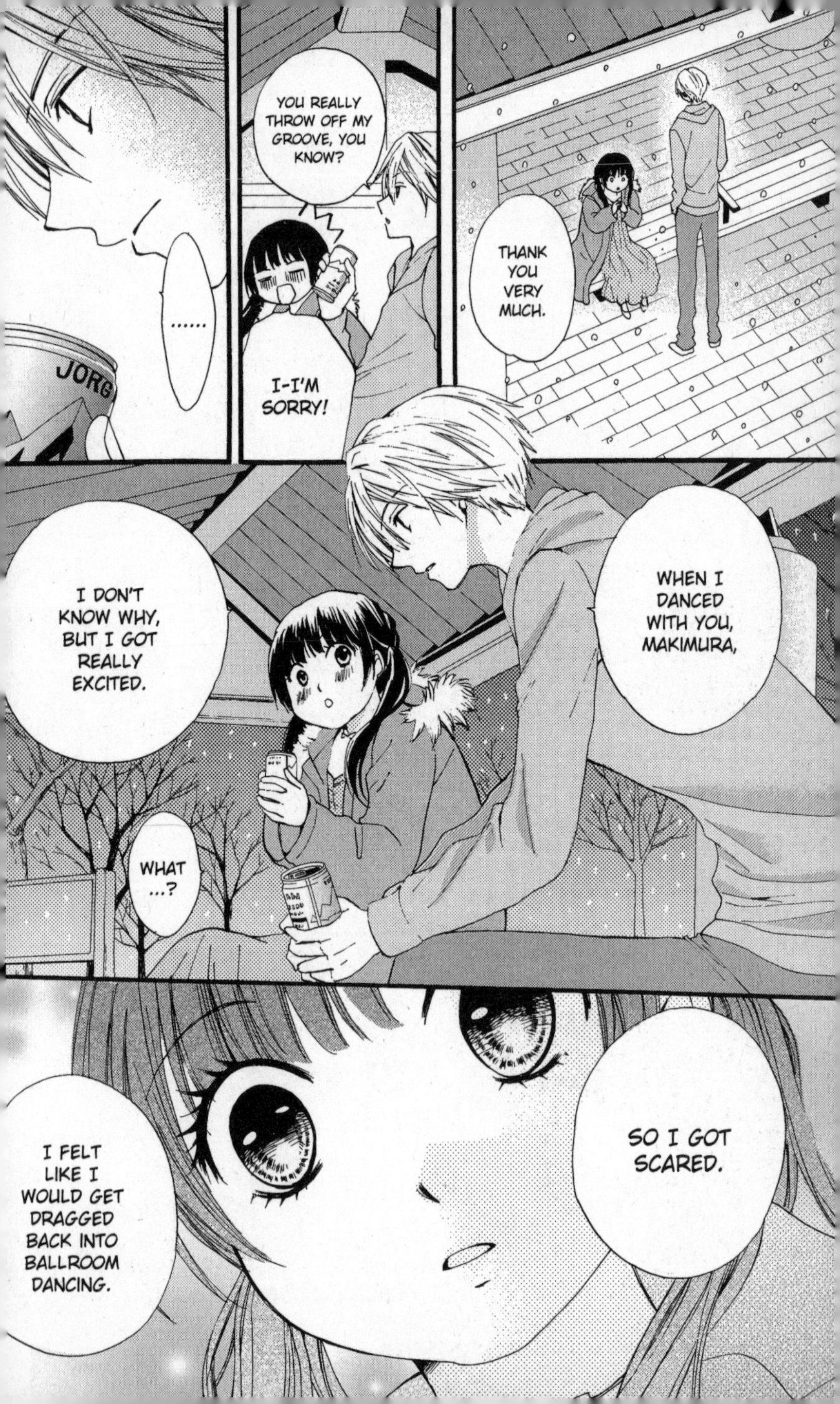
THANK YOU VERY MUCH.
YOU REALLY THROW OFF MY GROOVE, YOU KNOW?
I-I'M SORRY!
......
WHEN I DANCED WITH YOU, MAKIMURA,
I DON'T KNOW WHY, BUT I GOT REALLY EXCITED.
WHAT ...?
SO I GOT SCARED.
I FELT LIKE I WOULD GET DRAGGED BACK INTO BALLROOM DANCING.

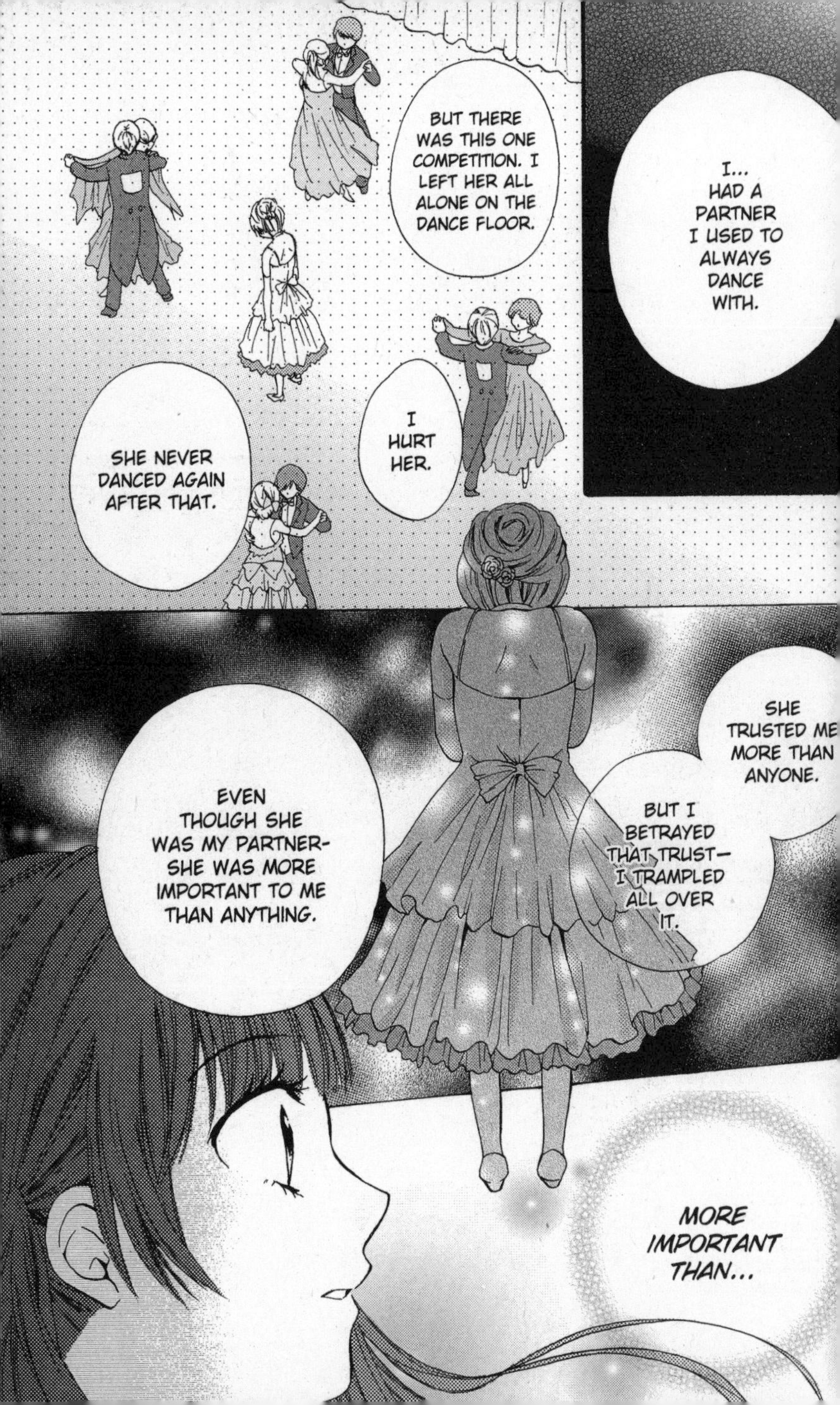
I... HAD A PARTNER I USED TO ALWAYS DANCE WITH.
BUT THERE WAS THIS ONE COMPETITION. I LEFT HER ALL ALONE ON THE DANCE FLOOR.
I HURT HER.
SHE NEVER DANCED AGAIN AFTER THAT.
SHE TRUSTED ME MORE THAN ANYONE.
BUT I BETRAYED THAT TRUST— I TRAMPLED ALL OVER IT.
EVEN THOUGH SHE WAS MY PARTNER- SHE WAS MORE IMPORTANT TO ME THAN ANYTHING.
MORE IMPORTANT THAN...

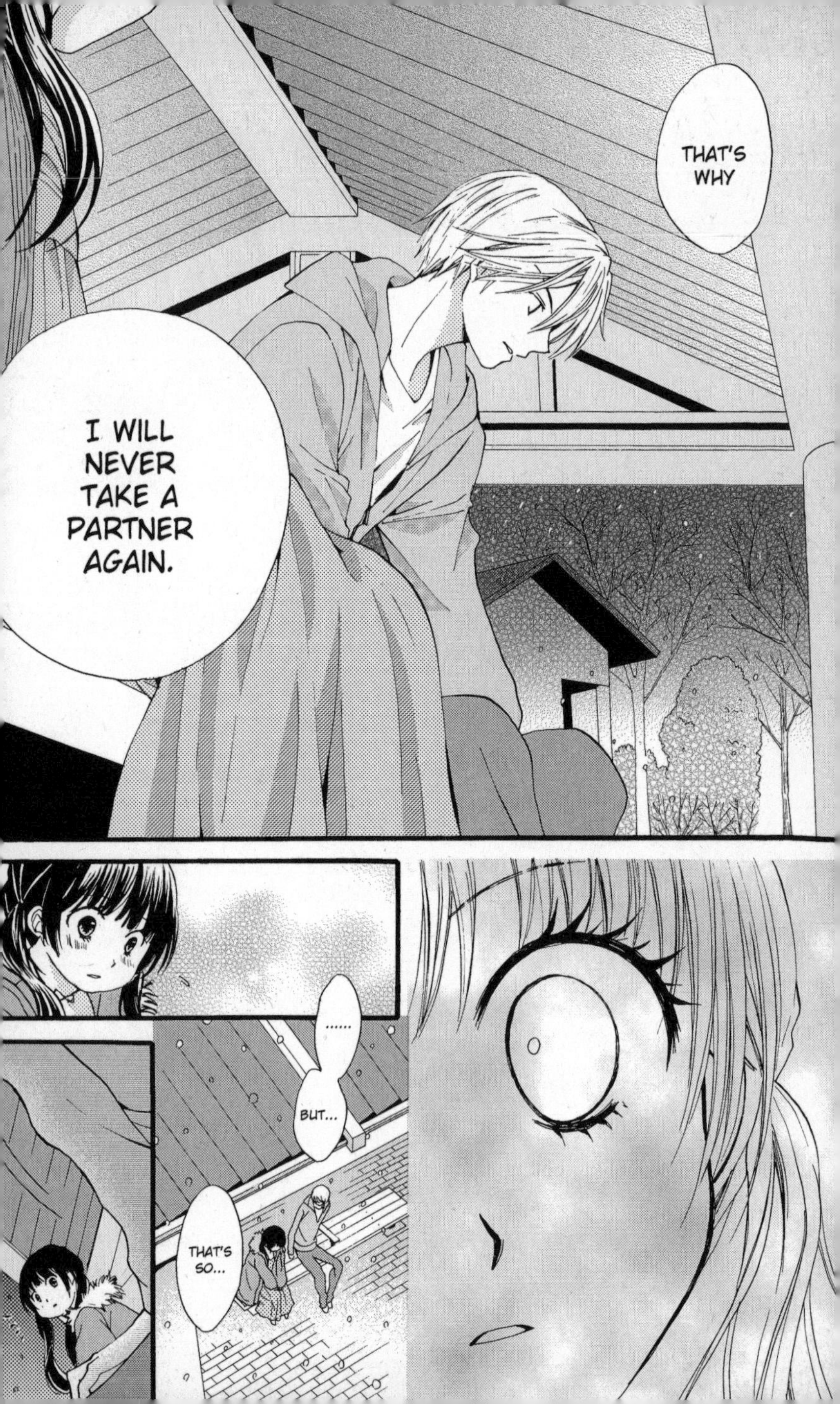
THAT'S WHY
I WILL NEVER TAKE A PARTNER AGAIN.
......
BUT...
THAT'S SO...

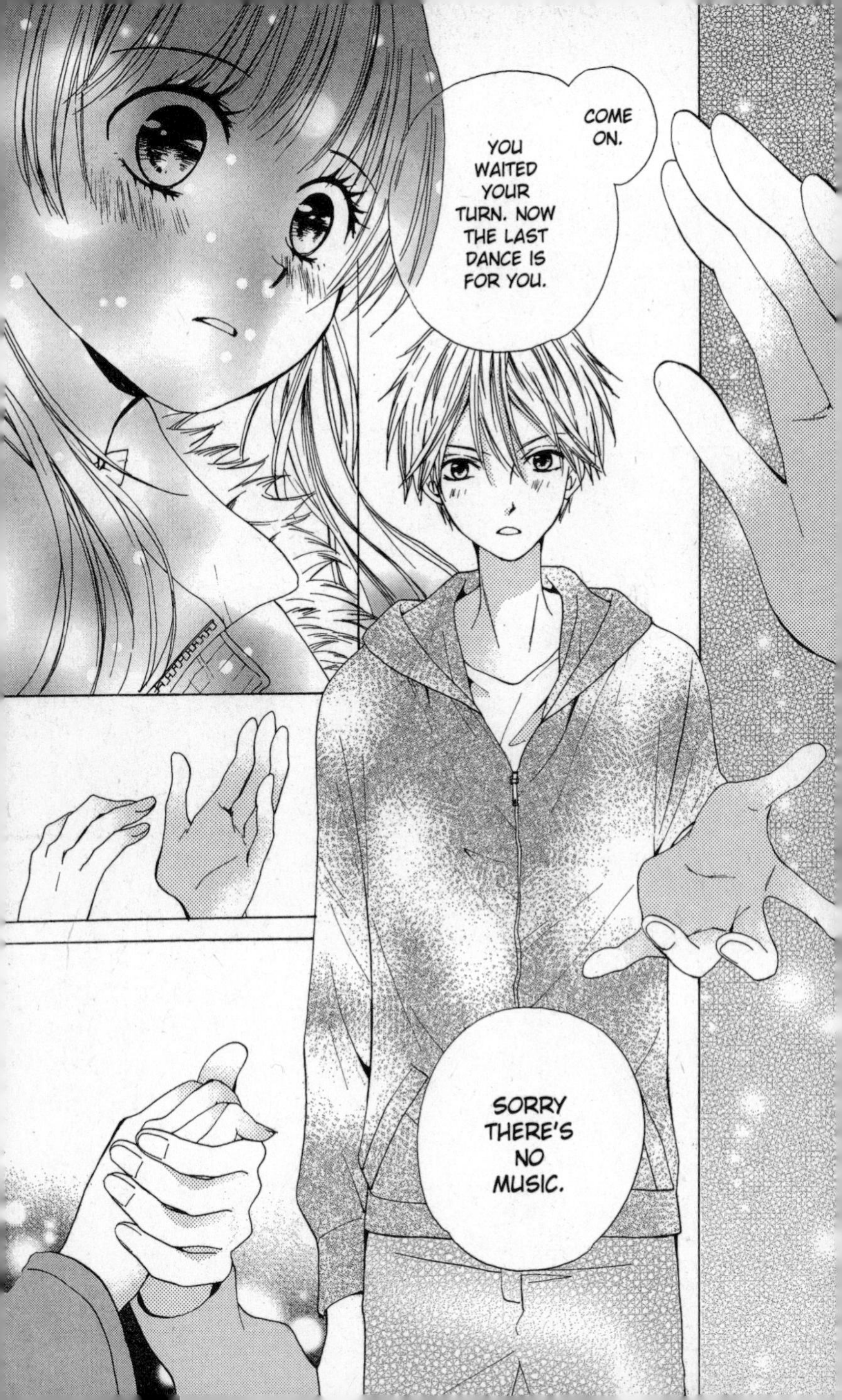
COME ON.
YOU WAITED YOUR TURN. NOW THE LAST DANCE IS FOR YOU.
SORRY THERE'S NO MUSIC.

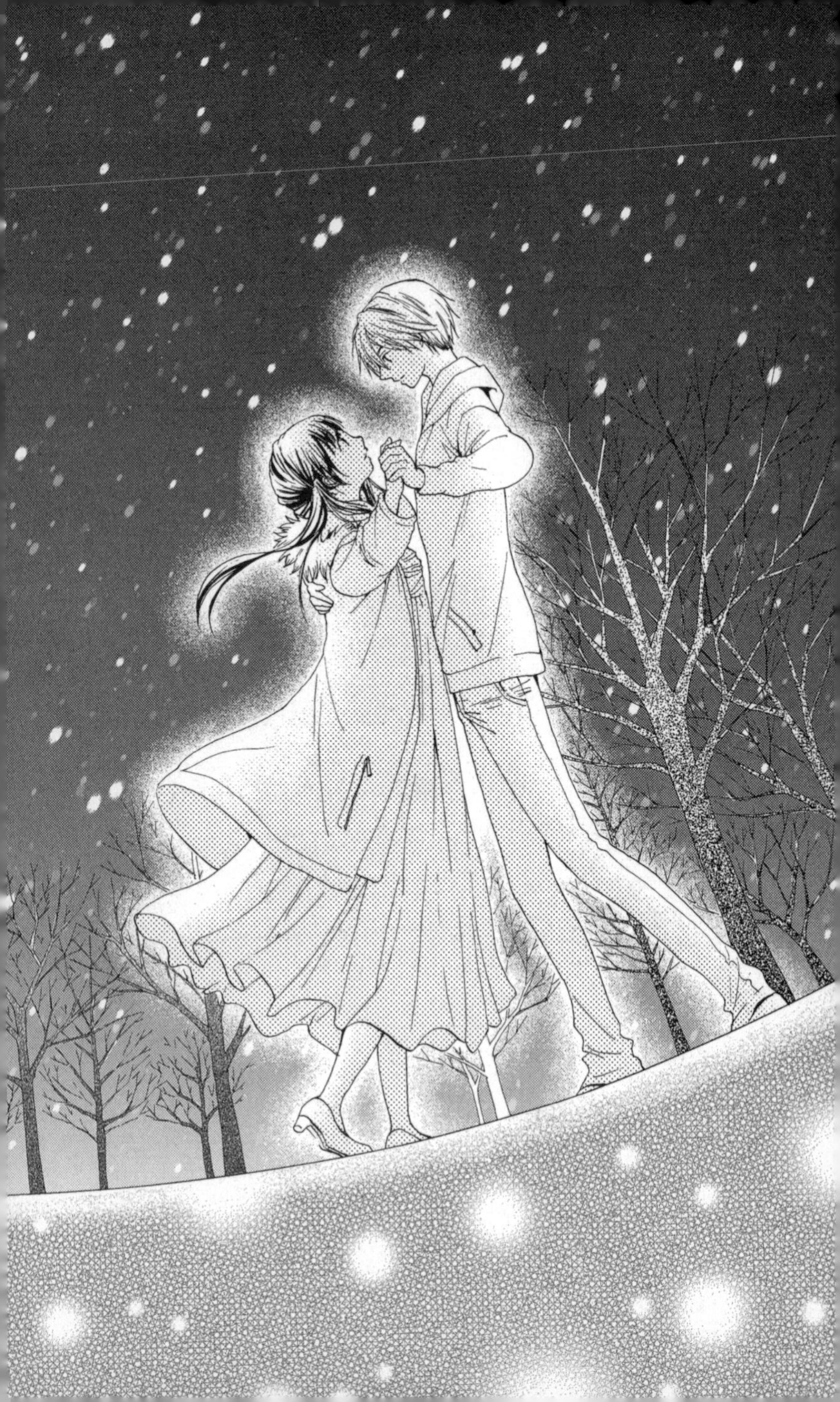

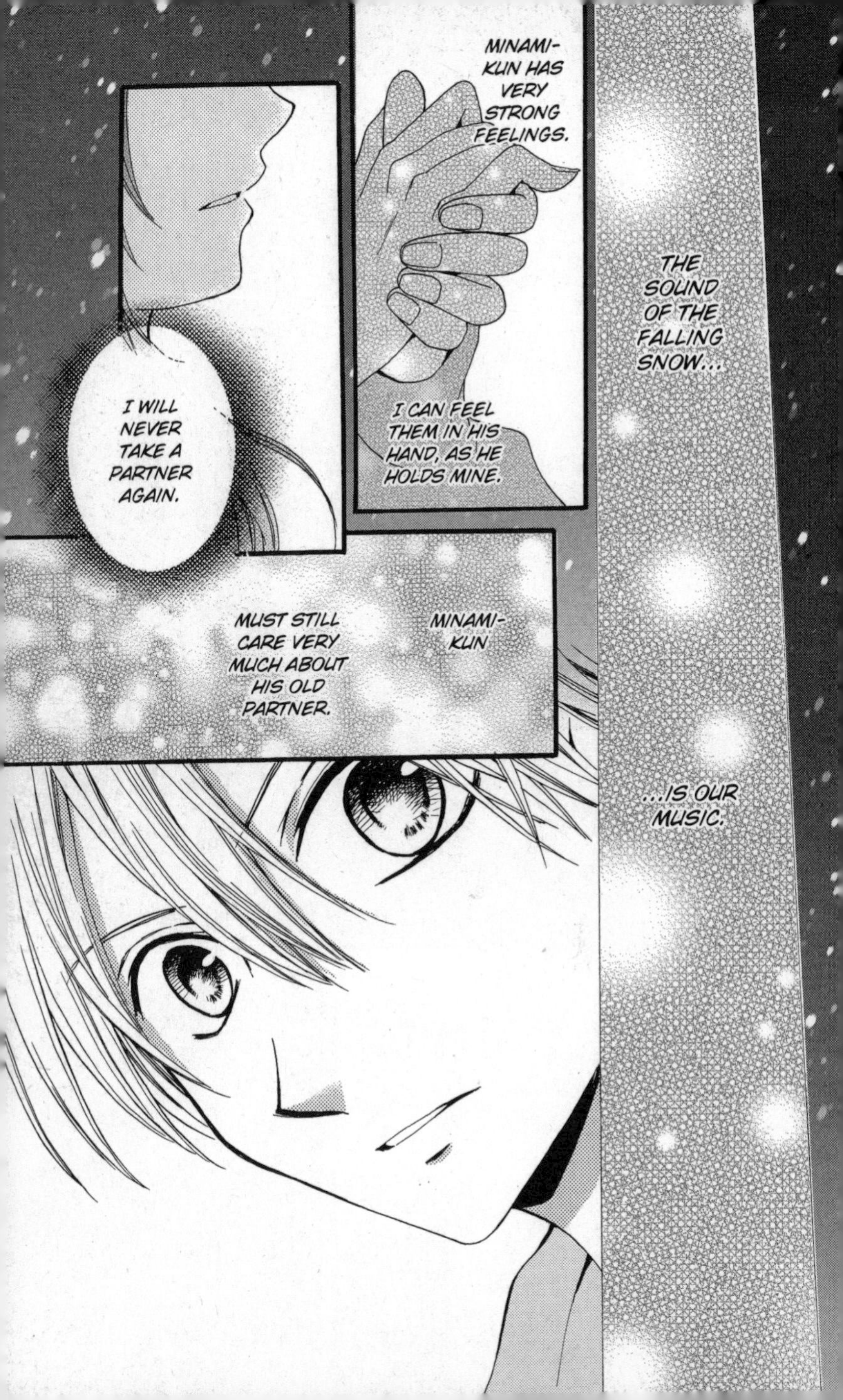
THE SOUND OF THE FALLING SNOW...
...IS OUR MUSIC.
MINAMI-KUN HAS VERY STRONG FEELINGS.
I CAN FEEL THEM IN HIS HAND, AS HE HOLDS MINE.
I WILL NEVER TAKE A PARTNER AGAIN.
MINAMI-KUN
MUST STILL CARE VERY MUCH ABOUT HIS OLD PARTNER.

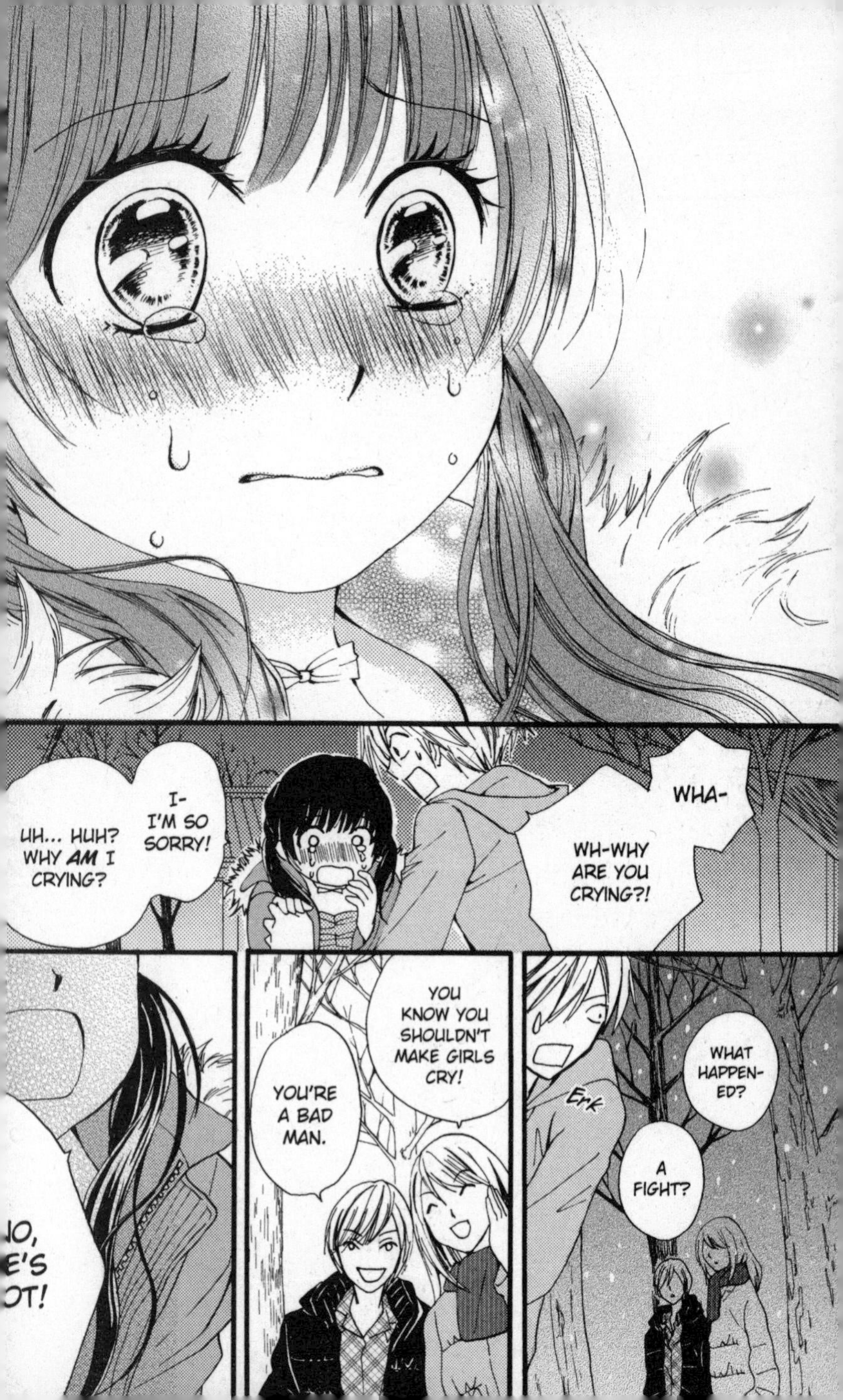
WHA-
WH-WHY ARE YOU CRYING?!
I- I'M SO SORRY!
UH... HUH? WHY *AM* I CRYING?
WHAT HAPPEN-ED?
A FIGHT?
Erk
YOU KNOW YOU SHOULDN'T MAKE GIRLS CRY!
YOU'RE A BAD MAN.

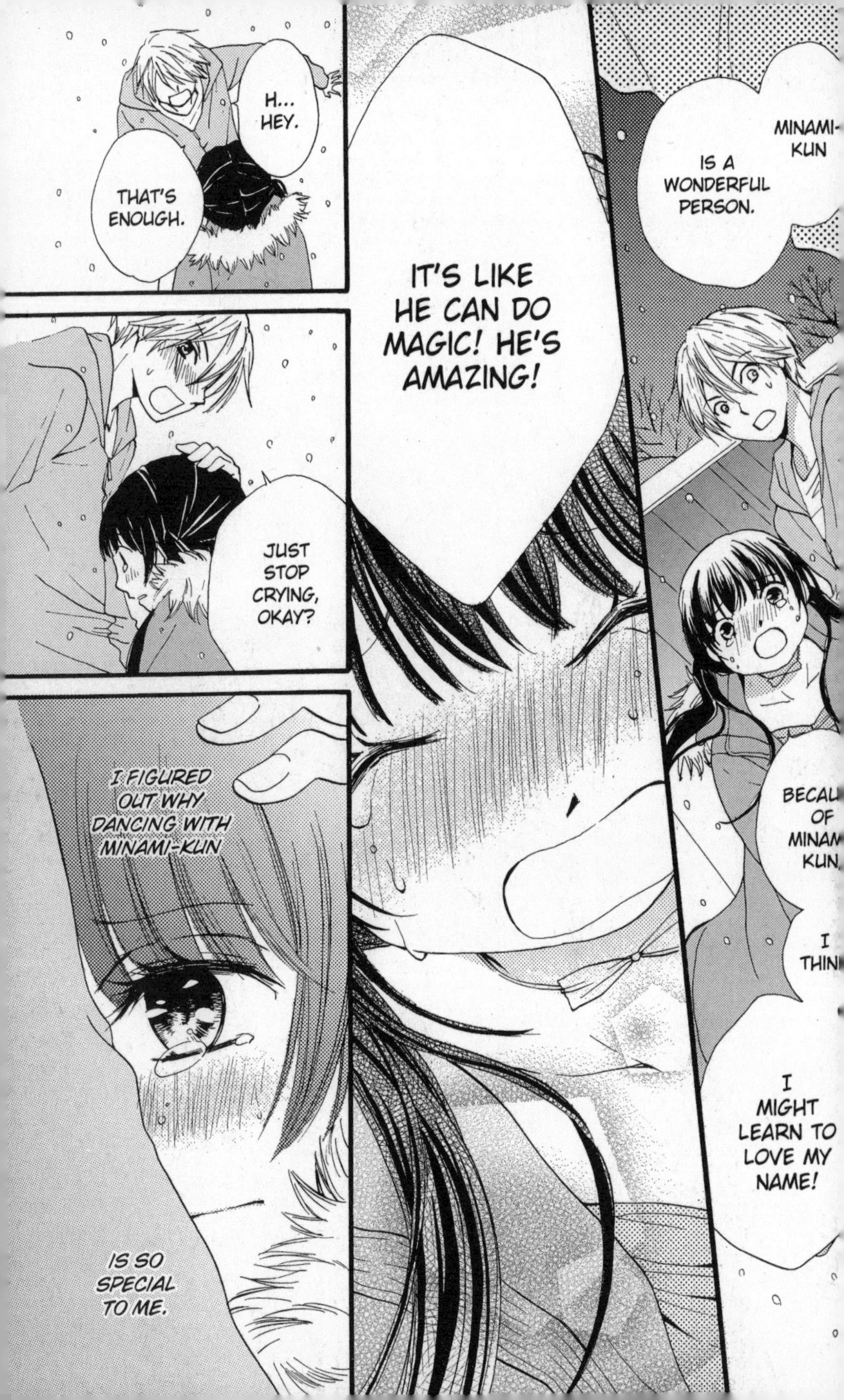
MINAMI-KUN
IS A WONDERFUL PERSON.
BECAU OF MINAM KUN,
I THIN
I MIGHT LEARN TO LOVE MY NAME!
IT'S LIKE HE CAN DO MAGIC! HE'S AMAZING!
H... HEY.
THAT'S ENOUGH.
JUST STOP CRYING, OKAY?
I FIGURED OUT WHY DANCING WITH MINAMI-KUN
IS SO SPECIAL TO ME.

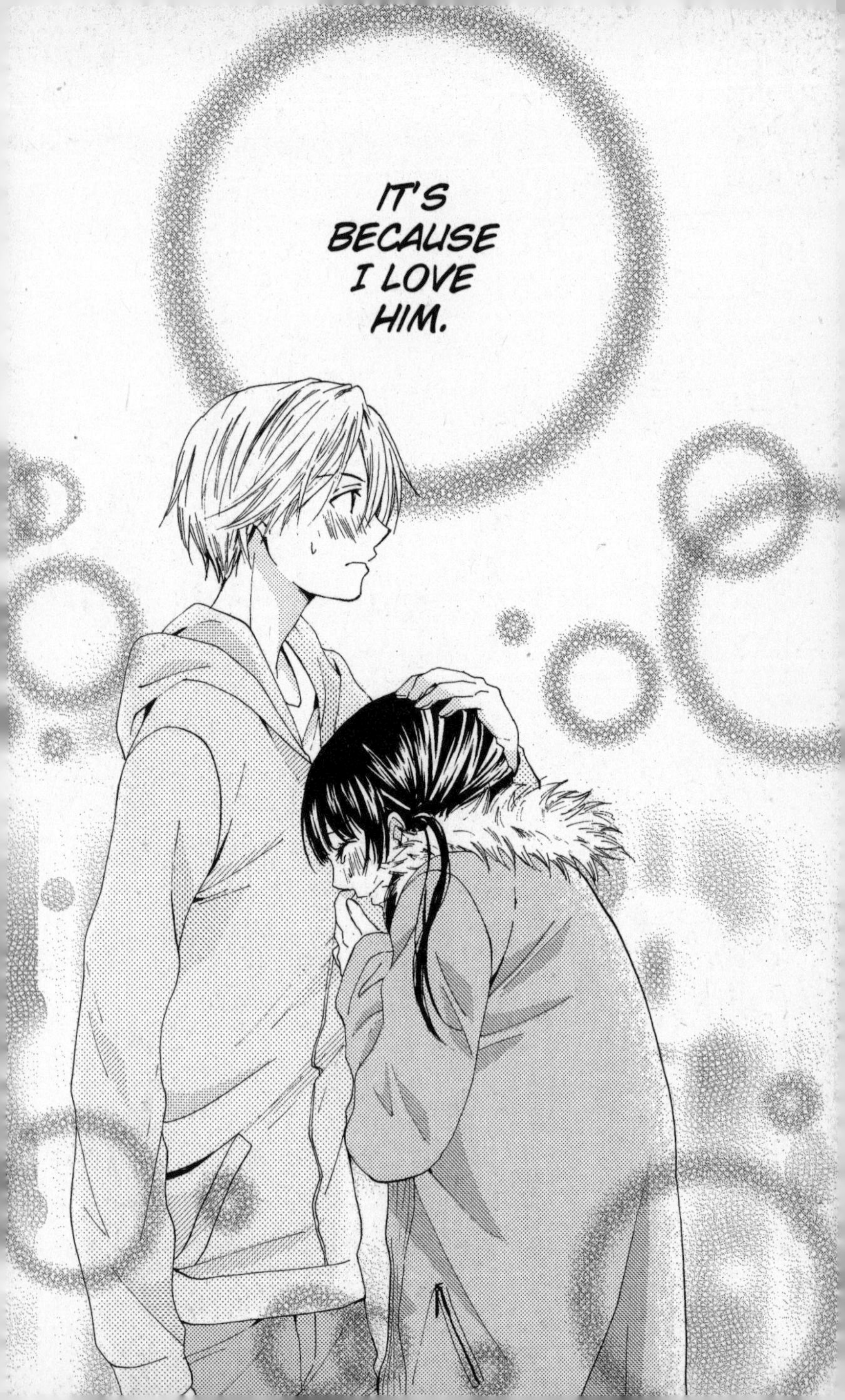
IT'S BECAUSE I LOVE HIM.

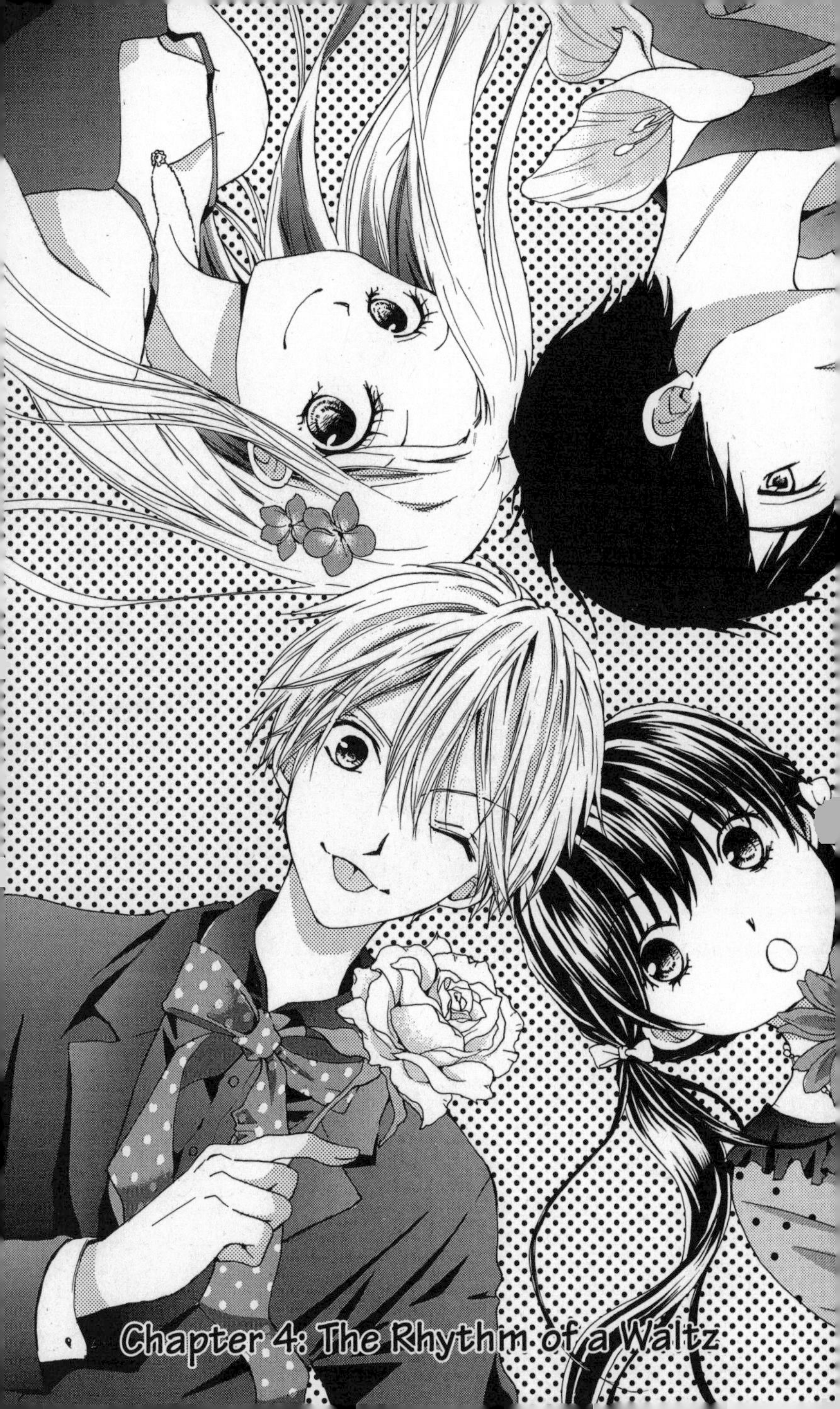

Chapter 4: The Rhythm of a Waltz

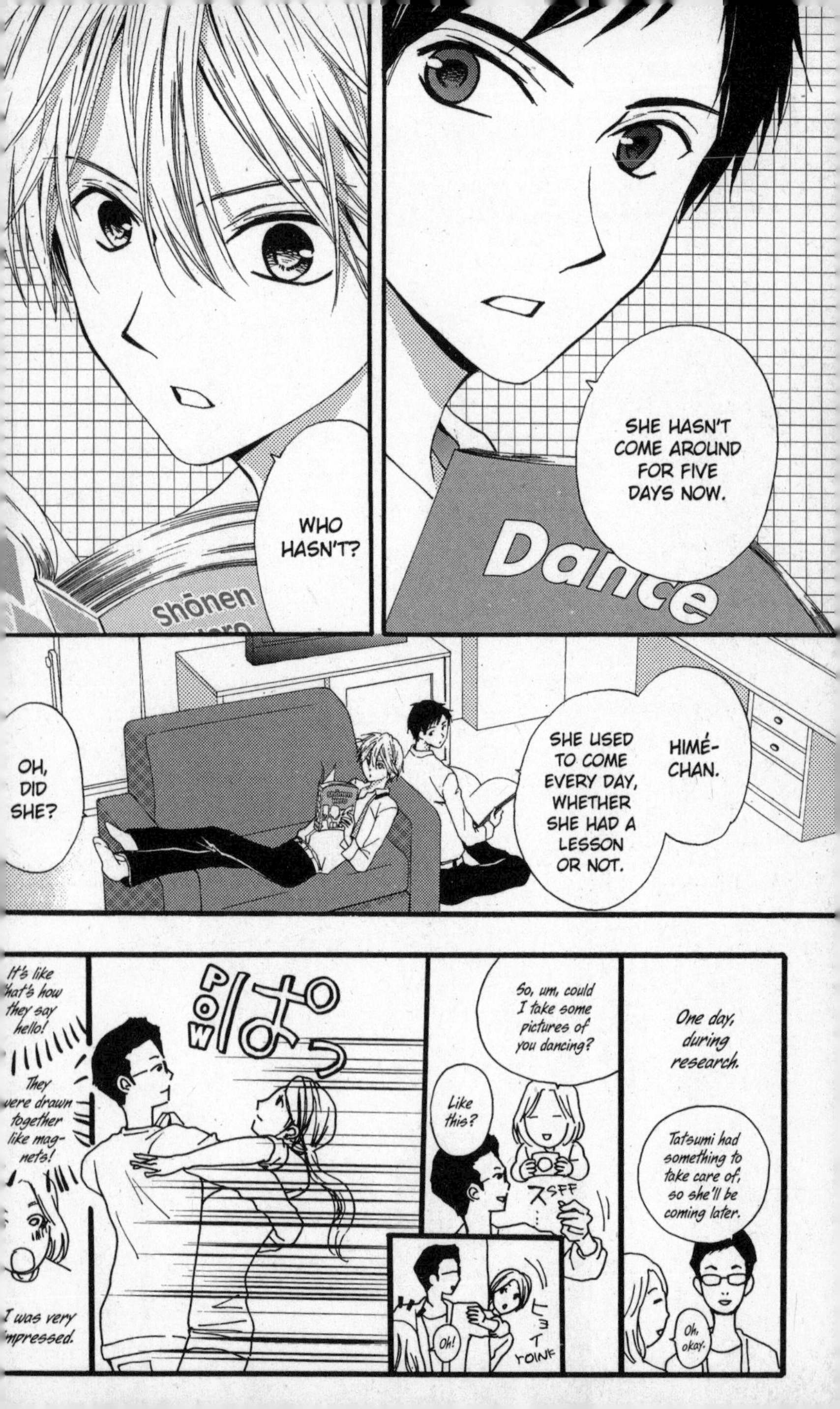

SHE HASN'T COME AROUND FOR FIVE DAYS NOW.
Dance
WHO HASN'T?
Shōnen
HIMÉ-CHAN.
SHE USED TO COME EVERY DAY, WHETHER SHE HAD A LESSON OR NOT.
OH, DID SHE?
One day, during research.
Tatsumi had something to take care of, so she'll be coming later.
Oh, okay.
So, um, could I take some pictures of you dancing?
Like this?
SFF
Oh!
YOINK
POW
It's like hat's how they say hello!
They vere drawn together like magnets!
I was very mpressed.

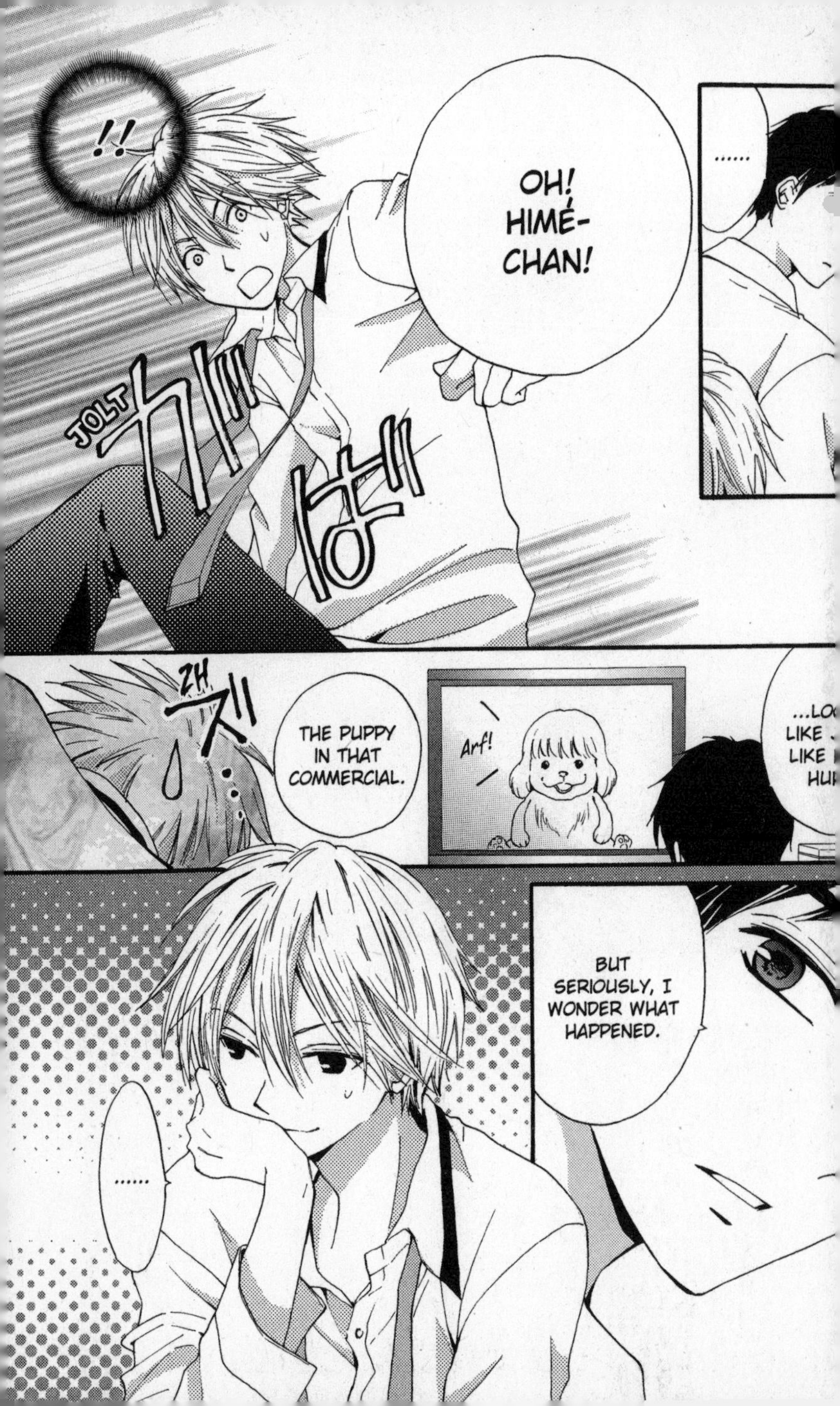
......
OH! HIMÉ-CHAN!
!!
JOLT
THE PUPPY IN THAT COMMERCIAL.
Arf!
ZH
BUT SERIOUSLY, I WONDER WHAT HAPPENED.
......

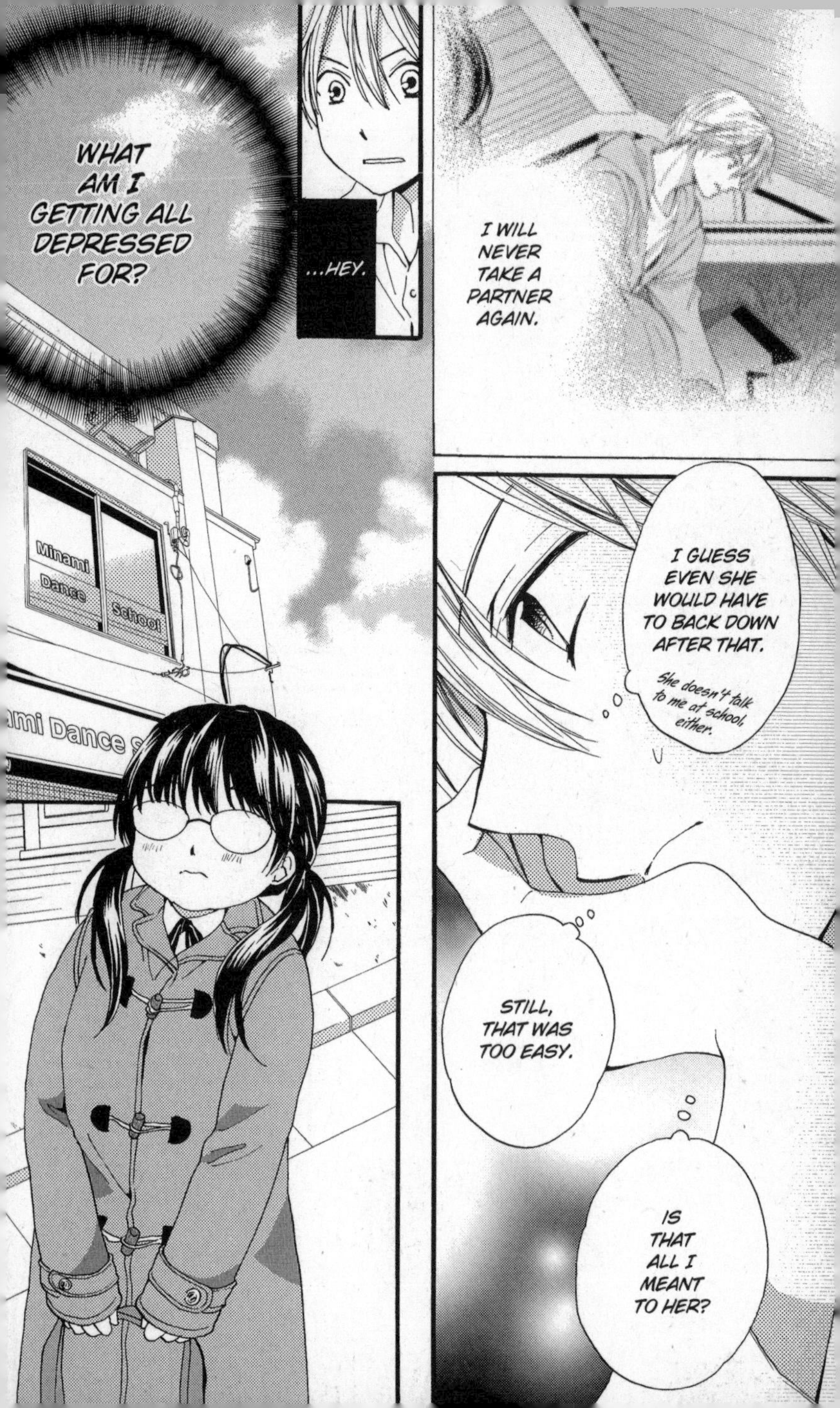
I WILL NEVER TAKE A PARTNER AGAIN.
I GUESS EVEN SHE WOULD HAVE TO BACK DOWN AFTER THAT.
She doesn't talk to me at school, either.
STILL, THAT WAS TOO EASY.
IS THAT ALL I MEANT TO HER?
...HEY.
WHAT AM I GETTING ALL DEPRESSED FOR?
Minami Dance School

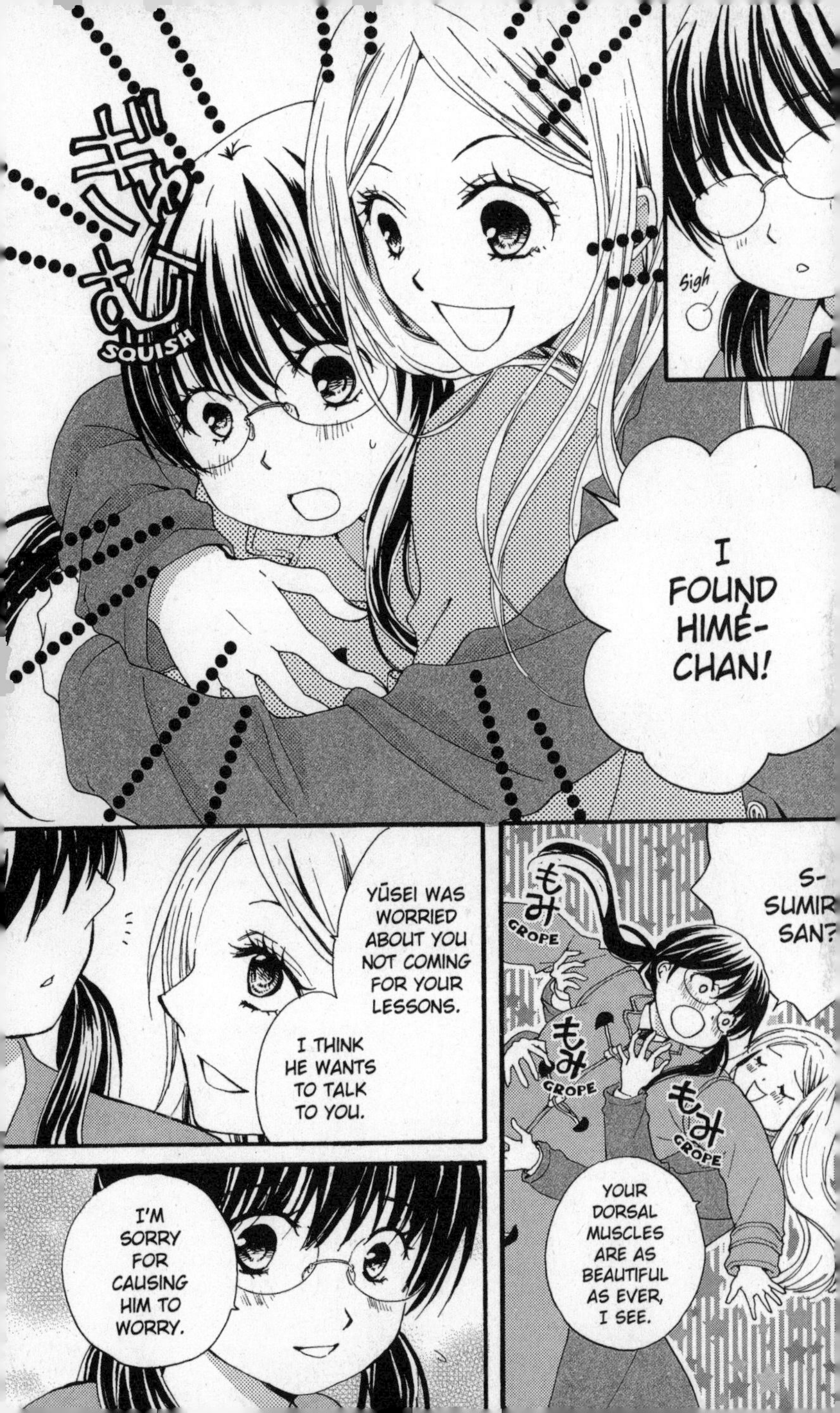
Sigh
SQUISH
I FOUND HIMÉ-CHAN!
S-SUMIR SAN?
もみ GROPE
もみ GROPE
もみ GROPE
YOUR DORSAL MUSCLES ARE AS BEAUTIFUL AS EVER, I SEE.
YŪSEI WAS WORRIED ABOUT YOU NOT COMING FOR YOUR LESSONS.
I THINK HE WANTS TO TALK TO YOU.
I'M SORRY FOR CAUSING HIM TO WORRY.

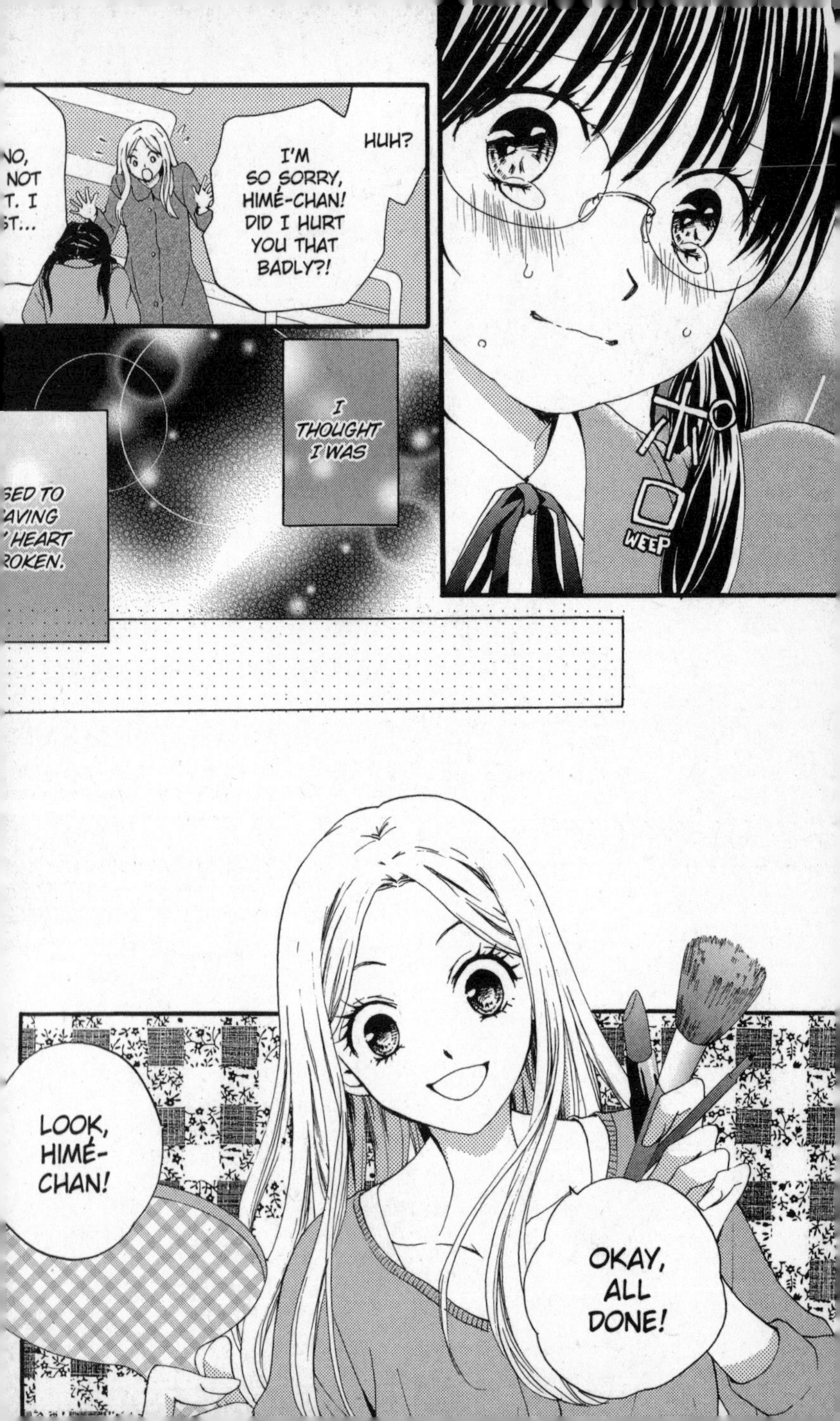
WEEP
HUH?
I'M SO SORRY, HIMÉ-CHAN! DID I HURT YOU THAT BADLY?!
NO, NOT T. I ST...
I THOUGHT I WAS
SED TO AVING HEART ROKEN.
OKAY, ALL DONE!
LOOK, HIMÉ-CHAN!

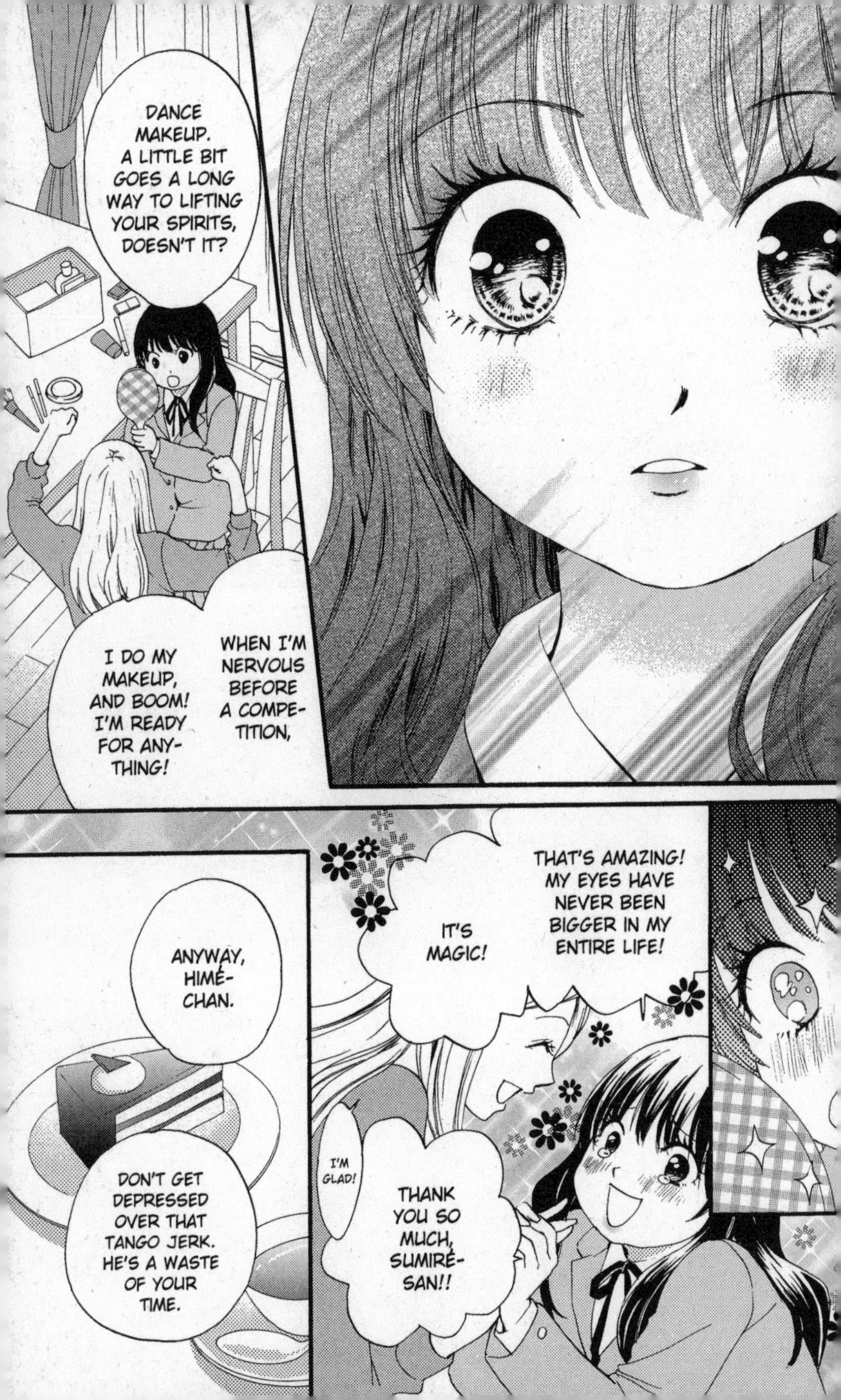
DANCE MAKEUP. A LITTLE BIT GOES A LONG WAY TO LIFTING YOUR SPIRITS, DOESN'T IT?
WHEN I'M NERVOUS BEFORE A COMPETITION,
I DO MY MAKEUP, AND BOOM! I'M READY FOR ANYTHING!
THAT'S AMAZING! MY EYES HAVE NEVER BEEN BIGGER IN MY ENTIRE LIFE!
IT'S MAGIC!
THANK YOU SO MUCH, SUMIRÉ-SAN!!
I'M GLAD!
ANYWAY, HIMÉ-CHAN.
DON'T GET DEPRESSED OVER THAT TANGO JERK. HE'S A WASTE OF YOUR TIME.

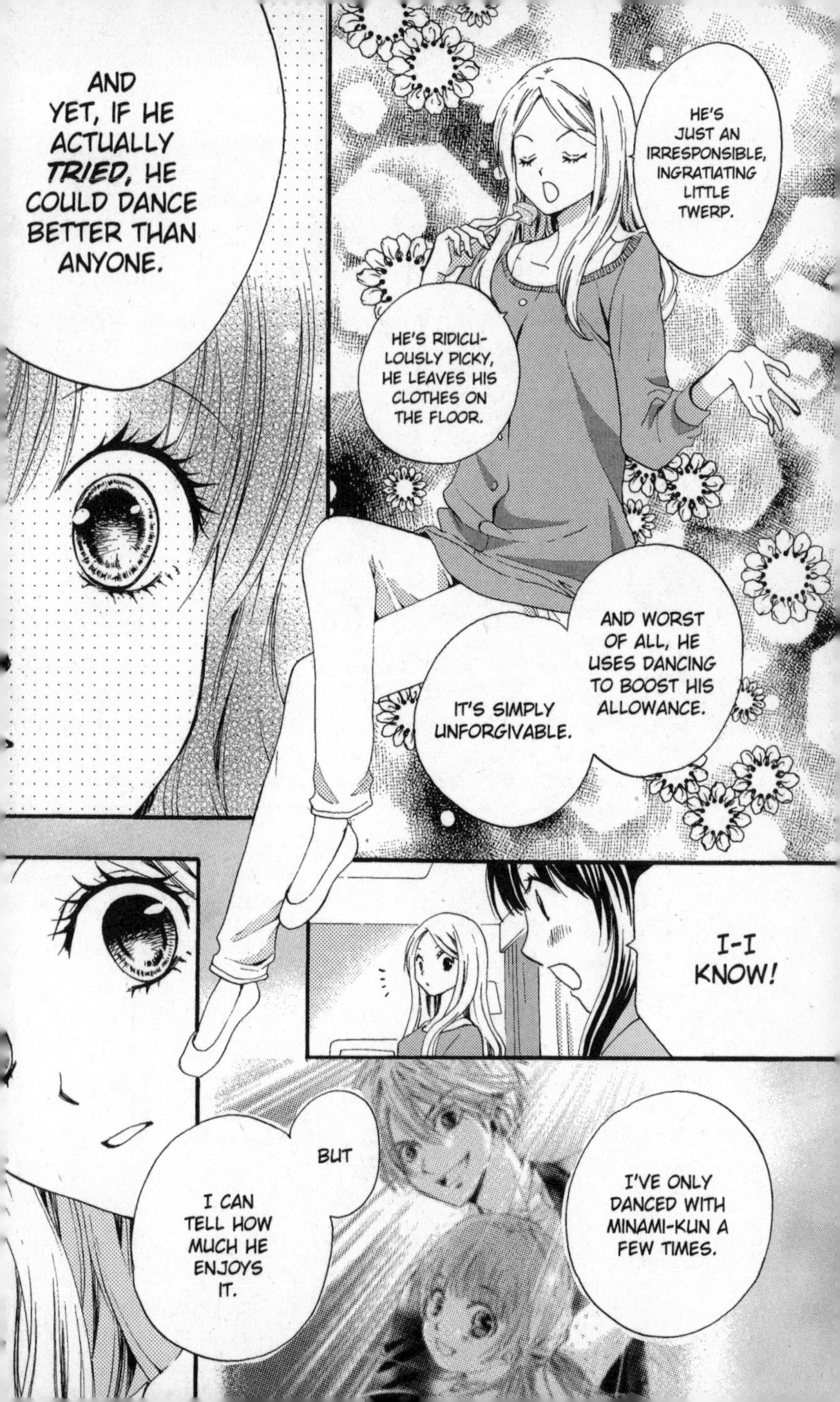
HE'S JUST AN IRRESPONSIBLE, INGRATIATING LITTLE TWERP.
HE'S RIDICULOUSLY PICKY, HE LEAVES HIS CLOTHES ON THE FLOOR.
AND WORST OF ALL, HE USES DANCING TO BOOST HIS ALLOWANCE.
IT'S SIMPLY UNFORGIVABLE.
AND YET, IF HE ACTUALLY *TRIED*, HE COULD DANCE BETTER THAN ANYONE.
I-I KNOW!
I'VE ONLY DANCED WITH MINAMI-KUN A FEW TIMES.
BUT
I CAN TELL HOW MUCH HE ENJOYS IT.

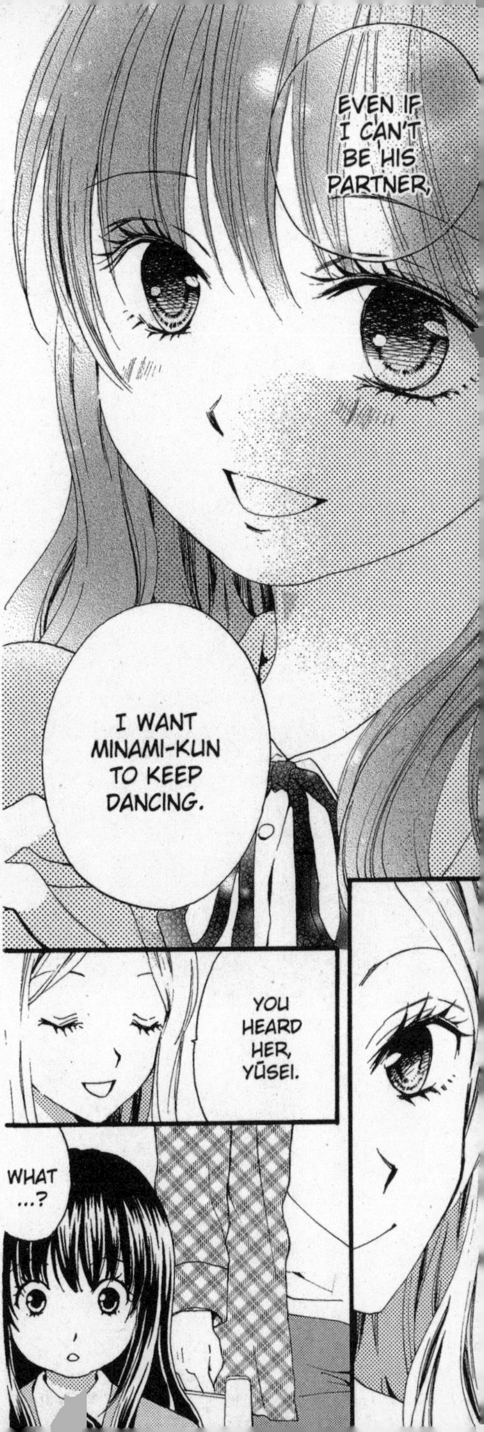
EVEN IF I CAN'T BE HIS PARTNER,
I WANT MINAMI-KUN TO KEEP DANCING.
YOU HEARD HER, YŪSEI.
WHAT ...?

M's Dance Academy
Wakashiro-sensei
Tatsumi-sensei

Special Thanks!!

Nakamura-sama
Miyaji-sama
My Editor-sama
Hirabayashi-sama
Everyone in the Editorial Department
Kawatani Design-sama
And all of my readers.

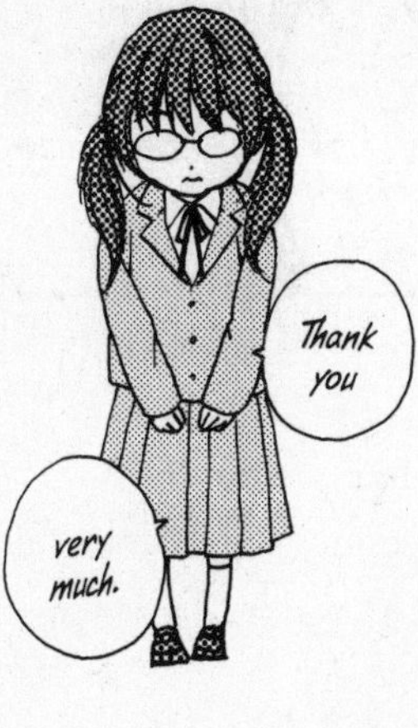
Thank you
very much.

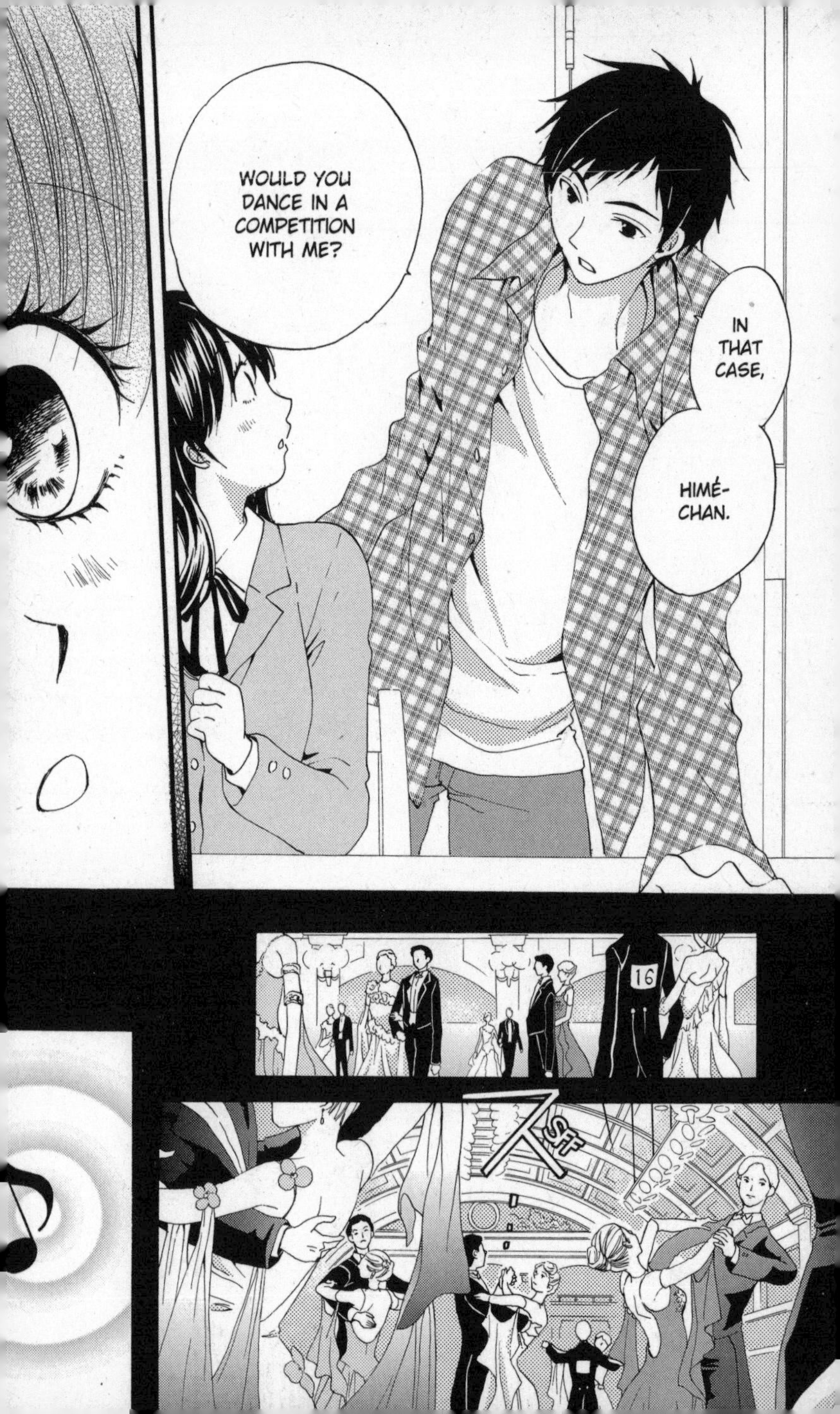
IN THAT CASE,
HIMÉ-CHAN.
WOULD YOU DANCE IN A COMPETITION WITH ME?
16
SFF

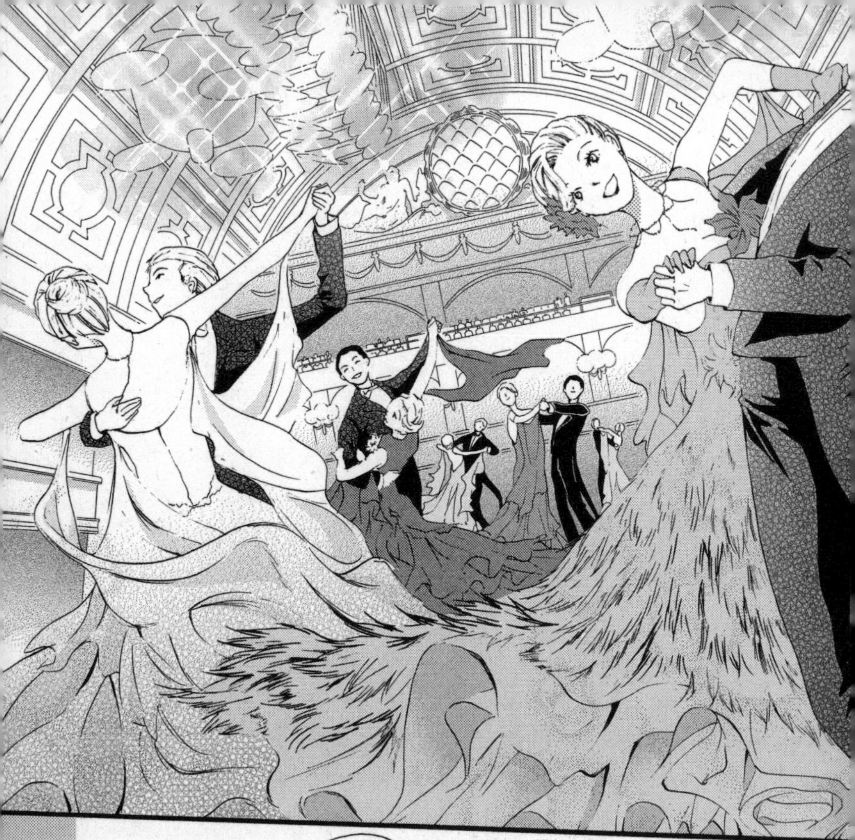

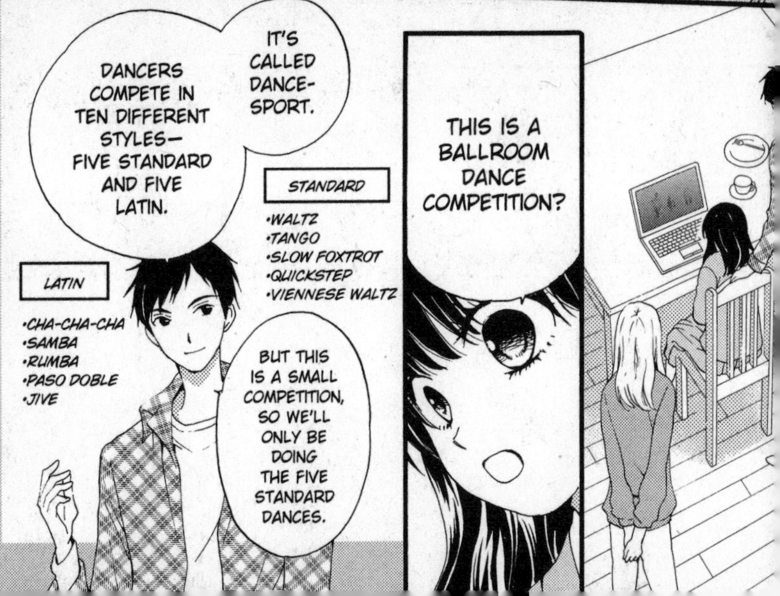
THIS IS A BALLROOM DANCE COMPETITION?
IT'S CALLED DANCE-SPORT.
DANCERS COMPETE IN TEN DIFFERENT STYLES— FIVE STANDARD AND FIVE LATIN.
STANDARD
•WALTZ
•TANGO
•SLOW FOXTROT
•QUICKSTEP
•VIENNESE WALTZ
LATIN
•CHA-CHA-CHA
•SAMBA
•RUMBA
•PASO DOBLE
•JIVE
BUT THIS IS A SMALL COMPETITION, SO WE'LL ONLY BE DOING THE FIVE STANDARD DANCES.

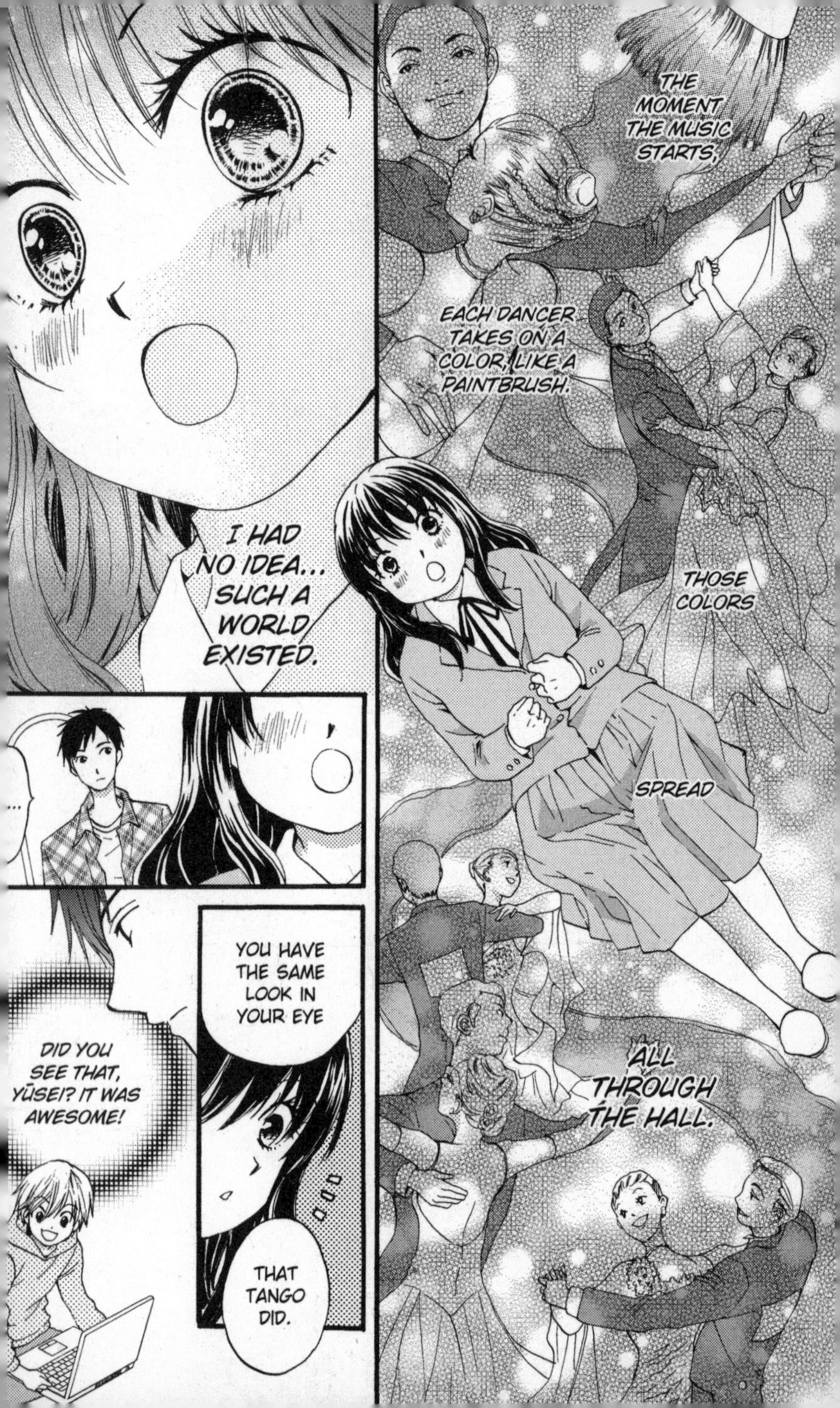
THE MOMENT THE MUSIC STARTS,
EACH DANCER TAKES ON A COLOR, LIKE A PAINTBRUSH.
THOSE COLORS
SPREAD
ALL THROUGH THE HALL.
I HAD NO IDEA... SUCH A WORLD EXISTED.
...
YOU HAVE THE SAME LOOK IN YOUR EYE
THAT TANGO DID.
DID YOU SEE THAT, YŪSEI? IT WAS AWESOME!

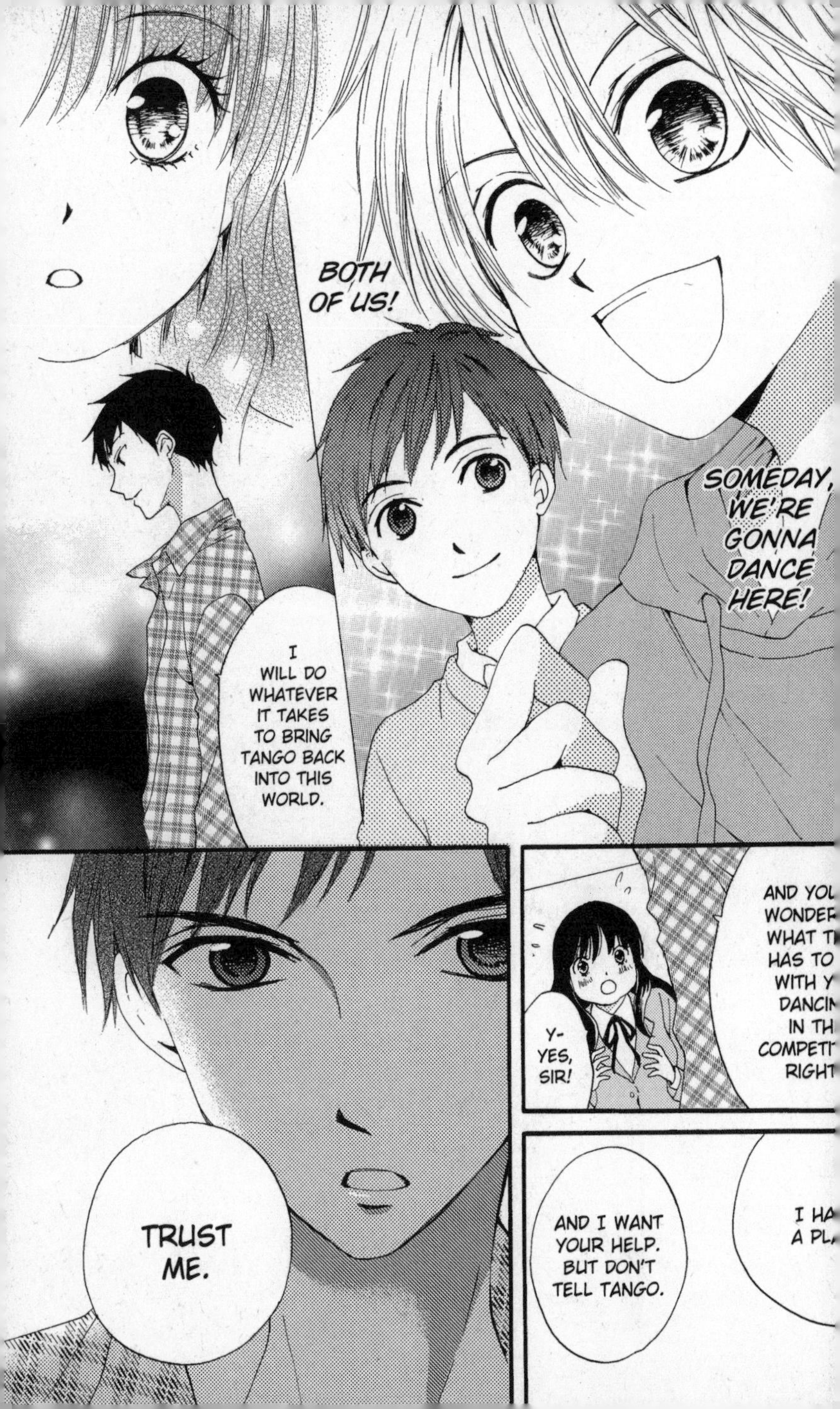
SOMEDAY, WE'RE GONNA DANCE HERE!
BOTH OF US!
I WILL DO WHATEVER IT TAKES TO BRING TANGO BACK INTO THIS WORLD.
AND YOU WONDER WHAT TH HAS TO WITH Y DANCIN IN TH COMPETI RIGHT
Y-YES, SIR!
I HA A PL
AND I WANT YOUR HELP. BUT DON'T TELL TANGO.
TRUST ME.

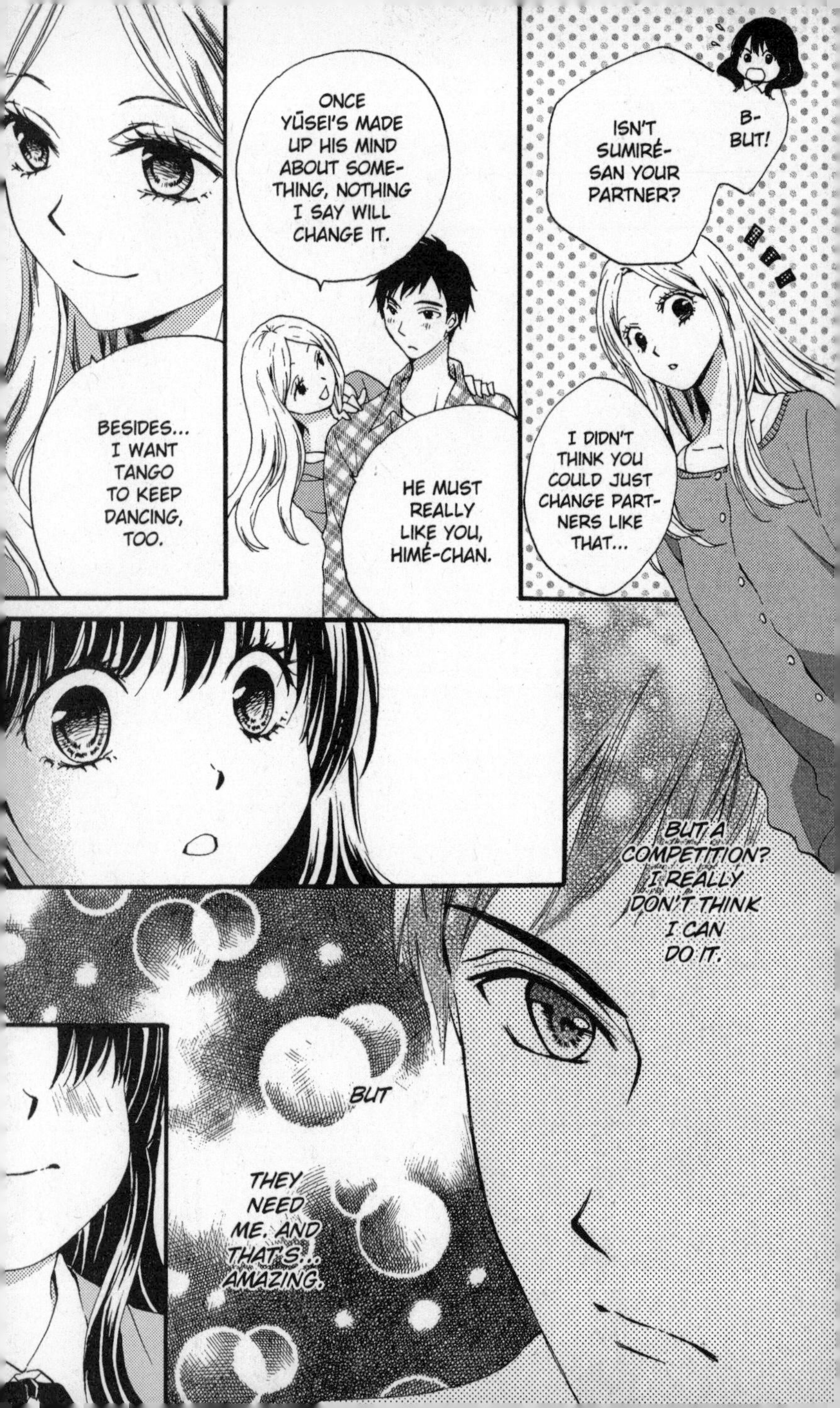
B-BUT!
ISN'T SUMIRÉ-SAN YOUR PARTNER?
I DIDN'T THINK YOU COULD JUST CHANGE PARTNERS LIKE THAT...
ONCE YŪSEI'S MADE UP HIS MIND ABOUT SOMETHING, NOTHING I SAY WILL CHANGE IT.
HE MUST REALLY LIKE YOU, HIMÉ-CHAN.
BESIDES... I WANT TANGO TO KEEP DANCING, TOO.
BUT A COMPETITION? I REALLY DON'T THINK I CAN DO IT.
BUT
THEY NEED ME. AND THAT'S... AMAZING.

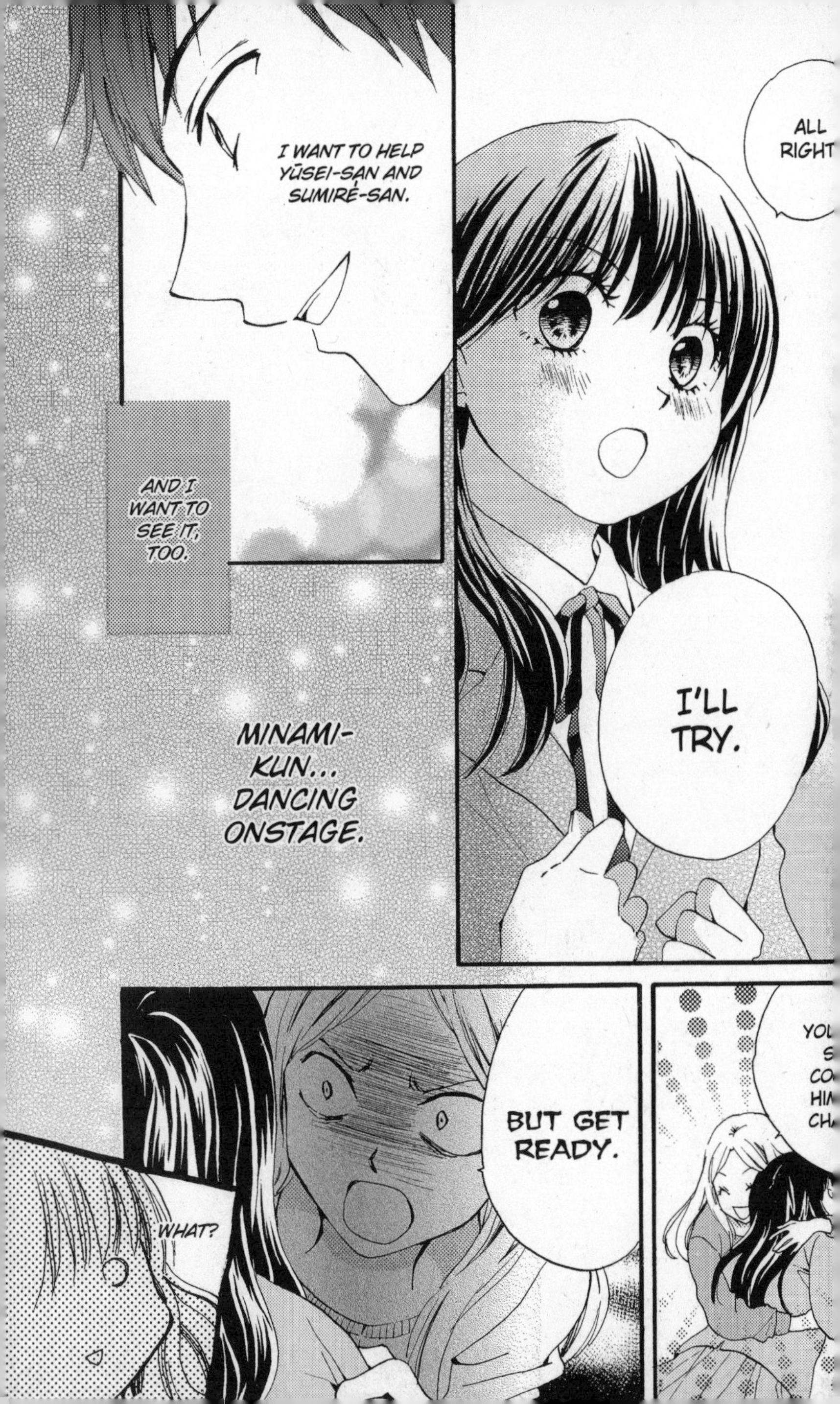
ALL RIGHT
I WANT TO HELP YŪSEI-SAN AND SUMIRÉ-SAN.
I'LL TRY.
AND I WANT TO SEE IT, TOO.
MINAMI-KUN... DANCING ONSTAGE.
BUT GET READY.
WHAT?

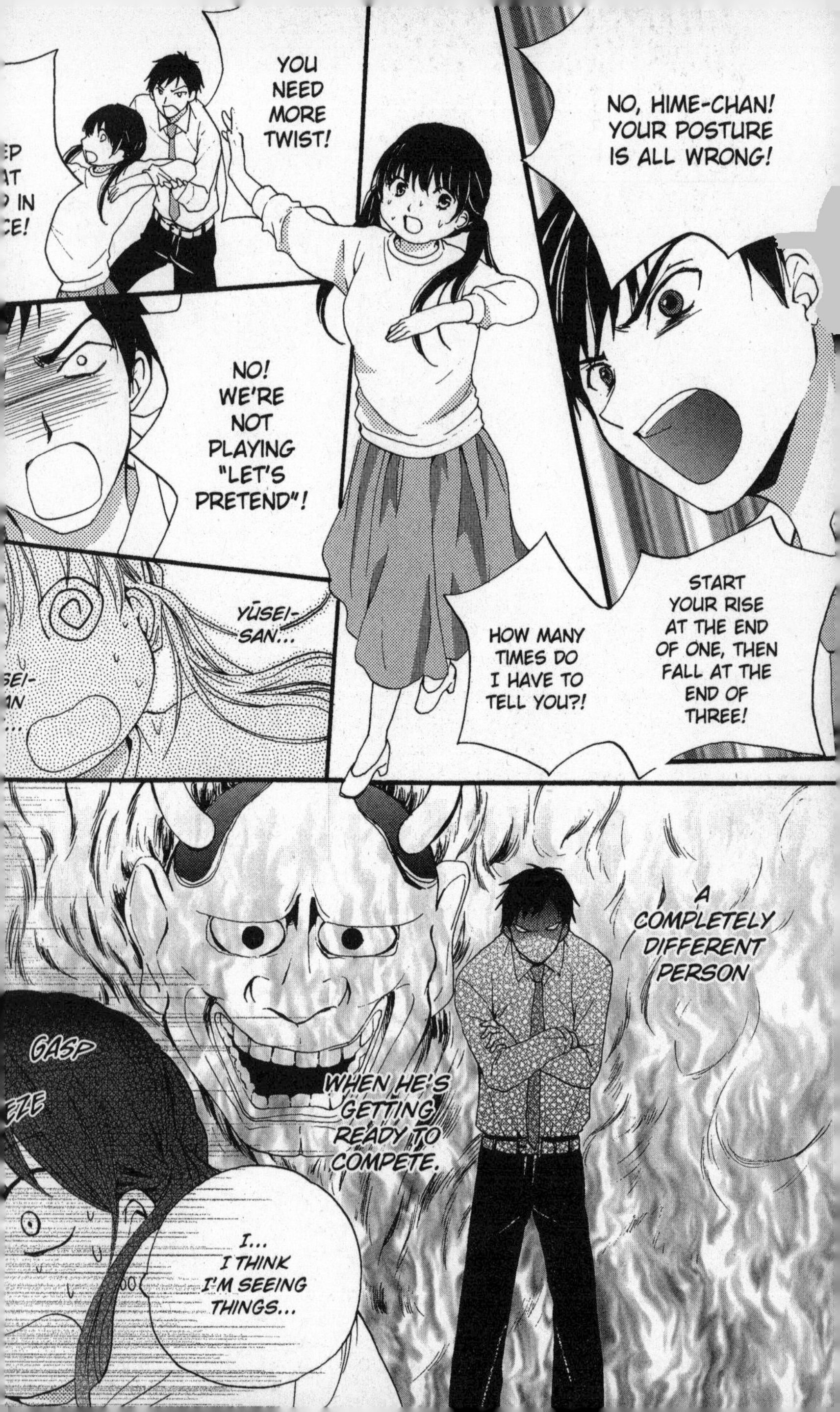
NO, HIME-CHAN! YOUR POSTURE IS ALL WRONG!
START YOUR RISE AT THE END OF ONE, THEN FALL AT THE END OF THREE!
HOW MANY TIMES DO I HAVE TO TELL YOU?!
YOU NEED MORE TWIST!
NO! WE'RE NOT PLAYING "LET'S PRETEND"!
YŪSEI-SAN...
A COMPLETELY DIFFERENT PERSON
WHEN HE'S GETTING READY TO COMPETE.
GASP
I... I THINK I'M SEEING THINGS...

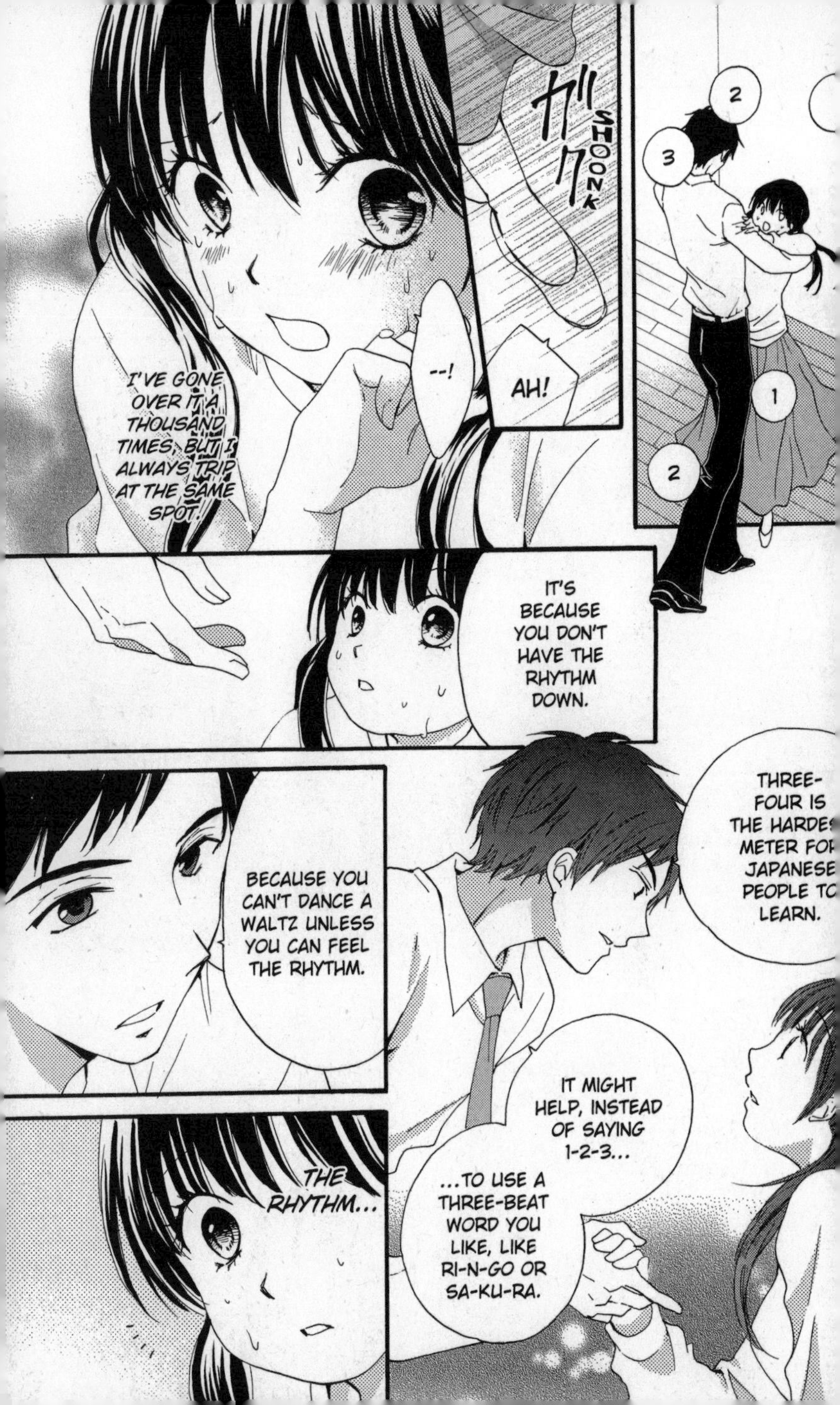
2
3
1
2
SHOONK
AH!
--!
I'VE GONE OVER IT A THOUSAND TIMES, BUT I ALWAYS TRIP AT THE SAME SPOT.
IT'S BECAUSE YOU DON'T HAVE THE RHYTHM DOWN.
THREE-FOUR IS THE HARDES METER FOR JAPANESE PEOPLE TO LEARN.
IT MIGHT HELP, INSTEAD OF SAYING 1-2-3...
...TO USE A THREE-BEAT WORD YOU LIKE, LIKE RI-N-GO OR SA-KU-RA.
BECAUSE YOU CAN'T DANCE A WALTZ UNLESS YOU CAN FEEL THE RHYTHM.
THE RHYTHM...

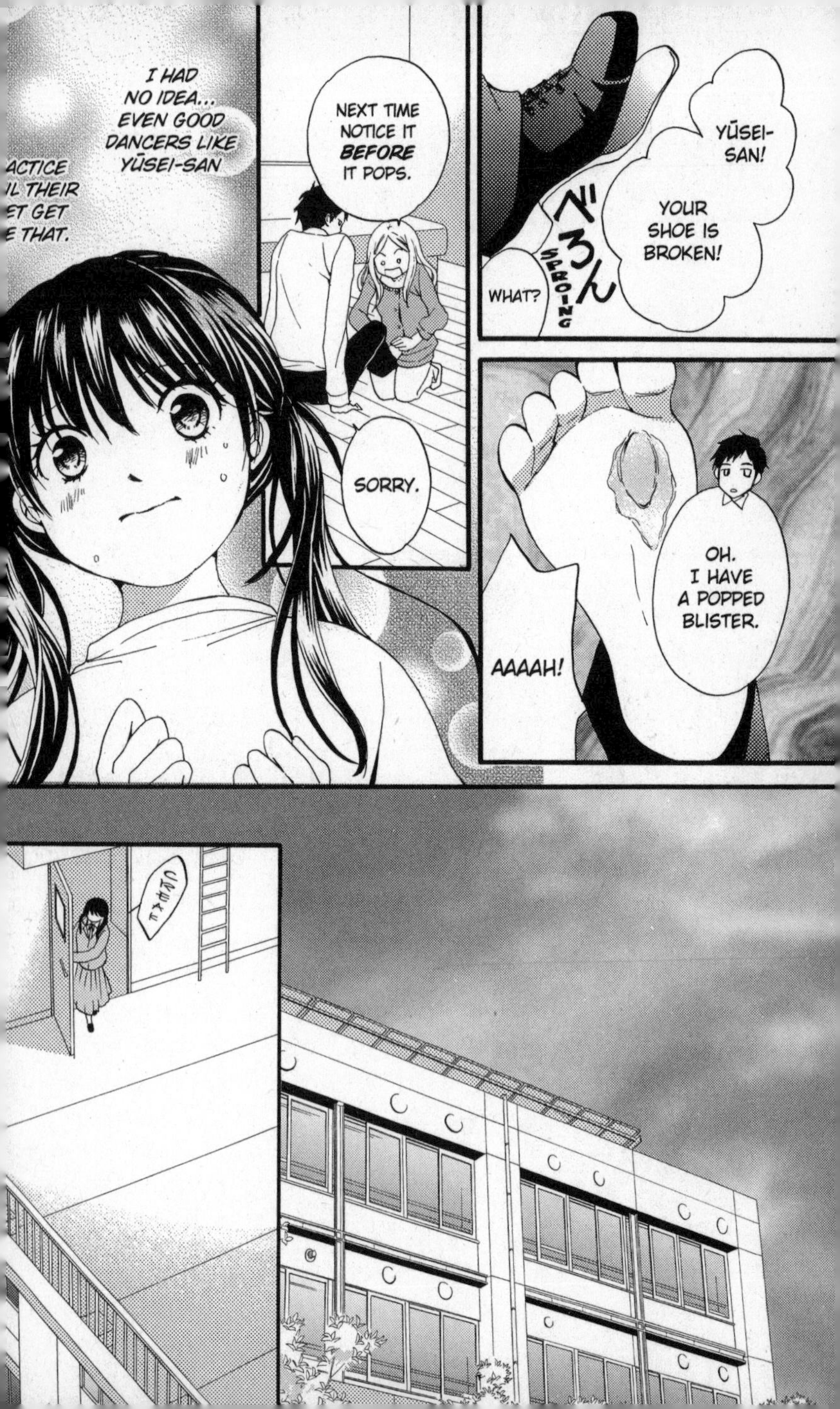
YŪSEI-SAN!
YOUR SHOE IS BROKEN!
べろん
SPROING
WHAT?
OH. I HAVE A POPPED BLISTER.
AAAAH!
NEXT TIME NOTICE IT *BEFORE* IT POPS.
SORRY.
I HAD NO IDEA... EVEN GOOD DANCERS LIKE YŪSEI-SAN
ACTICE IL THEIR ET GET E THAT.
CREAK

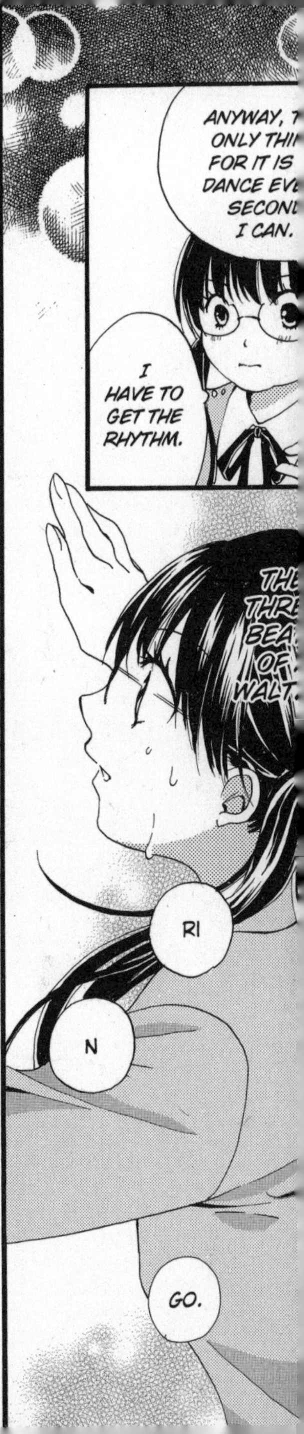
ANYWAY, T
ONLY THI
FOR IT IS
DANCE EV
SECON
I CAN.
I HAVE TO GET THE RHYTHM.
THE
THRE
BEA
OF
WALT
RI
N
GO.
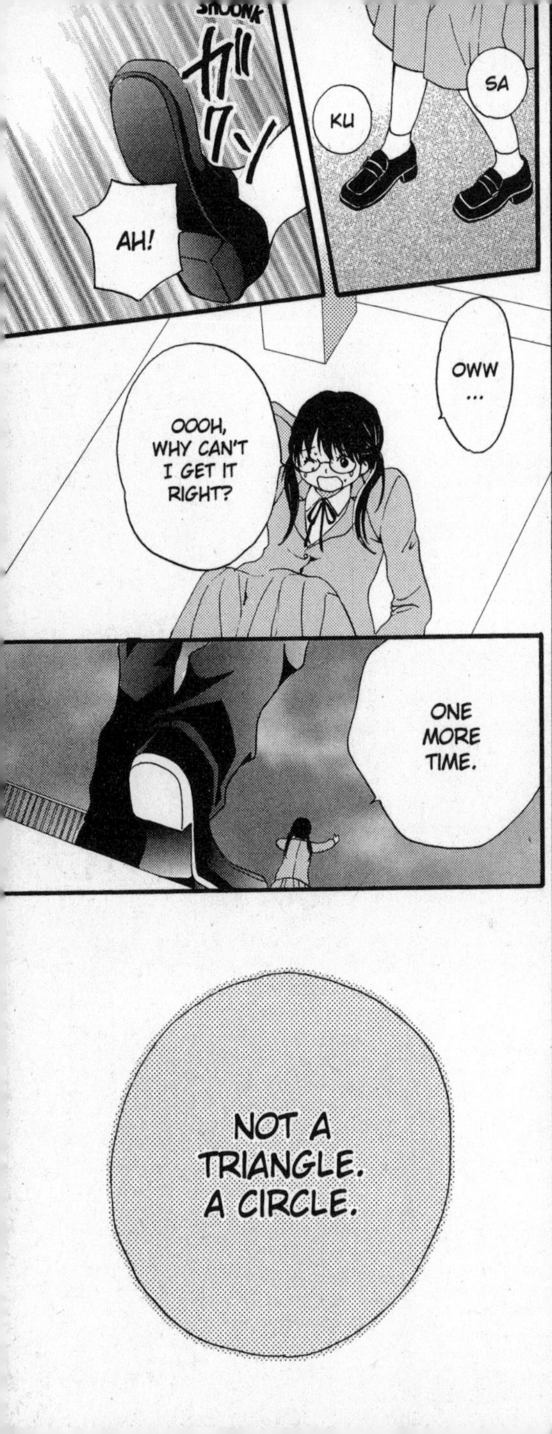
SA
KU
ガクン
AH!
OWW...
OOOH, WHY CAN'T I GET IT RIGHT?
ONE MORE TIME.
NOT A TRIANGLE. A CIRCLE.

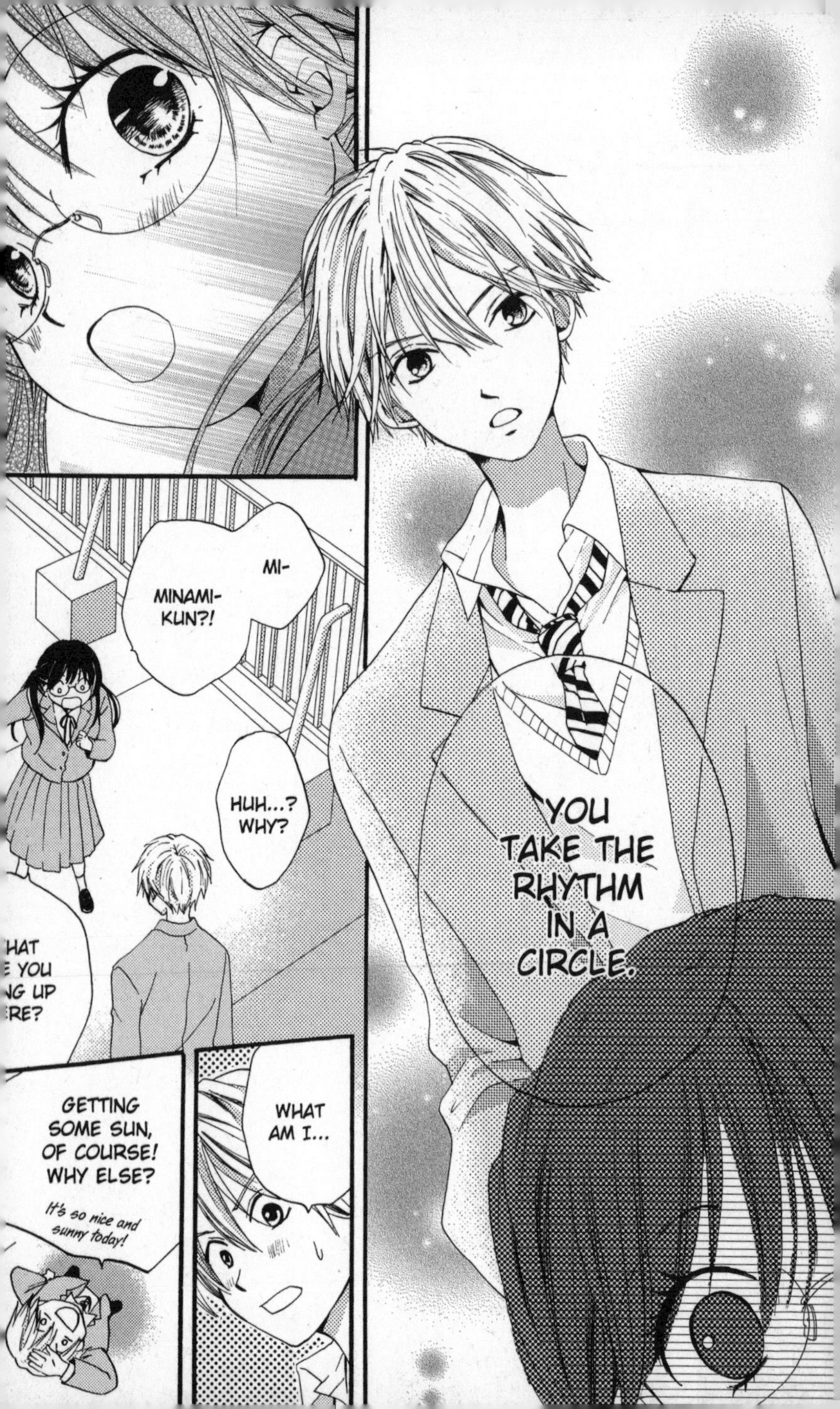
YOU TAKE THE RHYTHM IN A CIRCLE.
MI- MINAMI-KUN?!
HUH...? WHY?
HAT E YOU NG UP ERE?
WHAT AM I...
GETTING SOME SUN, OF COURSE! WHY ELSE?
It's so nice and sunny today!

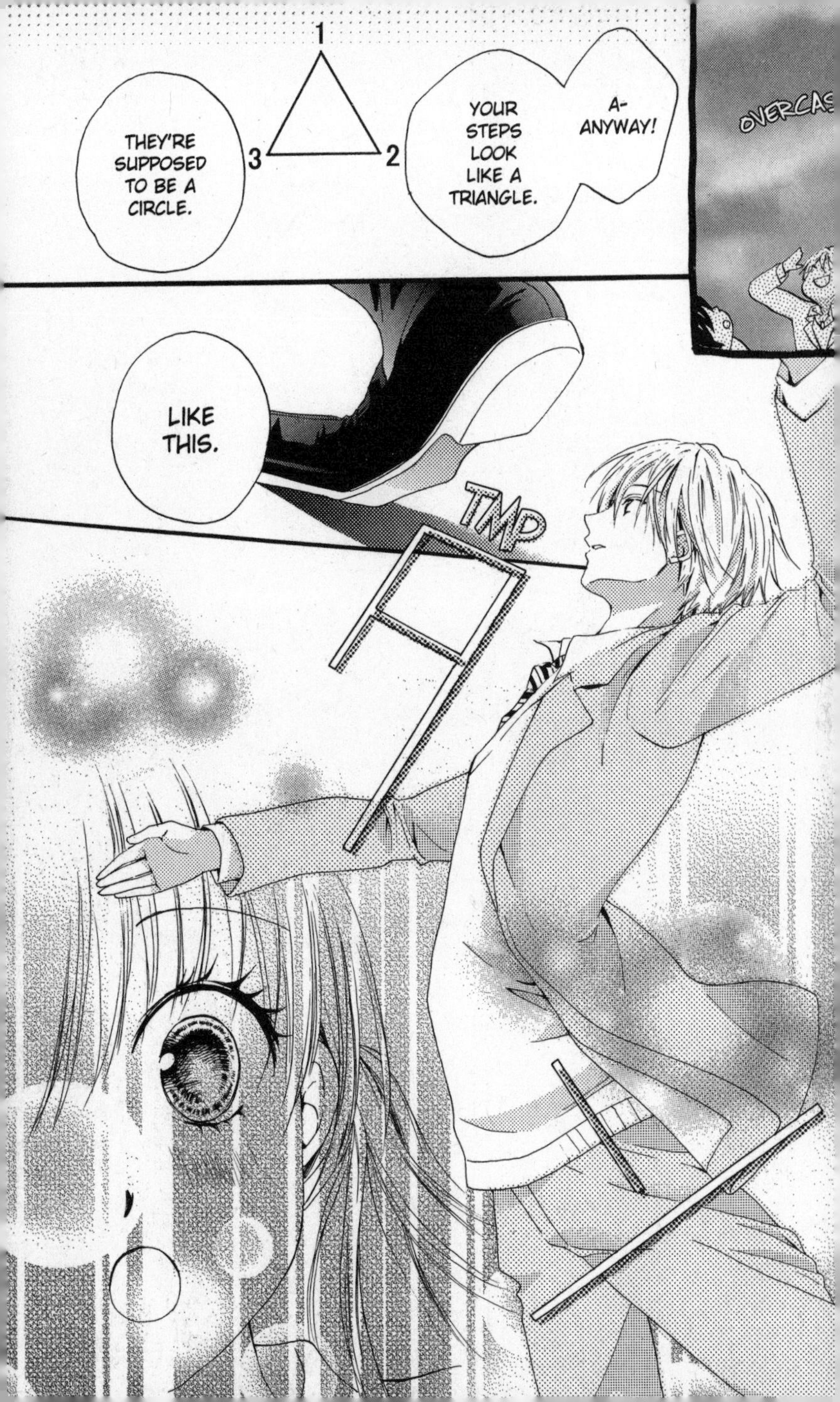

OVERCAS
A- ANYWAY!
YOUR STEPS LOOK LIKE A TRIANGLE.
1
2
3
THEY'RE SUPPOSED TO BE A CIRCLE.
LIKE THIS.
TMP

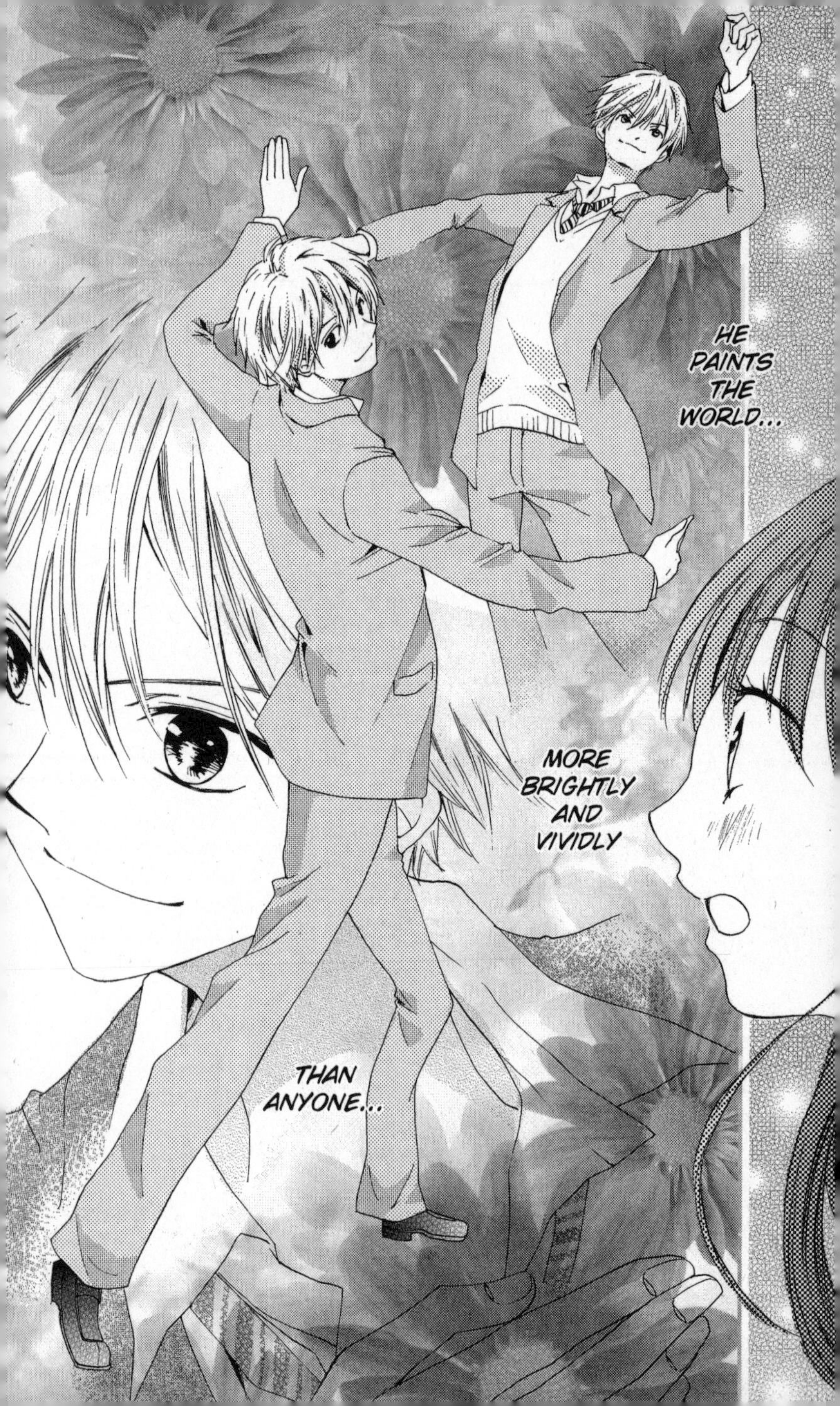
HE PAINTS THE WORLD...
MORE BRIGHTLY AND VIVIDLY
THAN ANYONE...

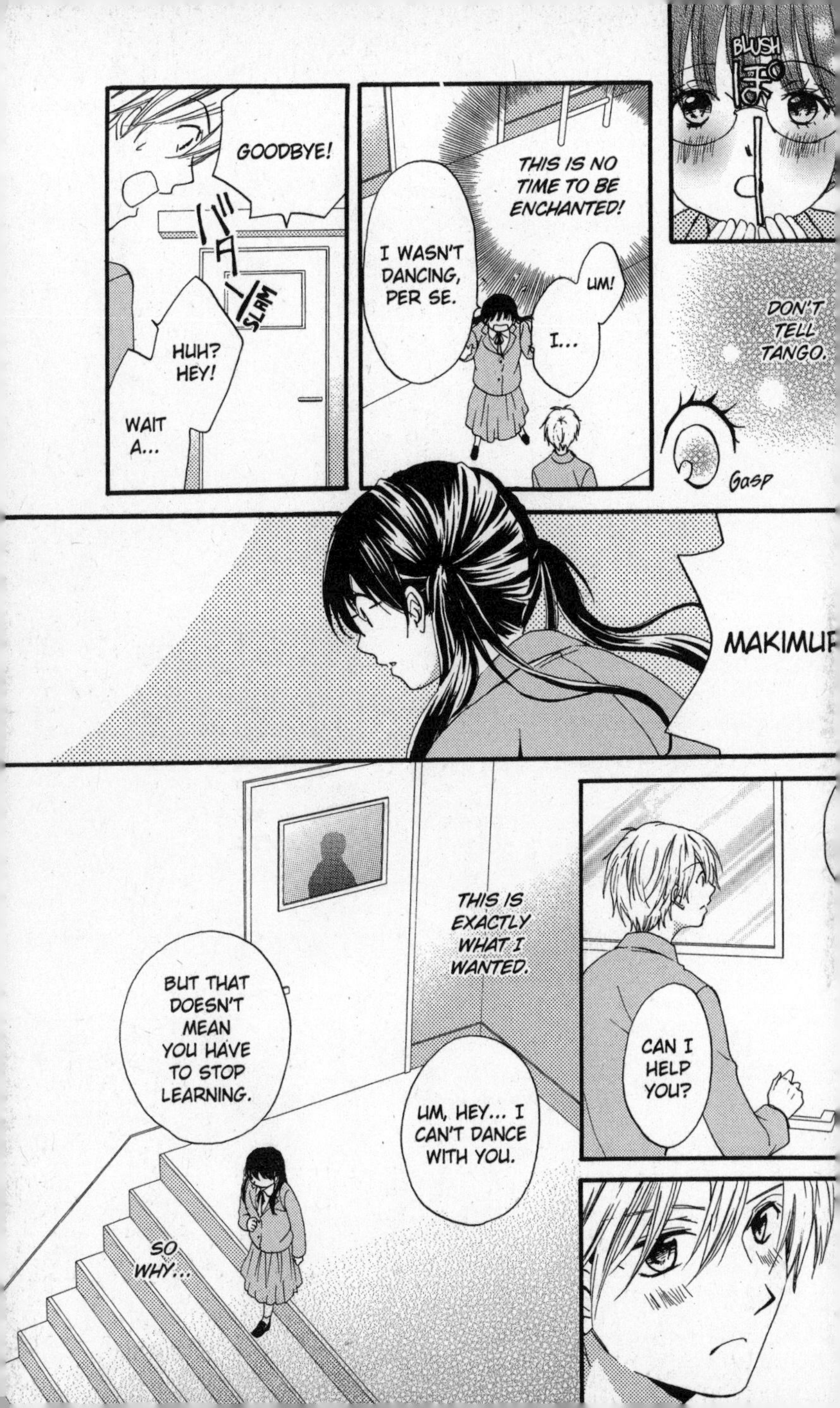
BLUSH
DON'T TELL TANGO.
Gasp
THIS IS NO TIME TO BE ENCHANTED!
UM!
I...
I WASN'T DANCING, PER SE.
GOODBYE!
SLAM
HUH? HEY!
WAIT A...
MAKIMUR
CAN I HELP YOU?
THIS IS EXACTLY WHAT I WANTED.
UM, HEY... I CAN'T DANCE WITH YOU.
BUT THAT DOESN'T MEAN YOU HAVE TO STOP LEARNING.
SO WHY...

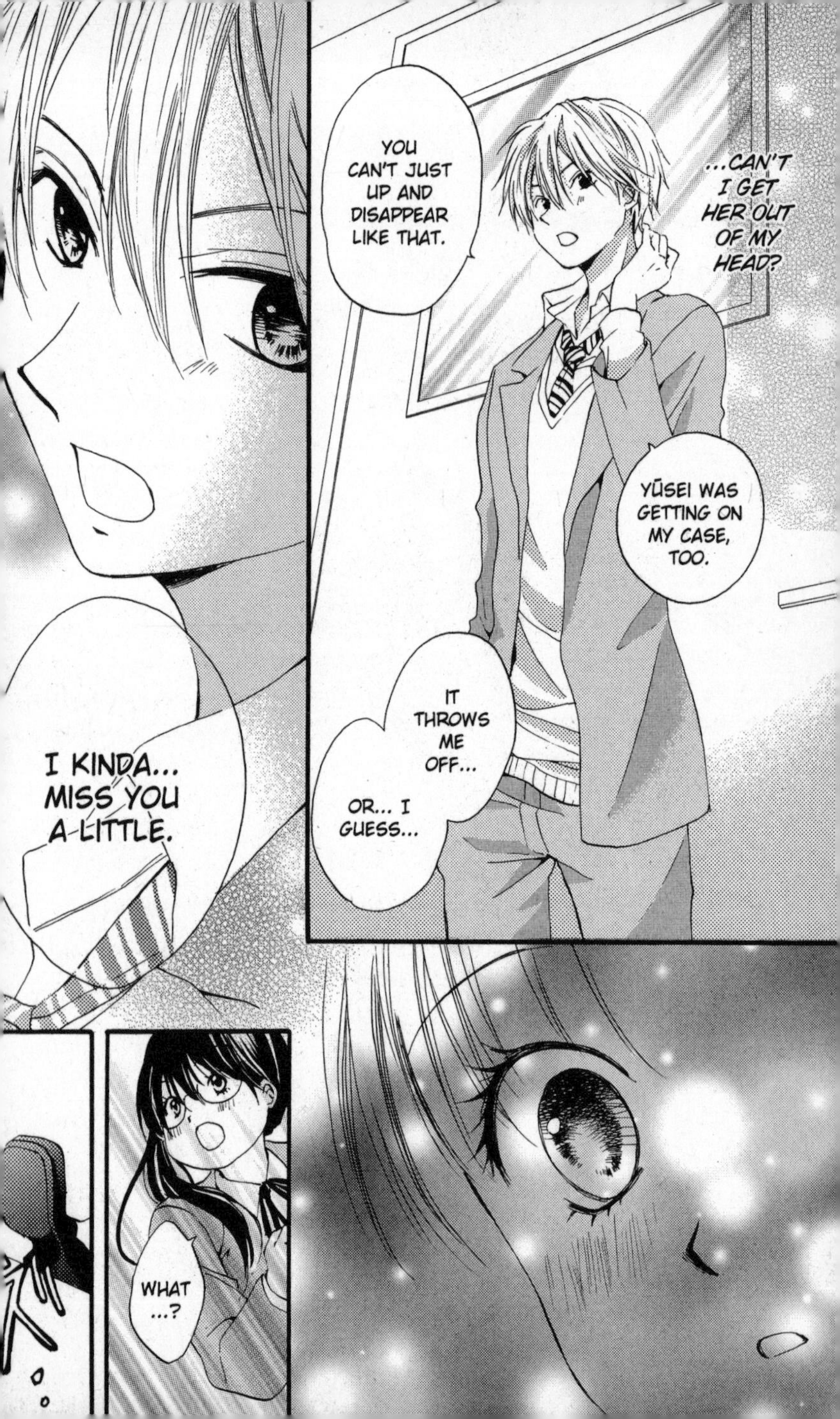
...CAN'T I GET HER OUT OF MY HEAD?
YOU CAN'T JUST UP AND DISAPPEAR LIKE THAT.
YŪSEI WAS GETTING ON MY CASE, TOO.
IT THROWS ME OFF...
OR... I GUESS...
I KINDA... MISS YOU A LITTLE.
WHAT ...?

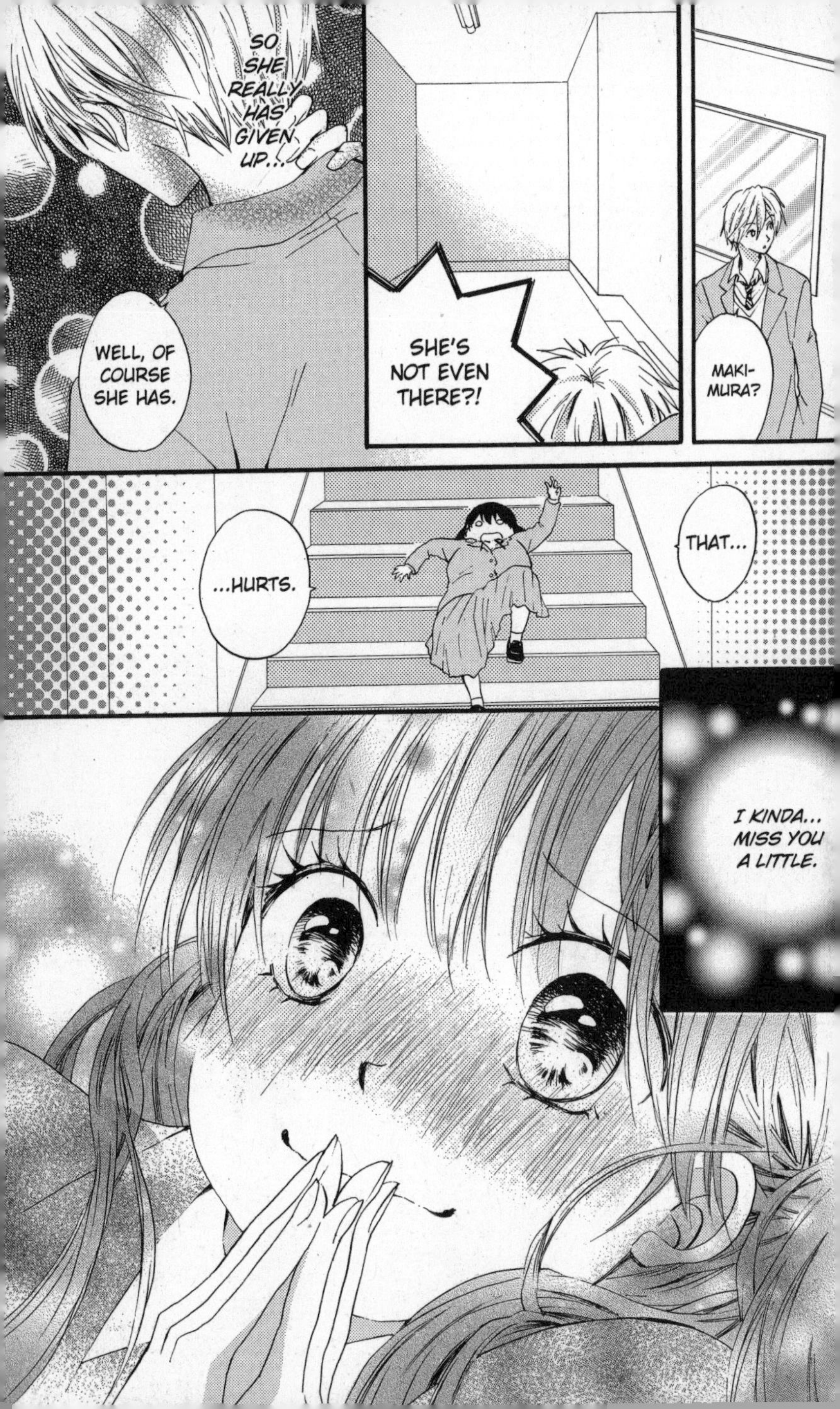
MAKI-MURA?
SHE'S NOT EVEN THERE?!
SO SHE REALLY HAS GIVEN UP...
WELL, OF COURSE SHE HAS.
THAT...
...HURTS.
I KINDA... MISS YOU A LITTLE.

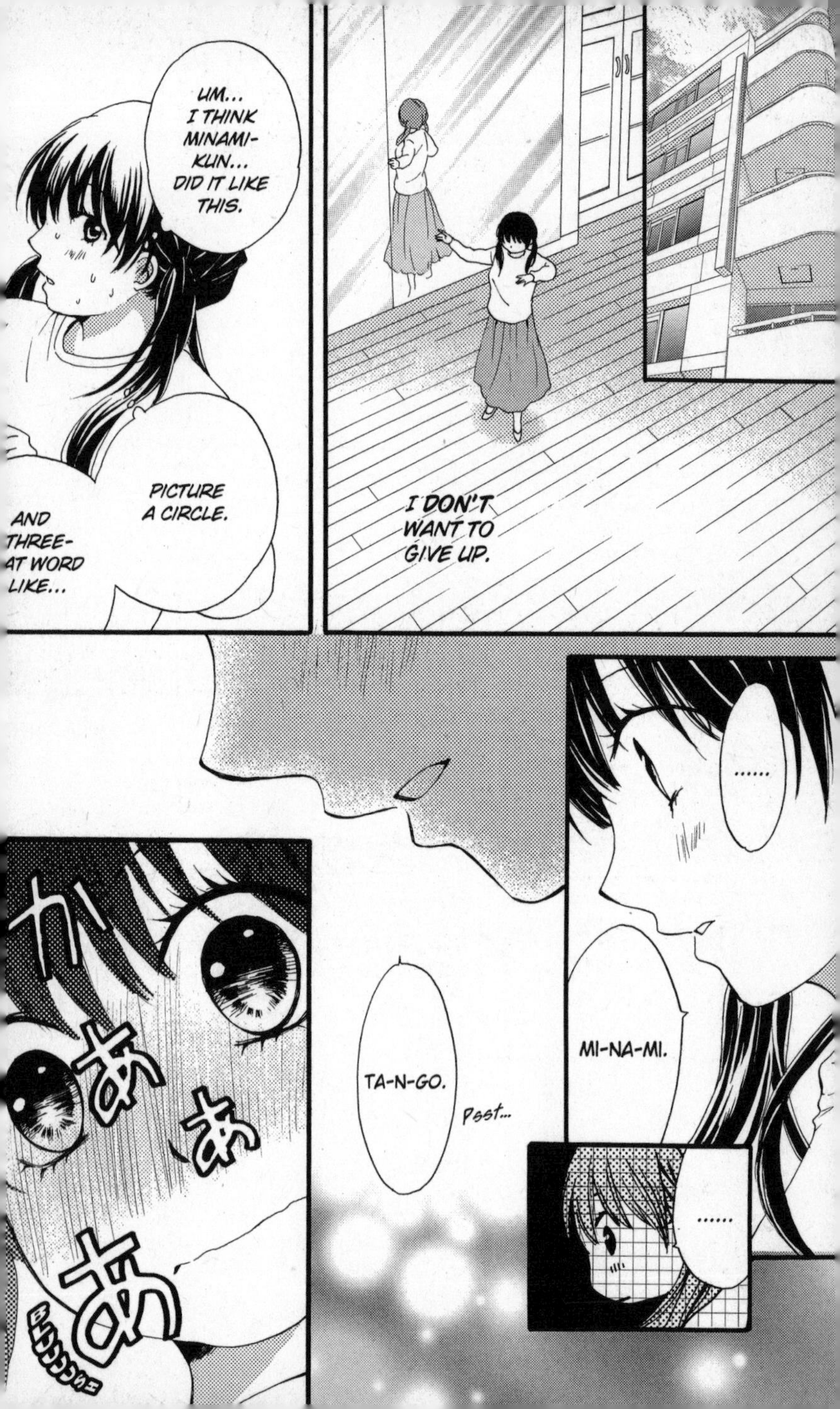

I DON'T WANT TO GIVE UP.
UM... I THINK MINAMI-KUN... DID IT LIKE THIS.
PICTURE A CIRCLE.
AND THREE-
AT WORD LIKE...
......
MI-NA-MI.
......
TA-N-GO.
Psst...
かあああ

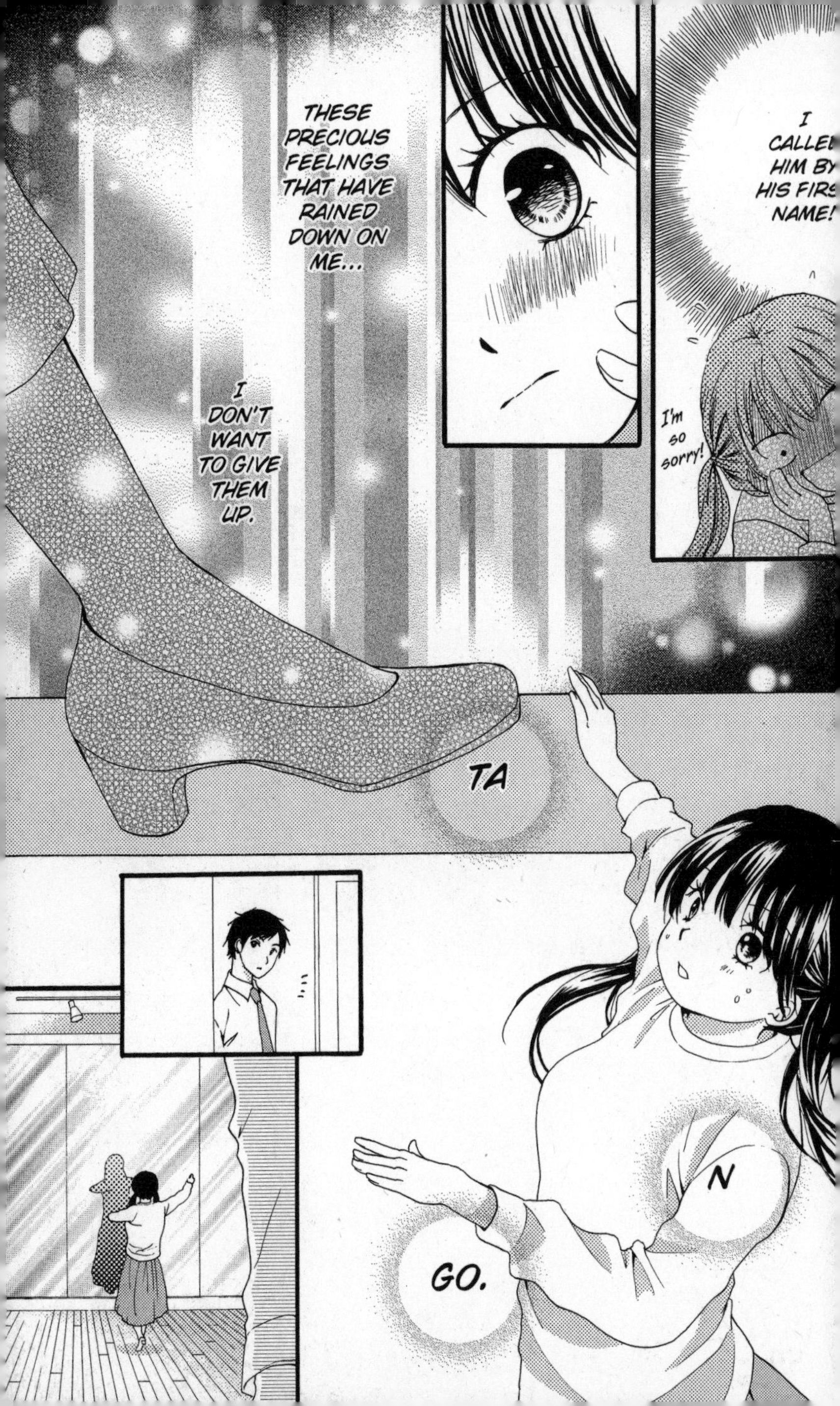
I CALLEI HIM BY HIS FIRS NAME!
I'm so sorry!
THESE PRECIOUS FEELINGS THAT HAVE RAINED DOWN ON ME...
I DON'T WANT TO GIVE THEM UP.
TA
N
GO.

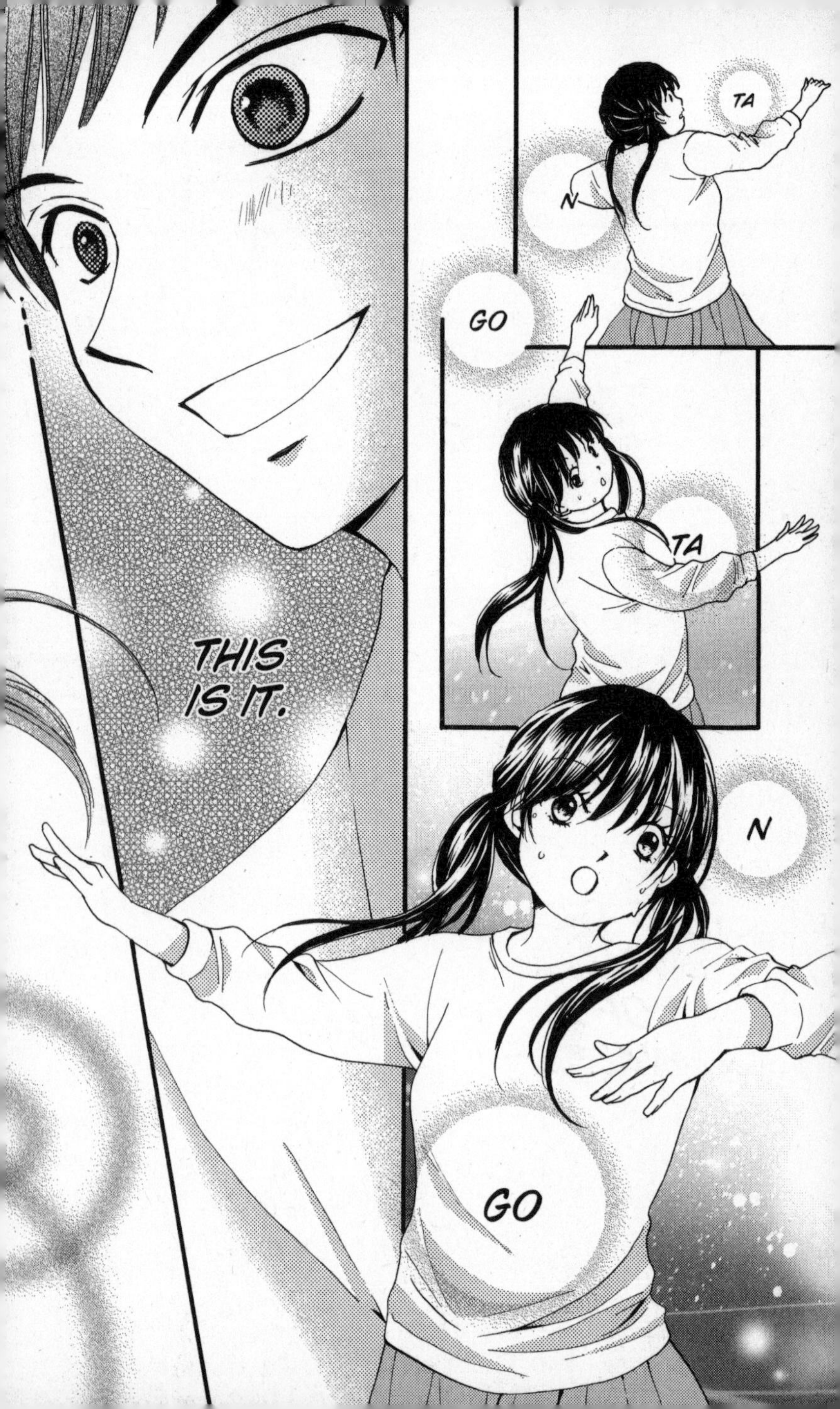
TA
N
GO
TA
N
GO
THIS IS IT.

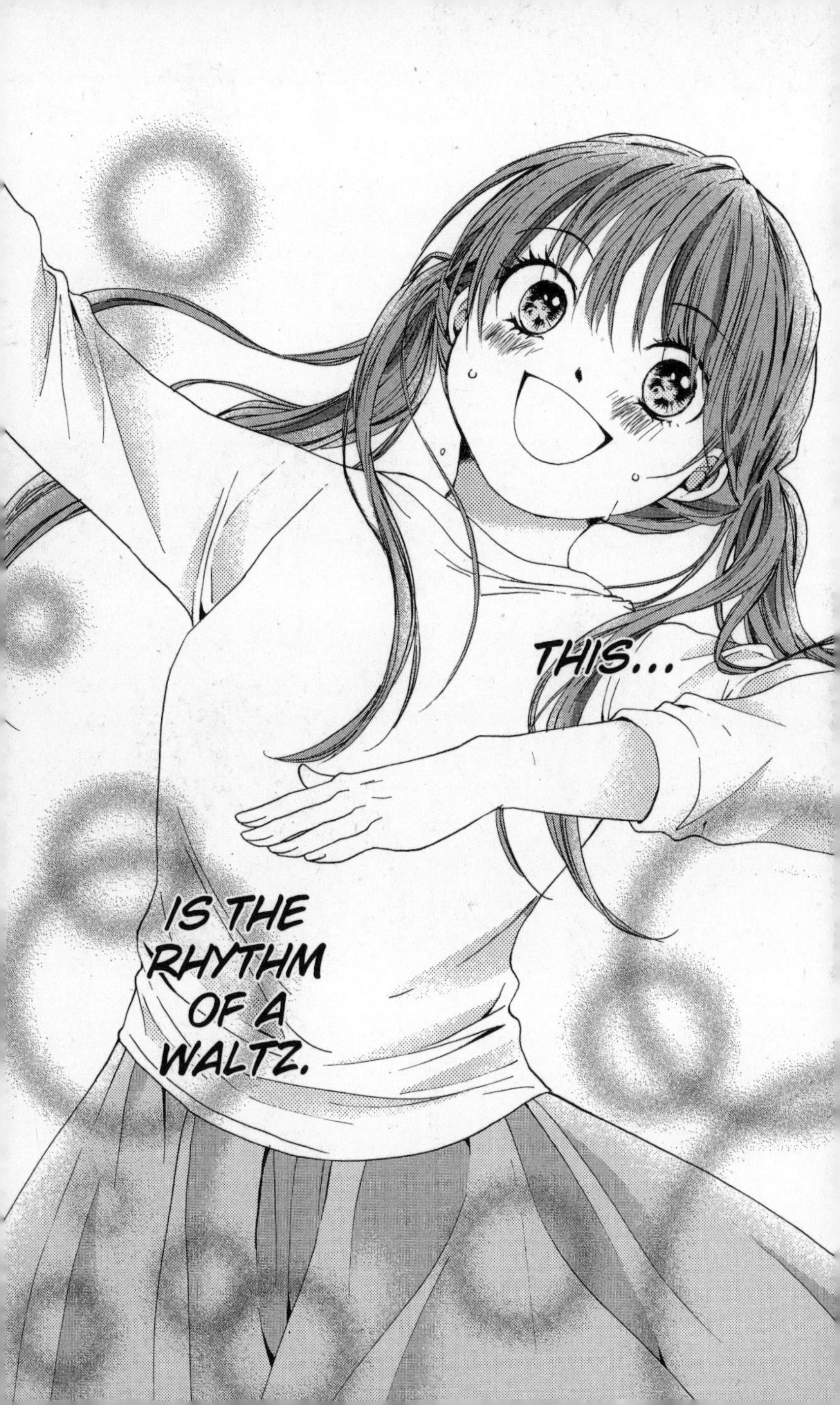
THIS...
IS THE RHYTHM OF A WALTZ.

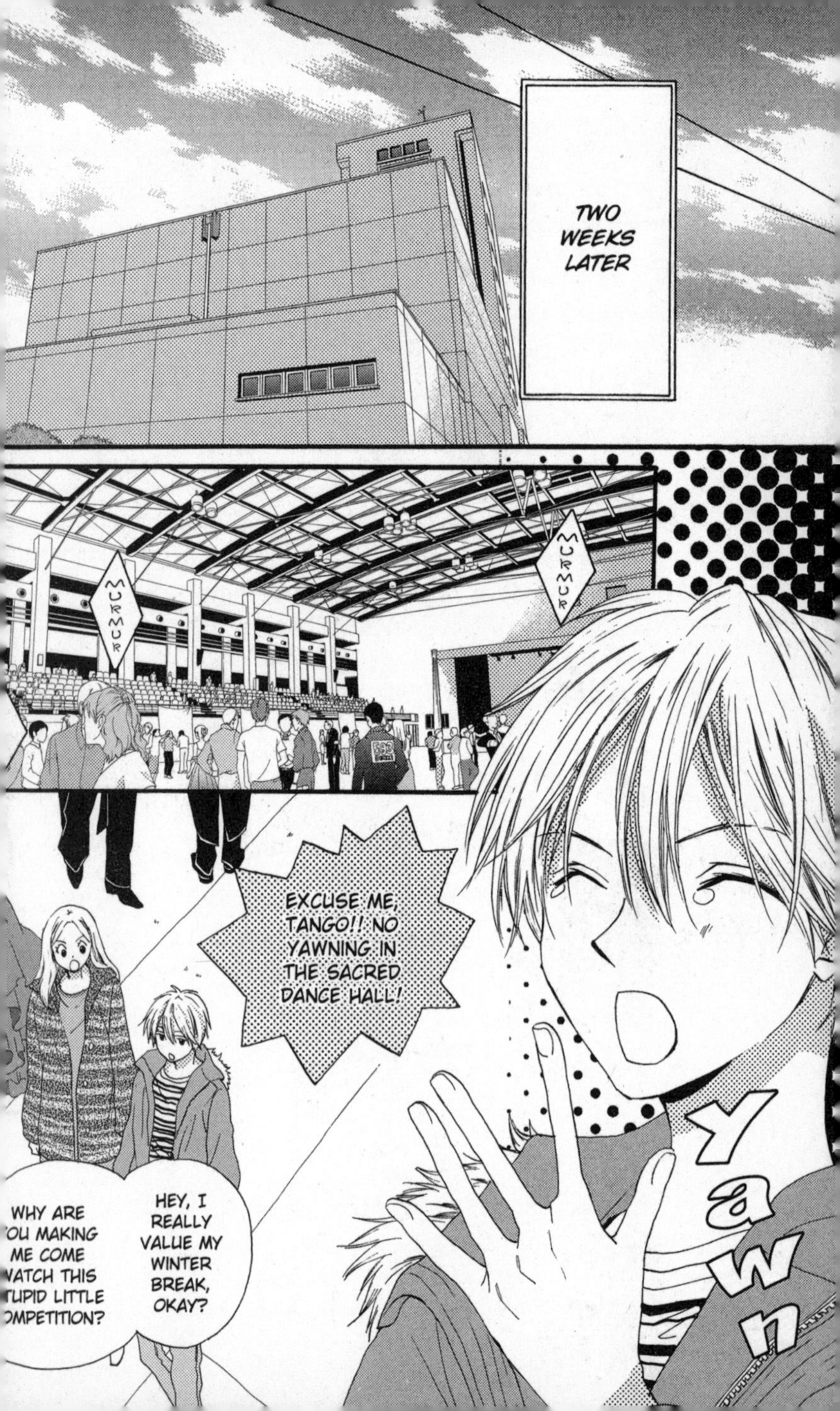
TWO WEEKS LATER
MURMUR
MURMUR
EXCUSE ME, TANGO!! NO YAWNING IN THE SACRED DANCE HALL!
YAWN
HEY, I REALLY VALUE MY WINTER BREAK, OKAY?
WHY ARE YOU MAKING ME COME WATCH THIS STUPID LITTLE COMPETITION?

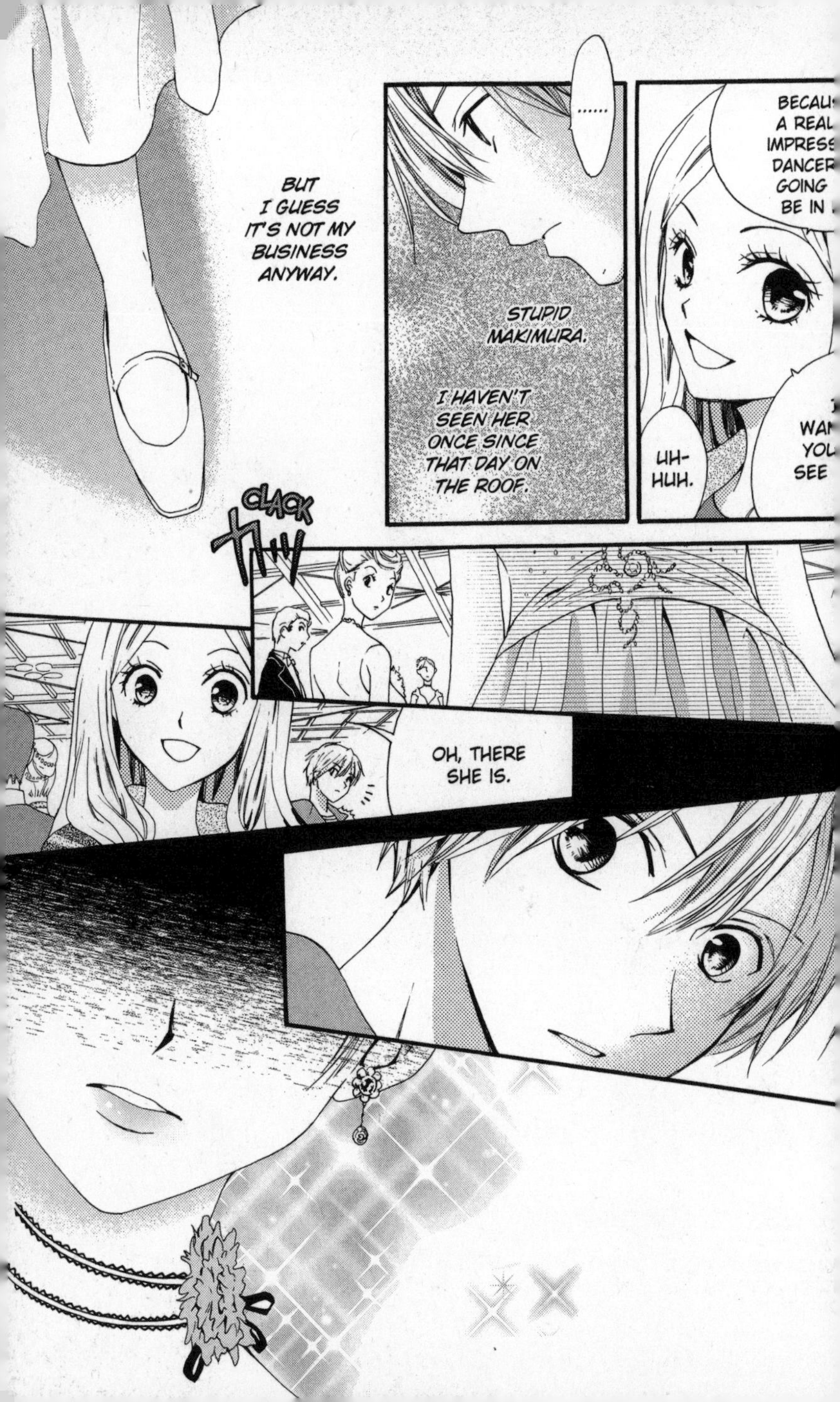
BECAU A REAL IMPRESS DANCER GOING BE IN
UH-HUH.
WAN YOU SEE
......
STUPID MAKIMURA.
I HAVEN'T SEEN HER ONCE SINCE THAT DAY ON THE ROOF.
BUT I GUESS IT'S NOT MY BUSINESS ANYWAY.
CLACK
OH, THERE SHE IS.

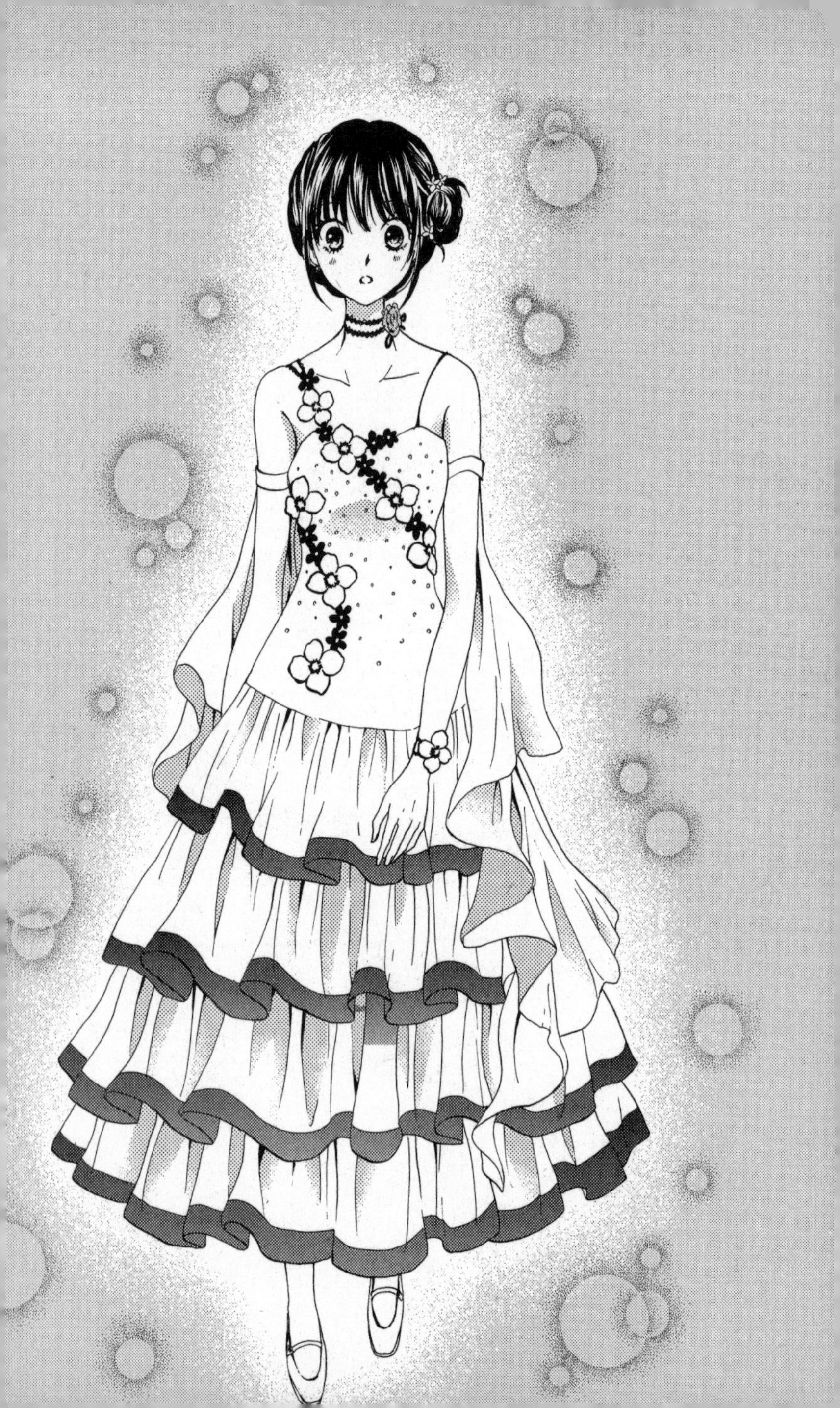

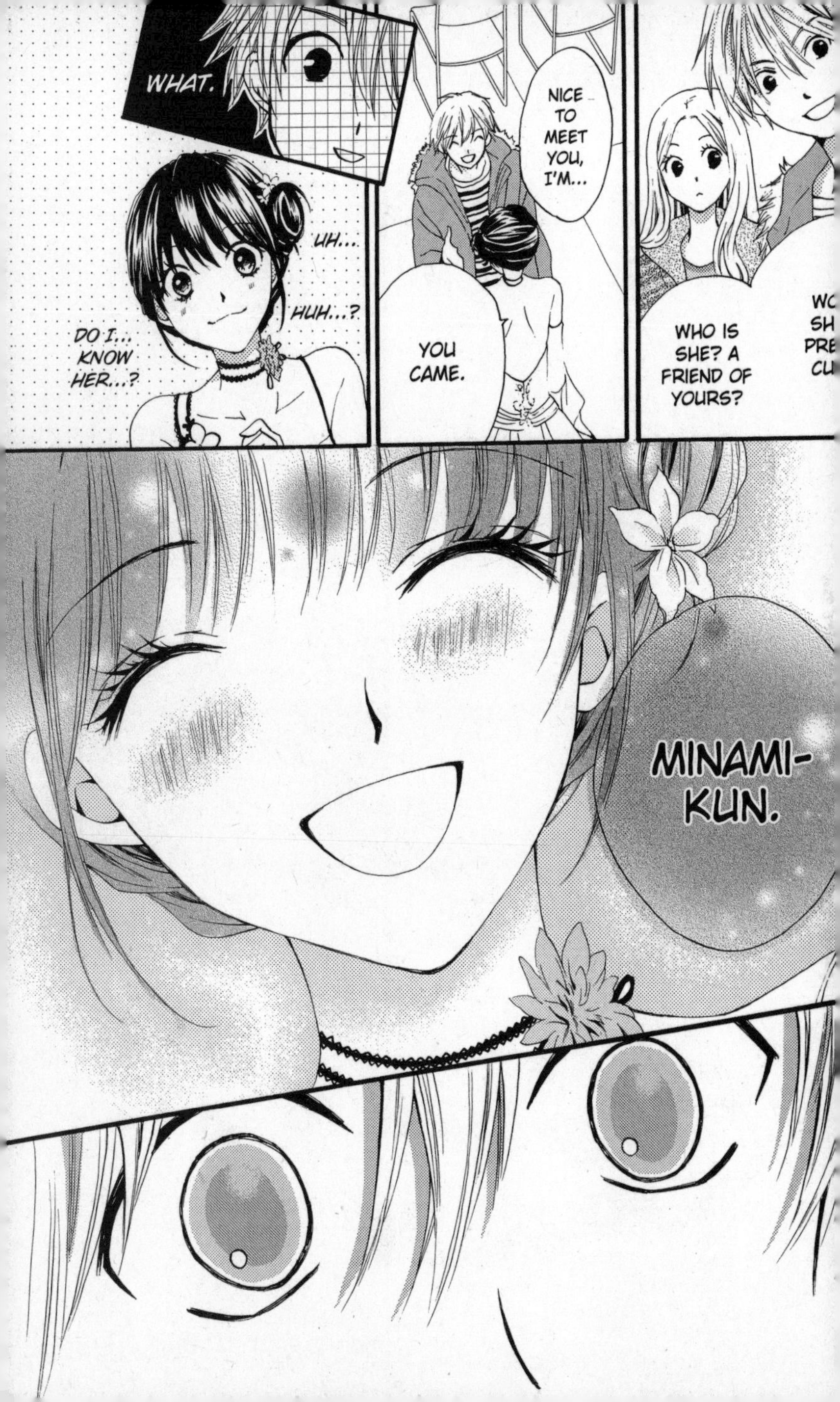
WHO IS SHE? A FRIEND OF YOURS?
NICE TO MEET YOU, I'M...
YOU CAME.
WHAT.
UH...
HUH...?
DO I... KNOW HER...?
MINAMI-KUN.

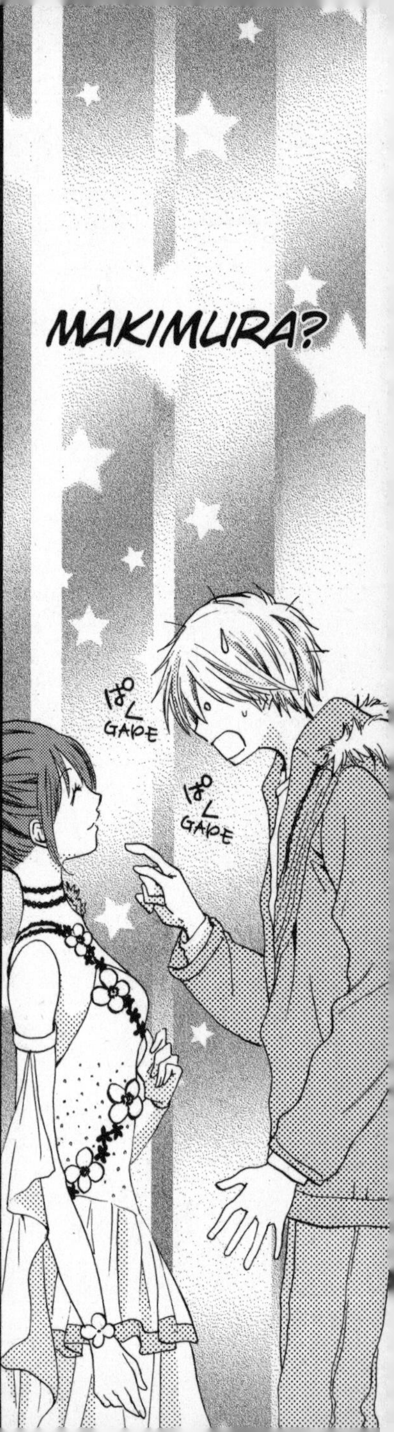
MAKIMURA?
GAPE
GAPE
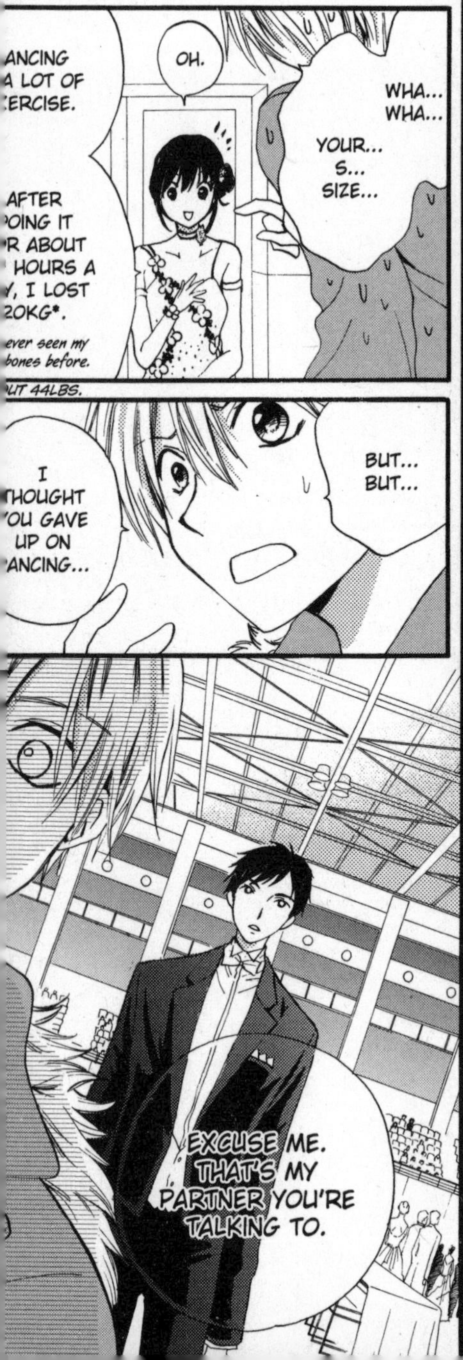
WHA... WHA...
YOUR... S... SIZE...
OH.
ANCING A LOT OF ERCISE.
AFTER OING IT R ABOUT HOURS A Y, I LOST 20KG*.
ever seen my bones before.
UT 44LBS.
BUT... BUT...
I THOUGHT OU GAVE UP ON ANCING...
EXCUSE ME. THAT'S MY PARTNER YOU'RE TALKING TO.

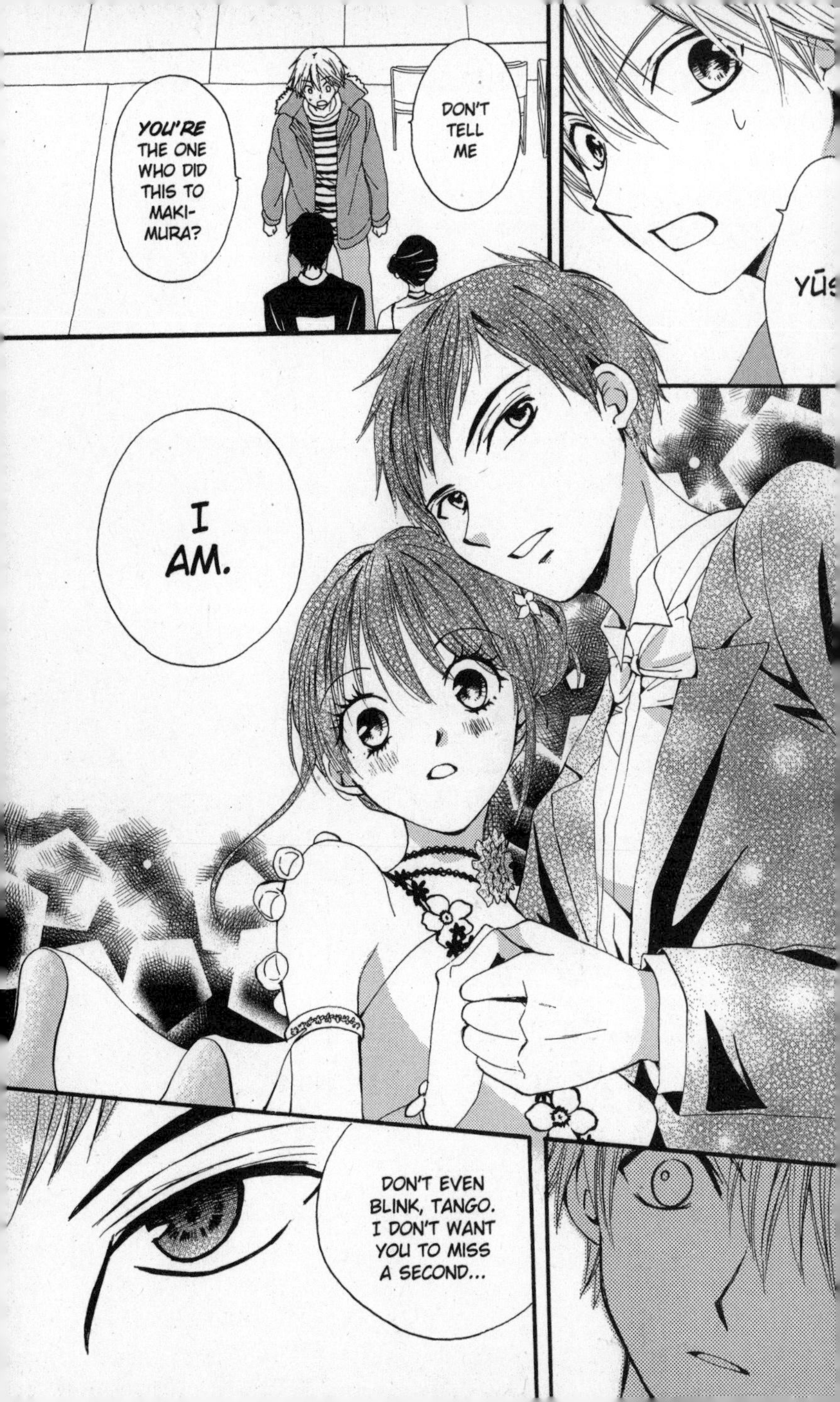
YŪS
DON'T TELL ME
YOU'RE THE ONE WHO DID THIS TO MAKI-MURA?
I AM.
DON'T EVEN BLINK, TANGO. I DON'T WANT YOU TO MISS A SECOND...

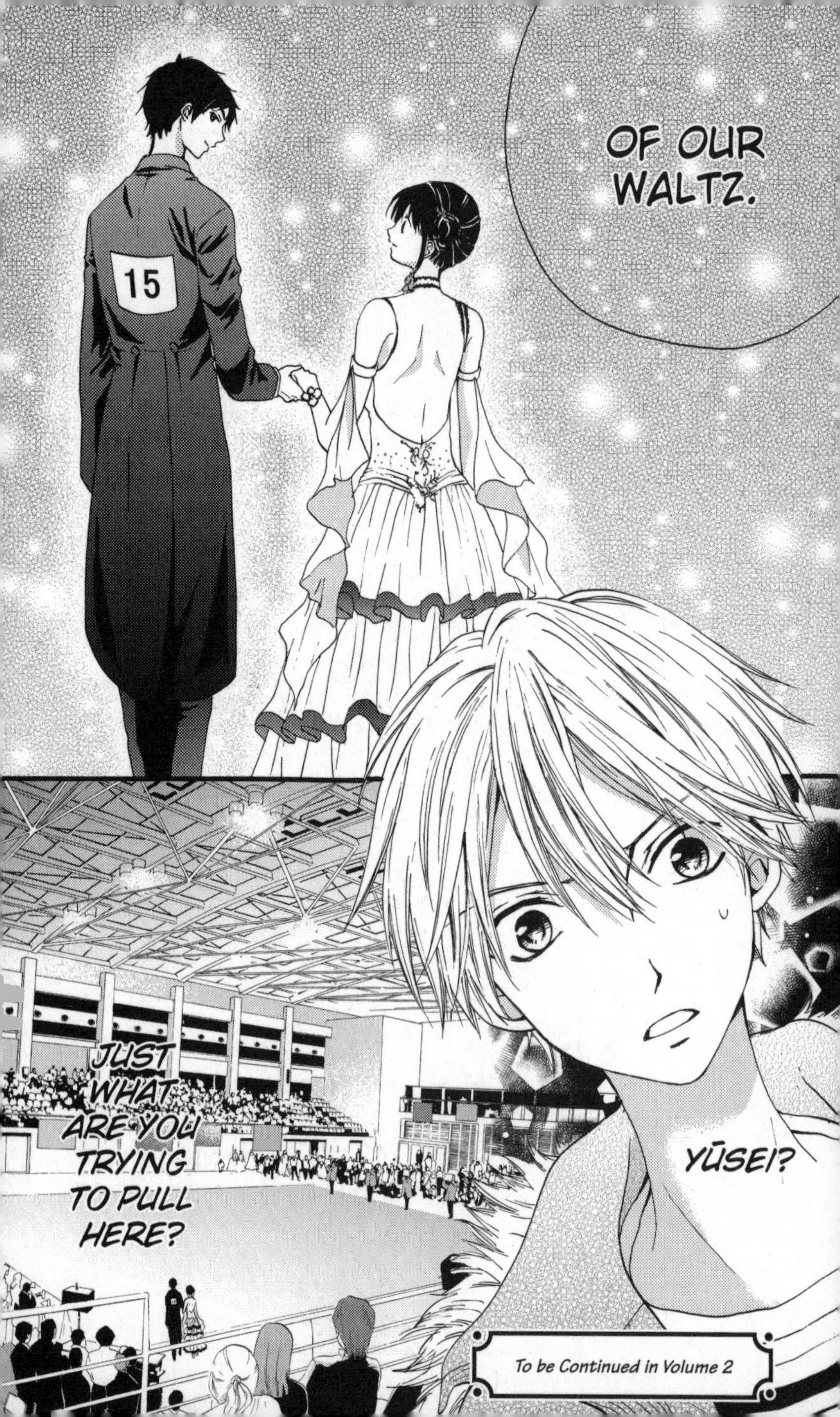
OF OUR WALTZ.
15
YŪSEI?
JUST WHAT ARE YOU TRYING TO PULL HERE?
To be Continued in Volume 2

LET'S READ A FOUR-PANEL COMIC

EVERYONE'S SPECIALTIES

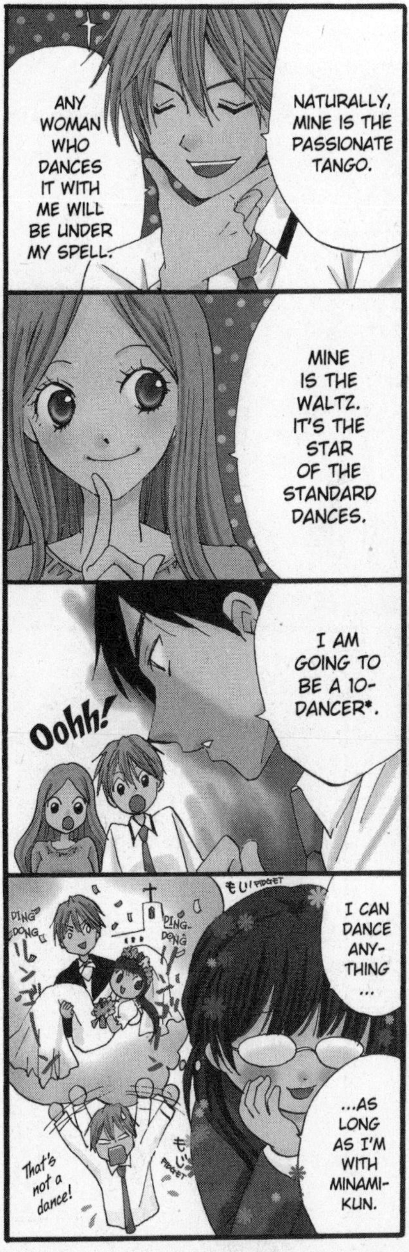
NATURALLY, MINE IS THE PASSIONATE TANGO.
ANY WOMAN WHO DANCES IT WITH ME WILL BE UNDER MY SPELL.
MINE IS THE WALTZ. IT'S THE STAR OF THE STANDARD DANCES.
I AM GOING TO BE A 10-DANCER*.
Oohh!
I CAN DANCE ANY-THING ...
もじ FIDGET
DING-DONG
DING DONG
...AS LONG AS I'M WITH MINAMI-KUN.
もじ FIDGET
That's not a dance!

*10-DANCER: SOMEONE WHO HAS BEEN AWARDED AN A-RANK IN ALL TEN COMPETITIVE DANCE STYLES. THERE ARE ONLY A HANDFUL OF THEM IN ALL OF JAPAN!

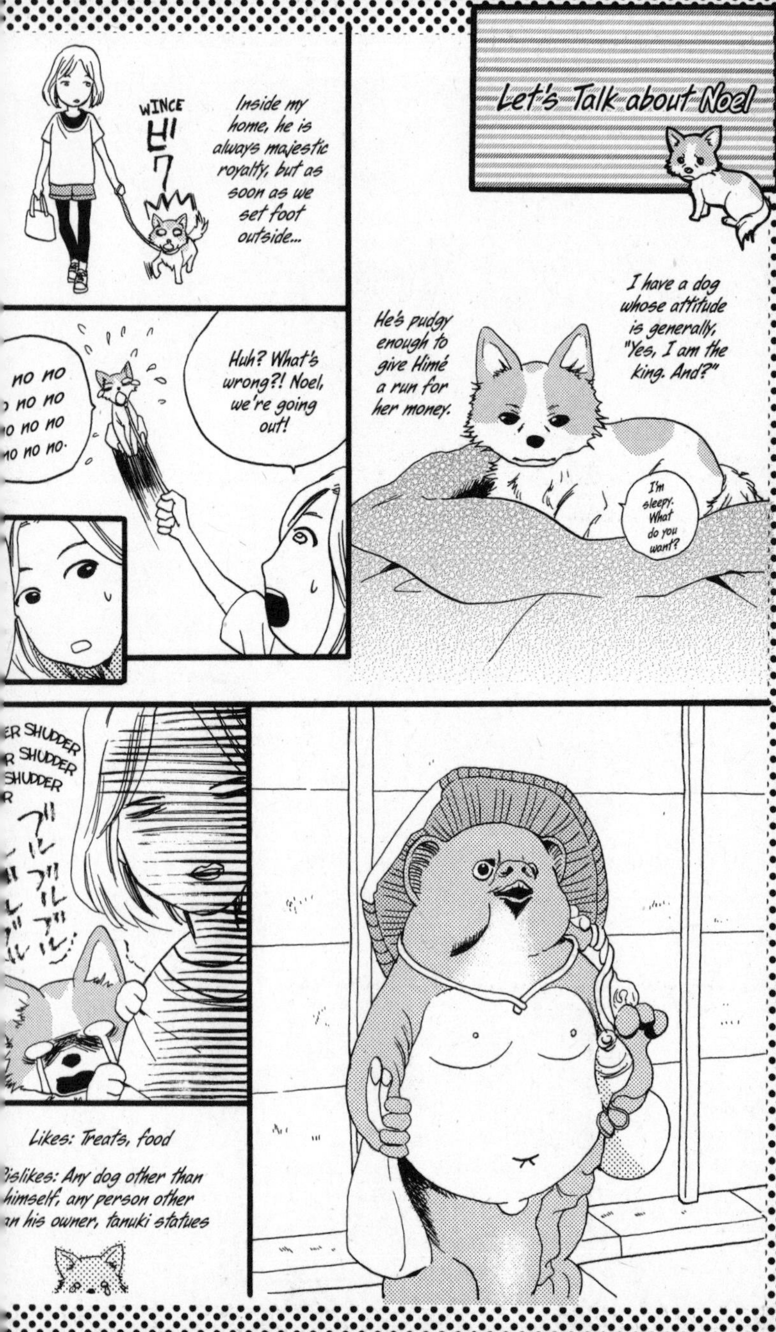
Let's Talk about Noel
I have a dog whose attitude is generally, "Yes, I am the king. And?"
He's pudgy enough to give Himé a run for her money.
I'm sleepy. What do you want?
Inside my home, he is always majestic royalty, but as soon as we set foot outside...
WINCE
Huh? What's wrong?! Noel, we're going out!
no no
no no
no no
no no no.
SHUDDER
SHUDDER
SHUDDER
Likes: Treats, food
Dislikes: Any dog other than himself, any person other than his owner, tanuki statues

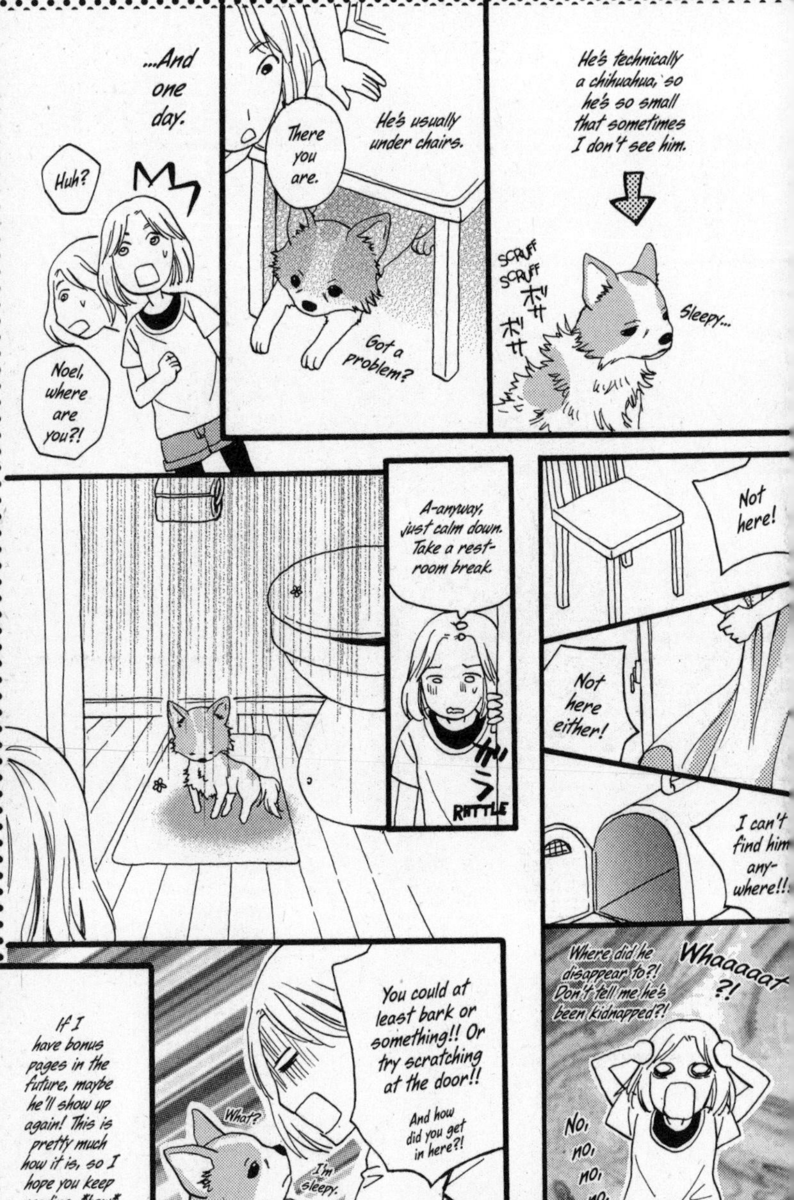
He's technically a chihuahua, so he's so small that sometimes I don't see him.
SCRUFF SCRUFF
ボサ ボサ
Sleepy...
He's usually under chairs.
There you are.
Got a problem?
...And one day.
Huh?
Noel, where are you?!
Not here!
Not here either!
I can't find him anywhere!!
A-anyway, just calm down. Take a rest-room break.
ガラ
RATTLE
Whaaaaat?!
Where did he disappear to?! Don't tell me he's been kidnapped?!
No, no, no, no.
You could at least bark or something!! Or try scratching at the door!!
And how did you get in here?!
What?
I'm sleepy.
If I have bonus pages in the future, maybe he'll show up again! This is pretty much how it is, so I hope you keep reading. *bow*

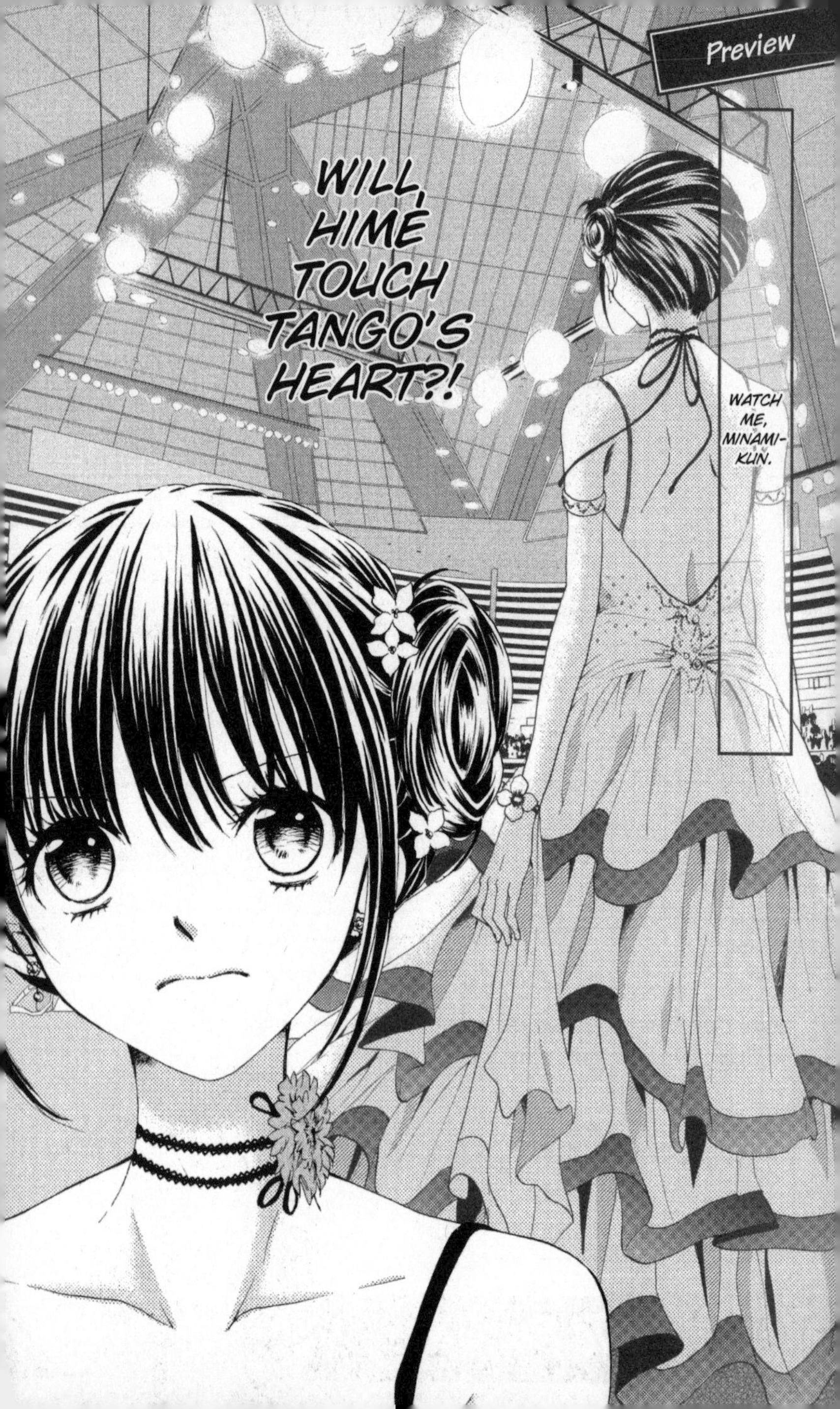
Preview
WATCH ME, MINAMI-KUN.
WILL HIME TOUCH TANGO'S HEART?!

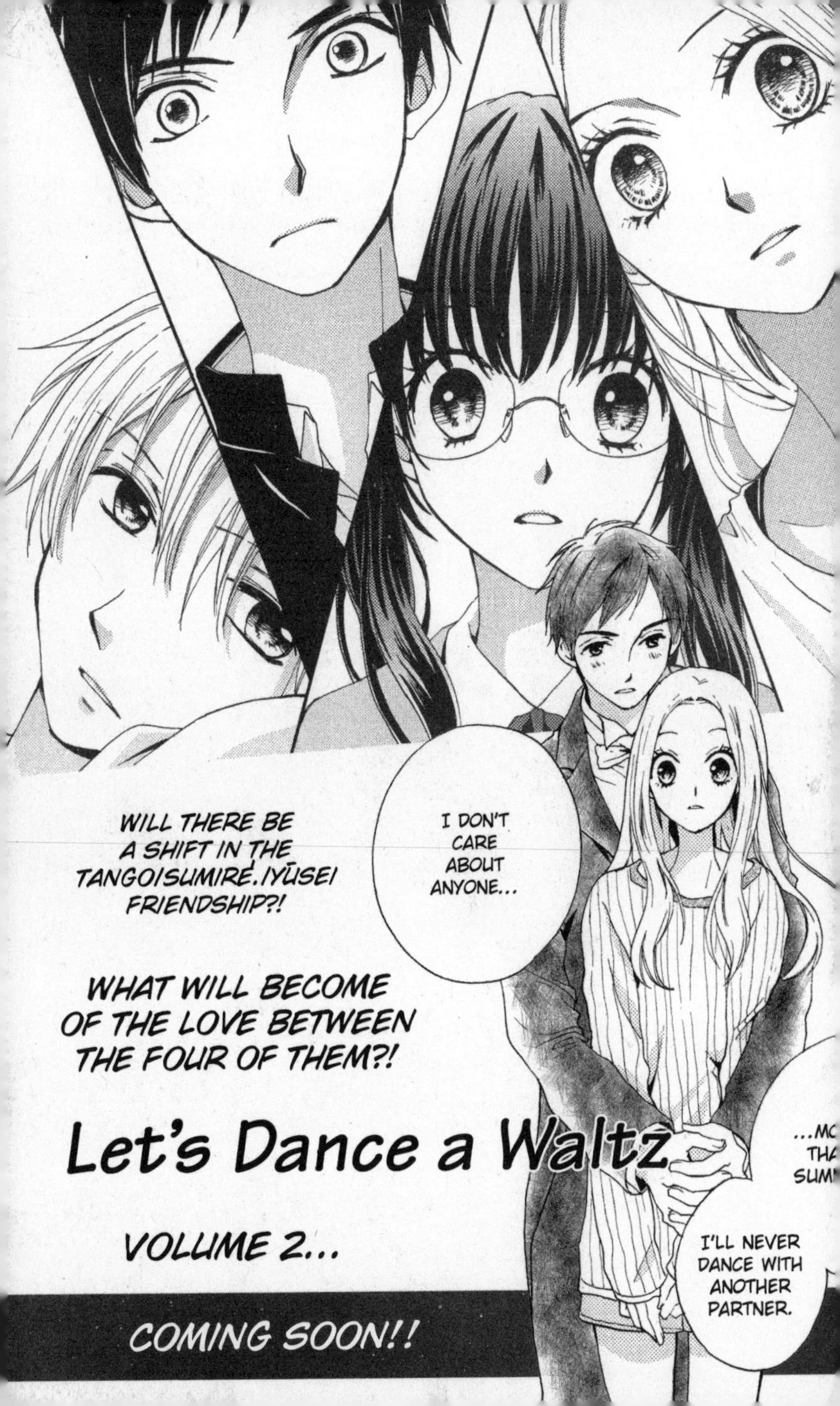

I DON'T CARE ABOUT ANYONE...
WILL THERE BE A SHIFT IN THE TANGO/SUMIRE/YŪSEI FRIENDSHIP?!
WHAT WILL BECOME OF THE LOVE BETWEEN THE FOUR OF THEM?!
I'LL NEVER DANCE WITH ANOTHER PARTNER.
Let's Dance a Waltz
VOLUME 2...
COMING SOON!!

AUTHOR'S COMMENT

I GO SEE A LOT OF BALLROOM DANCE COMPETITIONS,
BUT I'M STILL SURPRISED AT HOW DIFFERENT THEY ARE
FROM A REGULAR BALL. THEY'RE TEEMING WITH INTENSE
POWER! THEY'RE SO INTENSE, IT'S OVERWHELMING.
I HOPE I CAN CONVEY THAT IN MY MANGA, TOO.

Minami-kun... what are you eating?
Ice cream. So?

What!
They make ice cream servings that small?
Uh, it's a normal size.

At the Makimura Home
Minami-kun has never seen a normal-sized serving of ice cream.
Poor boy...
Industrial size
Curry spoon
Himé! I bought you more ice cream!

Let's Eat Some Snacks

Translation Notes

...nese is a tricky language for most Westerners, and translation is often more art than
...nce. For your edification and reading pleasure, here are notes on some of the places
...e we could have gone in a different direction with our translation of the work, or
...e a Japanese cultural reference is used.

...-a-date, page 14

...ne Japanese version, Sumire actually used the English word
...st." Not to be confused with a game show host or the host of
...arty, in Japan, the word "host" refers to a man whose job it is
...ntertain lonely women.

...one will ever find out, page 18

...ne of our readers might be wondering how Tango can
...sibly think he'll ever get all the way through middle school
...nout anyone making the connection between the name
...go and ballroom dancing. Fortunately for Tango, he goes
...chool in Japan, where boys' names ending in *go* are not
...ommon. Also, *tango* is a Japanese word which can mean
...cabulary" (maybe Tango's parents were linguistics geeks)
...oy's Day, a holiday celebrated on March 5.

...ess Himé, page 26

...translators asked Tango to do them a favor and translate
...é's name, for the benefit of our English-speaking readers.
...*e* is the Japanese word for "princess," so of course
...go knows that any time he says her name, he's saying
...word "princess."

Shall we dance?, page 64

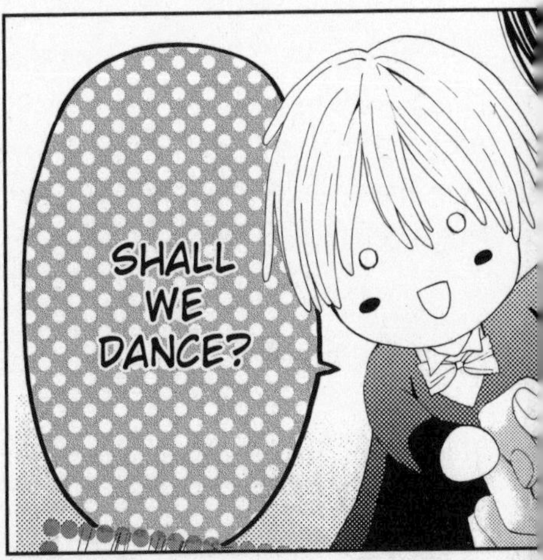
SHALL WE DANCE?

While this is a typical way to invite someone to dance, the specific way that the sentence is written in the original Japanese—the "shall we" written in English followed by "dance (or dansu)" spelled out in Japanese characters—is a reference to a 1996 Japanese movie of that title. It might go without saying that the movie is about ballroom dancing. An American remake was released in 2004, starring Rich Gere and Jennifer Lopez.

He's an idiot; he'll get over it in no time, page 95

There is a Japanese axiom that states, "fools don't catch cold." Tango's mother must be surprised that he managed to catch a cold in the first place, but now that it allegedly has happened, she's confident that his idiocy will help him to a swift recovery.

can do magic, page 125

re literally, Himé says that Tango is like a *mahō-tsukai,* or "magic
r." Usually this term gets translated to "wizard," or some such,
in Japan, it is also the term used in fairy tales for important
gic-using characters, including Cinderella's fairy godmother.
né likely made the comparison because Tango is helping her
ive up to her name and become a true princess, much like
derella's fairy godmother helped her.

e-four time, page 143

hout getting too technical, "three-four time" is a way of
scribing a type of musical rhythm—in this case, the rhythm
d for waltzes. Basically what this means is that, to keep the
hm, it helps to count "**one**-two-three, **one**-two-three,"
ere the first beat is stressed more heavily than the other
. It is considered to be a difficult rhythm for natives of
an to master, for unknown reasons. The translators found
theory that this is because the rhythm is based on the
hm of a horse's footsteps, and historically very few Japanese
ple have ridden horses. Another possibility is that the
anese words for one, two, and three (*ichi, ni,* and *san*)
e it difficult to count in an even rhythm. This also explains
ei's suggestion that Himé use three-syllable (three-beat)
rds instead of counting. The readers may have noticed
he uses an N all by itself to count as a beat. In English,
word *ringo* (apple) would be considered two-syllables,
in Japanese, it is in fact three beats (linguistically known
nora), because the N is a *mora* unto itself.

My Little Monster

OPPOSITES ATTRACT...MAYBE?

Haru Yoshida is feared as an unstable and violent "monster." Mizutani Shizuku is a grade-obsessed student with no friends. Fate brings these two together to form the most unlikely pair. Haru firmly believes he's in love with Mizutani and she firmly believes he's insane.

KODA[NSHA] COM[ICS]

KC
KODANSHA COMICS

i Tachibana has no friends — and says she doesn't need them!

everything changes when she accidentally roundhouse kicks the most
ular boy in school! However, Yamato Kurosawa isn't angry in the slightest—
act, he thinks his ordinary life could use an unusual girl like Mei. But winning
's trust will be a tough task. How long will she refuse to say, "I love you"?

SANKAREA

undying lov

"I ONLY LIKE ZOMBIE GIRLS."

Chihiro has an unusual connection to zombie movies. He doesn't feel b
the survivors – he wants to comfort the undead girls they slaughter! W
his pet passes away, he brews a resurrection potion. He's discovered b
local heiress Sanka Rea, and she serves as his first test subject!

Kodansha Comics Trade Paperback Original.

t's Dance a Waltz volume 1 copyright © 2013 Natsumi Ando
glish translation copyright © 2015 Natsumi Ando

blished in the United States by Kodansha Comics, an imprint of dansha USA Publishing, LLC, New York.

blication rights for this English edition arranged through Kodansha Ltd., kyo.

st published in Japan in 2013 by Kodansha Ltd., Tokyo as *Waltz no kan*, volume 1.

N 978-1-63236-046-5

nted in the United States of America.

w.kodanshacomics.com

7 6 5 4 3 2 1   4843

nslator: Alethea Nibley & Athena Nibley
tering: Jennifer Skarupa